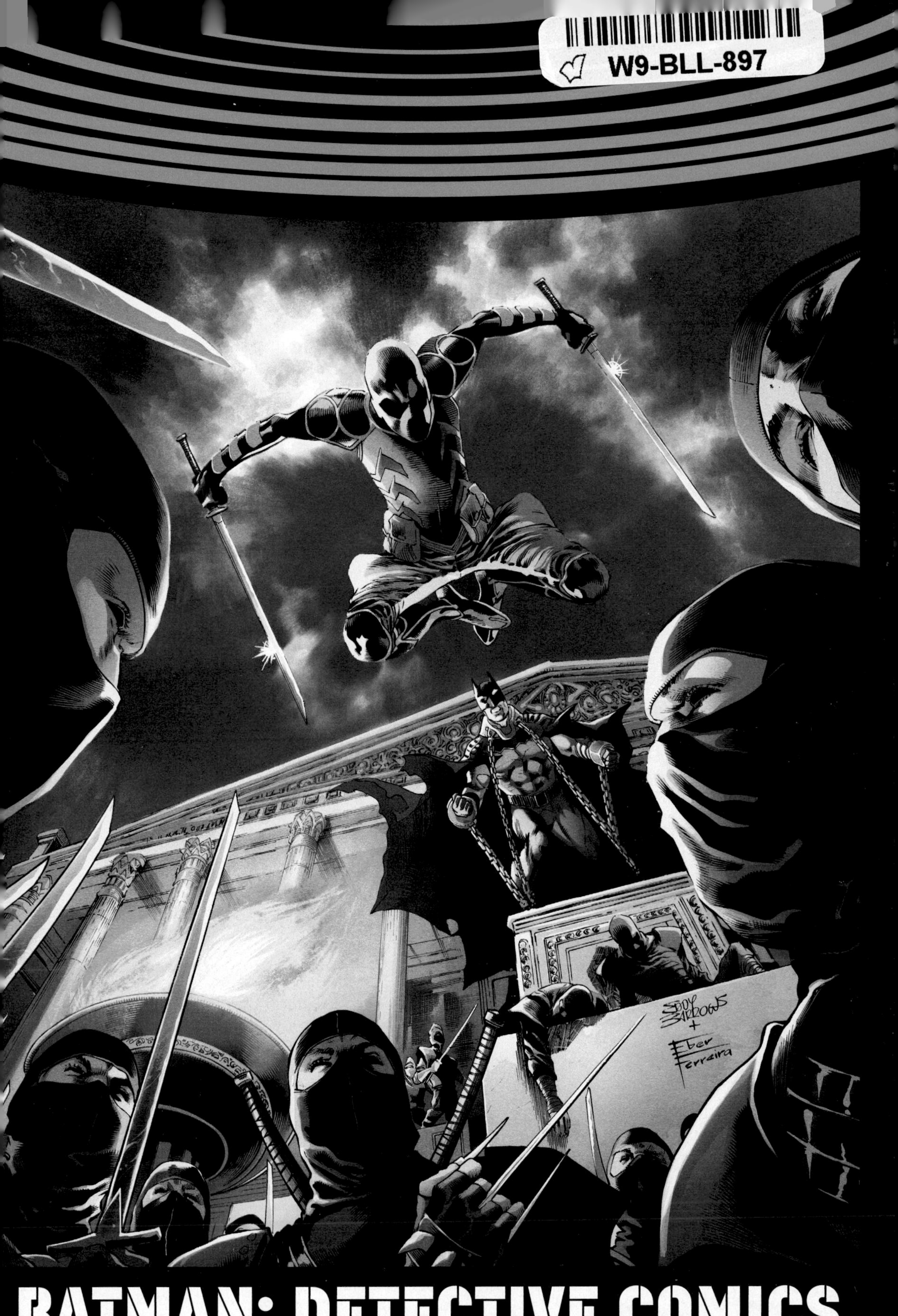
EDDY BARROWS
+
Eber
Ferreira

BATMAN: DETECTIVE COMICS

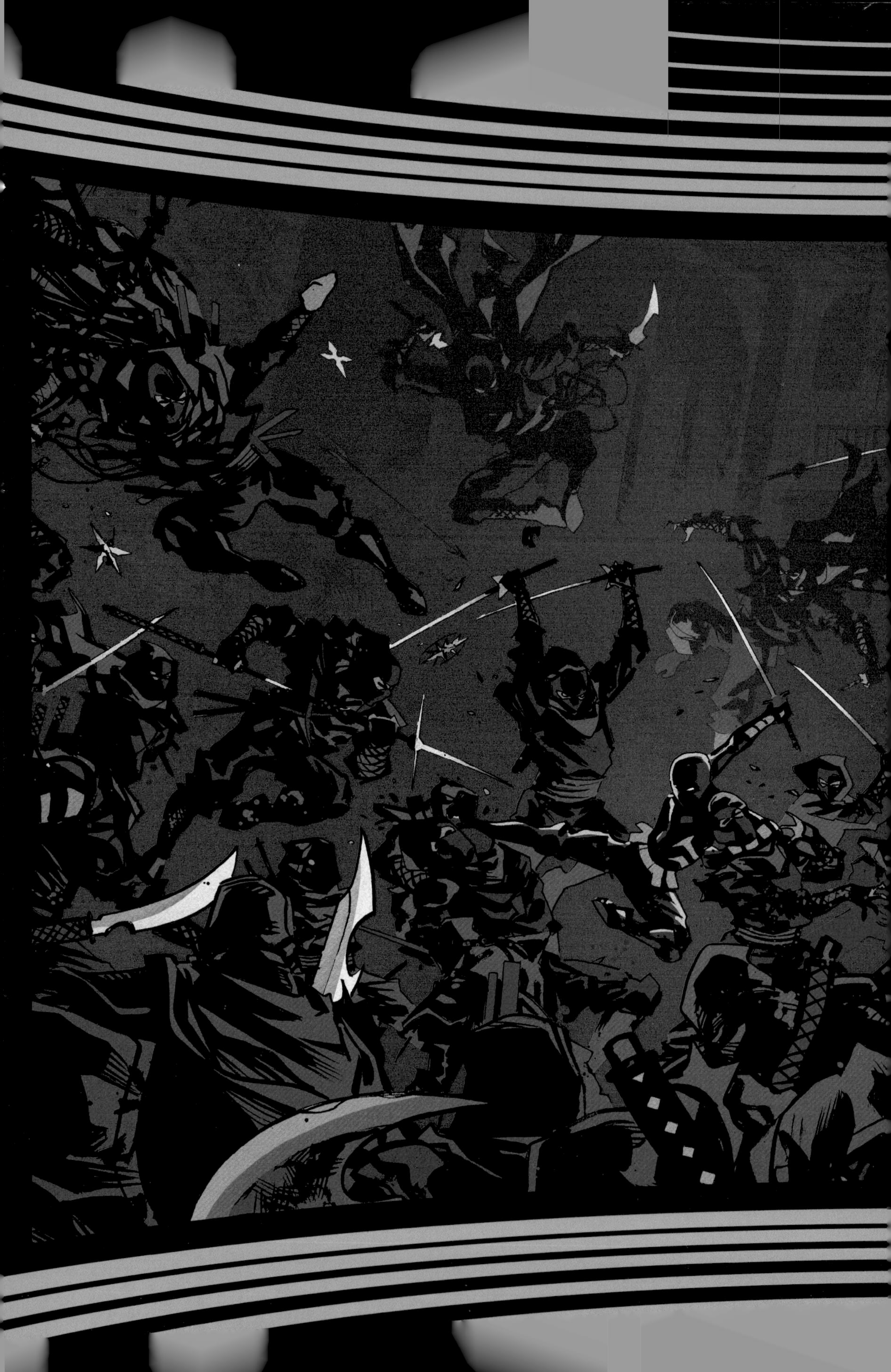

BATMAN: DETECTIVE COMICS
VOL.3 LEAGUE OF SHADOWS

JAMES TYNION IV
writer

MARCIO TAKARA ✳ **CHRISTIAN DUCE**
FERNANDO BLANCO ✳ ALVARO MARTINEZ ✳ RAUL FERNANDEZ
EDDY BARROWS ✳ EBER FERREIRA
artists

MARCELO MAIOLO ✳ **ALEX SINCLAIR**
DEAN WHITE ✳ ALLEN PASSALAQUA ✳ BRAD ANDERSON
ADRIANO LUCAS ✳ JOHN RAUCH
colorists

SAL CIPRIANO ✳ **MARILYN PATRIZIO**
letterers

EDDY BARROWS, EBER FERREIRA & ADRIANO LUCAS
collection cover artists

BATMAN created by BOB KANE with BILL FINGER

CHRIS CONROY Editor - Original Series ✳ **DAVE WIELGOSZ** Assistant Editor - Original Series
JEB WOODARD Group Editor - Collected Editions ✳ **ROBIN WILDMAN** Editor - Collected Edition
STEVE COOK Design Director - Books ✳ **MONIQUE GRUSPE** Publication Design

BOB HARRAS Senior VP - Editor-in-Chief, DC Comics
PAT McCALLUM Executive Editor, DC Comics

DIANE NELSON President ✳ **DAN DiDIO** Publisher ✳ **JIM LEE** Publisher ✳ **GEOFF JOHNS** President & Chief Creative Officer
AMIT DESAI Executive VP - Business & Marketing Strategy, Direct to Consumer & Global Franchise Management
SAM ADES Senior VP & General Manager, Digital Services ✳ **BOBBIE CHASE** VP & Executive Editor, Young Reader & Talent Development
MARK CHIARELLO Senior VP - Art, Design & Collected Editions ✳ **JOHN CUNNINGHAM** Senior VP - Sales & Trade Marketing
ANNE DePIES Senior VP - Business Strategy, Finance & Administration ✳ **DON FALLETTI** VP - Manufacturing Operations
LAWRENCE GANEM VP - Editorial Administration & Talent Relations ✳ **ALISON GILL** Senior VP - Manufacturing & Operations
HANK KANALZ Senior VP - Editorial Strategy & Administration ✳ **JAY KOGAN** VP - Legal Affairs ✳ **JACK MAHAN** VP - Business Affairs
NICK J. NAPOLITANO VP - Manufacturing Administration ✳ **EDDIE SCANNELL** VP - Consumer Marketing
COURTNEY SIMMONS Senior VP - Publicity & Communications ✳ **JIM (SKI) SOKOLOWSKI** VP - Comic Book Specialty Sales & Trade Marketing
NANCY SPEARS VP - Mass, Book, Digital Sales & Trade Marketing ✳ **MICHELE R. WELLS** VP - Content Strategy

BATMAN: DETECTIVE COMICS VOLUME 3—LEAGUE OF SHADOWS

DC Comics, 2900 West Alameda Ave., Burbank, CA 91505.
Printed by LSC Communications, Kendallville, IN, USA. 9/1/17. First Printing.
ISBN: 978-1-4012-7609-6

Library of Congress Cataloging-in-Publication Data is available.

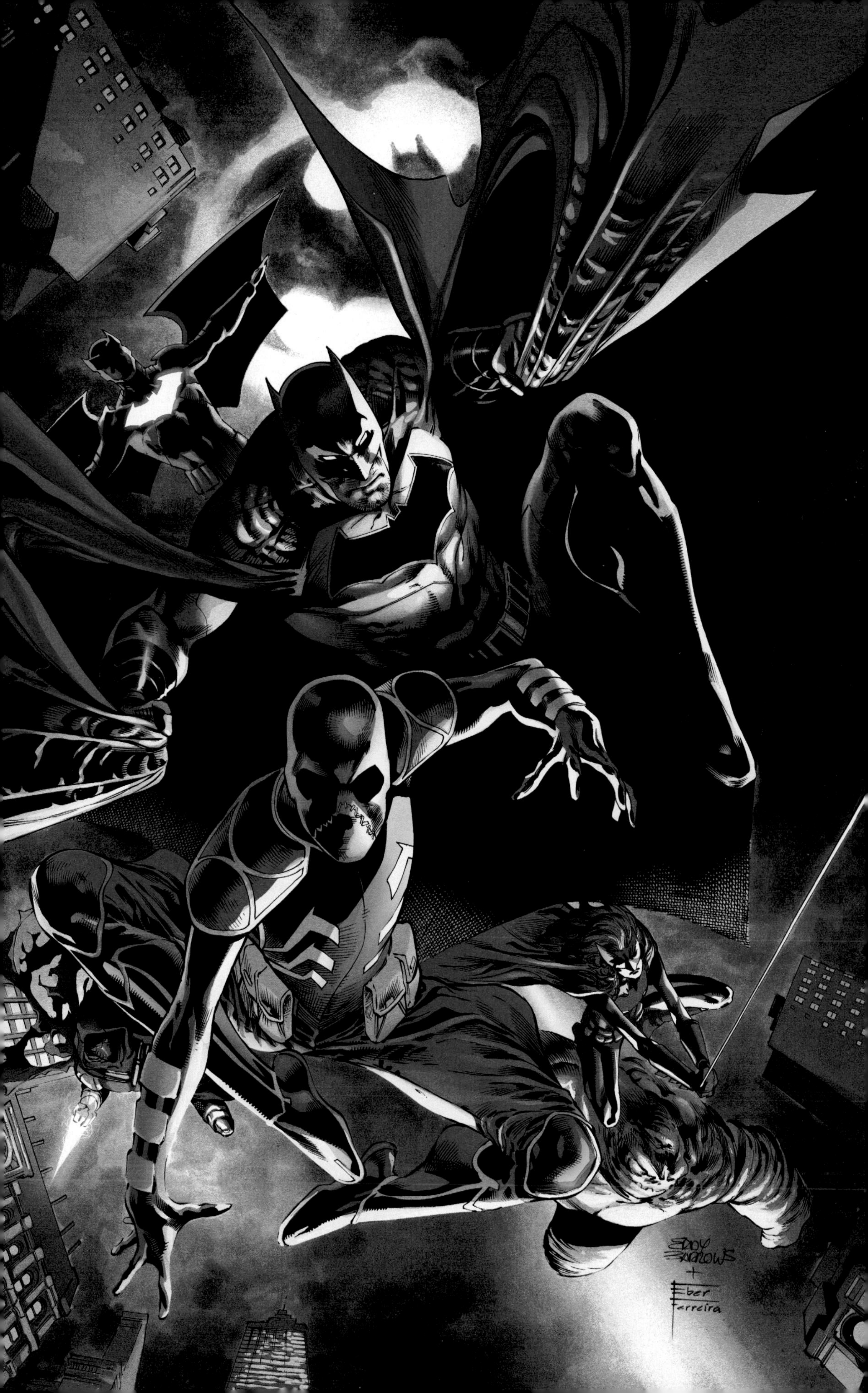
EDDY BARROWS
+
Eber Ferreira

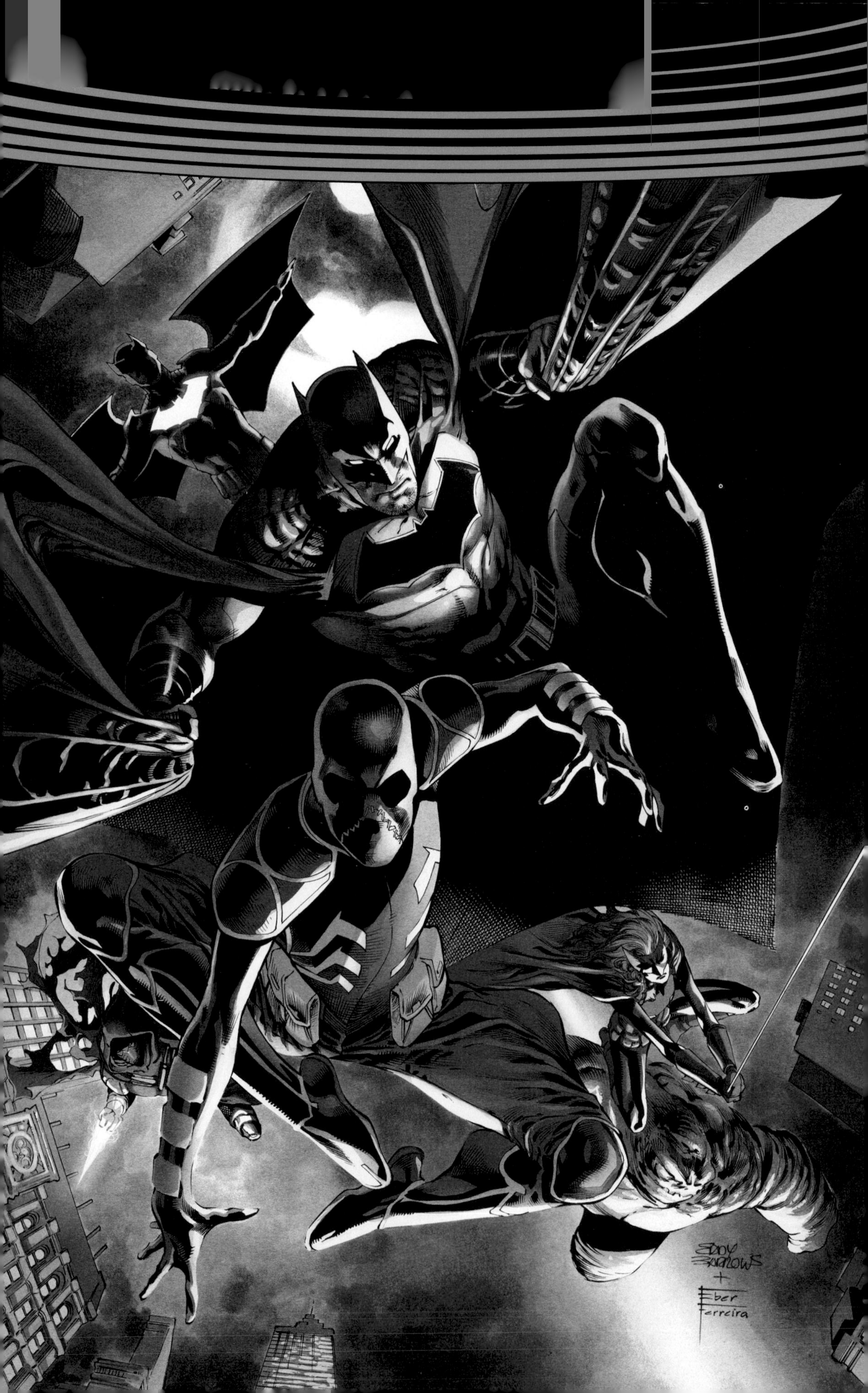
EDDY BARROWS
+
Eber Ferreira

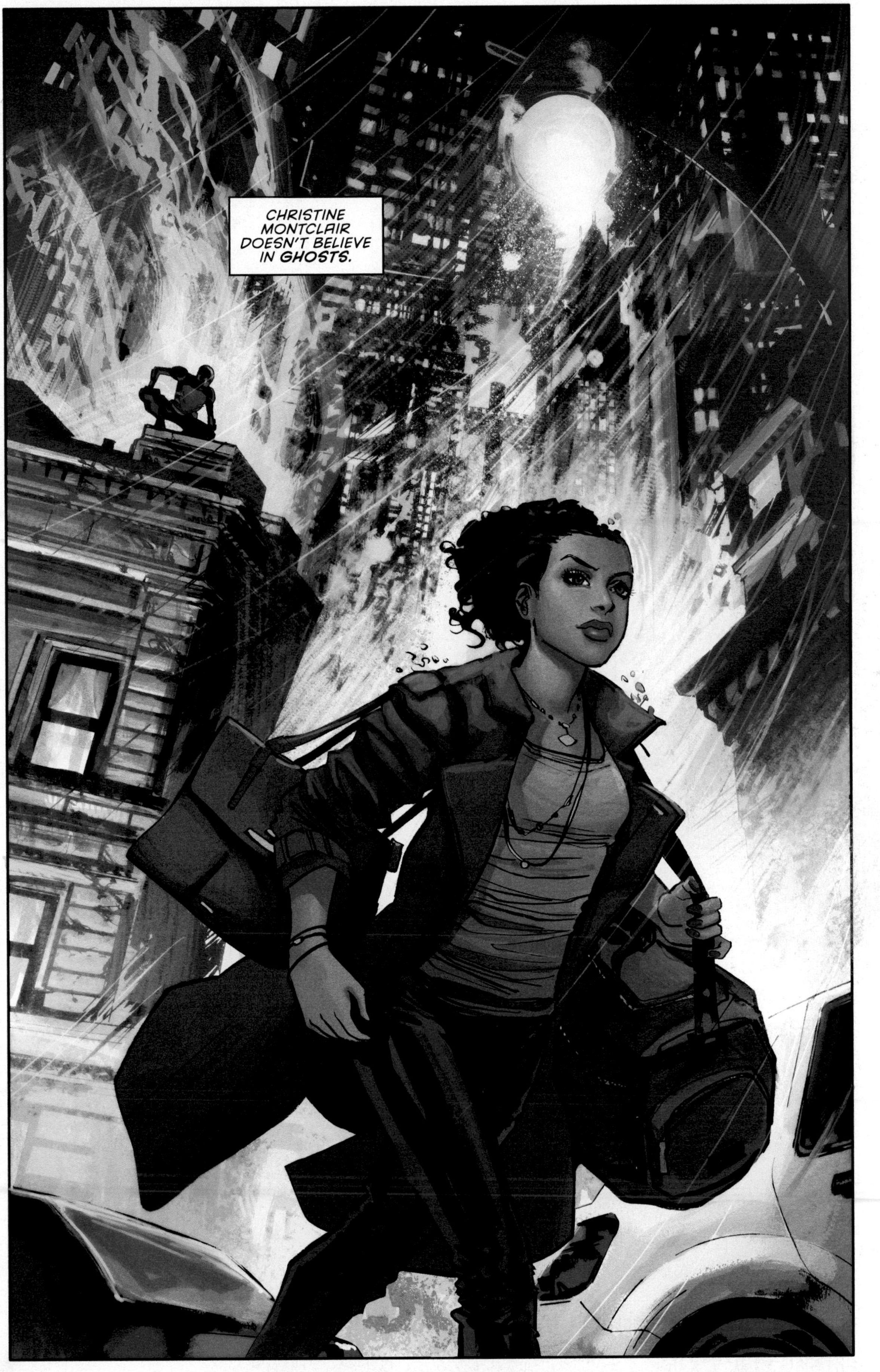
CHRISTINE MONTCLAIR DOESN'T BELIEVE IN GHOSTS.

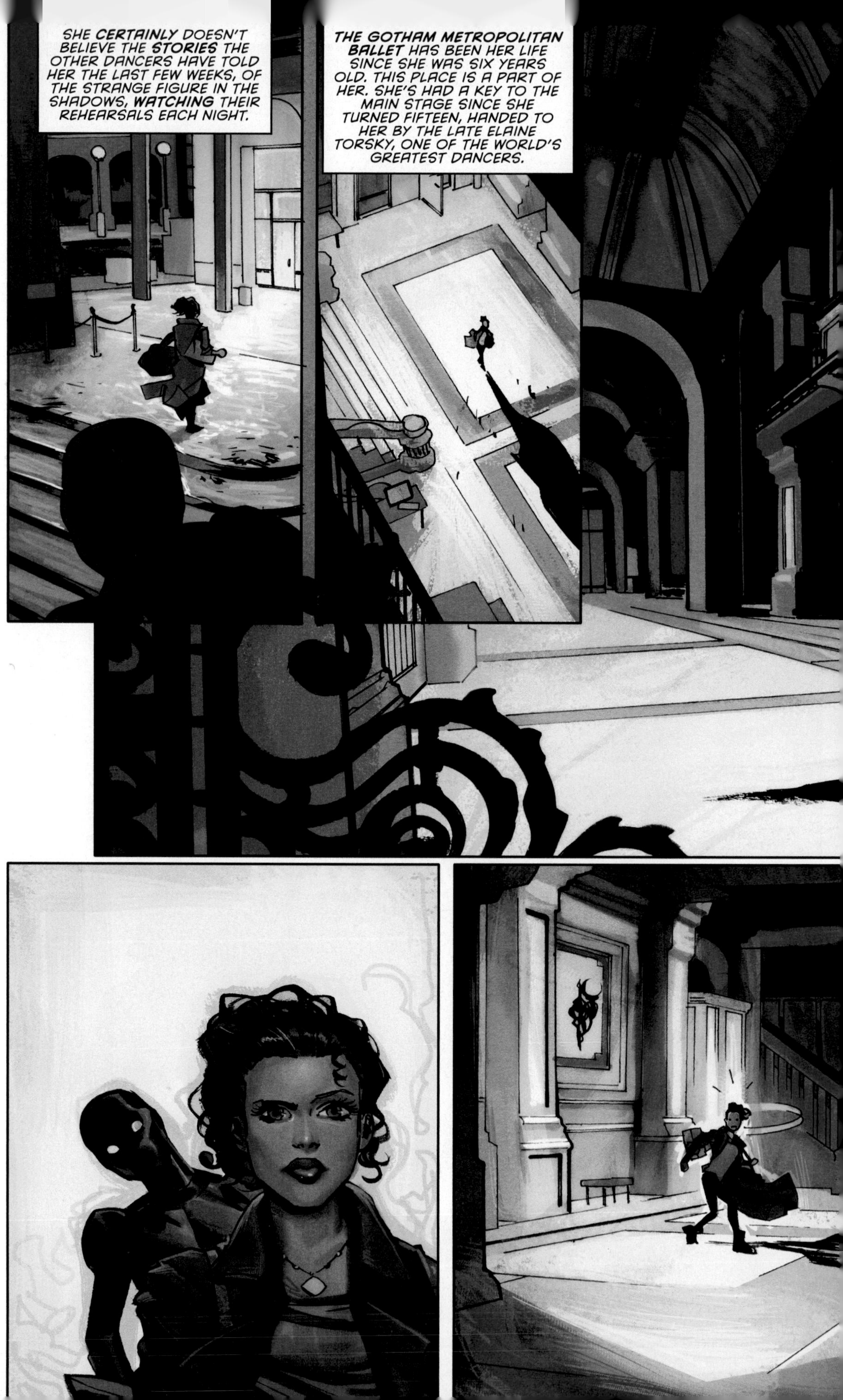
SHE CERTAINLY DOESN'T BELIEVE THE STORIES THE OTHER DANCERS HAVE TOLD HER THE LAST FEW WEEKS, OF THE STRANGE FIGURE IN THE SHADOWS, WATCHING THEIR REHEARSALS EACH NIGHT.
THE GOTHAM METROPOLITAN BALLET HAS BEEN HER LIFE SINCE SHE WAS SIX YEARS OLD. THIS PLACE IS A PART OF HER. SHE'S HAD A KEY TO THE MAIN STAGE SINCE SHE TURNED FIFTEEN, HANDED TO HER BY THE LATE ELAINE TORSKY, ONE OF THE WORLD'S GREATEST DANCERS.

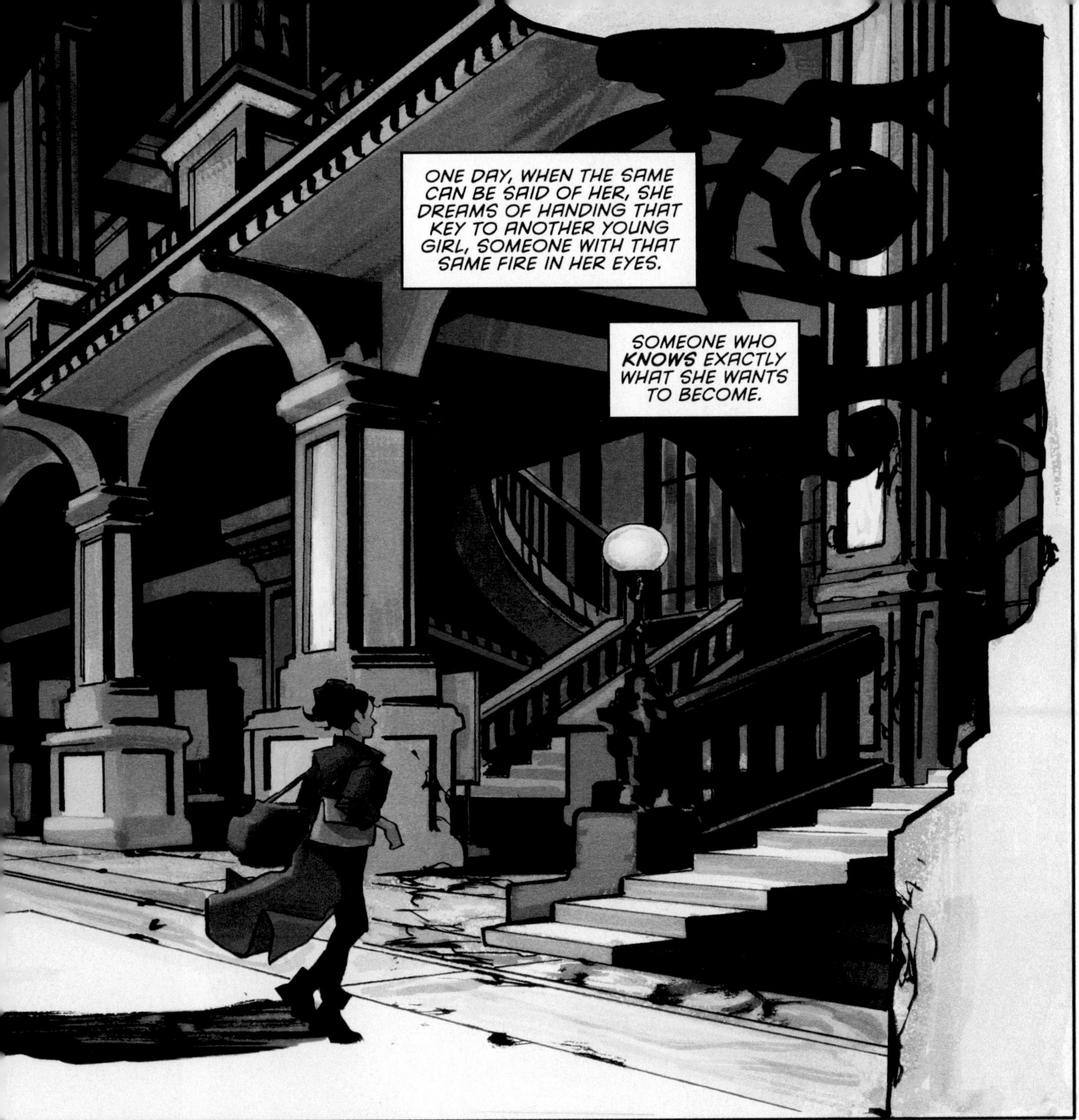
ONE DAY, WHEN THE SAME CAN BE SAID OF HER, SHE DREAMS OF HANDING THAT KEY TO ANOTHER YOUNG GIRL, SOMEONE WITH THAT SAME FIRE IN HER EYES.
SOMEONE WHO **KNOWS** EXACTLY WHAT SHE WANTS TO BECOME.

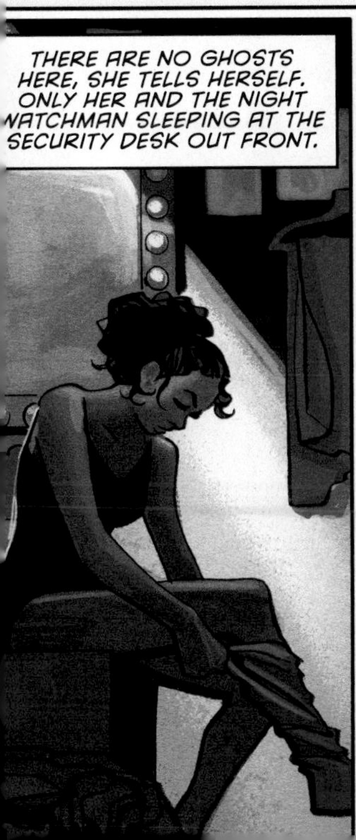
THERE ARE NO GHOSTS HERE, SHE TELLS HERSELF. ONLY HER AND THE NIGHT WATCHMAN SLEEPING AT THE SECURITY DESK OUT FRONT.

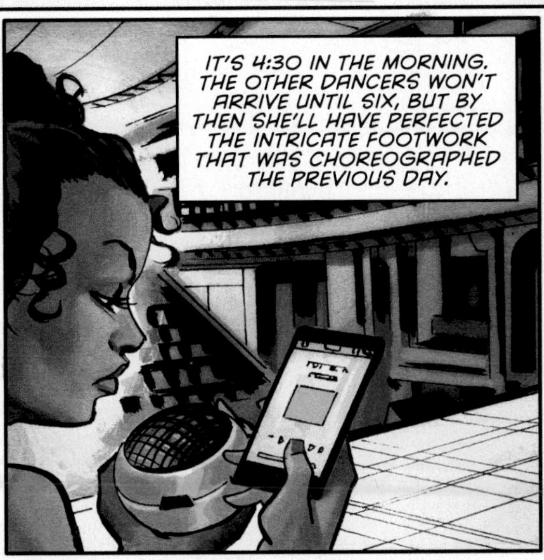
IT'S 4:30 IN THE MORNING. THE OTHER DANCERS WON'T ARRIVE UNTIL SIX, BUT BY THEN SHE'LL HAVE PERFECTED THE INTRICATE FOOTWORK THAT WAS CHOREOGRAPHED THE PREVIOUS DAY.

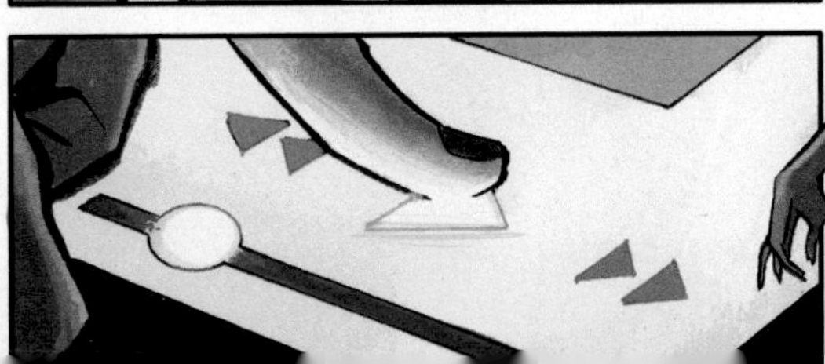

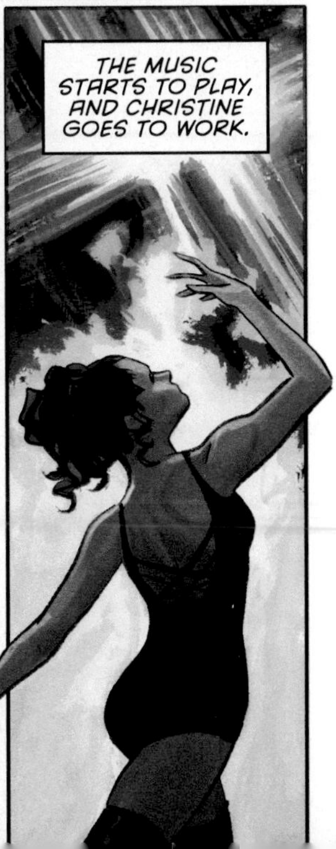
THE MUSIC STARTS TO PLAY, AND CHRISTINE GOES TO WORK.

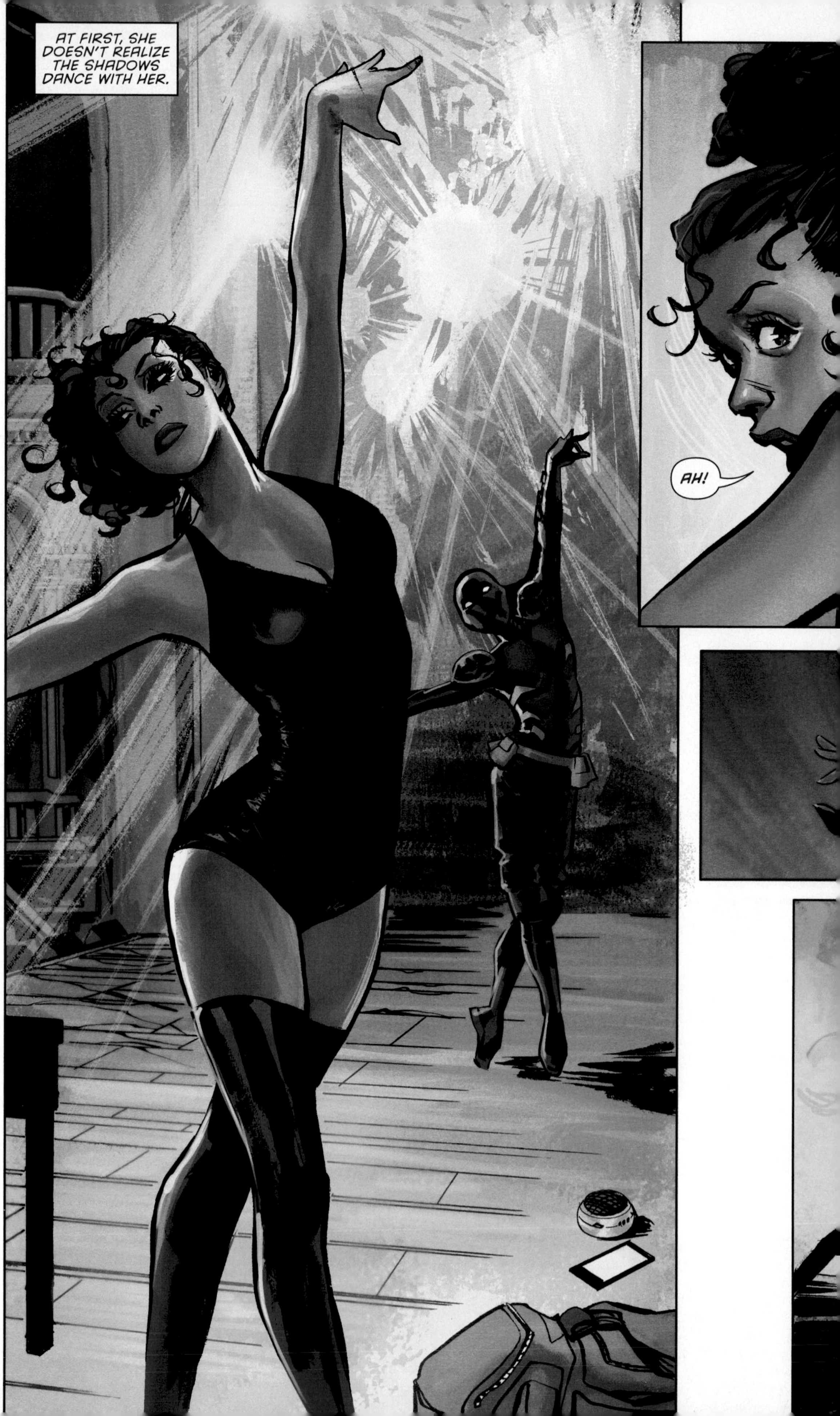
AT FIRST, SHE DOESN'T REALIZE THE SHADOWS DANCE WITH HER.
AH!

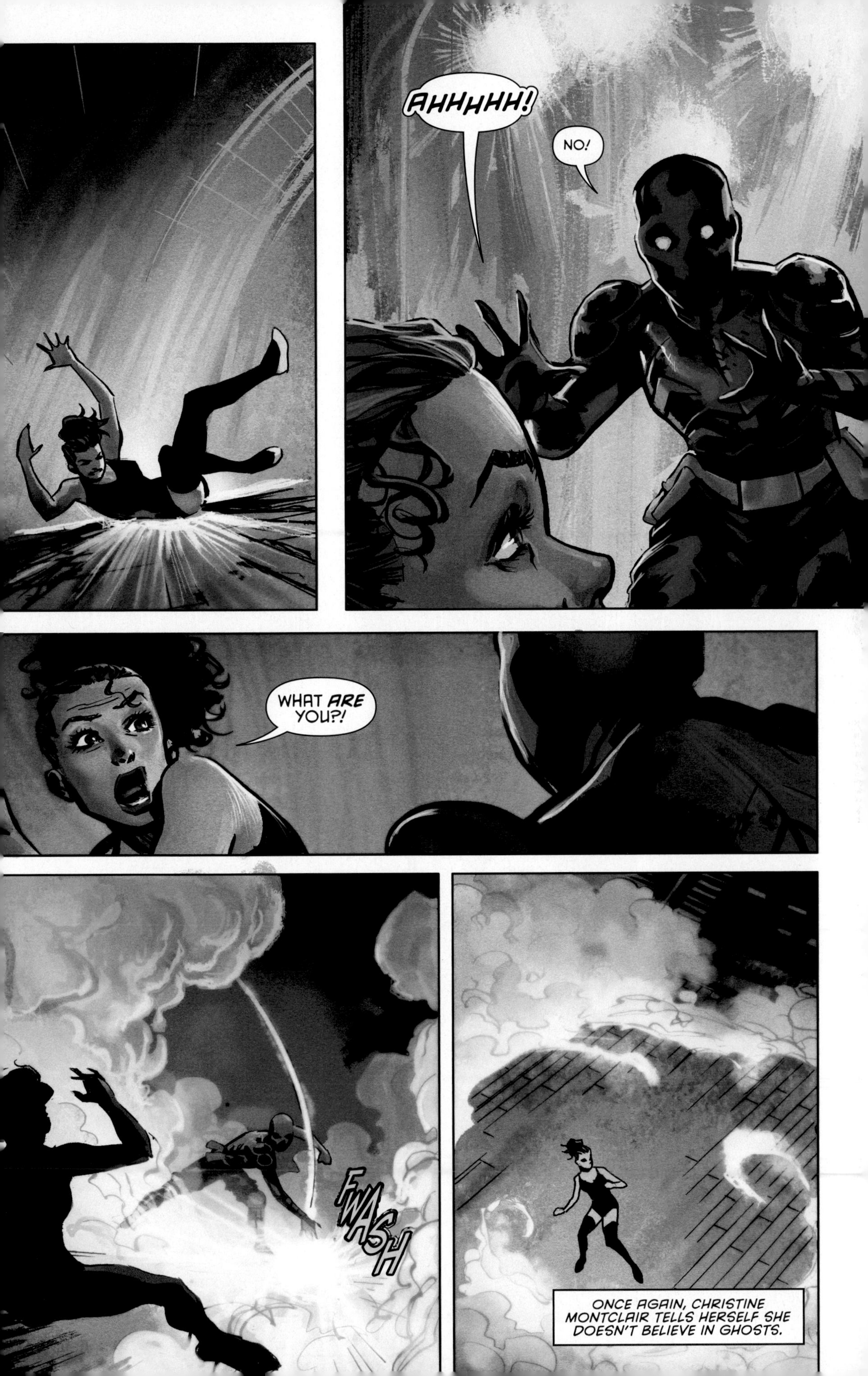
AHHHHH!
NO!
WHAT ARE YOU?!
FWASH
ONCE AGAIN, CHRISTINE MONTCLAIR TELLS HERSELF SHE DOESN'T BELIEVE IN GHOSTS.

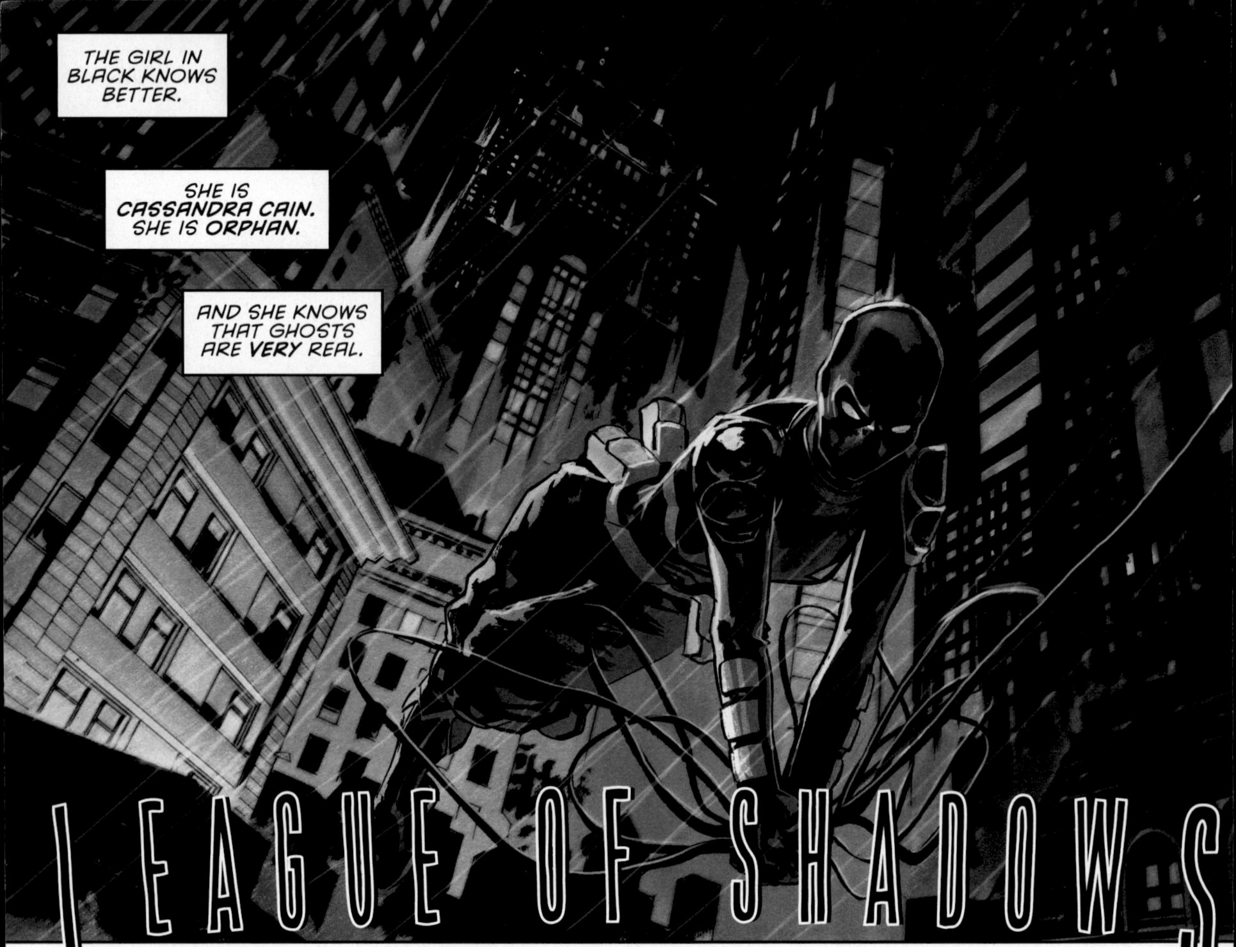
THE GIRL IN BLACK KNOWS BETTER.
SHE IS CASSANDRA CAIN. SHE IS ORPHAN.
AND SHE KNOWS THAT GHOSTS ARE VERY REAL.

LEAGUE OF SHADOWS

PROLOGUE: SHADOW OF A TEAR

JAMES TYNION IV Writer MARCIO TAKARA Artist DEAN WHITE Colors MARILYN PATRIZIO Letters
EDDY BARROWS, EBER FERREIRA & ADRIANO LUCAS Cover RAFAEL ALBUQUERQUE Variant Cover
DAVE WIELGOSZ Asst. Editor CHRIS CONROY Editor MARK DOYLE Group Editor
BATMAN CREATED BY BOB KANE WITH BILL FINGER

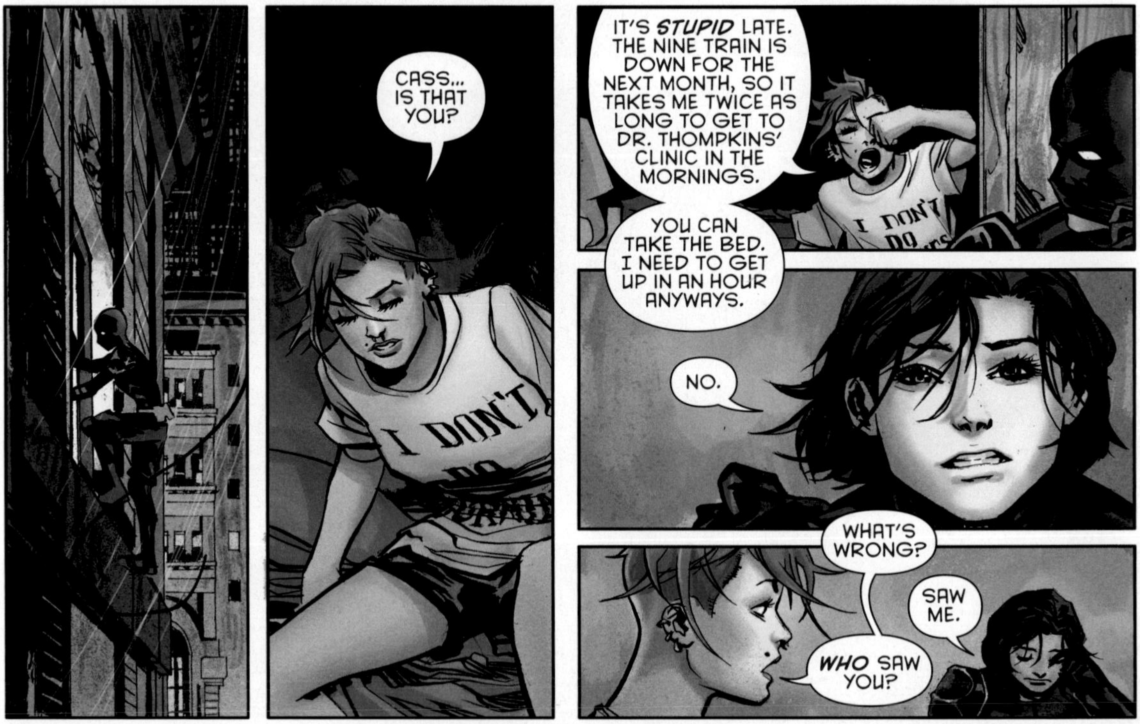
CASS... IS THAT YOU?
IT'S STUPID LATE. THE NINE TRAIN IS DOWN FOR THE NEXT MONTH, SO IT TAKES ME TWICE AS LONG TO GET TO DR. THOMPKINS' CLINIC IN THE MORNINGS.
YOU CAN TAKE THE BED. I NEED TO GET UP IN AN HOUR ANYWAYS.
NO.
WHAT'S WRONG?
SAW ME.
WHO SAW YOU?

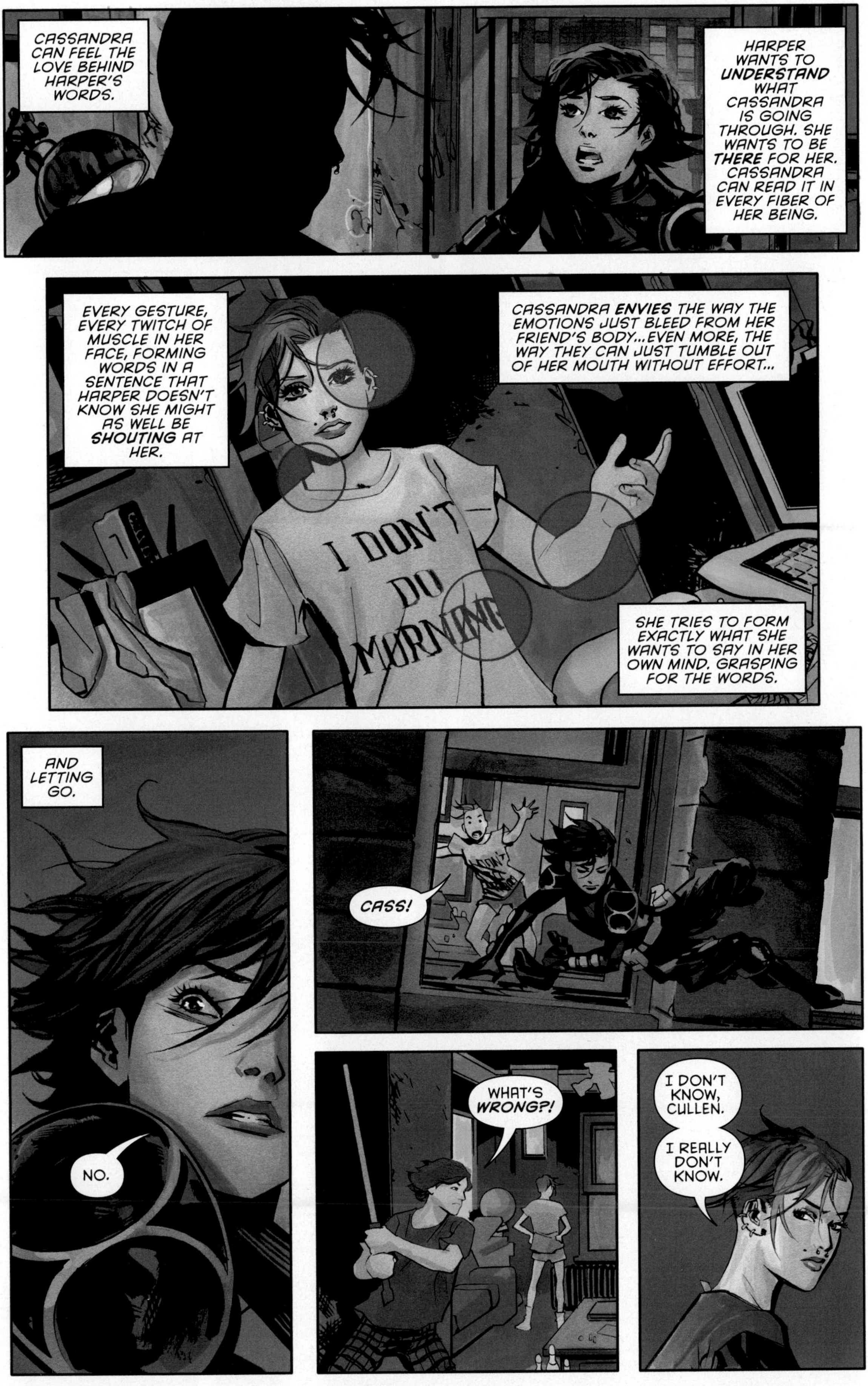
CASSANDRA CAN FEEL THE LOVE BEHIND HARPER'S WORDS.
HARPER WANTS TO **UNDERSTAND** WHAT CASSANDRA IS GOING THROUGH. SHE WANTS TO BE **THERE** FOR HER. CASSANDRA CAN READ IT IN EVERY FIBER OF HER BEING.
EVERY GESTURE, EVERY TWITCH OF MUSCLE IN HER FACE, FORMING WORDS IN A SENTENCE THAT HARPER DOESN'T KNOW SHE MIGHT AS WELL BE **SHOUTING** AT HER.
CASSANDRA **ENVIES** THE WAY THE EMOTIONS JUST BLEED FROM HER FRIEND'S BODY...EVEN MORE, THE WAY THEY CAN JUST TUMBLE OUT OF HER MOUTH WITHOUT EFFORT...
I DON'T DO MORNING
SHE TRIES TO FORM EXACTLY WHAT SHE WANTS TO SAY IN HER OWN MIND. GRASPING FOR THE WORDS.
AND LETTING GO.
NO.
CASS!
WHAT'S **WRONG?!**
I DON'T KNOW, CULLEN.
I REALLY DON'T KNOW.

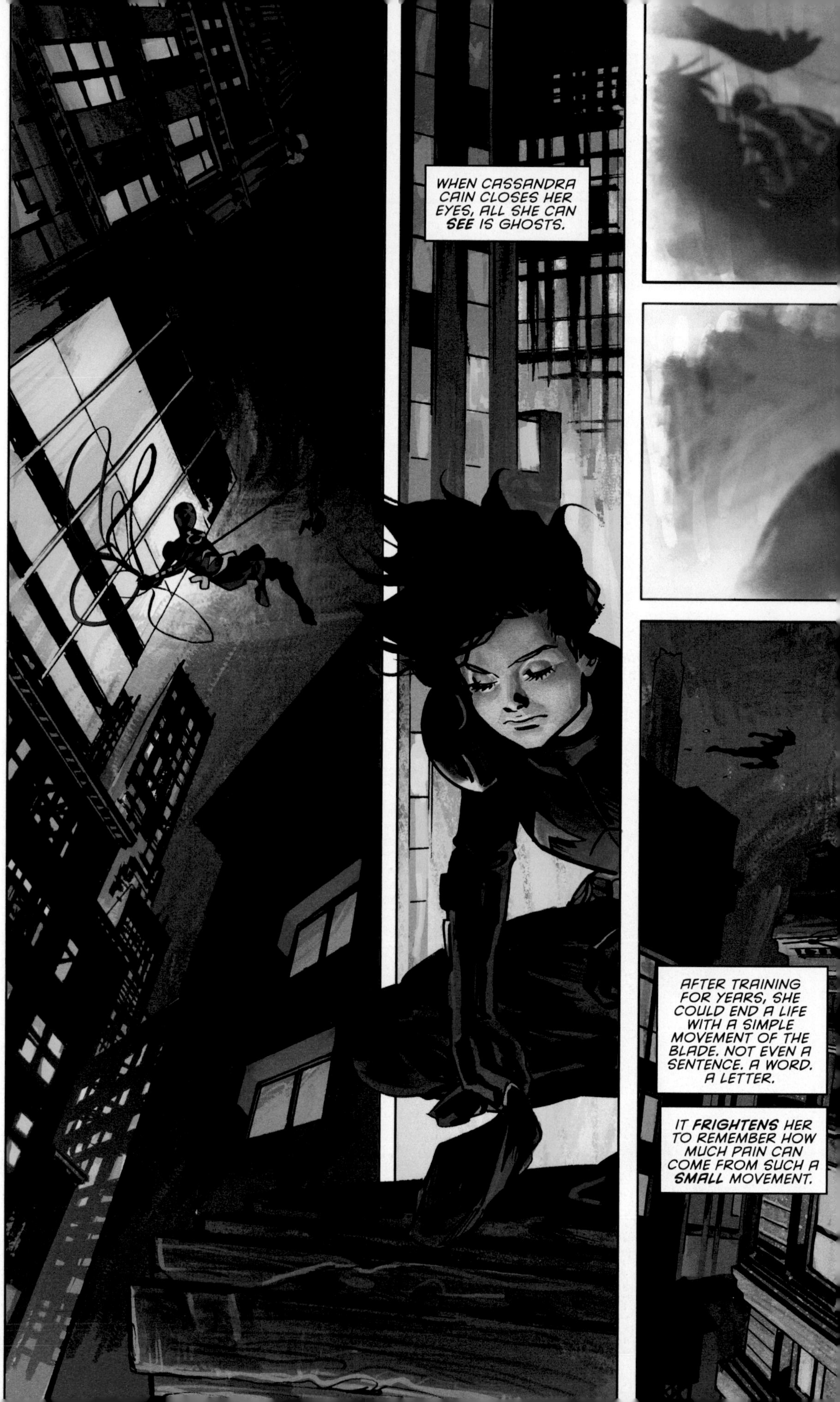

WHEN CASSANDRA CAIN CLOSES HER EYES, ALL SHE CAN **SEE** IS GHOSTS.
AFTER TRAINING FOR YEARS, SHE COULD END A LIFE WITH A SIMPLE MOVEMENT OF THE BLADE. NOT EVEN A SENTENCE. A WORD. A LETTER.
IT **FRIGHTENS** HER TO REMEMBER HOW MUCH PAIN CAN COME FROM SUCH A **SMALL** MOVEMENT.

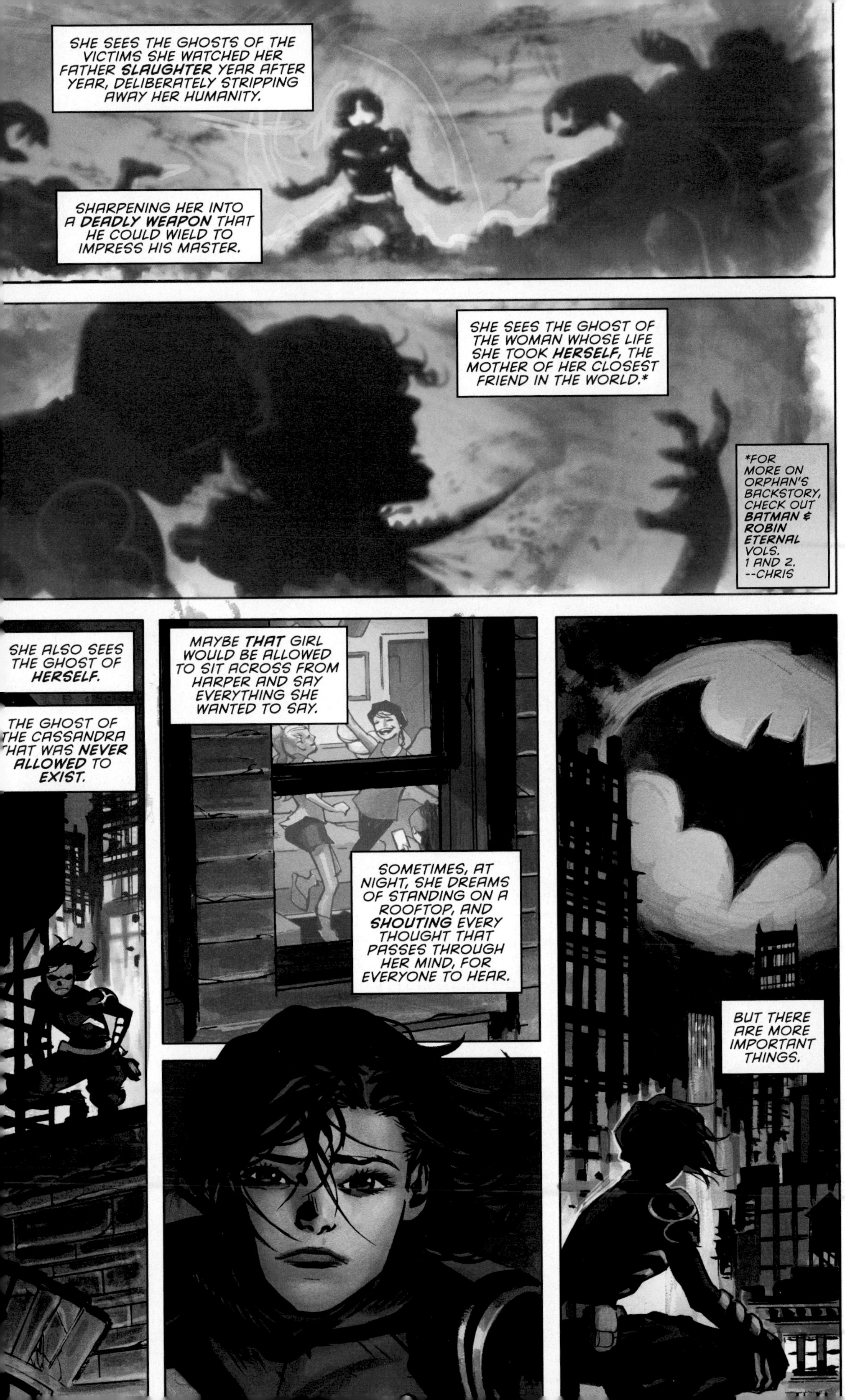
SHE SEES THE GHOSTS OF THE VICTIMS SHE WATCHED HER FATHER SLAUGHTER YEAR AFTER YEAR, DELIBERATELY STRIPPING AWAY HER HUMANITY.
SHARPENING HER INTO A DEADLY WEAPON THAT HE COULD WIELD TO IMPRESS HIS MASTER.
SHE SEES THE GHOST OF THE WOMAN WHOSE LIFE SHE TOOK HERSELF, THE MOTHER OF HER CLOSEST FRIEND IN THE WORLD.*
*FOR MORE ON ORPHAN'S BACKSTORY, CHECK OUT BATMAN & ROBIN ETERNAL VOLS. 1 AND 2. --CHRIS
SHE ALSO SEES THE GHOST OF HERSELF.
THE GHOST OF THE CASSANDRA THAT WAS NEVER ALLOWED TO EXIST.
MAYBE THAT GIRL WOULD BE ALLOWED TO SIT ACROSS FROM HARPER AND SAY EVERYTHING SHE WANTED TO SAY.
SOMETIMES, AT NIGHT, SHE DREAMS OF STANDING ON A ROOFTOP, AND SHOUTING EVERY THOUGHT THAT PASSES THROUGH HER MIND, FOR EVERYONE TO HEAR.
BUT THERE ARE MORE IMPORTANT THINGS.

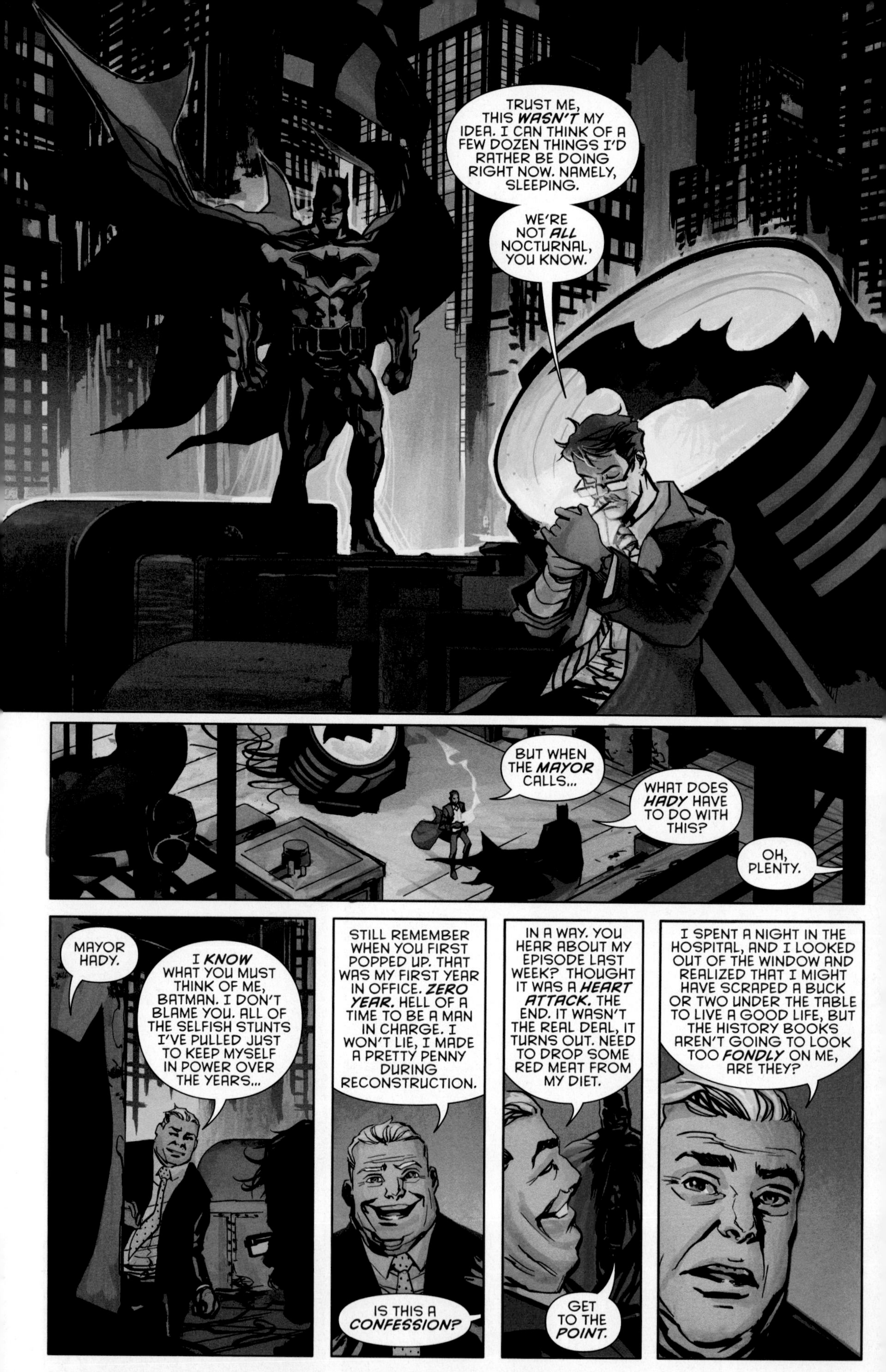
TRUST ME, THIS *WASN'T* MY IDEA. I CAN THINK OF A FEW DOZEN THINGS I'D RATHER BE DOING RIGHT NOW. NAMELY, SLEEPING.
WE'RE NOT *ALL* NOCTURNAL, YOU KNOW.
BUT WHEN THE *MAYOR* CALLS...
WHAT DOES *HADY* HAVE TO DO WITH THIS?
OH, PLENTY.
MAYOR HADY.
I *KNOW* WHAT YOU MUST THINK OF ME, BATMAN. I DON'T BLAME YOU. ALL OF THE SELFISH STUNTS I'VE PULLED JUST TO KEEP MYSELF IN POWER OVER THE YEARS...
STILL REMEMBER WHEN YOU FIRST POPPED UP. THAT WAS MY FIRST YEAR IN OFFICE. *ZERO YEAR.* HELL OF A TIME TO BE A MAN IN CHARGE. I WON'T LIE, I MADE A PRETTY PENNY DURING RECONSTRUCTION.
IS THIS A *CONFESSION?*
IN A WAY. YOU HEAR ABOUT MY EPISODE LAST WEEK? THOUGHT IT WAS A *HEART ATTACK.* THE END. IT WASN'T THE REAL DEAL, IT TURNS OUT. NEED TO DROP SOME RED MEAT FROM MY DIET.
GET TO THE *POINT.*
I SPENT A NIGHT IN THE HOSPITAL, AND I LOOKED OUT OF THE WINDOW AND REALIZED THAT I MIGHT HAVE SCRAPED A BUCK OR TWO UNDER THE TABLE TO LIVE A GOOD LIFE, BUT THE HISTORY BOOKS AREN'T GOING TO LOOK TOO *FONDLY* ON ME, ARE THEY?

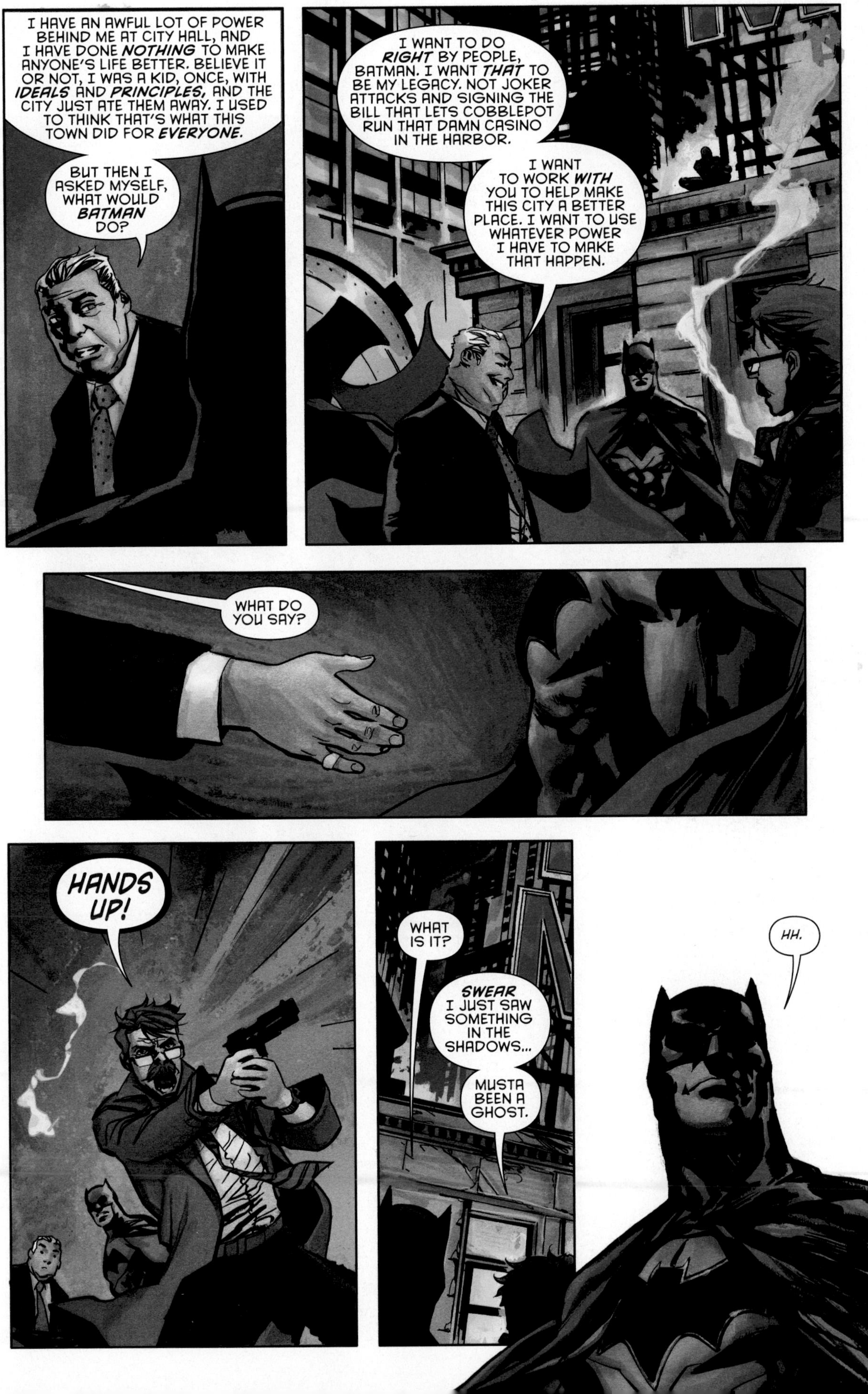
I HAVE AN AWFUL LOT OF POWER BEHIND ME AT CITY HALL, AND I HAVE DONE NOTHING TO MAKE ANYONE'S LIFE BETTER. BELIEVE IT OR NOT, I WAS A KID, ONCE, WITH IDEALS AND PRINCIPLES, AND THE CITY JUST ATE THEM AWAY. I USED TO THINK THAT'S WHAT THIS TOWN DID FOR EVERYONE.
BUT THEN I ASKED MYSELF, WHAT WOULD BATMAN DO?
I WANT TO DO RIGHT BY PEOPLE, BATMAN. I WANT THAT TO BE MY LEGACY. NOT JOKER ATTACKS AND SIGNING THE BILL THAT LETS COBBLEPOT RUN THAT DAMN CASINO IN THE HARBOR.
I WANT TO WORK WITH YOU TO HELP MAKE THIS CITY A BETTER PLACE. I WANT TO USE WHATEVER POWER I HAVE TO MAKE THAT HAPPEN.
WHAT DO YOU SAY?
HANDS UP!
WHAT IS IT?
SWEAR I JUST SAW SOMETHING IN THE SHADOWS...
MUSTA BEEN A GHOST.
HH.

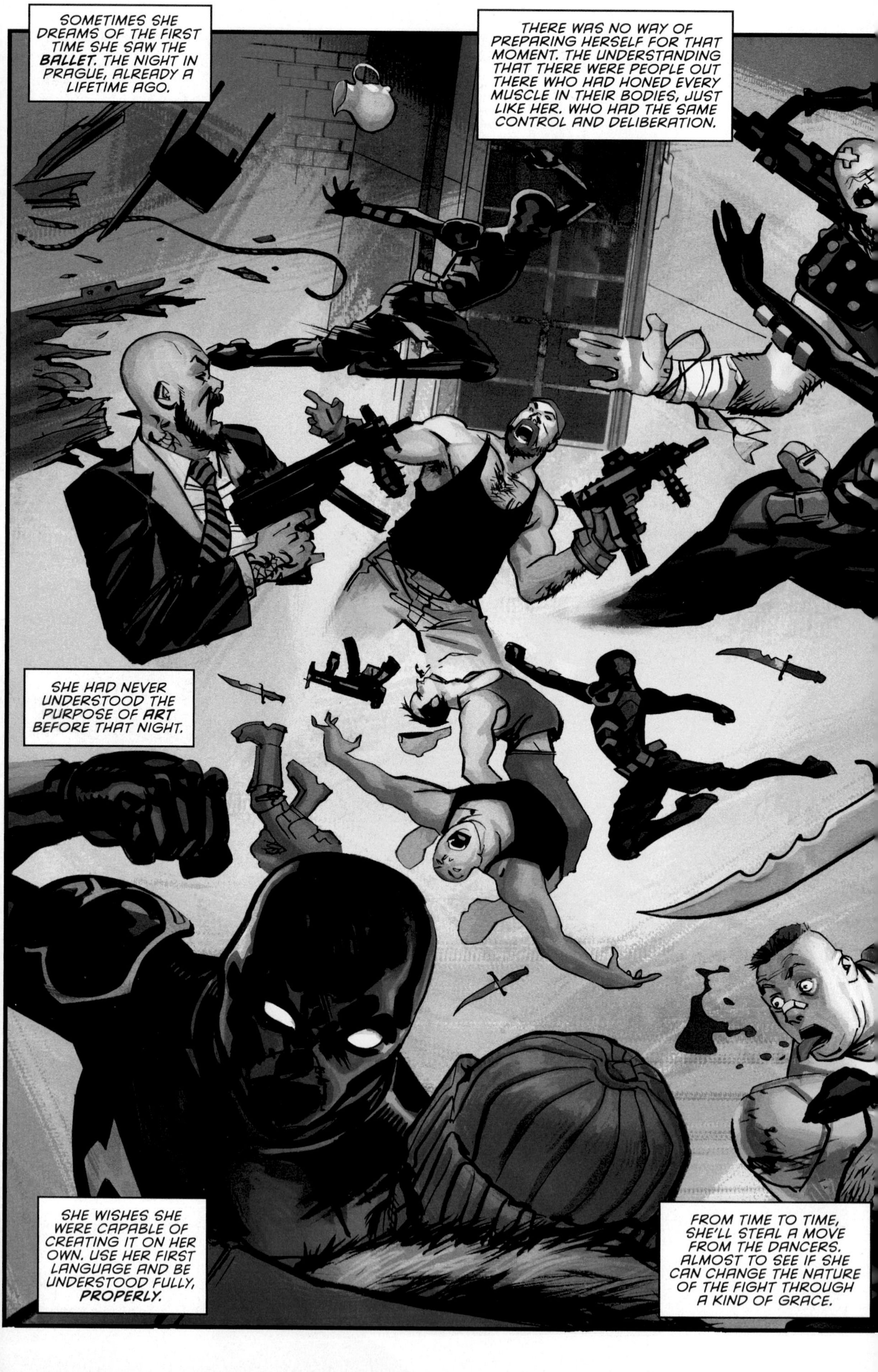
SOMETIMES SHE DREAMS OF THE FIRST TIME SHE SAW THE BALLET. THE NIGHT IN PRAGUE, ALREADY A LIFETIME AGO.
THERE WAS NO WAY OF PREPARING HERSELF FOR THAT MOMENT. THE UNDERSTANDING THAT THERE WERE PEOPLE OUT THERE WHO HAD HONED EVERY MUSCLE IN THEIR BODIES, JUST LIKE HER. WHO HAD THE SAME CONTROL AND DELIBERATION.
SHE HAD NEVER UNDERSTOOD THE PURPOSE OF ART BEFORE THAT NIGHT.
SHE WISHES SHE WERE CAPABLE OF CREATING IT ON HER OWN. USE HER FIRST LANGUAGE AND BE UNDERSTOOD FULLY, PROPERLY.
FROM TIME TO TIME, SHE'LL STEAL A MOVE FROM THE DANCERS. ALMOST TO SEE IF SHE CAN CHANGE THE NATURE OF THE FIGHT THROUGH A KIND OF GRACE.

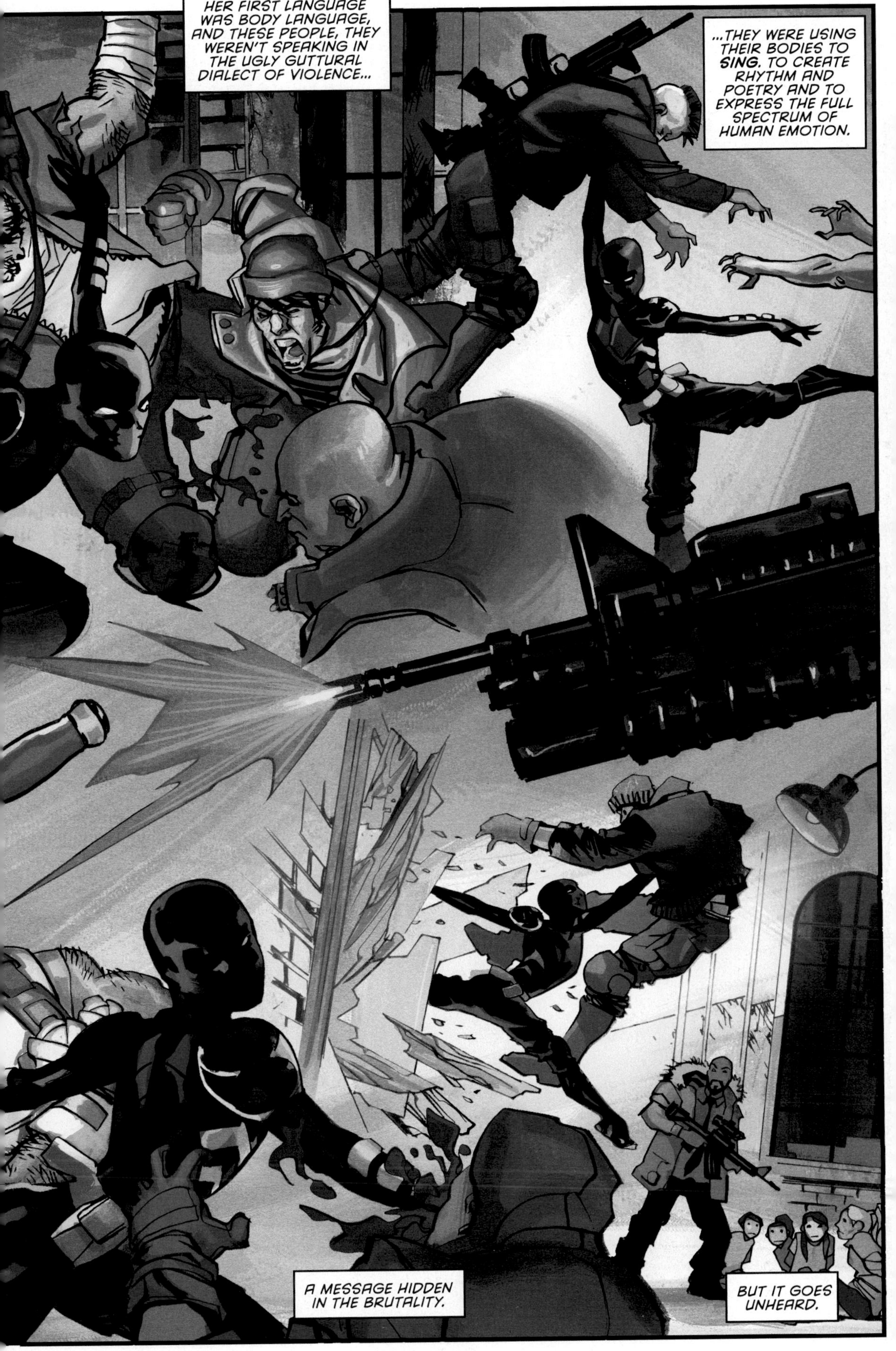
HER FIRST LANGUAGE WAS BODY LANGUAGE, AND THESE PEOPLE, THEY WEREN'T SPEAKING IN THE UGLY GUTTURAL DIALECT OF VIOLENCE...
...THEY WERE USING THEIR BODIES TO SING. TO CREATE RHYTHM AND POETRY AND TO EXPRESS THE FULL SPECTRUM OF HUMAN EMOTION.
A MESSAGE HIDDEN IN THE BRUTALITY.
BUT IT GOES UNHEARD.

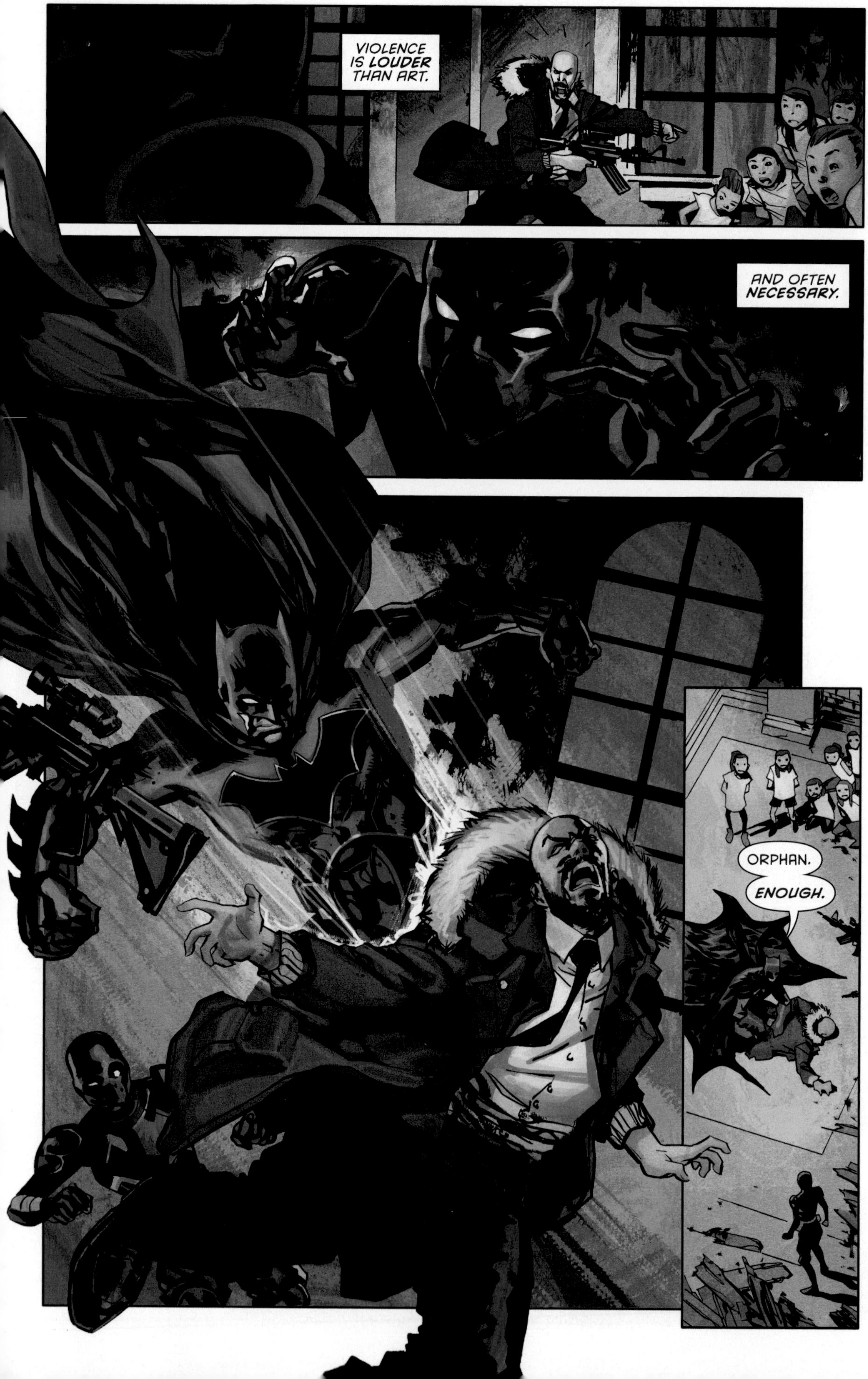
VIOLENCE IS LOUDER THAN ART.
AND OFTEN NECESSARY.
ORPHAN.
ENOUGH.

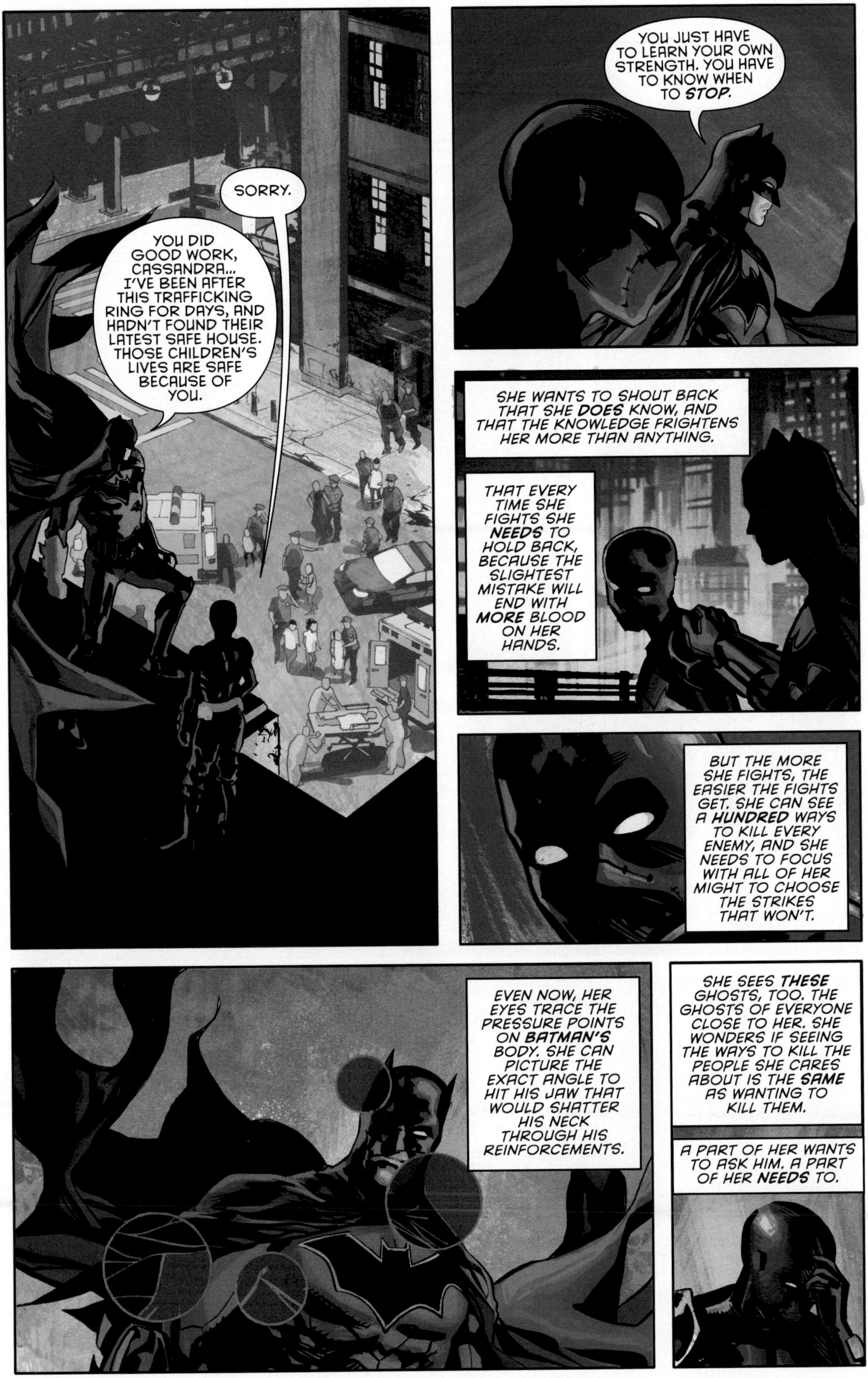
SORRY.
YOU DID GOOD WORK, CASSANDRA... I'VE BEEN AFTER THIS TRAFFICKING RING FOR DAYS, AND HADN'T FOUND THEIR LATEST SAFE HOUSE. THOSE CHILDREN'S LIVES ARE SAFE BECAUSE OF YOU.
YOU JUST HAVE TO LEARN YOUR OWN STRENGTH. YOU HAVE TO KNOW WHEN TO STOP.
SHE WANTS TO SHOUT BACK THAT SHE DOES KNOW, AND THAT THE KNOWLEDGE FRIGHTENS HER MORE THAN ANYTHING.
THAT EVERY TIME SHE FIGHTS SHE NEEDS TO HOLD BACK, BECAUSE THE SLIGHTEST MISTAKE WILL END WITH MORE BLOOD ON HER HANDS.
BUT THE MORE SHE FIGHTS, THE EASIER THE FIGHTS GET. SHE CAN SEE A HUNDRED WAYS TO KILL EVERY ENEMY, AND SHE NEEDS TO FOCUS WITH ALL OF HER MIGHT TO CHOOSE THE STRIKES THAT WON'T.
EVEN NOW, HER EYES TRACE THE PRESSURE POINTS ON BATMAN'S BODY. SHE CAN PICTURE THE EXACT ANGLE TO HIT HIS JAW THAT WOULD SHATTER HIS NECK THROUGH HIS REINFORCEMENTS.
SHE SEES THESE GHOSTS, TOO. THE GHOSTS OF EVERYONE CLOSE TO HER. SHE WONDERS IF SEEING THE WAYS TO KILL THE PEOPLE SHE CARES ABOUT IS THE SAME AS WANTING TO KILL THEM.
A PART OF HER WANTS TO ASK HIM. A PART OF HER NEEDS TO.

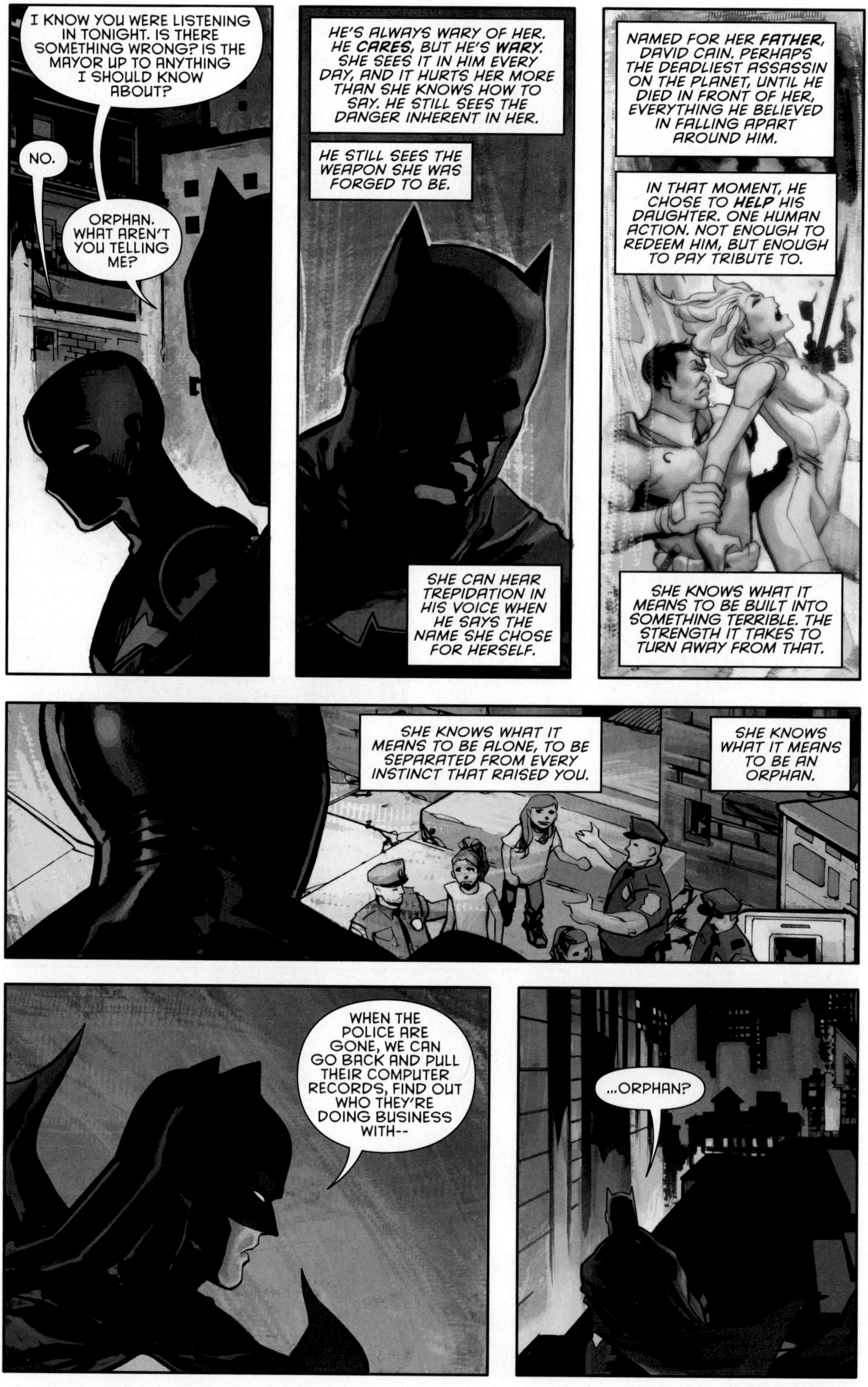
I KNOW YOU WERE LISTENING IN TONIGHT. IS THERE SOMETHING WRONG? IS THE MAYOR UP TO ANYTHING I SHOULD KNOW ABOUT?
NO.
ORPHAN. WHAT AREN'T YOU TELLING ME?
HE'S ALWAYS WARY OF HER. HE CARES, BUT HE'S WARY. SHE SEES IT IN HIM EVERY DAY, AND IT HURTS HER MORE THAN SHE KNOWS HOW TO SAY. HE STILL SEES THE DANGER INHERENT IN HER.
HE STILL SEES THE WEAPON SHE WAS FORGED TO BE.
SHE CAN HEAR TREPIDATION IN HIS VOICE WHEN HE SAYS THE NAME SHE CHOSE FOR HERSELF.
NAMED FOR HER FATHER, DAVID CAIN. PERHAPS THE DEADLIEST ASSASSIN ON THE PLANET, UNTIL HE DIED IN FRONT OF HER, EVERYTHING HE BELIEVED IN FALLING APART AROUND HIM.
IN THAT MOMENT, HE CHOSE TO HELP HIS DAUGHTER. ONE HUMAN ACTION. NOT ENOUGH TO REDEEM HIM, BUT ENOUGH TO PAY TRIBUTE TO.
SHE KNOWS WHAT IT MEANS TO BE BUILT INTO SOMETHING TERRIBLE. THE STRENGTH IT TAKES TO TURN AWAY FROM THAT.
SHE KNOWS WHAT IT MEANS TO BE ALONE, TO BE SEPARATED FROM EVERY INSTINCT THAT RAISED YOU.
SHE KNOWS WHAT IT MEANS TO BE AN ORPHAN.
WHEN THE POLICE ARE GONE, WE CAN GO BACK AND PULL THEIR COMPUTER RECORDS, FIND OUT WHO THEY'RE DOING BUSINESS WITH--
...ORPHAN?

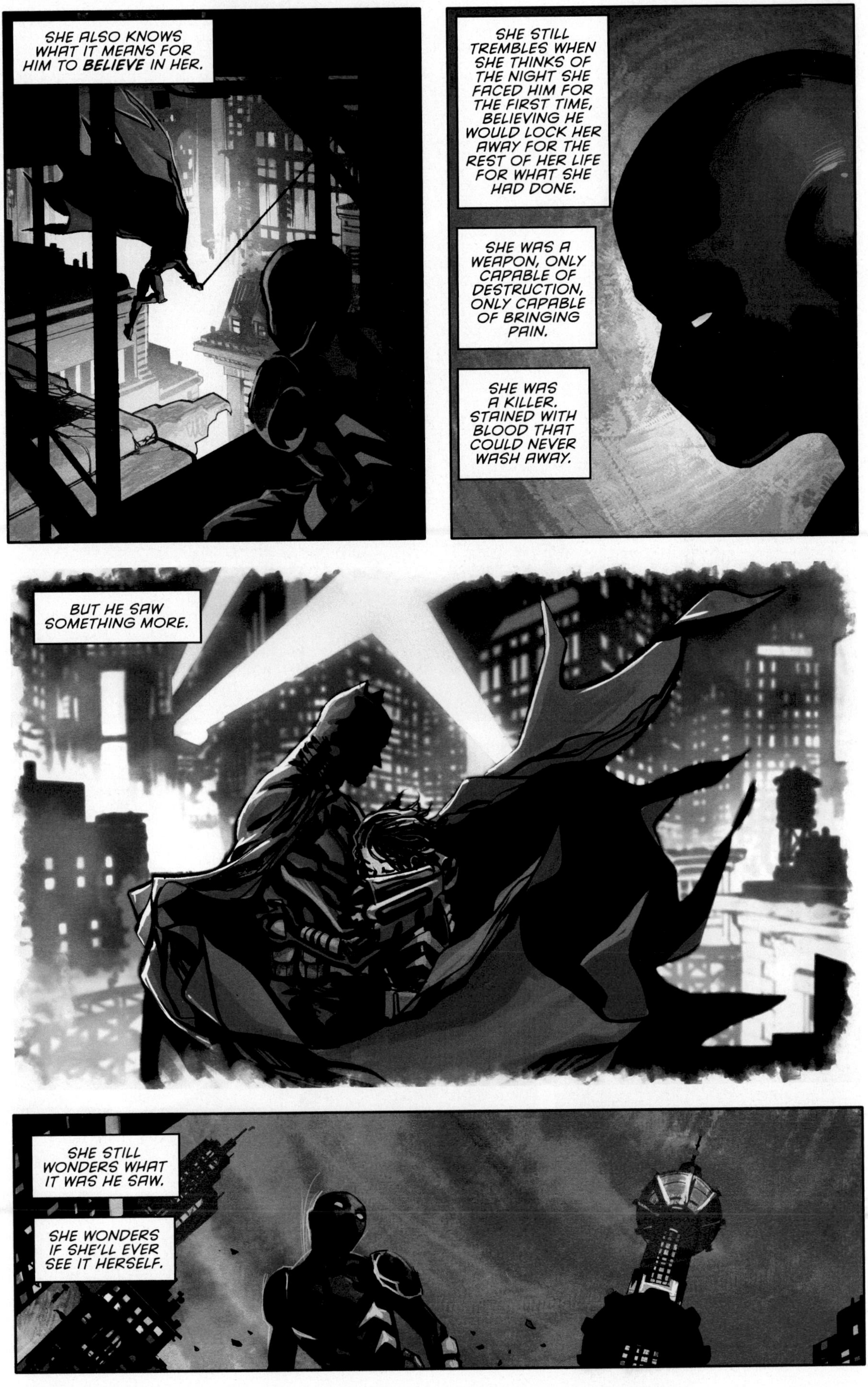
SHE ALSO KNOWS WHAT IT MEANS FOR HIM TO **BELIEVE** IN HER.
SHE STILL TREMBLES WHEN SHE THINKS OF THE NIGHT SHE FACED HIM FOR THE FIRST TIME, BELIEVING HE WOULD LOCK HER AWAY FOR THE REST OF HER LIFE FOR WHAT SHE HAD DONE.
SHE WAS A WEAPON, ONLY CAPABLE OF DESTRUCTION, ONLY CAPABLE OF BRINGING PAIN.
SHE WAS A KILLER. STAINED WITH BLOOD THAT COULD NEVER WASH AWAY.
BUT HE SAW SOMETHING MORE.
SHE STILL WONDERS WHAT IT WAS HE SAW.
SHE WONDERS IF SHE'LL EVER SEE IT HERSELF.

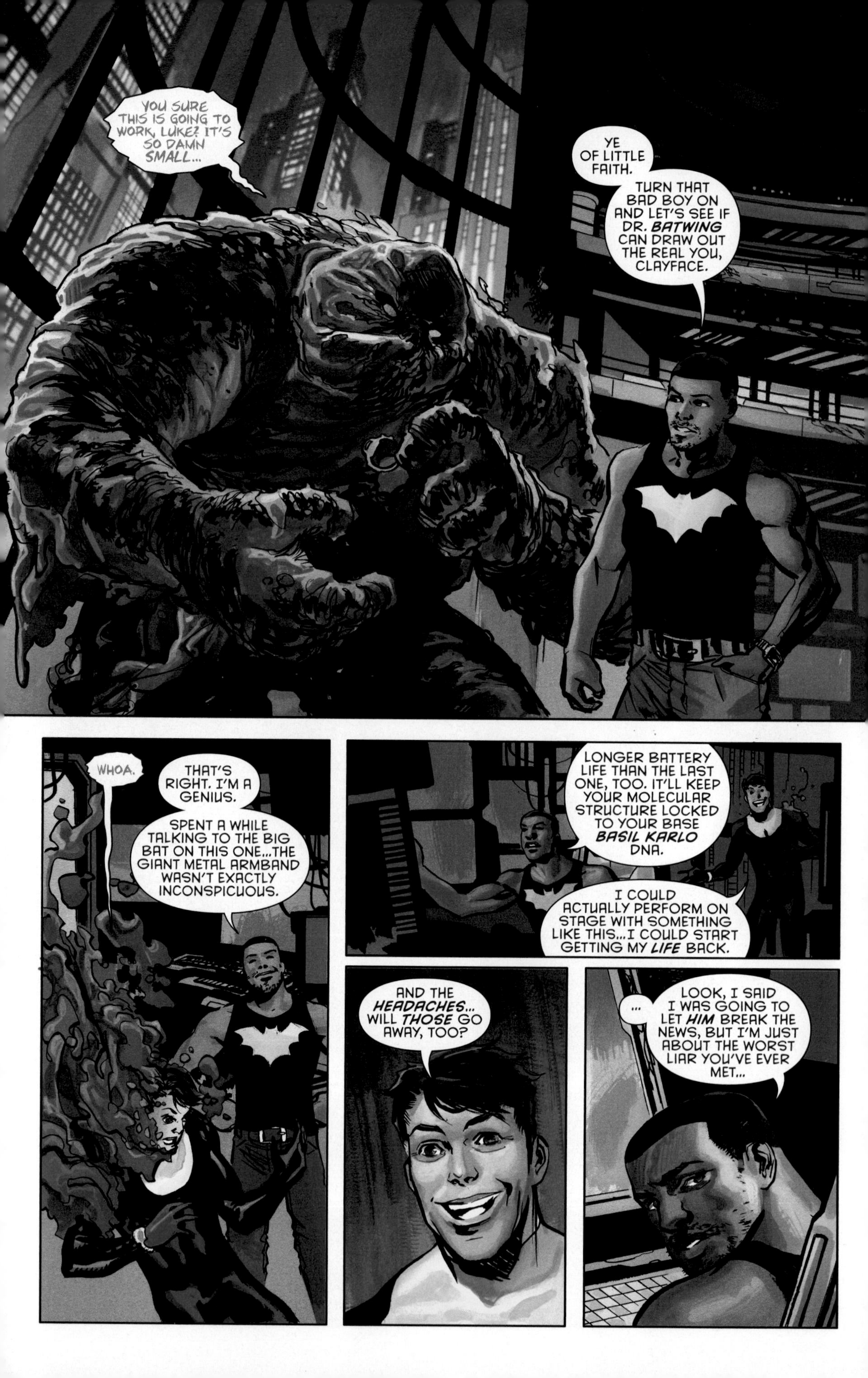
YOU SURE THIS IS GOING TO WORK, LUKE? IT'S SO DAMN SMALL...
YE OF LITTLE FAITH.
TURN THAT BAD BOY ON AND LET'S SEE IF DR. BATWING CAN DRAW OUT THE REAL YOU, CLAYFACE.
WHOA.
THAT'S RIGHT. I'M A GENIUS.
SPENT A WHILE TALKING TO THE BIG BAT ON THIS ONE...THE GIANT METAL ARMBAND WASN'T EXACTLY INCONSPICUOUS.
LONGER BATTERY LIFE THAN THE LAST ONE, TOO. IT'LL KEEP YOUR MOLECULAR STRUCTURE LOCKED TO YOUR BASE BASIL KARLO DNA.
I COULD ACTUALLY PERFORM ON STAGE WITH SOMETHING LIKE THIS...I COULD START GETTING MY LIFE BACK.
AND THE HEADACHES... WILL THOSE GO AWAY, TOO?
...
LOOK, I SAID I WAS GOING TO LET HIM BREAK THE NEWS, BUT I'M JUST ABOUT THE WORST LIAR YOU'VE EVER MET...

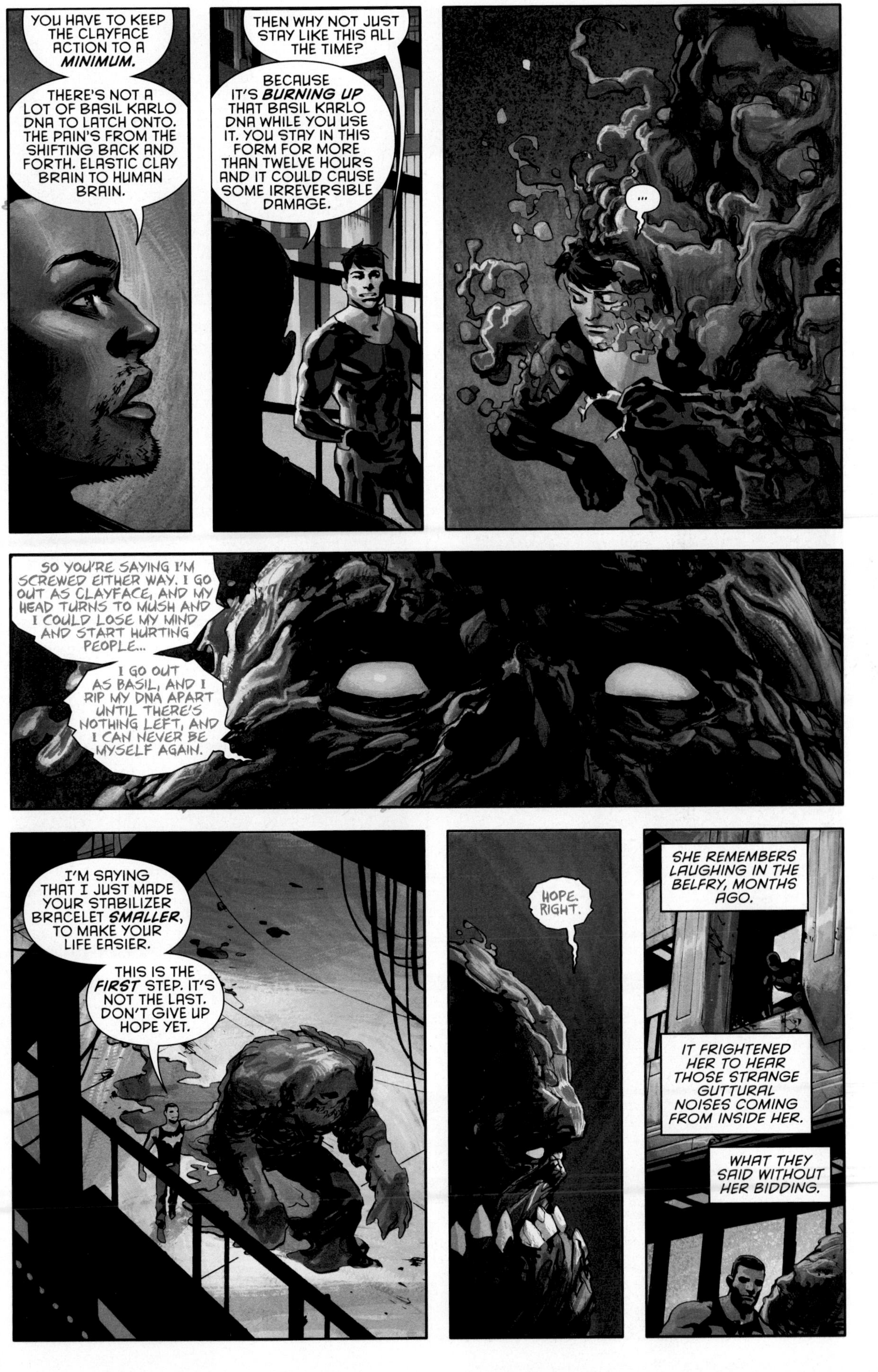
YOU HAVE TO KEEP THE CLAYFACE ACTION TO A *MINIMUM.*
THERE'S NOT A LOT OF BASIL KARLO DNA TO LATCH ONTO. THE PAIN'S FROM THE SHIFTING BACK AND FORTH. ELASTIC CLAY BRAIN TO HUMAN BRAIN.
THEN WHY NOT JUST STAY LIKE THIS ALL THE TIME?
BECAUSE IT'S *BURNING UP* THAT BASIL KARLO DNA WHILE YOU USE IT. YOU STAY IN THIS FORM FOR MORE THAN TWELVE HOURS AND IT COULD CAUSE SOME IRREVERSIBLE DAMAGE.
...
SO YOU'RE SAYING I'M SCREWED EITHER WAY. I GO OUT AS CLAYFACE, AND MY HEAD TURNS TO MUSH AND I COULD LOSE MY MIND AND START HURTING PEOPLE...
I GO OUT AS BASIL, AND I RIP MY DNA APART UNTIL THERE'S NOTHING LEFT, AND I CAN NEVER BE MYSELF AGAIN.
I'M SAYING THAT I JUST MADE YOUR STABILIZER BRACELET *SMALLER*, TO MAKE YOUR LIFE EASIER.
THIS IS THE *FIRST* STEP. IT'S NOT THE LAST. DON'T GIVE UP HOPE YET.
HOPE. RIGHT.
SHE REMEMBERS LAUGHING IN THE BELFRY, MONTHS AGO.
IT FRIGHTENED HER TO HEAR THOSE STRANGE GUTTURAL NOISES COMING FROM INSIDE HER.
WHAT THEY SAID WITHOUT HER BIDDING.

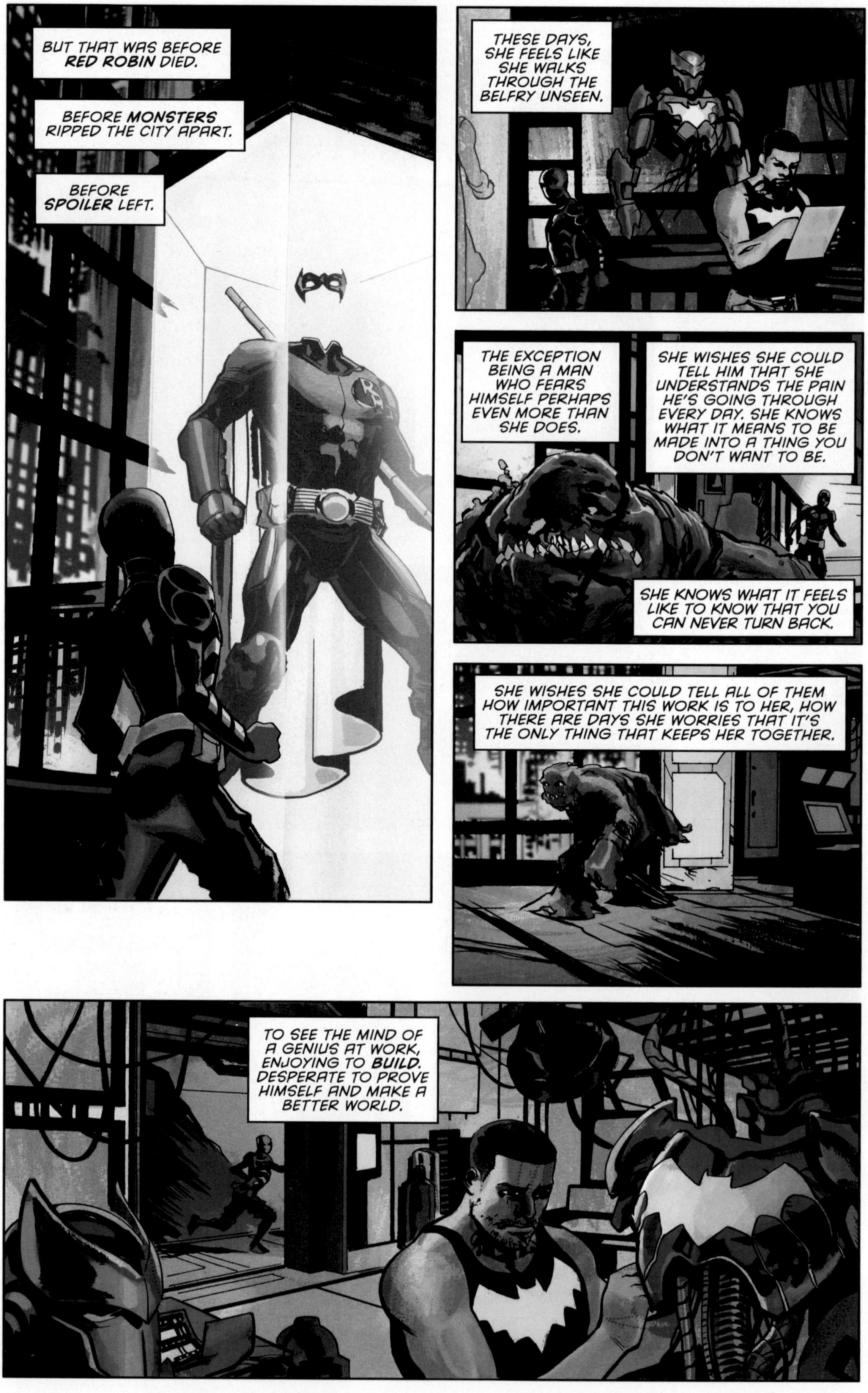
BUT THAT WAS BEFORE RED ROBIN DIED.
BEFORE MONSTERS RIPPED THE CITY APART.
BEFORE SPOILER LEFT.
THESE DAYS, SHE FEELS LIKE SHE WALKS THROUGH THE BELFRY UNSEEN.
THE EXCEPTION BEING A MAN WHO FEARS HIMSELF PERHAPS EVEN MORE THAN SHE DOES.
SHE WISHES SHE COULD TELL HIM THAT SHE UNDERSTANDS THE PAIN HE'S GOING THROUGH EVERY DAY. SHE KNOWS WHAT IT MEANS TO BE MADE INTO A THING YOU DON'T WANT TO BE.
SHE KNOWS WHAT IT FEELS LIKE TO KNOW THAT YOU CAN NEVER TURN BACK.
SHE WISHES SHE COULD TELL ALL OF THEM HOW IMPORTANT THIS WORK IS TO HER, HOW THERE ARE DAYS SHE WORRIES THAT IT'S THE ONLY THING THAT KEEPS HER TOGETHER.
TO SEE THE MIND OF A GENIUS AT WORK, ENJOYING TO BUILD. DESPERATE TO PROVE HIMSELF AND MAKE A BETTER WORLD.

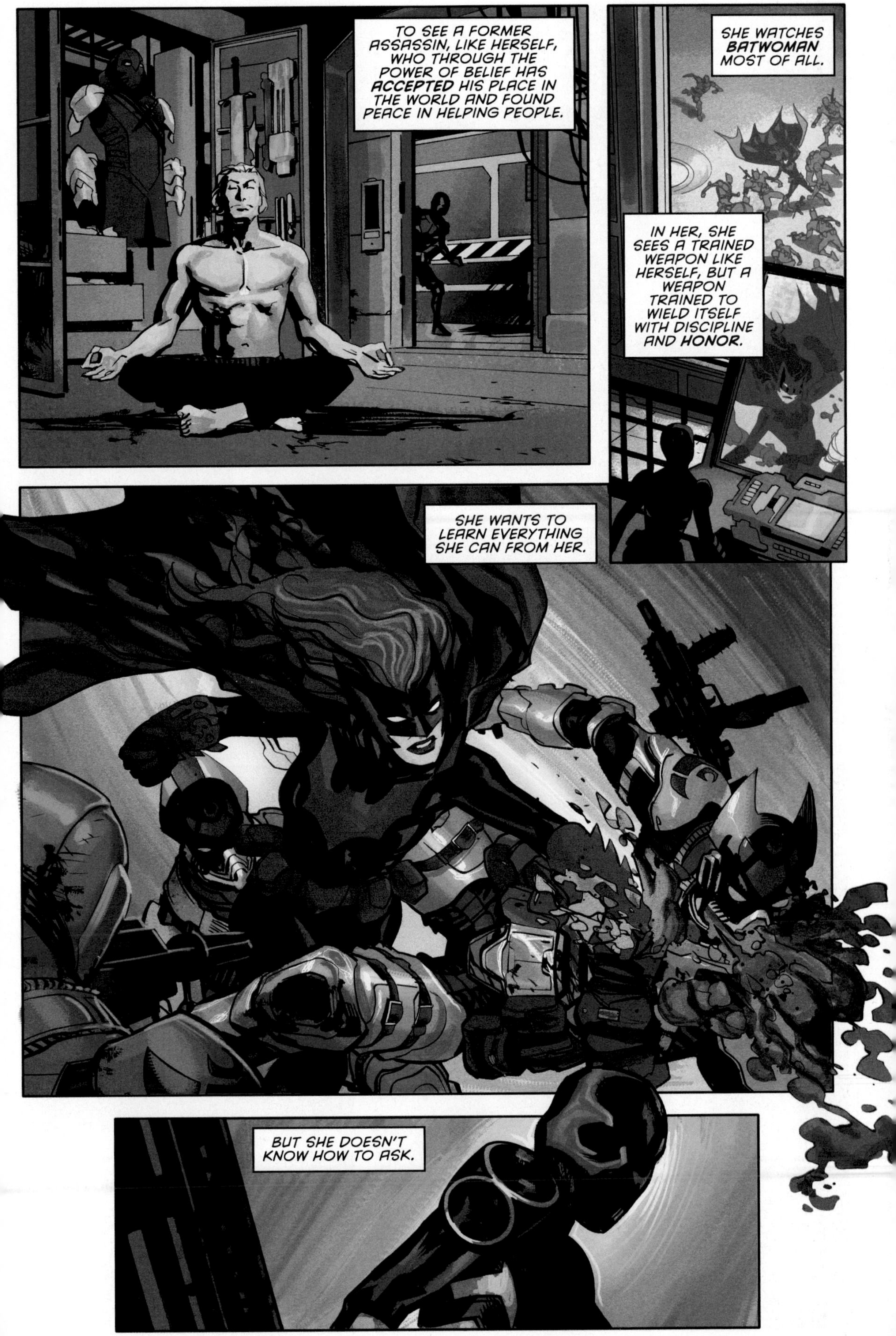
TO SEE A FORMER ASSASSIN, LIKE HERSELF, WHO THROUGH THE POWER OF BELIEF HAS ACCEPTED HIS PLACE IN THE WORLD AND FOUND PEACE IN HELPING PEOPLE.
SHE WATCHES BATWOMAN MOST OF ALL.
IN HER, SHE SEES A TRAINED WEAPON LIKE HERSELF, BUT A WEAPON TRAINED TO WIELD ITSELF WITH DISCIPLINE AND HONOR.
SHE WANTS TO LEARN EVERYTHING SHE CAN FROM HER.
BUT SHE DOESN'T KNOW HOW TO ASK.

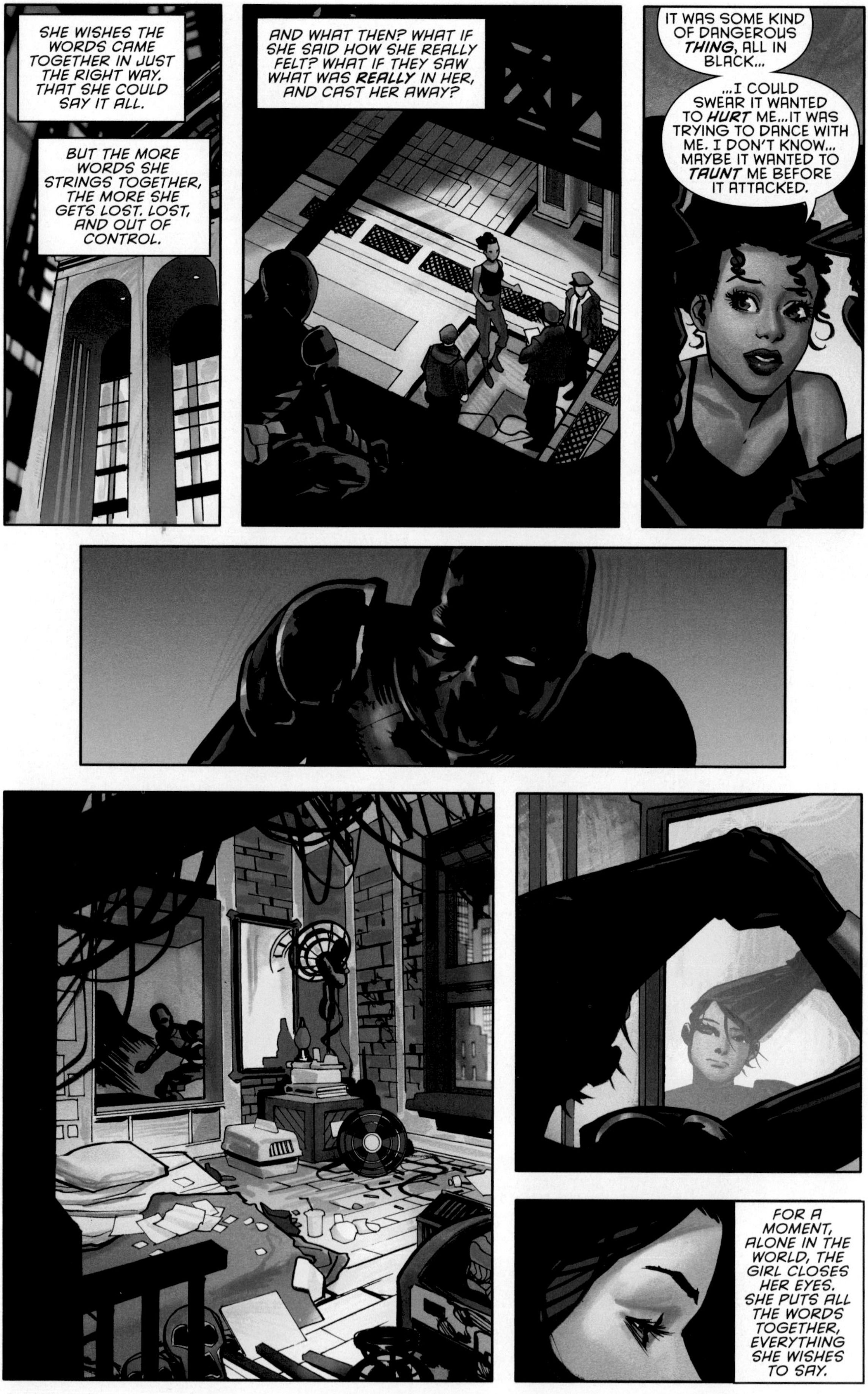
SHE WISHES THE WORDS CAME TOGETHER IN JUST THE RIGHT WAY. THAT SHE COULD SAY IT ALL.
BUT THE MORE WORDS SHE STRINGS TOGETHER, THE MORE SHE GETS LOST. LOST, AND OUT OF CONTROL.
AND WHAT THEN? WHAT IF SHE SAID HOW SHE REALLY FELT? WHAT IF THEY SAW WHAT WAS REALLY IN HER, AND CAST HER AWAY?
IT WAS SOME KIND OF DANGEROUS THING, ALL IN BLACK...
...I COULD SWEAR IT WANTED TO HURT ME...IT WAS TRYING TO DANCE WITH ME. I DON'T KNOW... MAYBE IT WANTED TO TAUNT ME BEFORE IT ATTACKED.
FOR A MOMENT, ALONE IN THE WORLD, THE GIRL CLOSES HER EYES. SHE PUTS ALL THE WORDS TOGETHER, EVERYTHING SHE WISHES TO SAY.

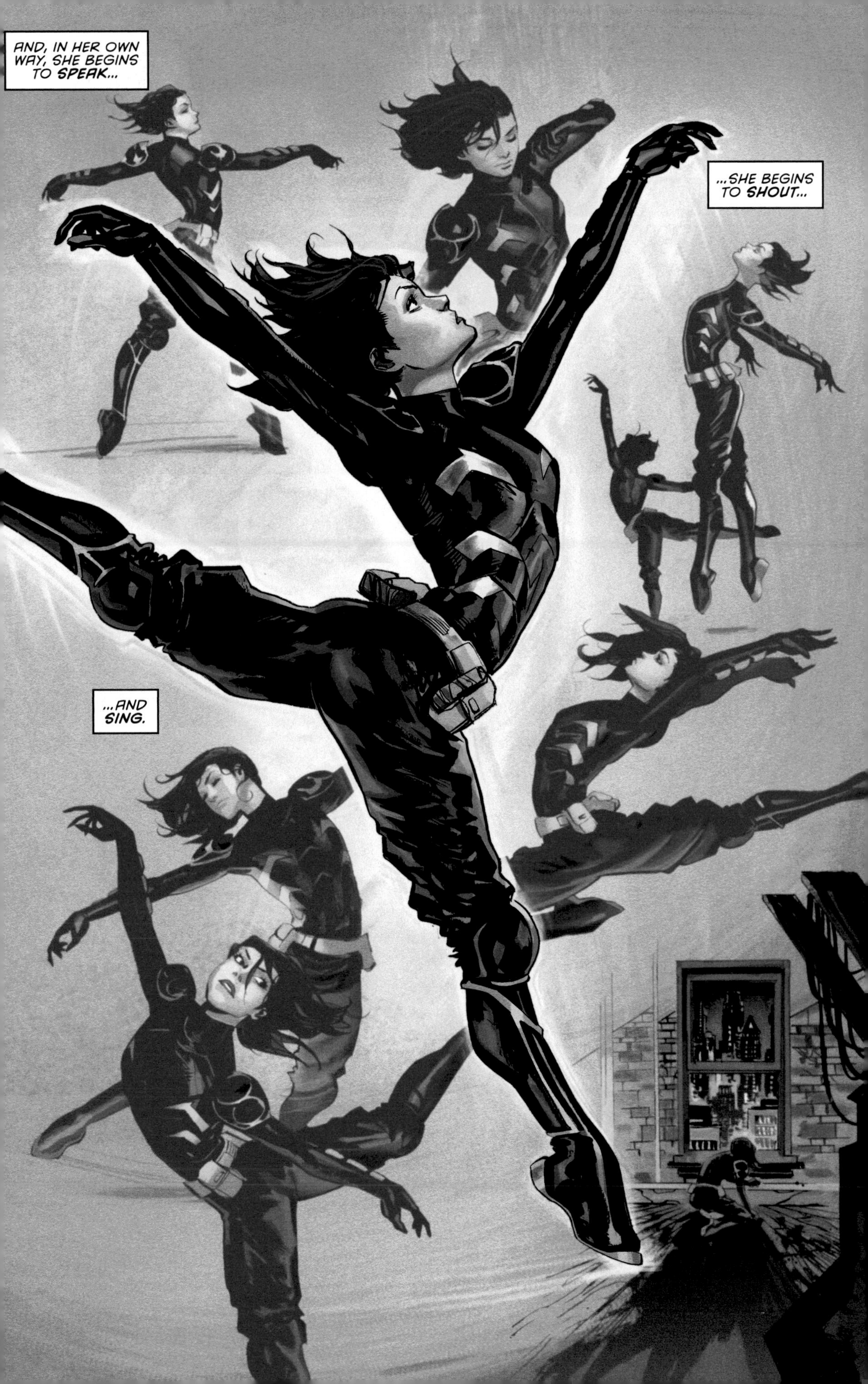
AND, IN HER OWN WAY, SHE BEGINS TO SPEAK...
...SHE BEGINS TO SHOUT...
...AND SING.

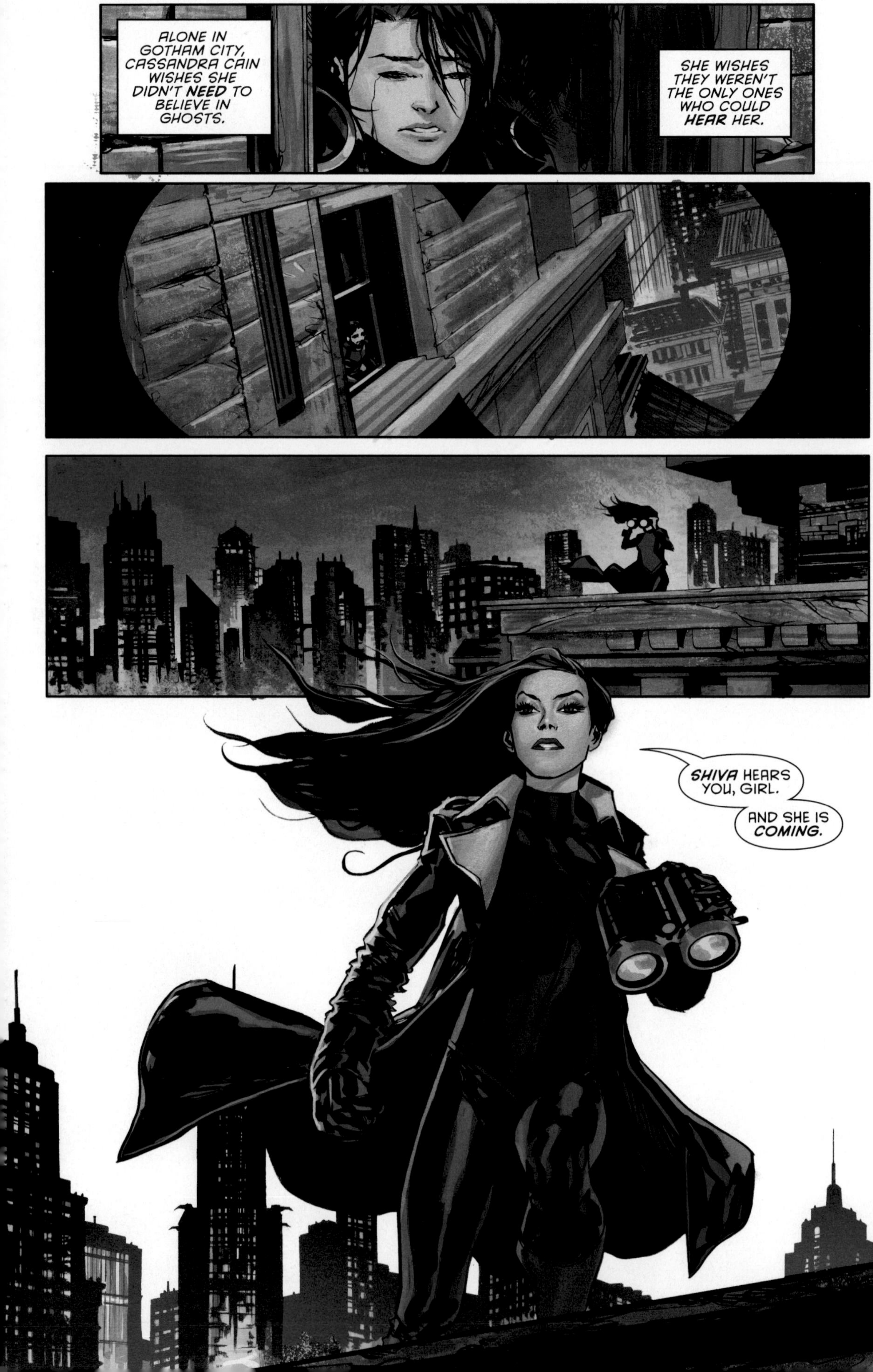
ALONE IN GOTHAM CITY, CASSANDRA CAIN WISHES SHE DIDN'T NEED TO BELIEVE IN GHOSTS.
SHE WISHES THEY WEREN'T THE ONLY ONES WHO COULD HEAR HER.
SHIVA HEARS YOU, GIRL.
AND SHE IS COMING.

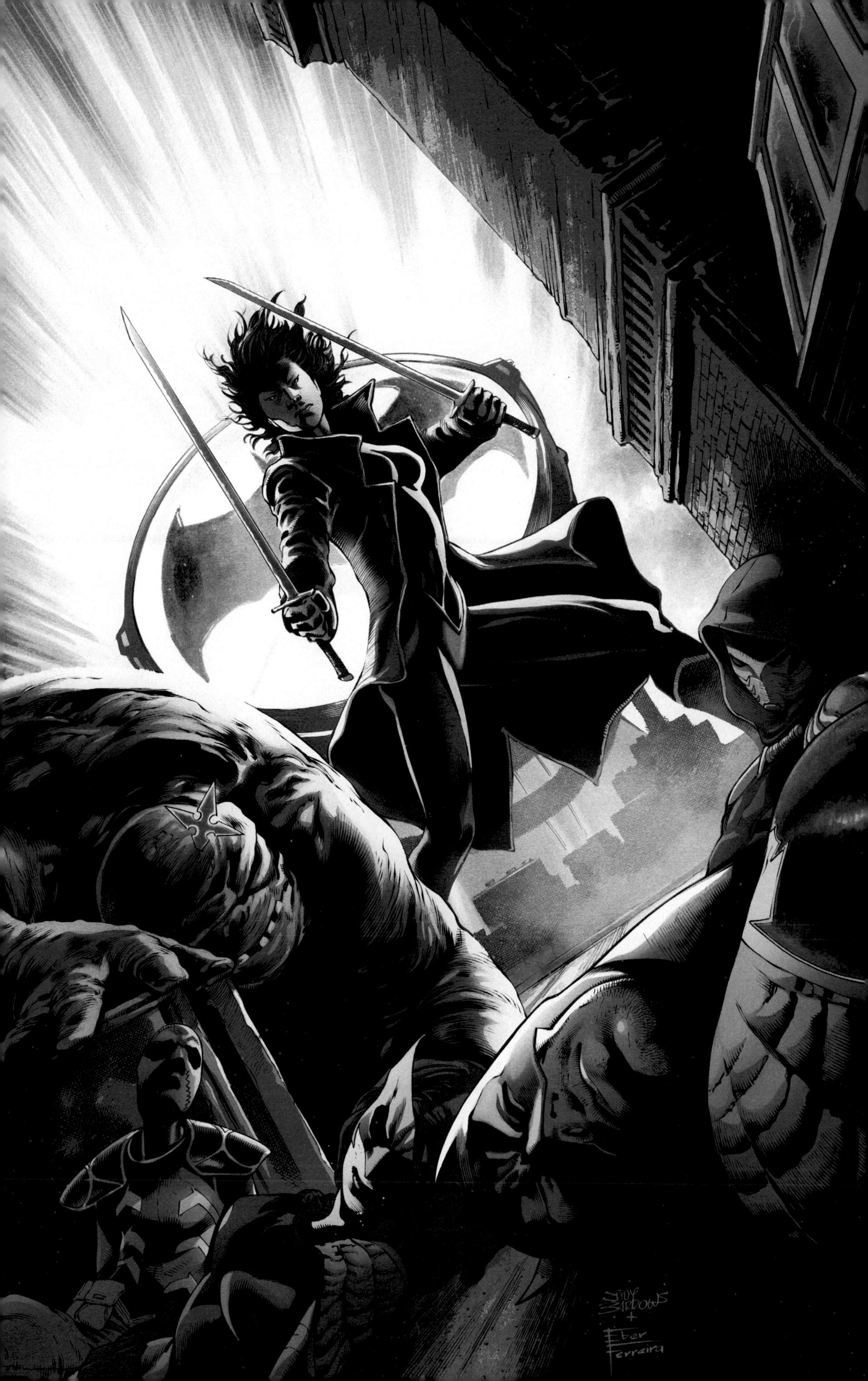

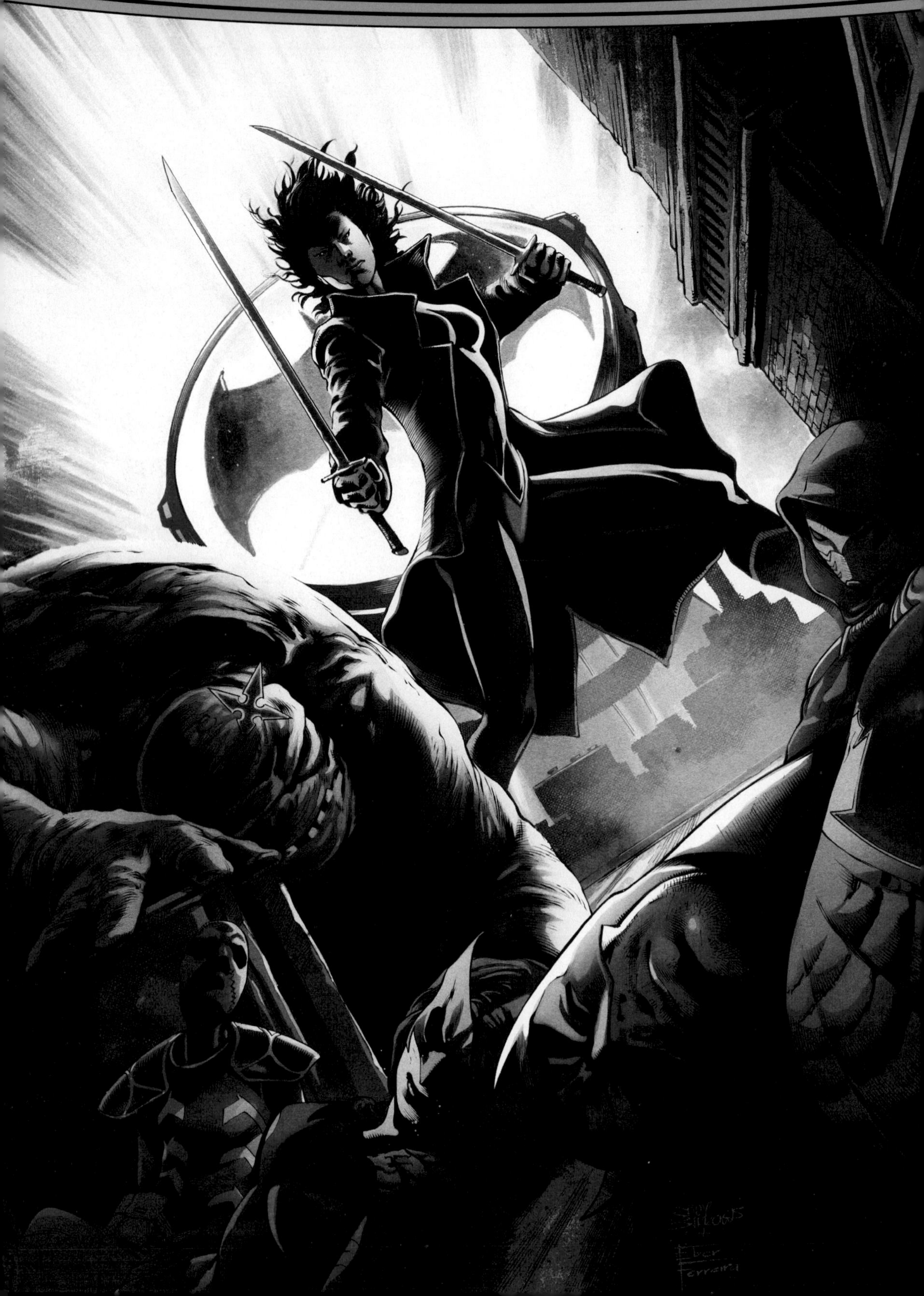

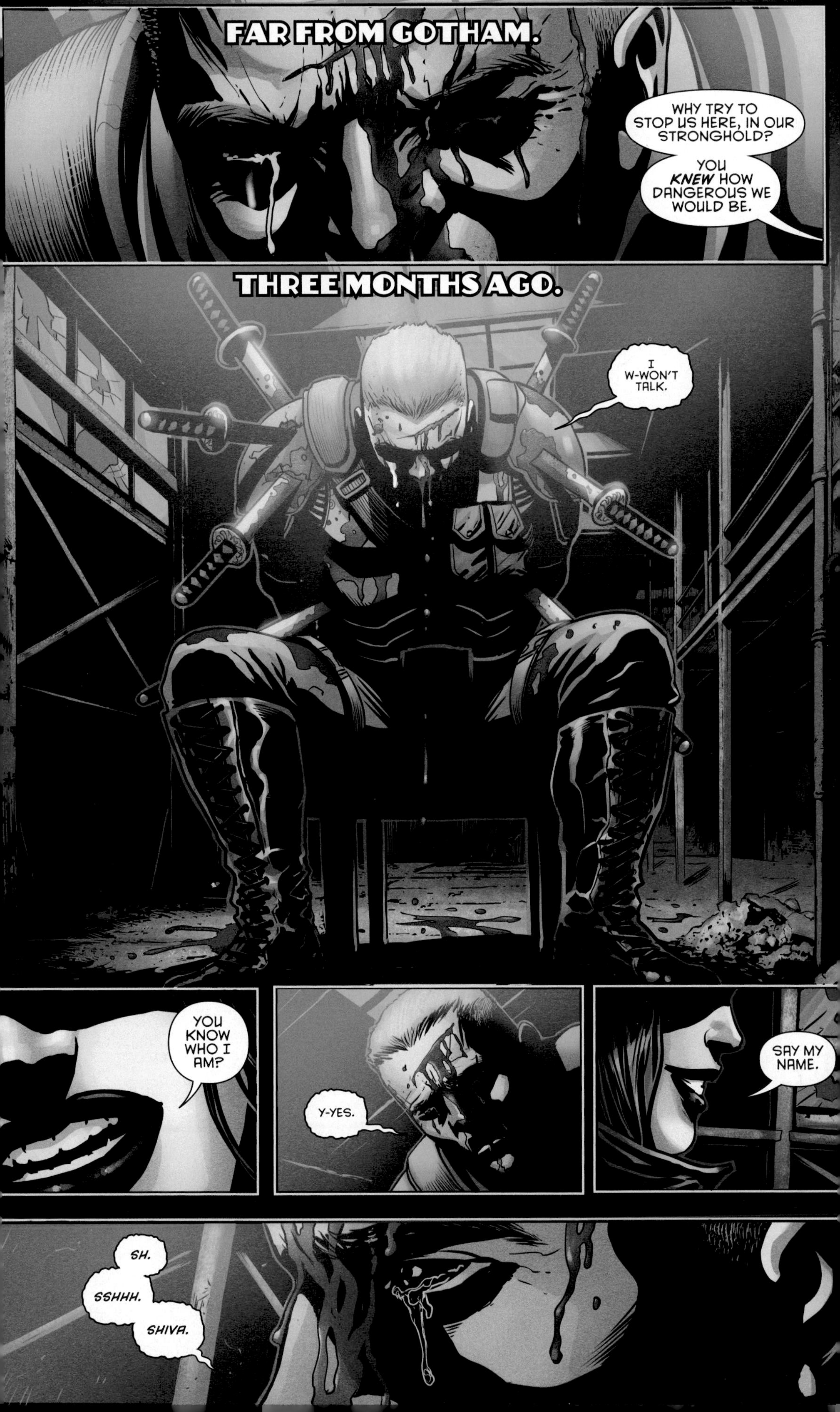
FAR FROM GOTHAM.
WHY TRY TO STOP US HERE, IN OUR STRONGHOLD?
YOU KNEW HOW DANGEROUS WE WOULD BE.
THREE MONTHS AGO.
I W-WON'T TALK.
YOU KNOW WHO I AM?
Y-YES.
SAY MY NAME.
SH.
SSHHH.
SHIVA.

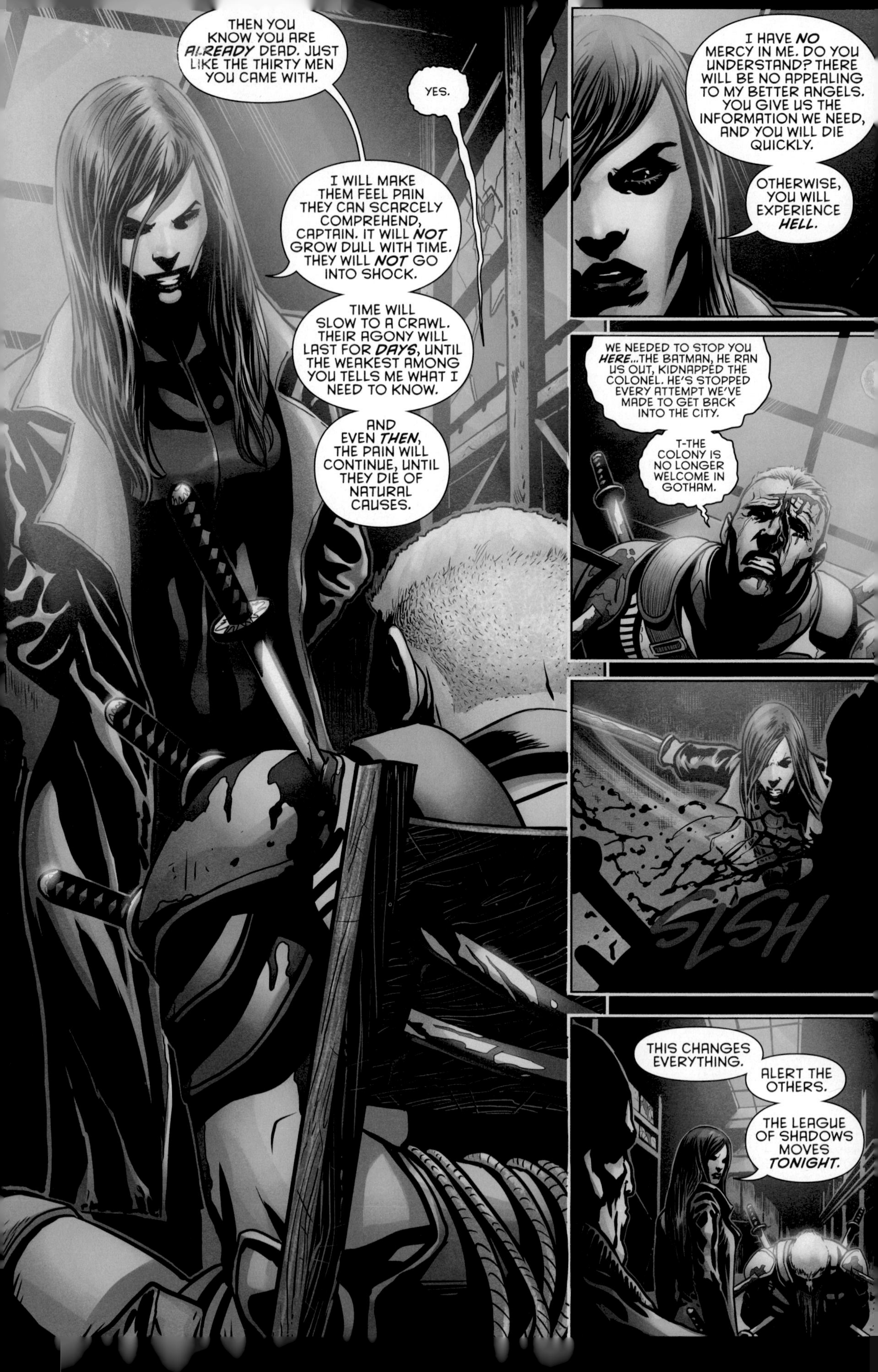
THEN YOU KNOW YOU ARE ALREADY DEAD. JUST LIKE THE THIRTY MEN YOU CAME WITH.
YES.
I WILL MAKE THEM FEEL PAIN THEY CAN SCARCELY COMPREHEND, CAPTAIN. IT WILL NOT GROW DULL WITH TIME. THEY WILL NOT GO INTO SHOCK.
TIME WILL SLOW TO A CRAWL. THEIR AGONY WILL LAST FOR DAYS, UNTIL THE WEAKEST AMONG YOU TELLS ME WHAT I NEED TO KNOW.
AND EVEN THEN, THE PAIN WILL CONTINUE, UNTIL THEY DIE OF NATURAL CAUSES.
I HAVE NO MERCY IN ME. DO YOU UNDERSTAND? THERE WILL BE NO APPEALING TO MY BETTER ANGELS. YOU GIVE US THE INFORMATION WE NEED, AND YOU WILL DIE QUICKLY.
OTHERWISE, YOU WILL EXPERIENCE HELL.
WE NEEDED TO STOP YOU HERE...THE BATMAN, HE RAN US OUT, KIDNAPPED THE COLONEL. HE'S STOPPED EVERY ATTEMPT WE'VE MADE TO GET BACK INTO THE CITY.
T-THE COLONY IS NO LONGER WELCOME IN GOTHAM.
SLISH
THIS CHANGES EVERYTHING.
ALERT THE OTHERS.
THE LEAGUE OF SHADOWS MOVES TONIGHT.

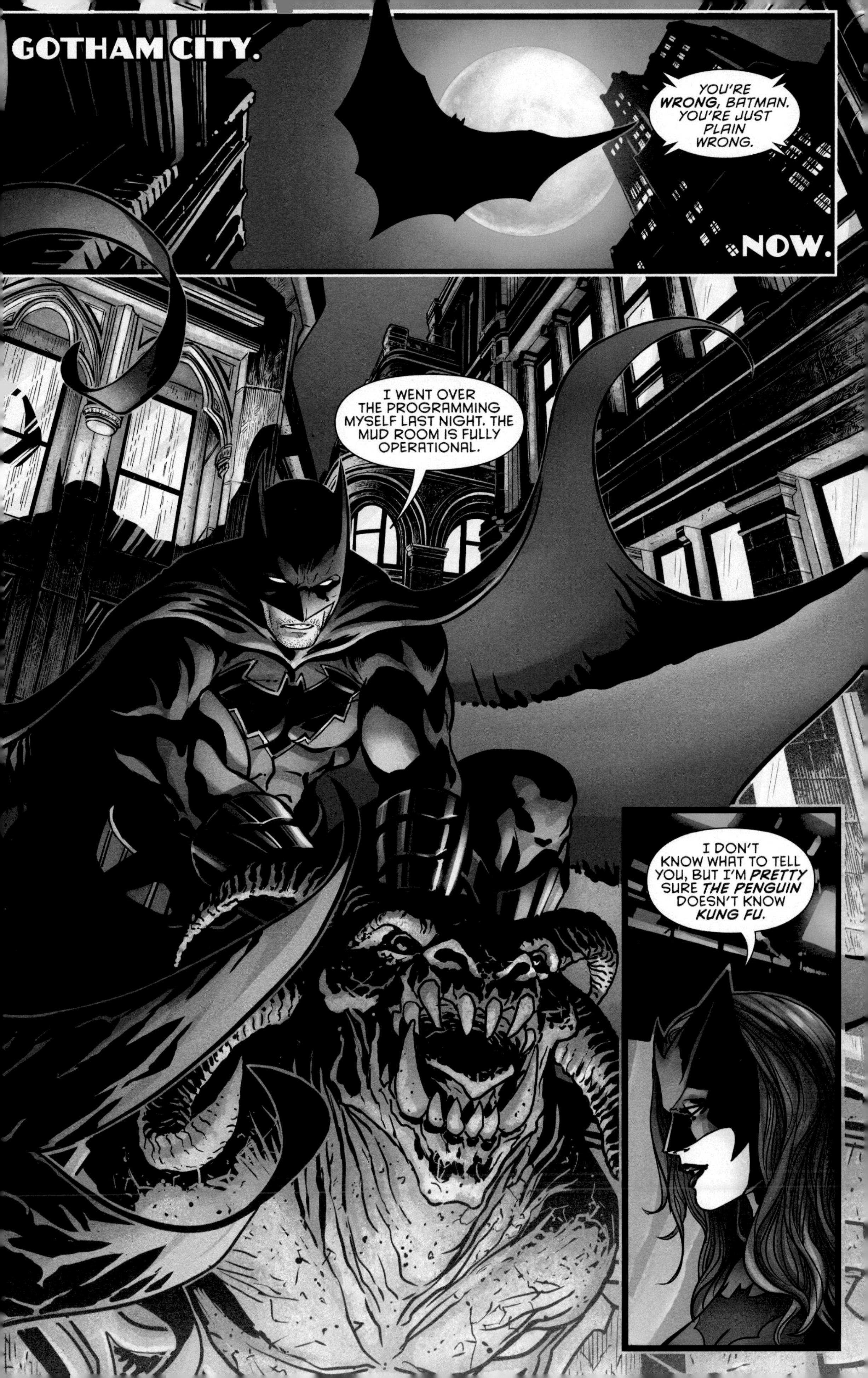

GOTHAM CITY.
YOU'RE WRONG, BATMAN. YOU'RE JUST PLAIN WRONG.
...NOW.
I WENT OVER THE PROGRAMMING MYSELF LAST NIGHT. THE MUD ROOM IS FULLY OPERATIONAL.
I DON'T KNOW WHAT TO TELL YOU, BUT I'M PRETTY SURE THE PENGUIN DOESN'T KNOW KUNG FU.

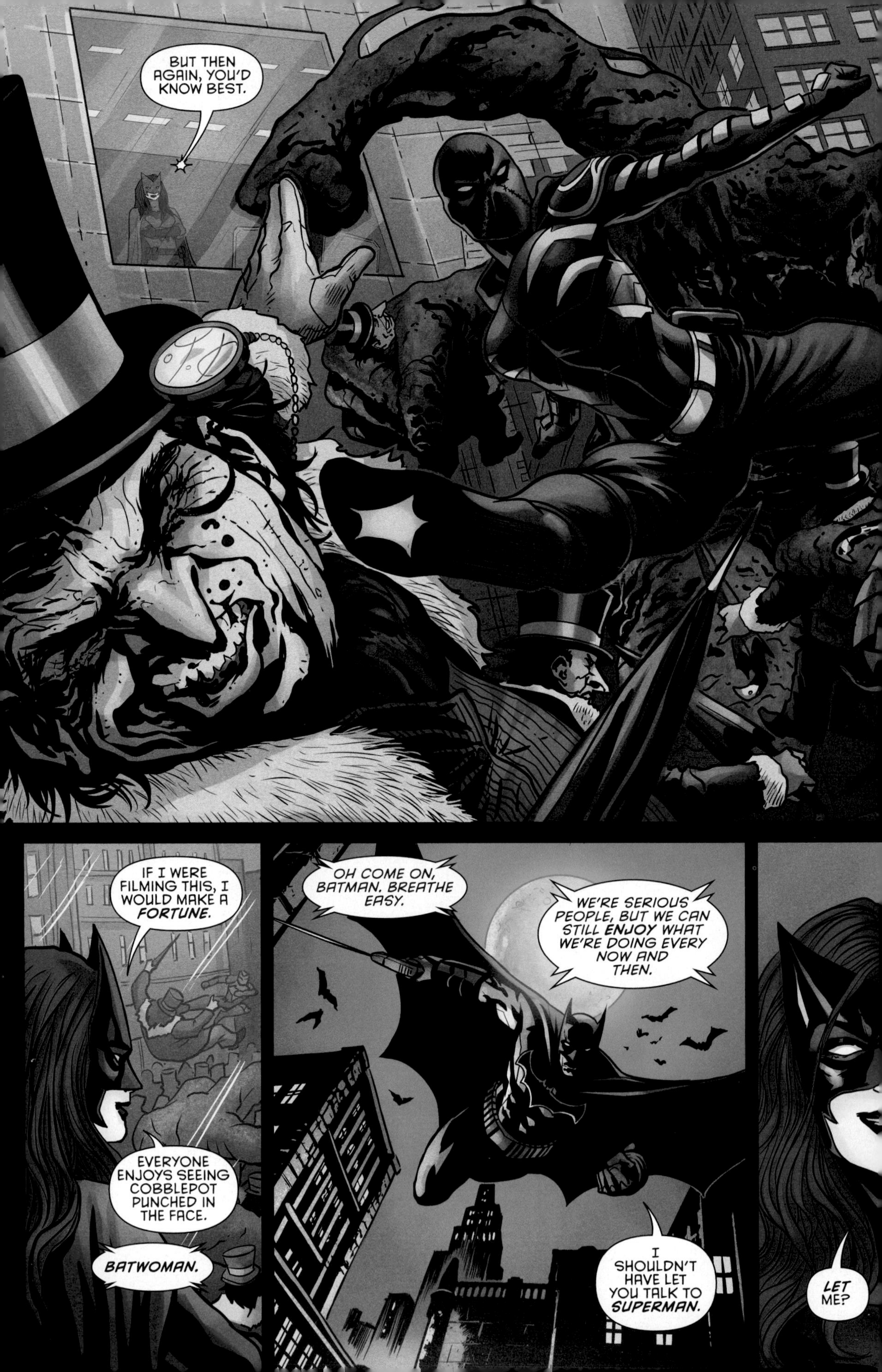
BUT THEN AGAIN, YOU'D KNOW BEST.
IF I WERE FILMING THIS, I WOULD MAKE A *FORTUNE.*
EVERYONE ENJOYS SEEING COBBLEPOT PUNCHED IN THE FACE.
BATWOMAN.
OH COME ON, BATMAN. BREATHE EASY.
WE'RE SERIOUS PEOPLE, BUT WE CAN STILL ***ENJOY*** *WHAT WE'RE DOING EVERY NOW AND THEN.*
I SHOULDN'T HAVE LET YOU TALK TO ***SUPERMAN.***
LET ME?

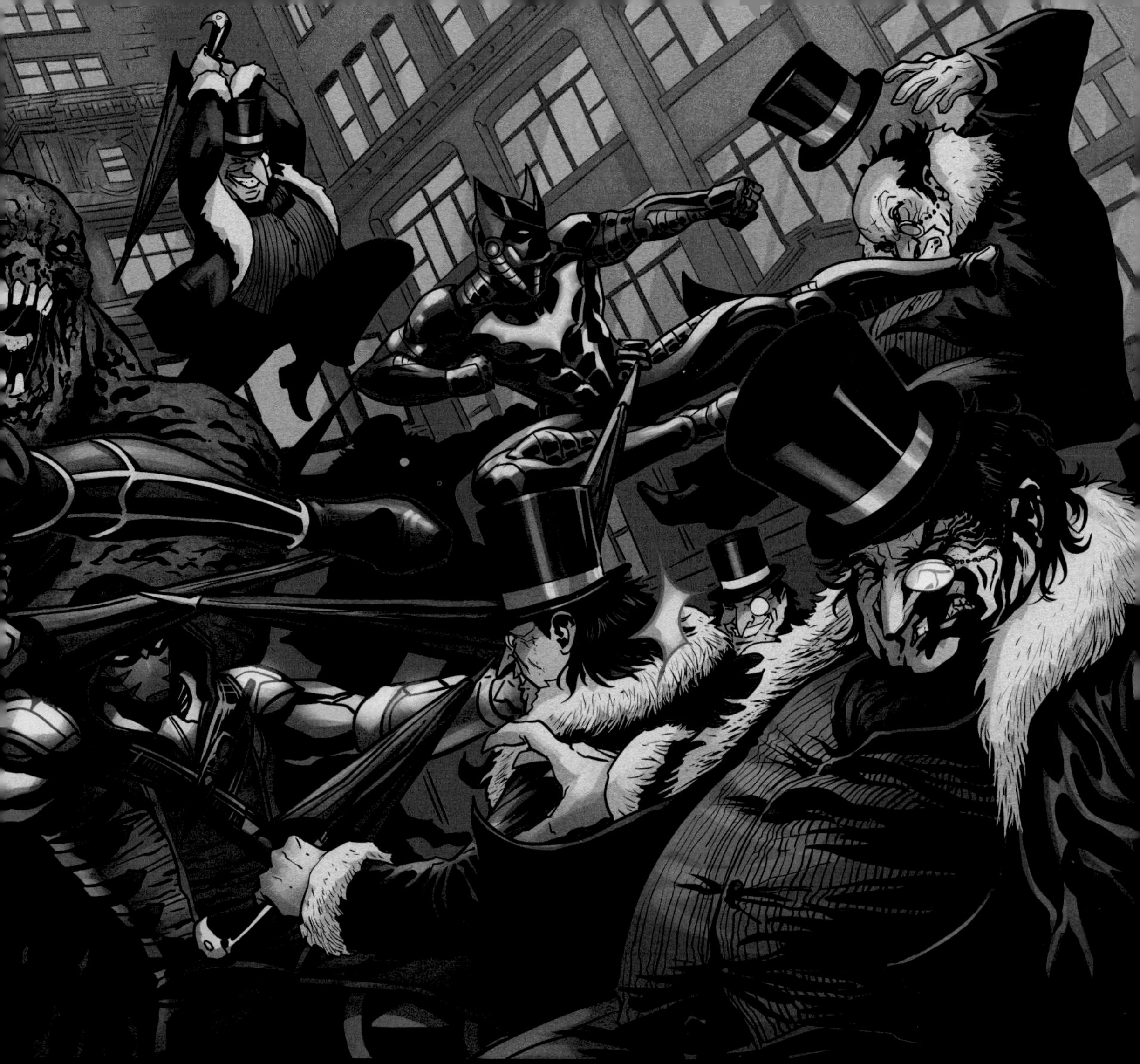

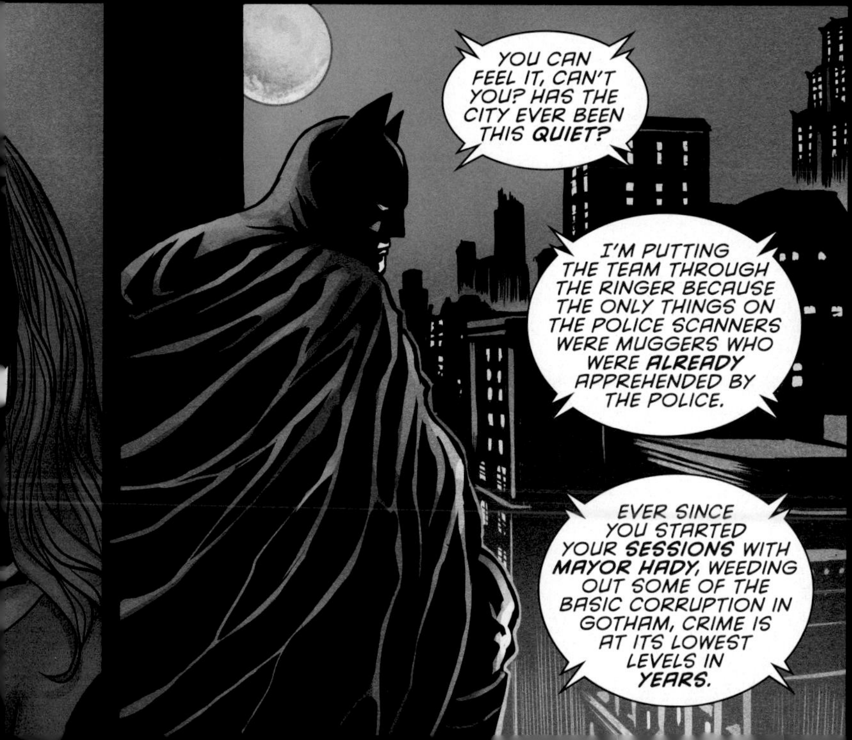

YOU CAN FEEL IT, CAN'T YOU? HAS THE CITY EVER BEEN THIS QUIET?
I'M PUTTING THE TEAM THROUGH THE RINGER BECAUSE THE ONLY THINGS ON THE POLICE SCANNERS WERE MUGGERS WHO WERE ALREADY APPREHENDED BY THE POLICE.
EVER SINCE YOU STARTED YOUR SESSIONS WITH MAYOR HADY, WEEDING OUT SOME OF THE BASIC CORRUPTION IN GOTHAM, CRIME IS AT ITS LOWEST LEVELS IN YEARS.

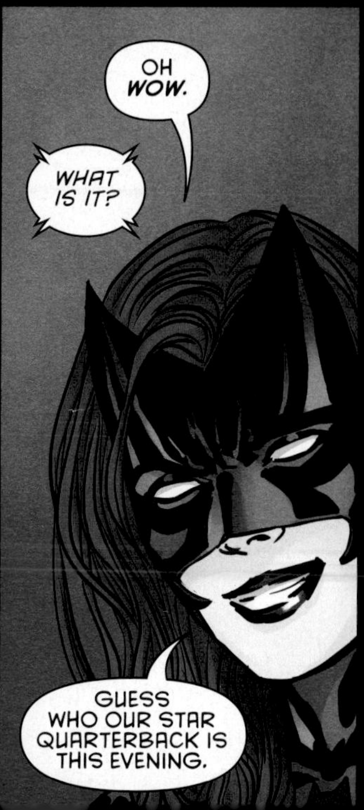

OH WOW.
WHAT IS IT?
GUESS WHO OUR STAR QUARTERBACK IS THIS EVENING.

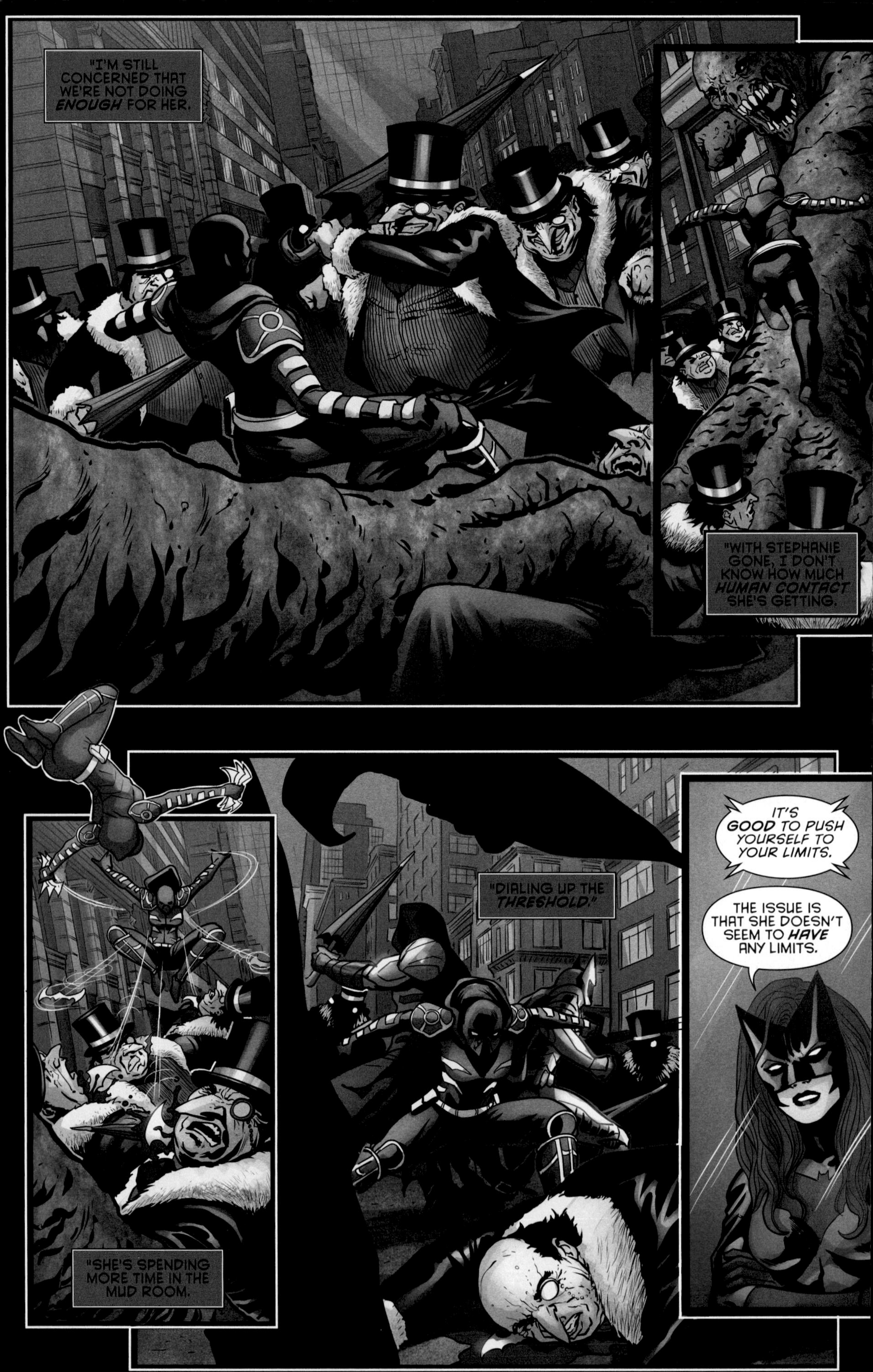
"I'M STILL CONCERNED THAT WE'RE NOT DOING ENOUGH FOR HER.
"WITH STEPHANIE GONE, I DON'T KNOW HOW MUCH HUMAN CONTACT SHE'S GETTING.
"SHE'S SPENDING MORE TIME IN THE MUD ROOM.
"DIALING UP THE THRESHOLD."
IT'S GOOD TO PUSH YOURSELF TO YOUR LIMITS.
THE ISSUE IS THAT SHE DOESN'T SEEM TO HAVE ANY LIMITS.

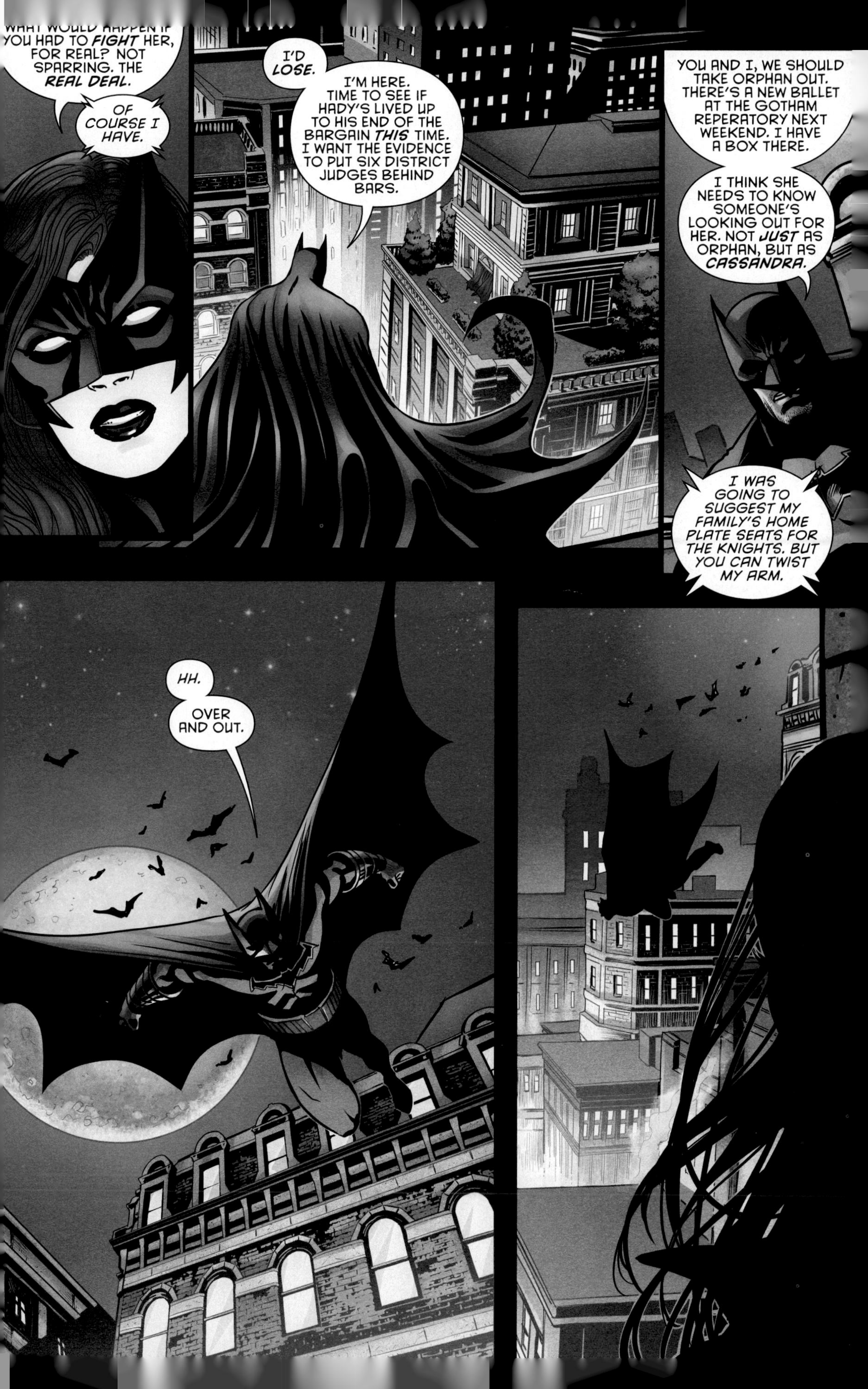
WHAT WOULD HAPPEN IF YOU HAD TO FIGHT HER, FOR REAL? NOT SPARRING. THE REAL DEAL.
OF COURSE I HAVE.
I'D LOSE.
I'M HERE. TIME TO SEE IF HADY'S LIVED UP TO HIS END OF THE BARGAIN THIS TIME. I WANT THE EVIDENCE TO PUT SIX DISTRICT JUDGES BEHIND BARS.
YOU AND I, WE SHOULD TAKE ORPHAN OUT. THERE'S A NEW BALLET AT THE GOTHAM REPERATORY NEXT WEEKEND. I HAVE A BOX THERE.
I THINK SHE NEEDS TO KNOW SOMEONE'S LOOKING OUT FOR HER. NOT JUST AS ORPHAN, BUT AS CASSANDRA.
I WAS GOING TO SUGGEST MY FAMILY'S HOME PLATE SEATS FOR THE KNIGHTS. BUT YOU CAN TWIST MY ARM.
HH.
OVER AND OUT.

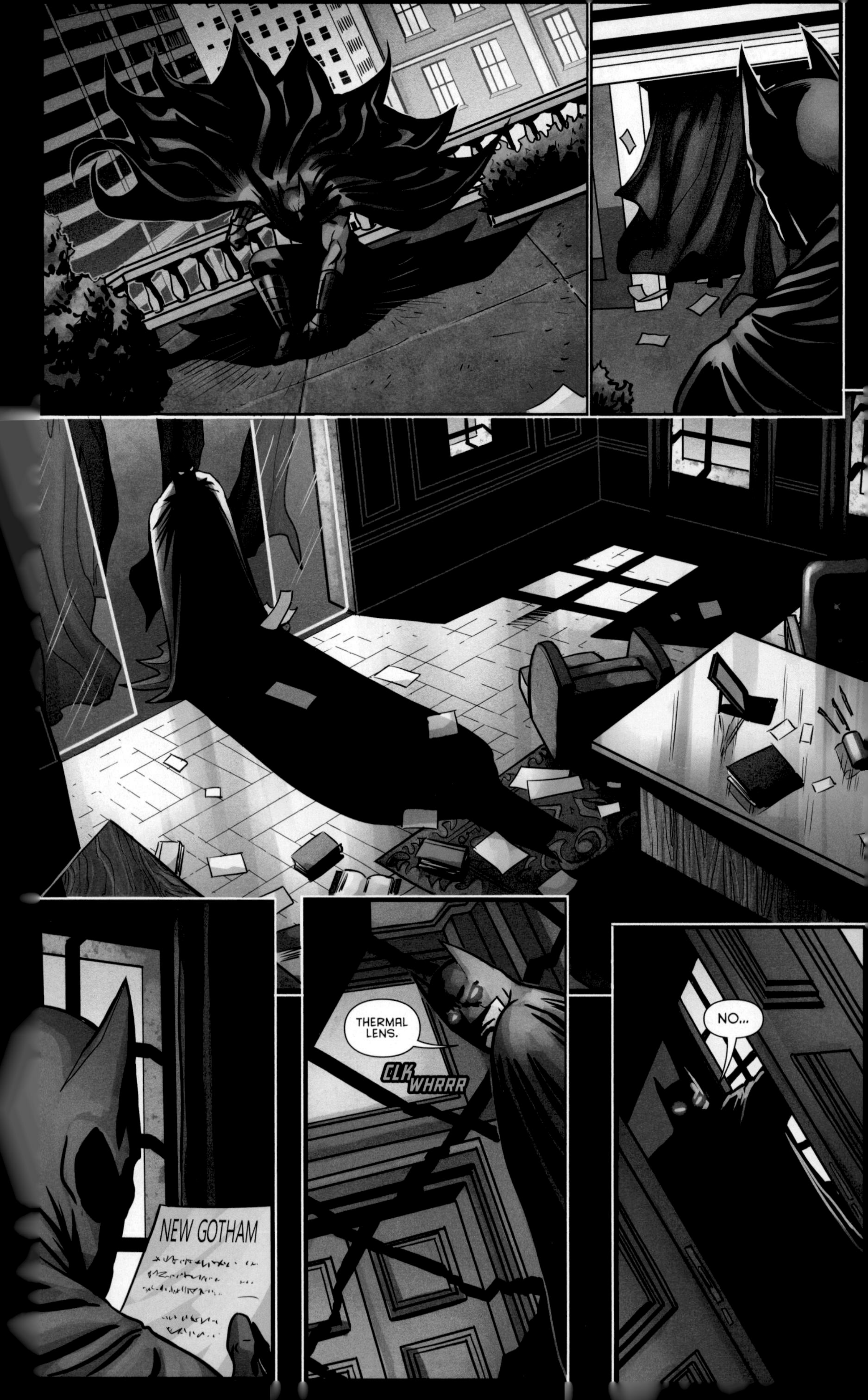

NEW GOTHAM
THERMAL LENS.
CLK
WHRRR
NO...

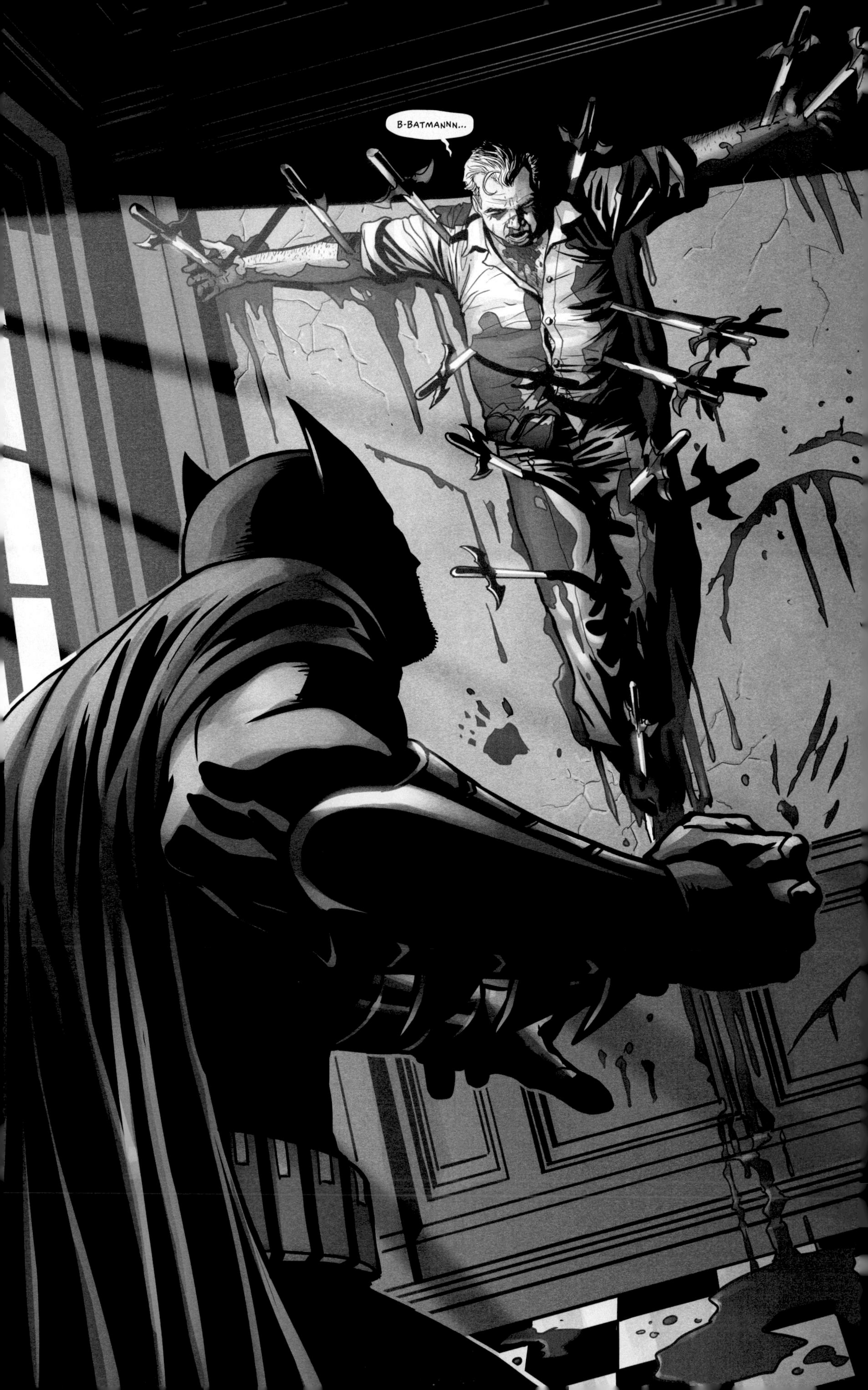
B-BATMANNN...

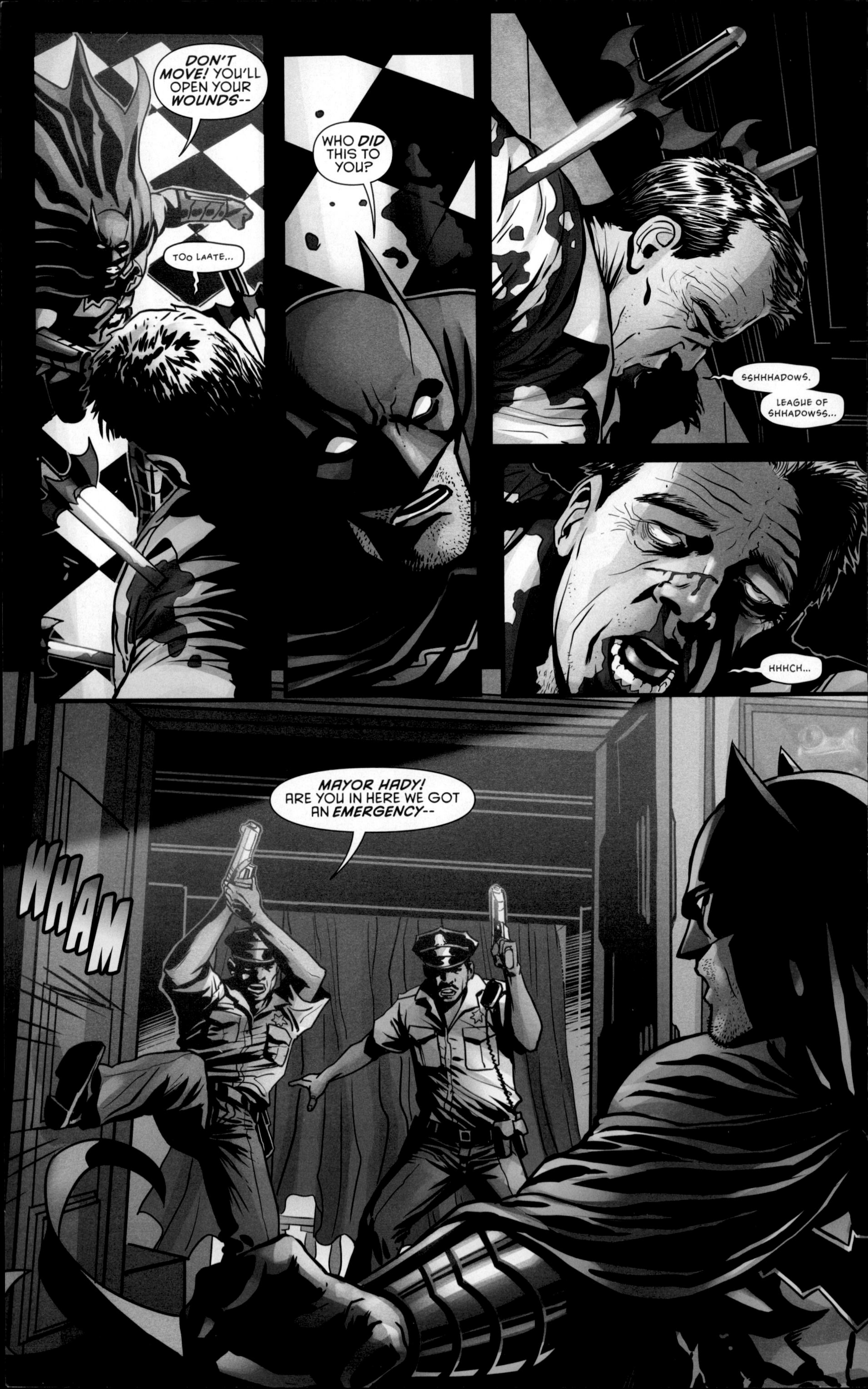
DON'T MOVE! YOU'LL OPEN YOUR WOUNDS--
TOo LAATE...
WHO DID THIS TO YOU?
SSHHHADOWS.
LEAGUE OF SHHADOWSS...
HHHCH...
MAYOR HADY! ARE YOU IN HERE WE GOT AN EMERGENCY--
WHAM

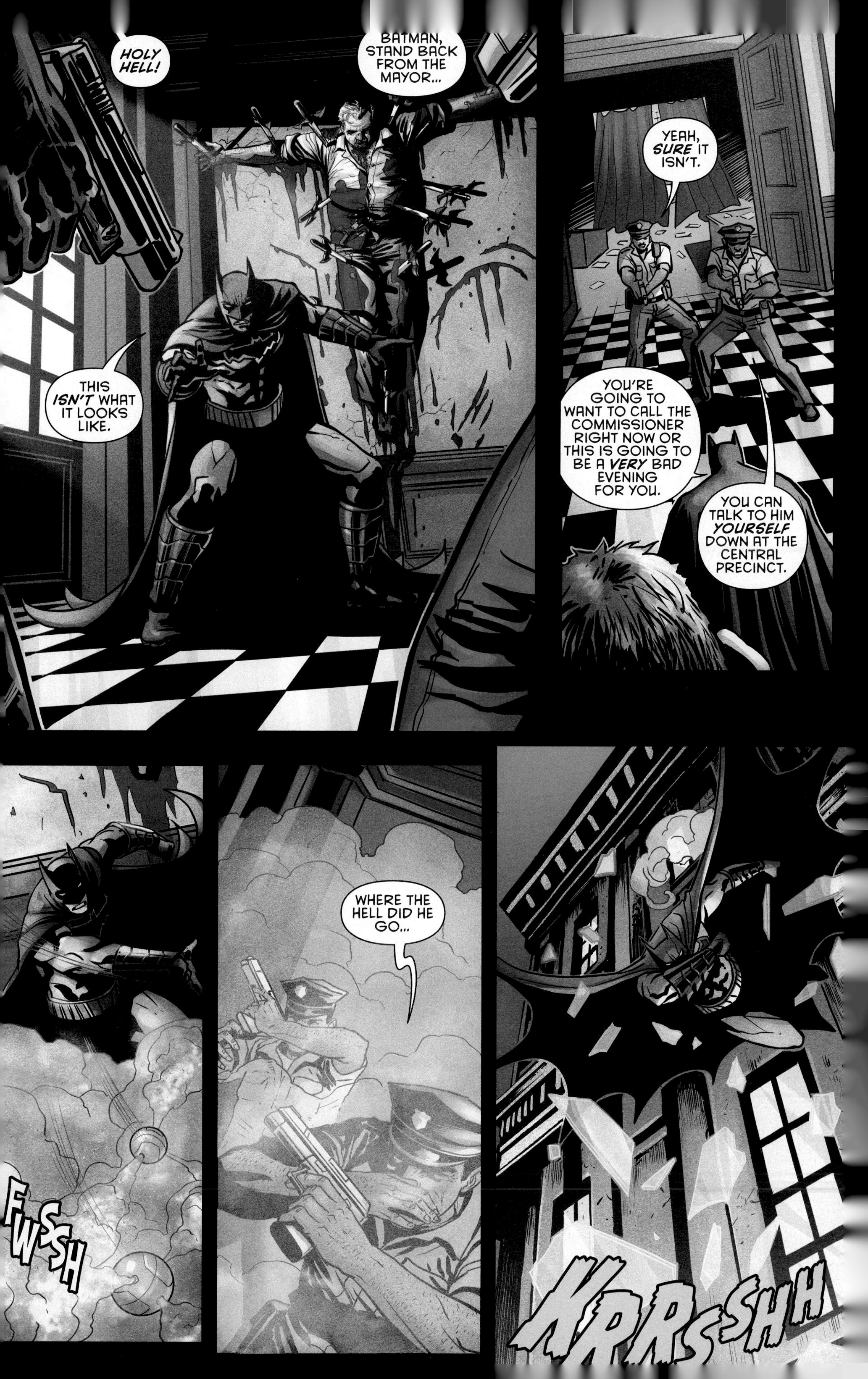
HOLY HELL!
BATMAN, STAND BACK FROM THE MAYOR...
THIS ISN'T WHAT IT LOOKS LIKE.
YEAH, SURE IT ISN'T.
YOU'RE GOING TO WANT TO CALL THE COMMISSIONER RIGHT NOW OR THIS IS GOING TO BE A VERY BAD EVENING FOR YOU.
YOU CAN TALK TO HIM YOURSELF DOWN AT THE CENTRAL PRECINCT.
FWSSH
WHERE THE HELL DID HE GO...
KRRSSHH

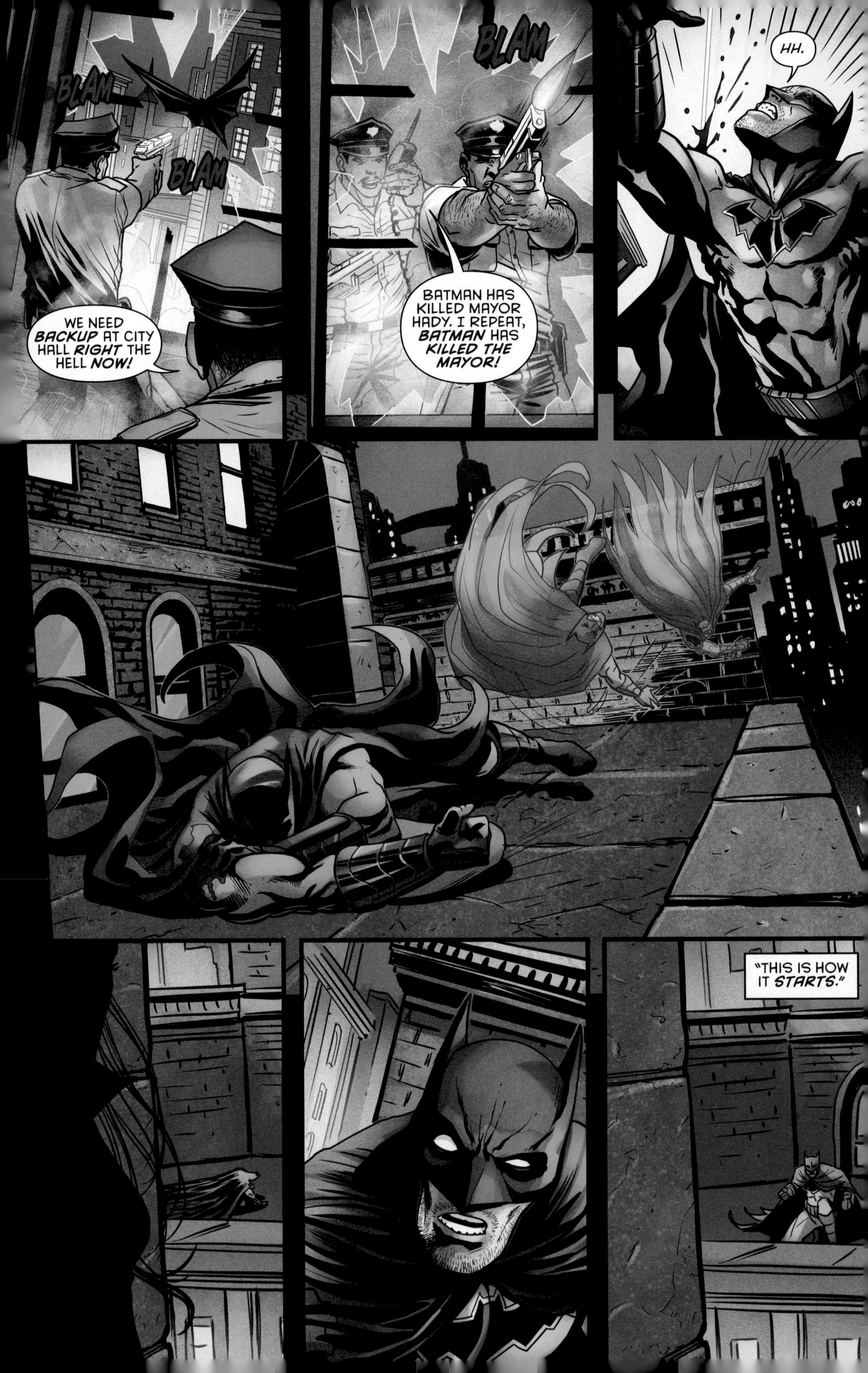
BLAM
BLAM
WE NEED BACKUP AT CITY HALL RIGHT THE HELL NOW!
BLAM
BATMAN HAS KILLED MAYOR HADY. I REPEAT, BATMAN HAS KILLED THE MAYOR!
HH.
"THIS IS HOW IT STARTS."

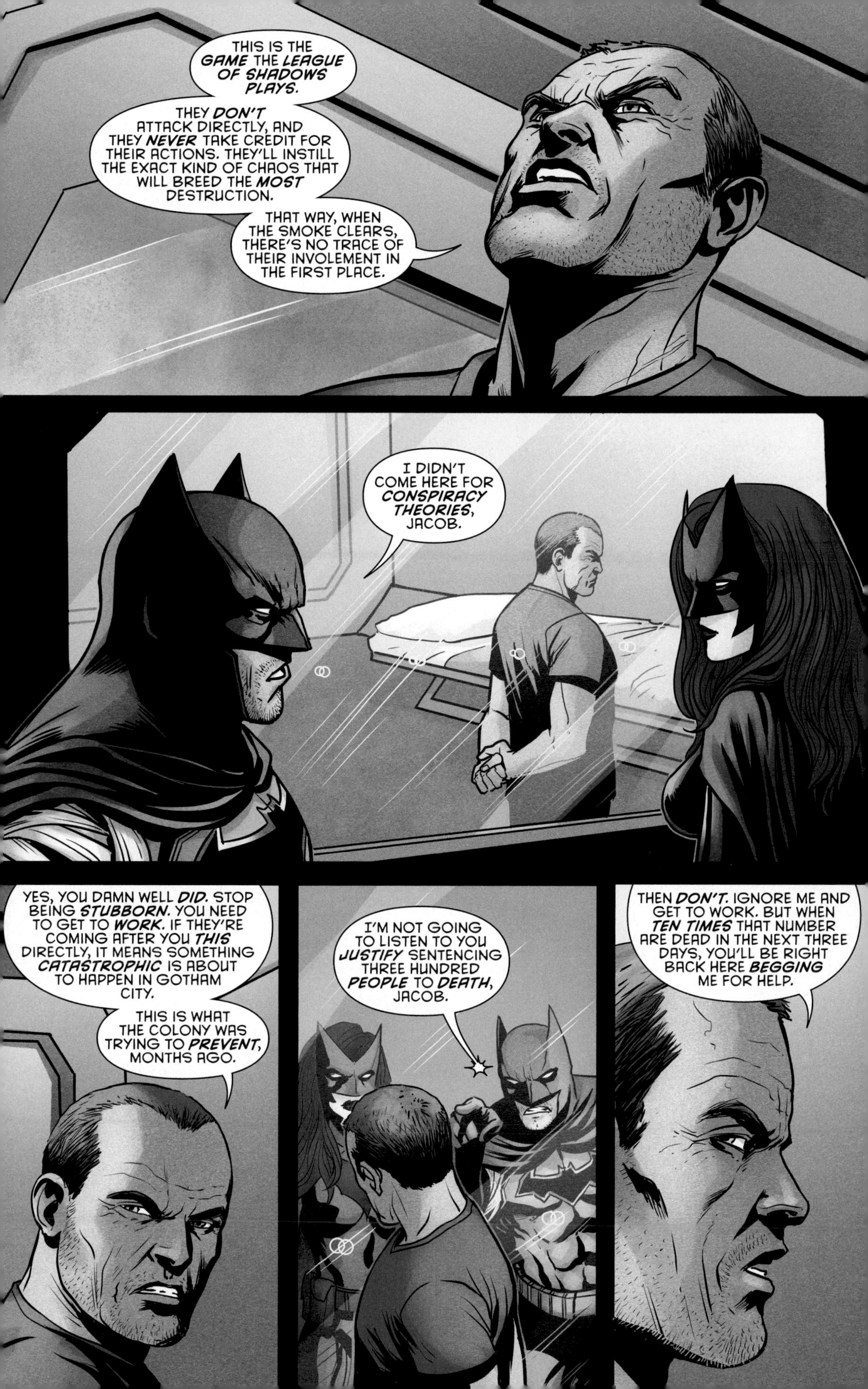
THIS IS THE GAME THE LEAGUE OF SHADOWS PLAYS.
THEY DON'T ATTACK DIRECTLY, AND THEY NEVER TAKE CREDIT FOR THEIR ACTIONS. THEY'LL INSTILL THE EXACT KIND OF CHAOS THAT WILL BREED THE MOST DESTRUCTION.
THAT WAY, WHEN THE SMOKE CLEARS, THERE'S NO TRACE OF THEIR INVOLEMENT IN THE FIRST PLACE.
I DIDN'T COME HERE FOR CONSPIRACY THEORIES, JACOB.
YES, YOU DAMN WELL DID. STOP BEING STUBBORN. YOU NEED TO GET TO WORK. IF THEY'RE COMING AFTER YOU THIS DIRECTLY, IT MEANS SOMETHING CATASTROPHIC IS ABOUT TO HAPPEN IN GOTHAM CITY.
THIS IS WHAT THE COLONY WAS TRYING TO PREVENT, MONTHS AGO.
I'M NOT GOING TO LISTEN TO YOU JUSTIFY SENTENCING THREE HUNDRED PEOPLE TO DEATH, JACOB.
THEN DON'T. IGNORE ME AND GET TO WORK. BUT WHEN TEN TIMES THAT NUMBER ARE DEAD IN THE NEXT THREE DAYS, YOU'LL BE RIGHT BACK HERE BEGGING ME FOR HELP.

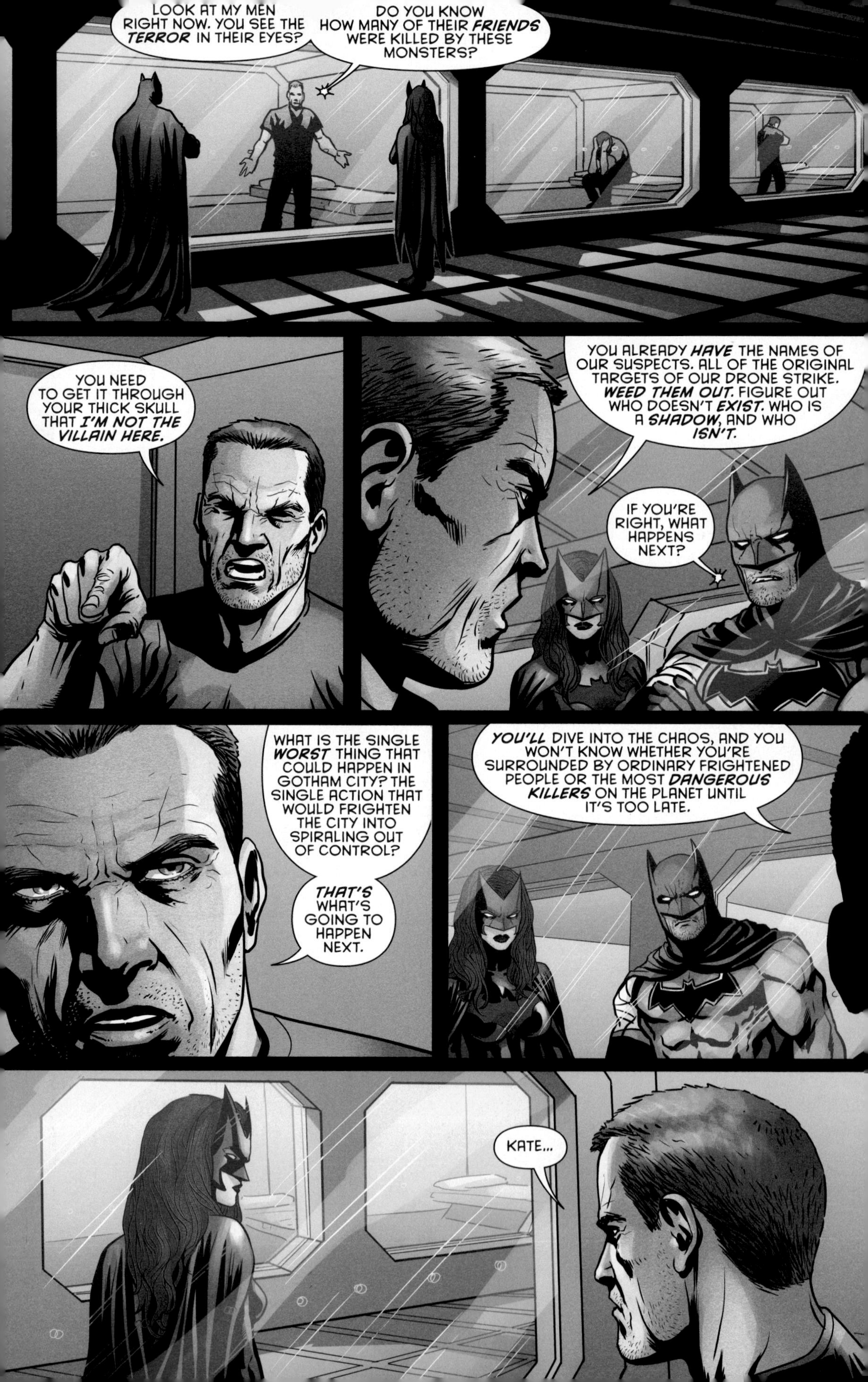
LOOK AT MY MEN RIGHT NOW. YOU SEE THE TERROR IN THEIR EYES?
DO YOU KNOW HOW MANY OF THEIR FRIENDS WERE KILLED BY THESE MONSTERS?
YOU NEED TO GET IT THROUGH YOUR THICK SKULL THAT I'M NOT THE VILLAIN HERE.
YOU ALREADY HAVE THE NAMES OF OUR SUSPECTS. ALL OF THE ORIGINAL TARGETS OF OUR DRONE STRIKE. WEED THEM OUT. FIGURE OUT WHO DOESN'T EXIST. WHO IS A SHADOW, AND WHO ISN'T.
IF YOU'RE RIGHT, WHAT HAPPENS NEXT?
WHAT IS THE SINGLE WORST THING THAT COULD HAPPEN IN GOTHAM CITY? THE SINGLE ACTION THAT WOULD FRIGHTEN THE CITY INTO SPIRALING OUT OF CONTROL?
THAT'S WHAT'S GOING TO HAPPEN NEXT.
YOU'LL DIVE INTO THE CHAOS, AND YOU WON'T KNOW WHETHER YOU'RE SURROUNDED BY ORDINARY FRIGHTENED PEOPLE OR THE MOST DANGEROUS KILLERS ON THE PLANET UNTIL IT'S TOO LATE.
KATE...

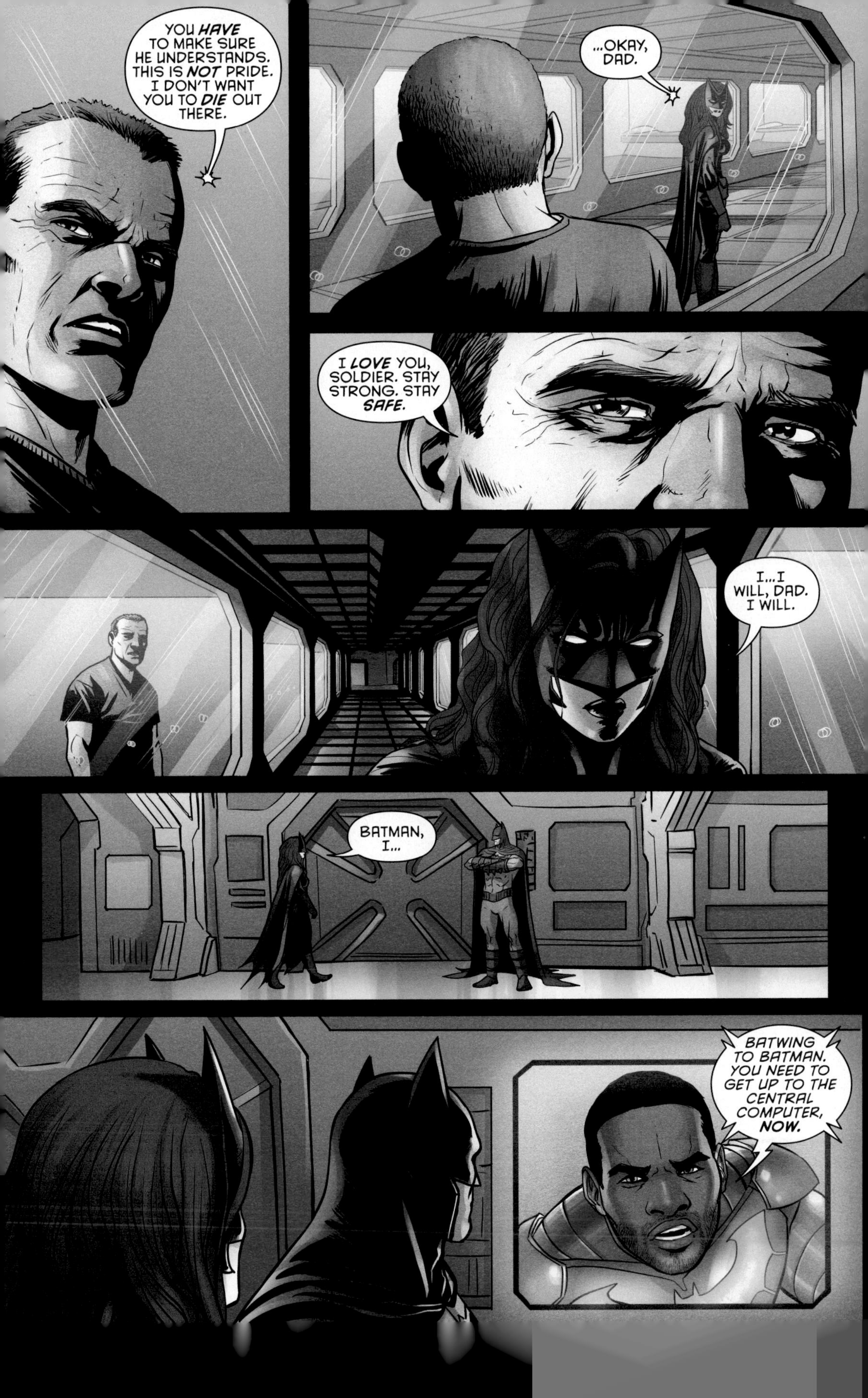
YOU **HAVE** TO MAKE SURE HE UNDERSTANDS. THIS IS **NOT** PRIDE. I DON'T WANT YOU TO **DIE** OUT THERE.
...OKAY, DAD.
I **LOVE** YOU, SOLDIER. STAY STRONG. STAY **SAFE**.
I...I WILL, DAD. I WILL.
BATMAN, I...
BATWING TO BATMAN. YOU NEED TO GET UP TO THE CENTRAL COMPUTER, **NOW**.

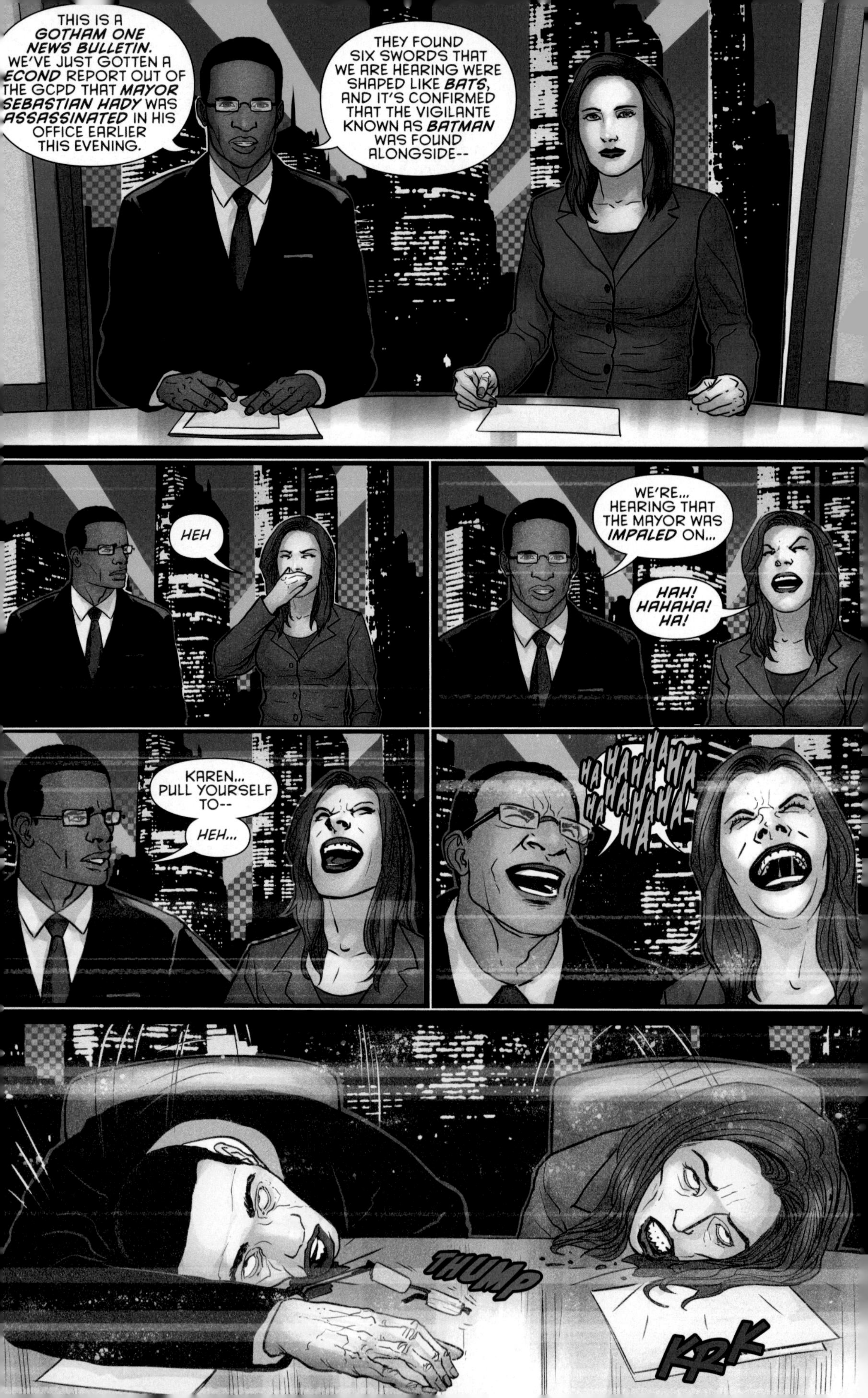
THIS IS A GOTHAM ONE NEWS BULLETIN. WE'VE JUST GOTTEN A ECOND REPORT OUT OF THE GCPD THAT MAYOR SEBASTIAN HADY WAS ASSASSINATED IN HIS OFFICE EARLIER THIS EVENING.
THEY FOUND SIX SWORDS THAT WE ARE HEARING WERE SHAPED LIKE BATS, AND IT'S CONFIRMED THAT THE VIGILANTE KNOWN AS BATMAN WAS FOUND ALONGSIDE--
HEH
WE'RE... HEARING THAT THE MAYOR WAS IMPALED ON...
HAH! HAHAHA! HA!
KAREN... PULL YOURSELF TO--
HEH...
HA HA HA HA HA HA HA HA HA HA HA HA HA HA
THUMP
KRK

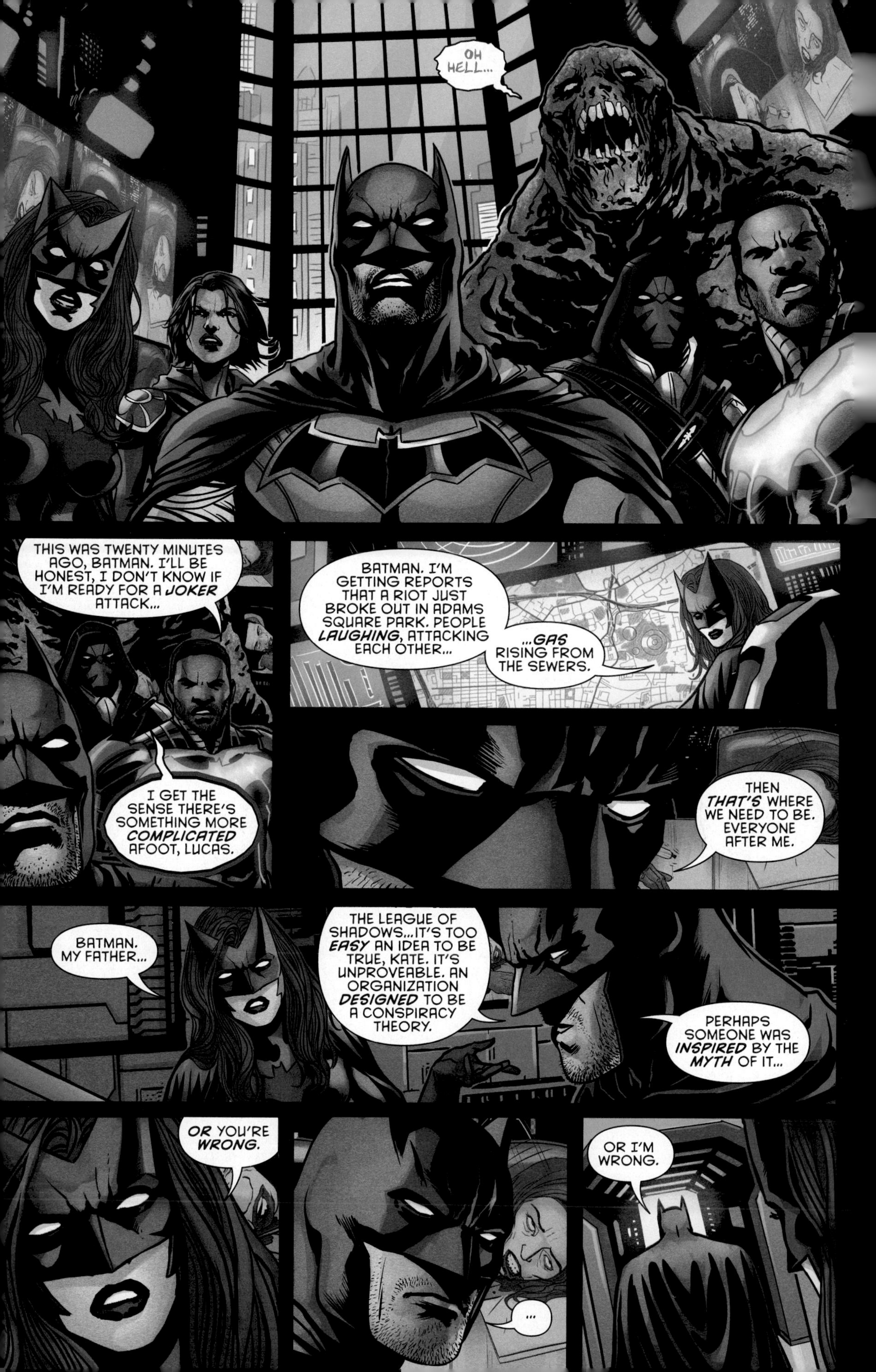
OH HELL...
THIS WAS TWENTY MINUTES AGO, BATMAN. I'LL BE HONEST, I DON'T KNOW IF I'M READY FOR A JOKER ATTACK...
I GET THE SENSE THERE'S SOMETHING MORE COMPLICATED AFOOT, LUCAS.
BATMAN. I'M GETTING REPORTS THAT A RIOT JUST BROKE OUT IN ADAMS SQUARE PARK. PEOPLE LAUGHING, ATTACKING EACH OTHER...
...GAS RISING FROM THE SEWERS.
THEN THAT'S WHERE WE NEED TO BE. EVERYONE AFTER ME.
BATMAN. MY FATHER...
THE LEAGUE OF SHADOWS...IT'S TOO EASY AN IDEA TO BE TRUE, KATE. IT'S UNPROVEABLE. AN ORGANIZATION DESIGNED TO BE A CONSPIRACY THEORY.
PERHAPS SOMEONE WAS INSPIRED BY THE MYTH OF IT...
OR YOU'RE WRONG.
...
OR I'M WRONG.

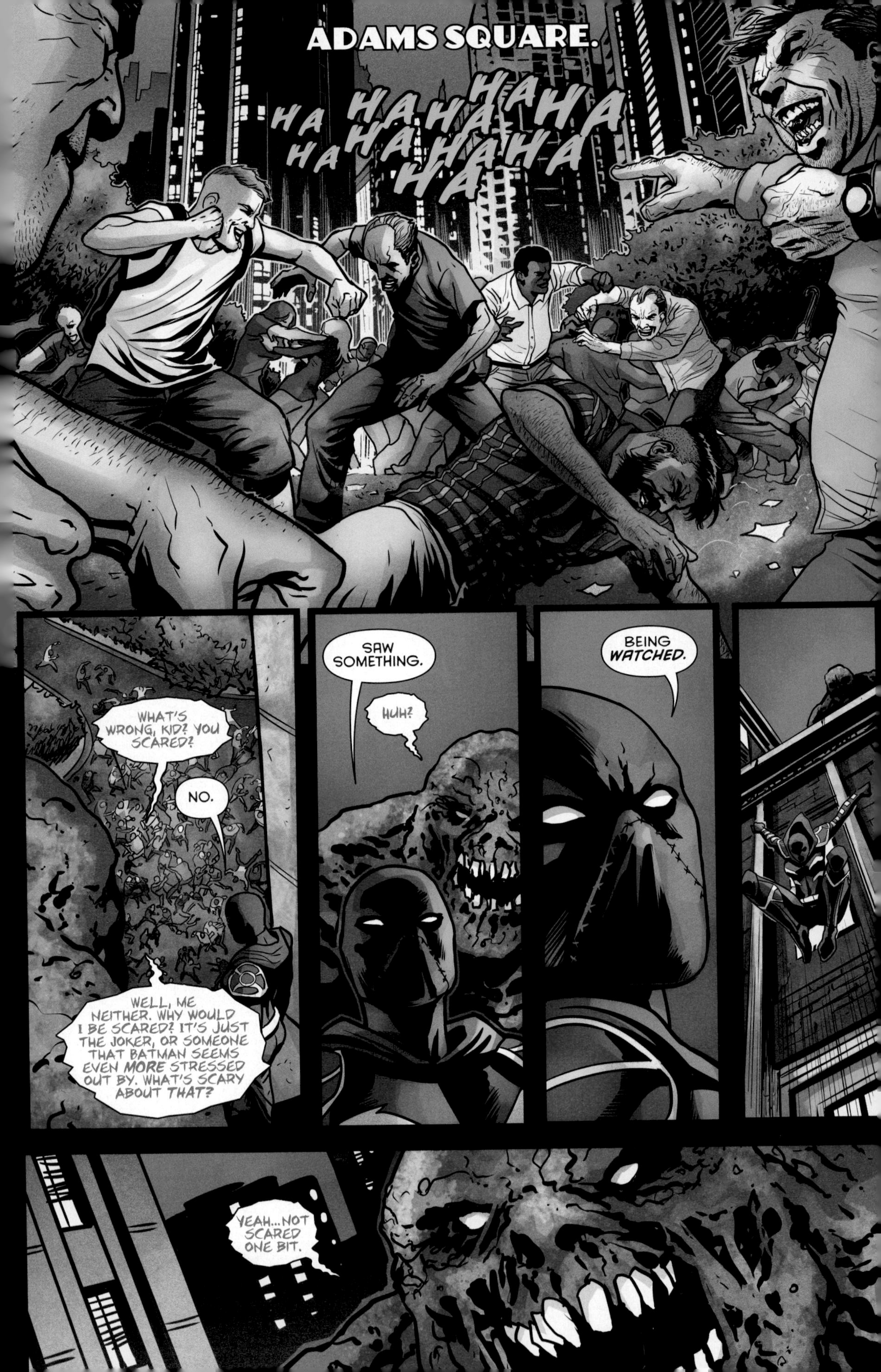
ADAMS SQUARE.
HA HAHA HAHA
HA HAHA HAHA
HA
WHAT'S WRONG, KID? YOU SCARED?
NO.
WELL, ME NEITHER. WHY WOULD I BE SCARED? IT'S JUST THE JOKER, OR SOMEONE THAT BATMAN SEEMS EVEN MORE STRESSED OUT BY. WHAT'S SCARY ABOUT THAT?
SAW SOMETHING.
HUH?
BEING WATCHED.
YEAH...NOT SCARED ONE BIT.

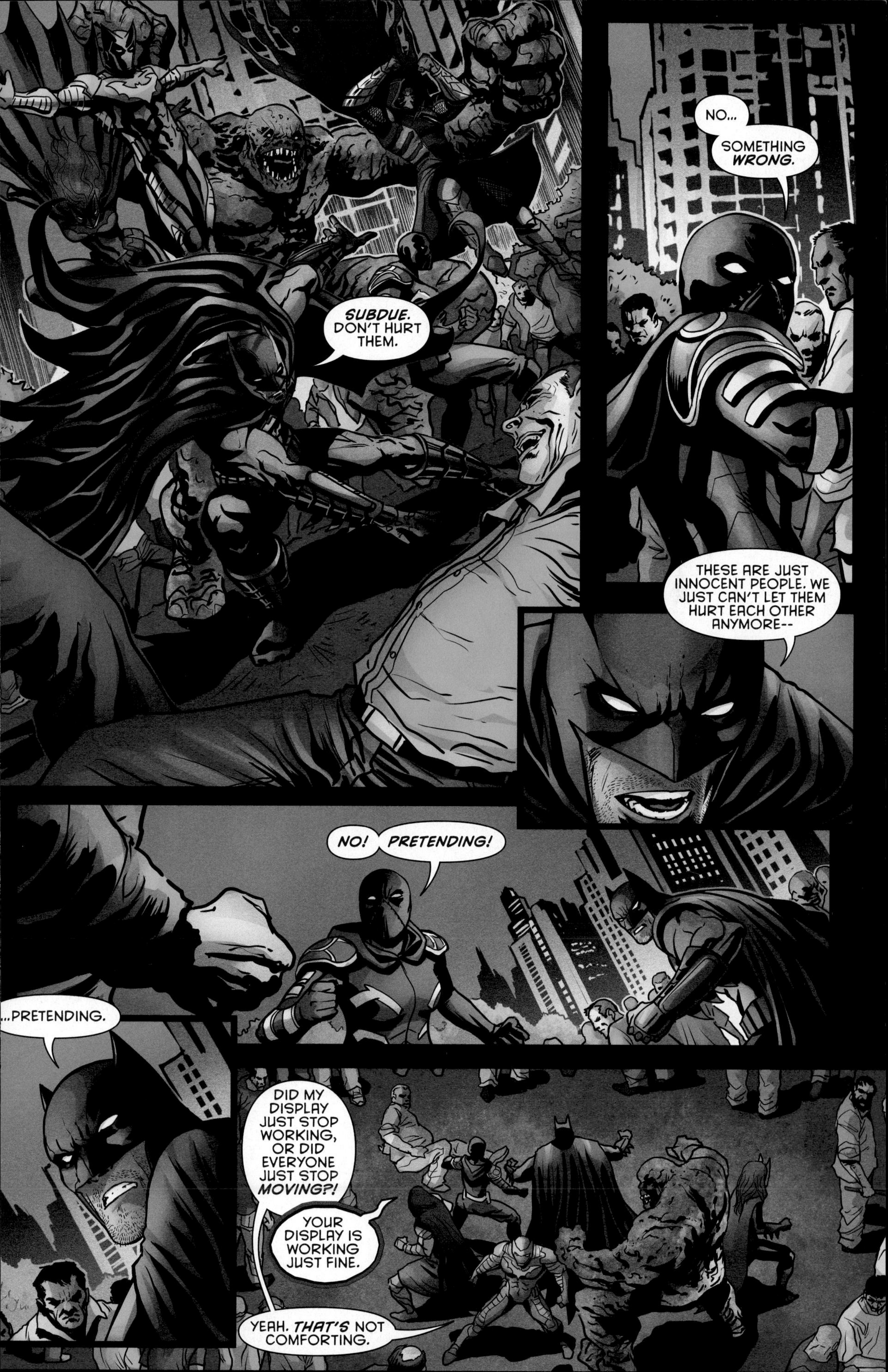
SUBDUE. DON'T HURT THEM.
NO...
SOMETHING WRONG.
THESE ARE JUST INNOCENT PEOPLE. WE JUST CAN'T LET THEM HURT EACH OTHER ANYMORE--
NO! PRETENDING!
...PRETENDING.
DID MY DISPLAY JUST STOP WORKING, OR DID EVERYONE JUST STOP MOVING?!
YOUR DISPLAY IS WORKING JUST FINE.
YEAH. THAT'S NOT COMFORTING.

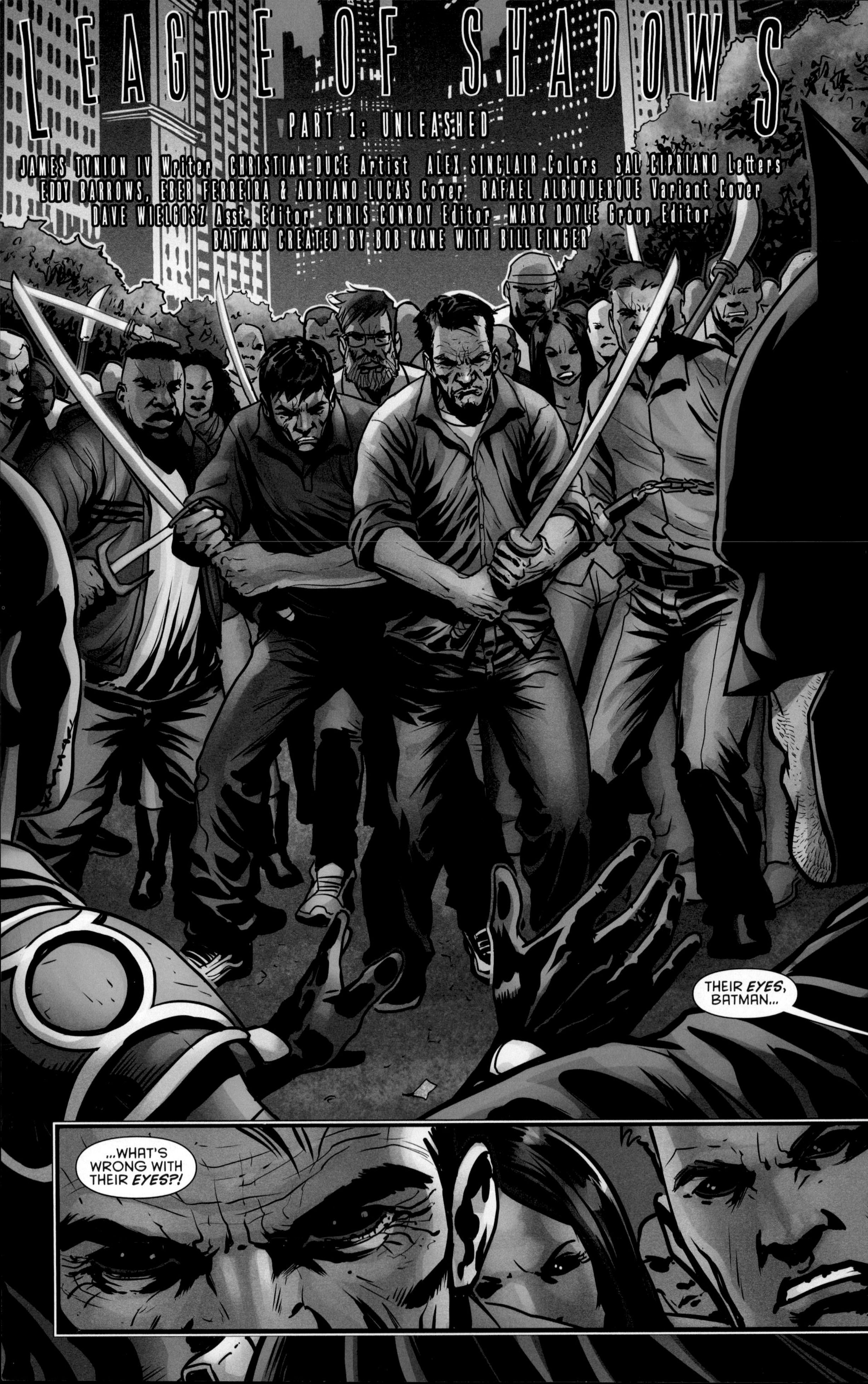
LEAGUE OF SHADOWS
PART 1: UNLEASHED
JAMES TYNION IV Writer CHRISTIAN DUCE Artist ALEX SINCLAIR Colors SAL CIPRIANO Letters
EDDY BARROWS, EBER FERREIRA & ADRIANO LUCAS Cover RAFAEL ALBUQUERQUE Variant Cover
DAVE WIELGOSZ Asst. Editor CHRIS CONROY Editor MARK DOYLE Group Editor
BATMAN CREATED BY BOB KANE WITH BILL FINGER
THEIR EYES, BATMAN...
...WHAT'S WRONG WITH THEIR EYES?!

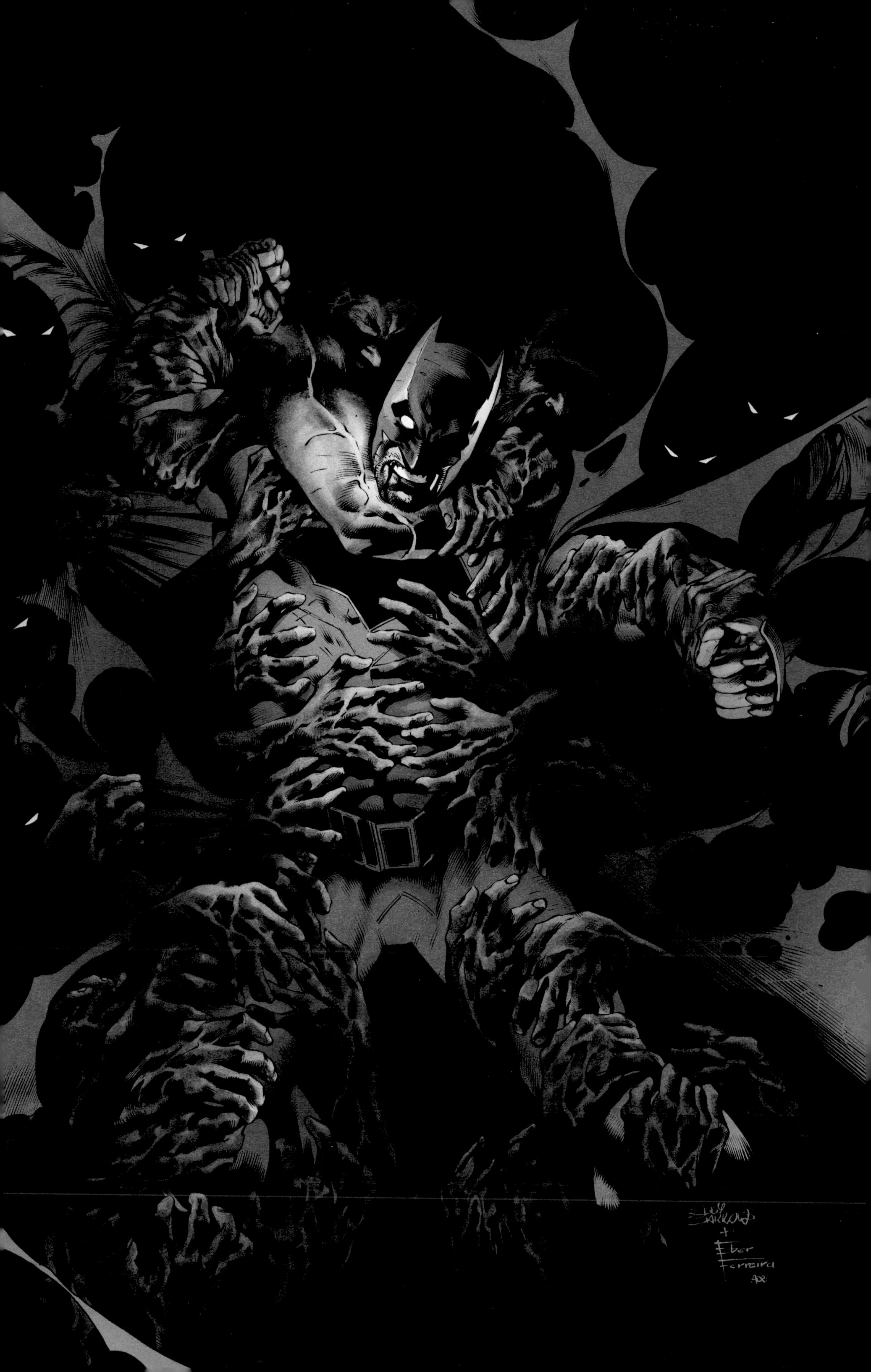
+
Eber
Ferreira

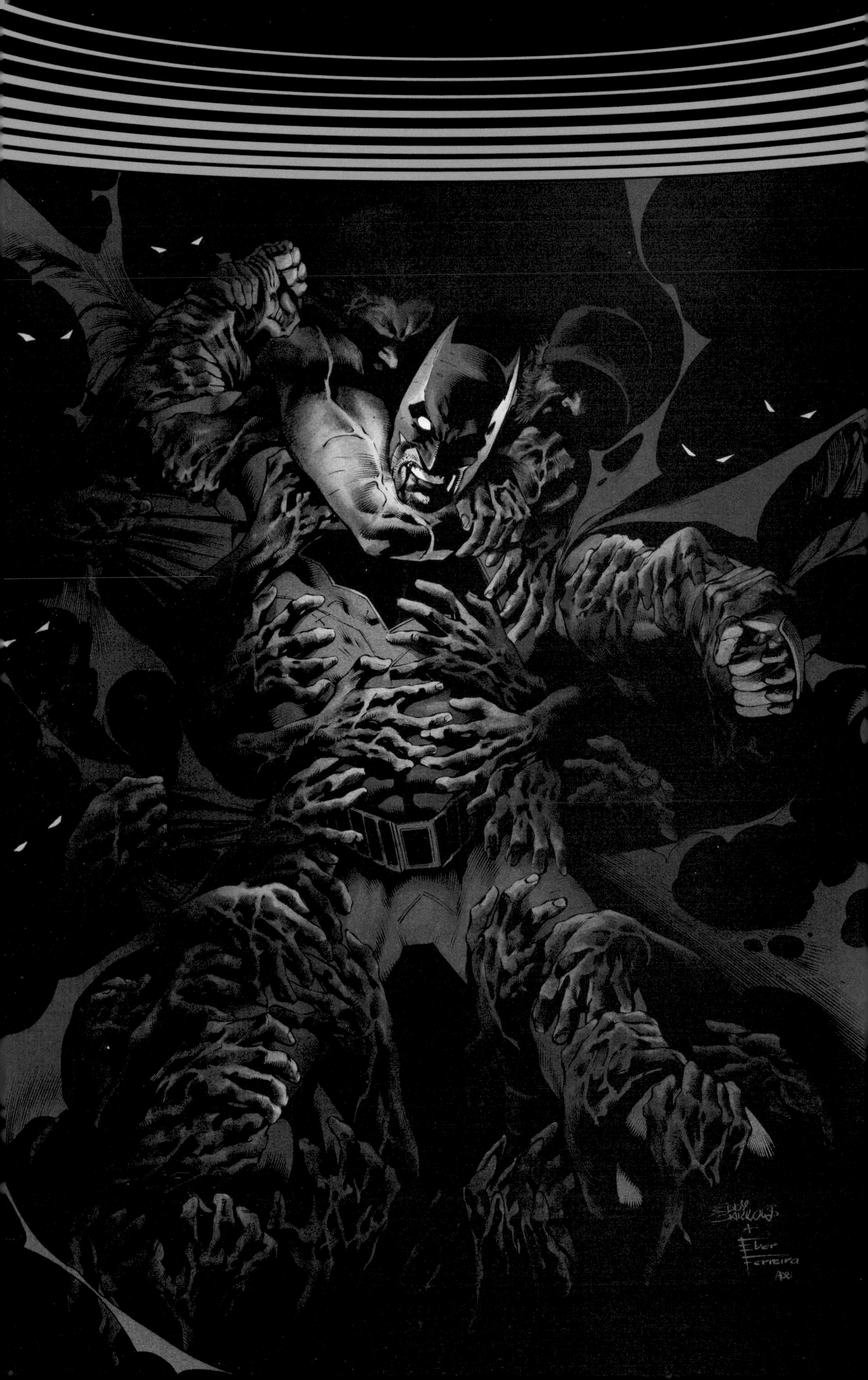

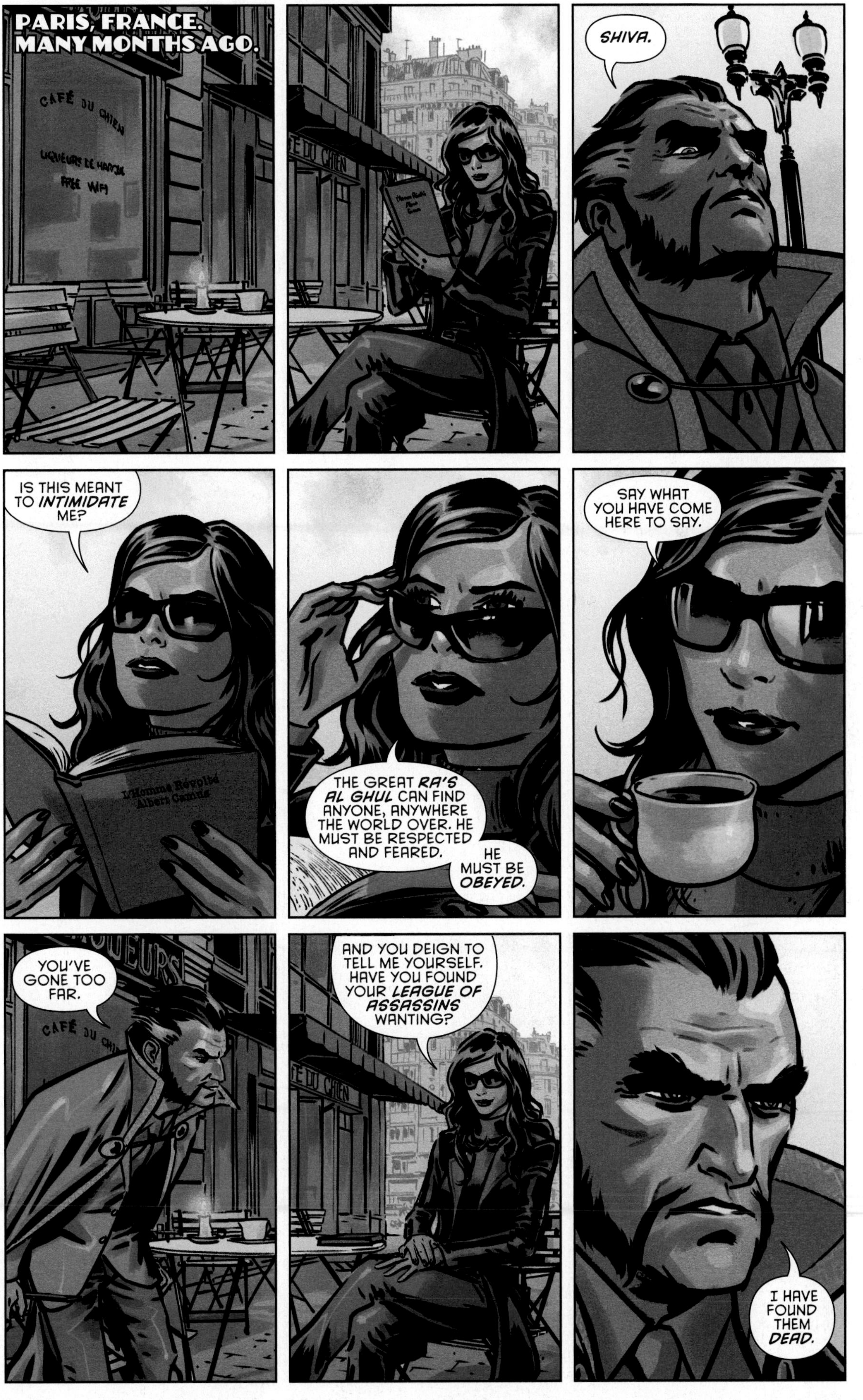
PARIS, FRANCE. MANY MONTHS AGO.
CAFÉ DU CHIEN
FREE WIFI
SHIVA.
IS THIS MEANT TO *INTIMIDATE* ME?
L'Homme Révolté
Albert Camus
THE GREAT *RA'S AL GHUL* CAN FIND ANYONE, ANYWHERE THE WORLD OVER. HE MUST BE RESPECTED AND FEARED.
HE MUST BE *OBEYED*.
SAY WHAT YOU HAVE COME HERE TO SAY.
YOU'VE GONE TOO FAR.
CAFÉ DU CHIEN
AND YOU DEIGN TO TELL ME YOURSELF. HAVE YOU FOUND YOUR *LEAGUE OF ASSASSINS* WANTING?
I HAVE FOUND THEM *DEAD*.

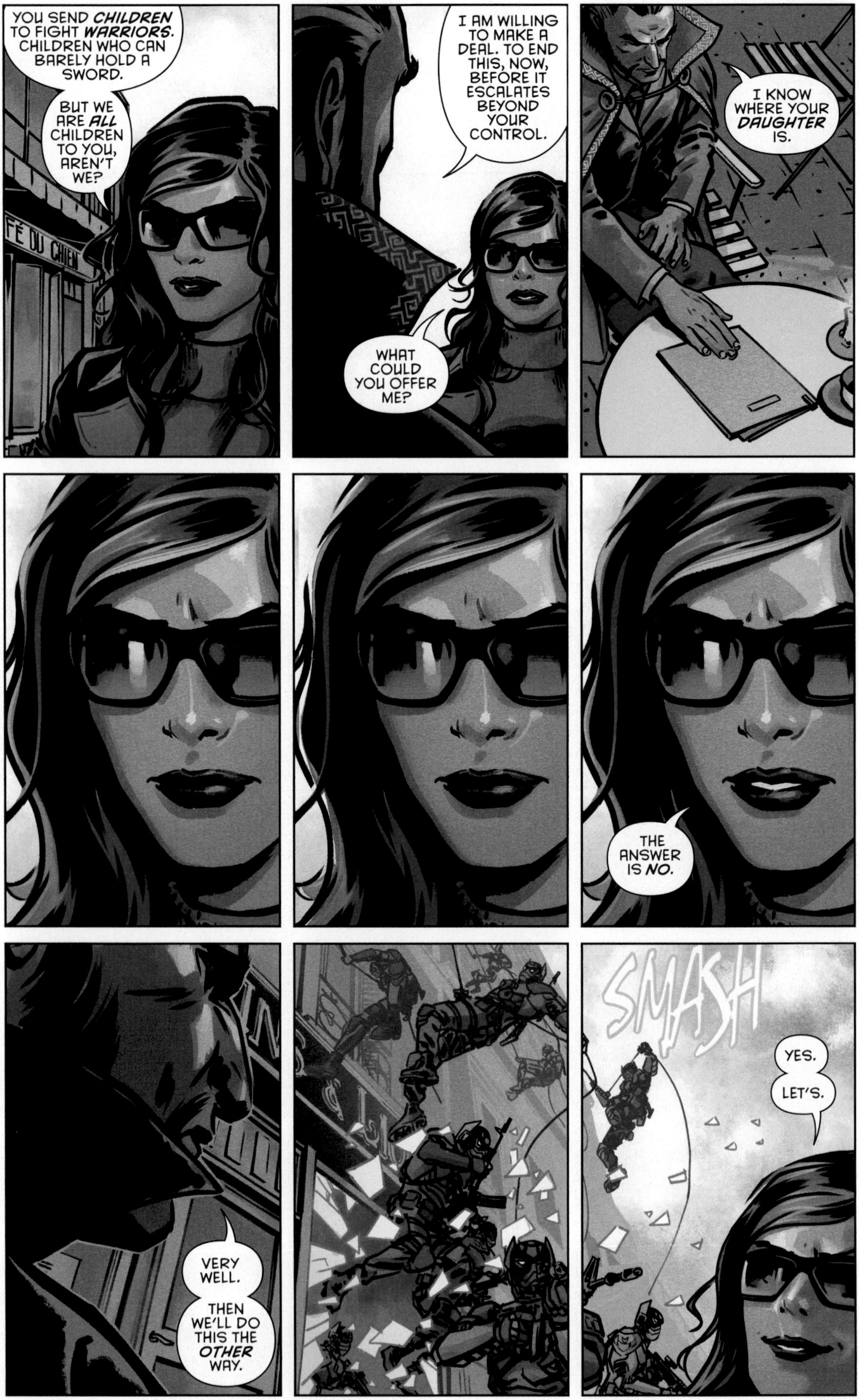

YOU SEND CHILDREN TO FIGHT WARRIORS. CHILDREN WHO CAN BARELY HOLD A SWORD.
BUT WE ARE ALL CHILDREN TO YOU, AREN'T WE?
FÉ DU CHIEN
I AM WILLING TO MAKE A DEAL. TO END THIS, NOW, BEFORE IT ESCALATES BEYOND YOUR CONTROL.
WHAT COULD YOU OFFER ME?
I KNOW WHERE YOUR DAUGHTER IS.
THE ANSWER IS NO.
VERY WELL.
THEN WE'LL DO THIS THE OTHER WAY.
SMASH
YES.
LET'S.

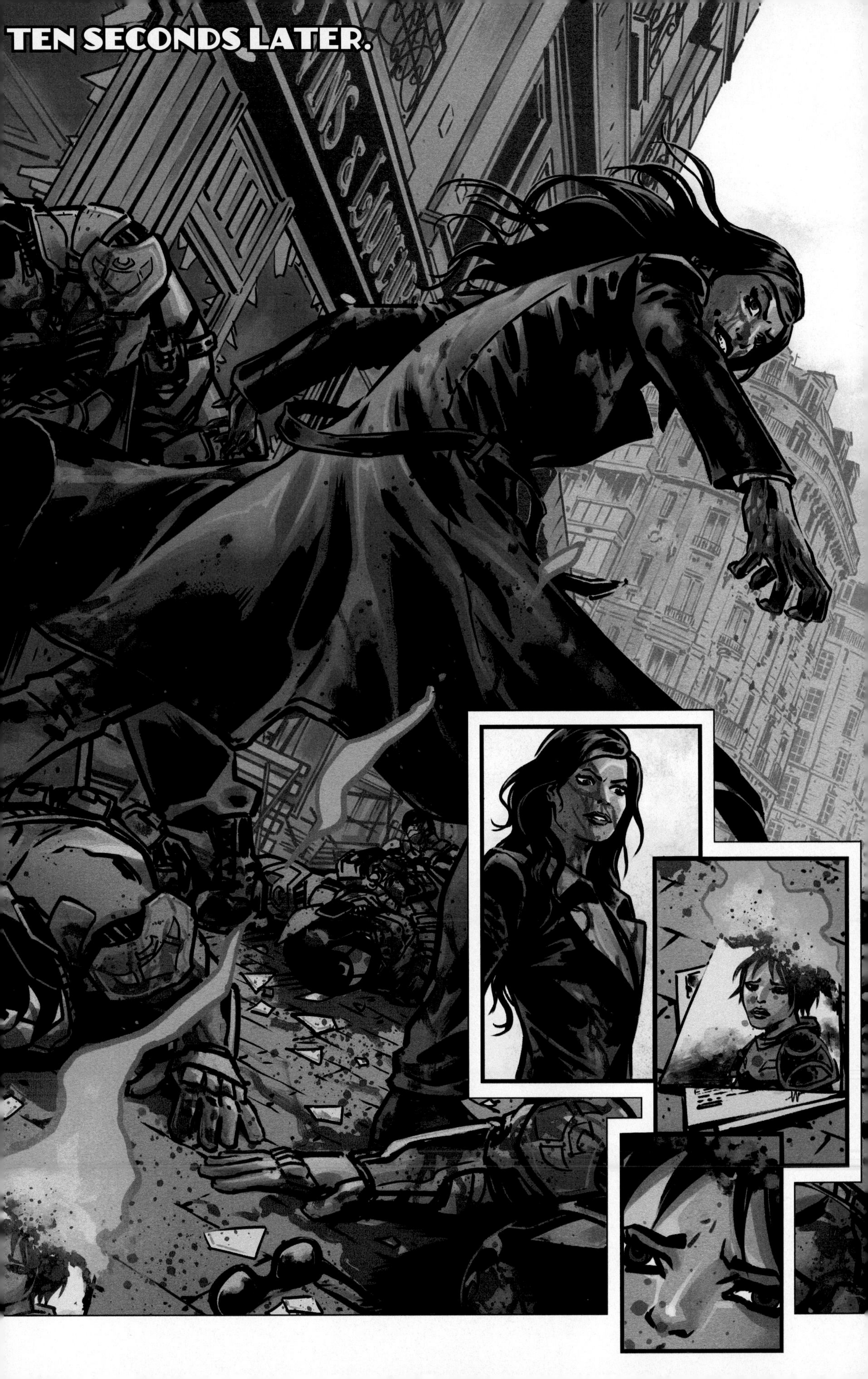
TEN SECONDS LATER.

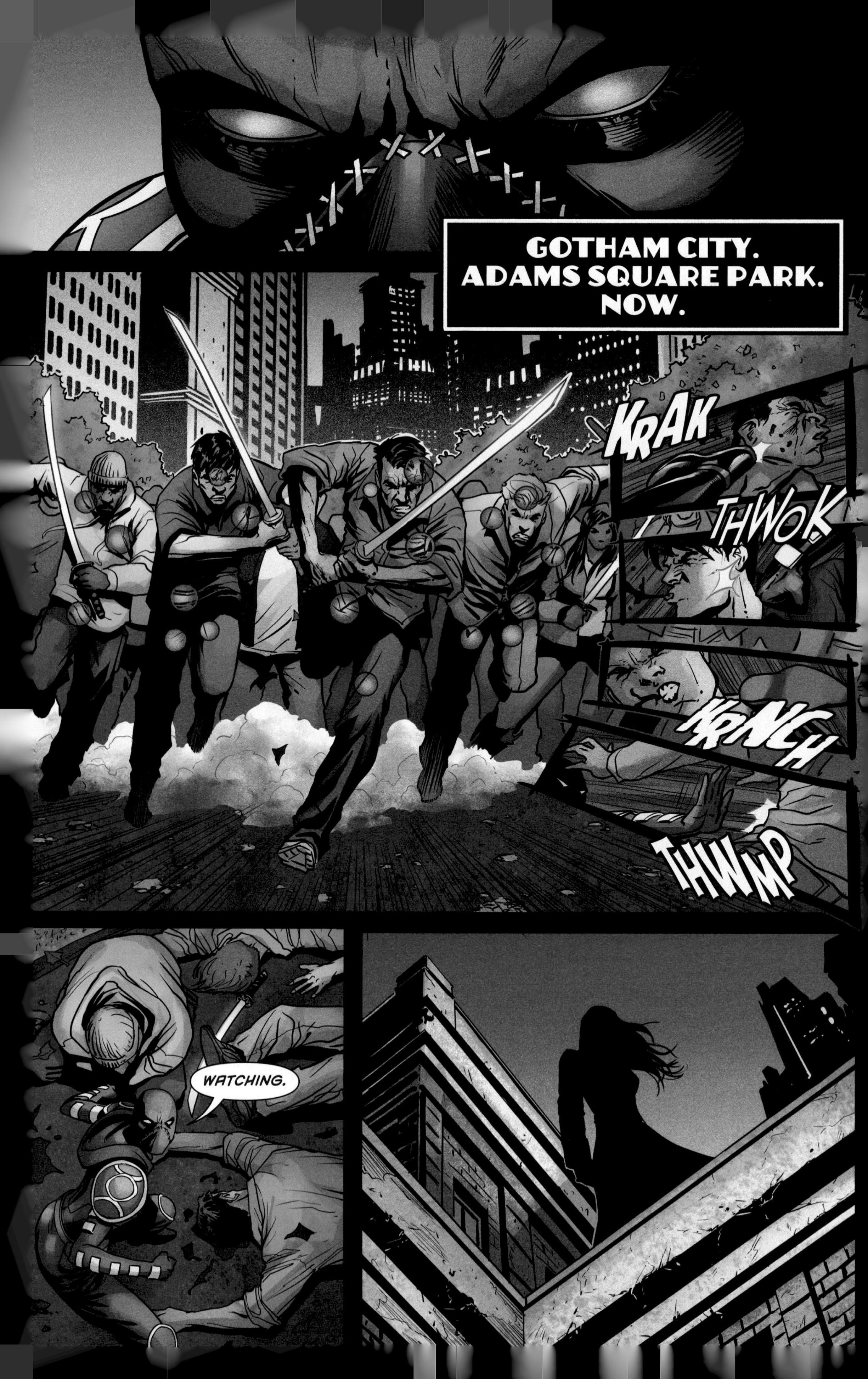
GOTHAM CITY.
ADAMS SQUARE PARK.
NOW.
KRAK
THWOK
KRNCH
THWMP
WATCHING.

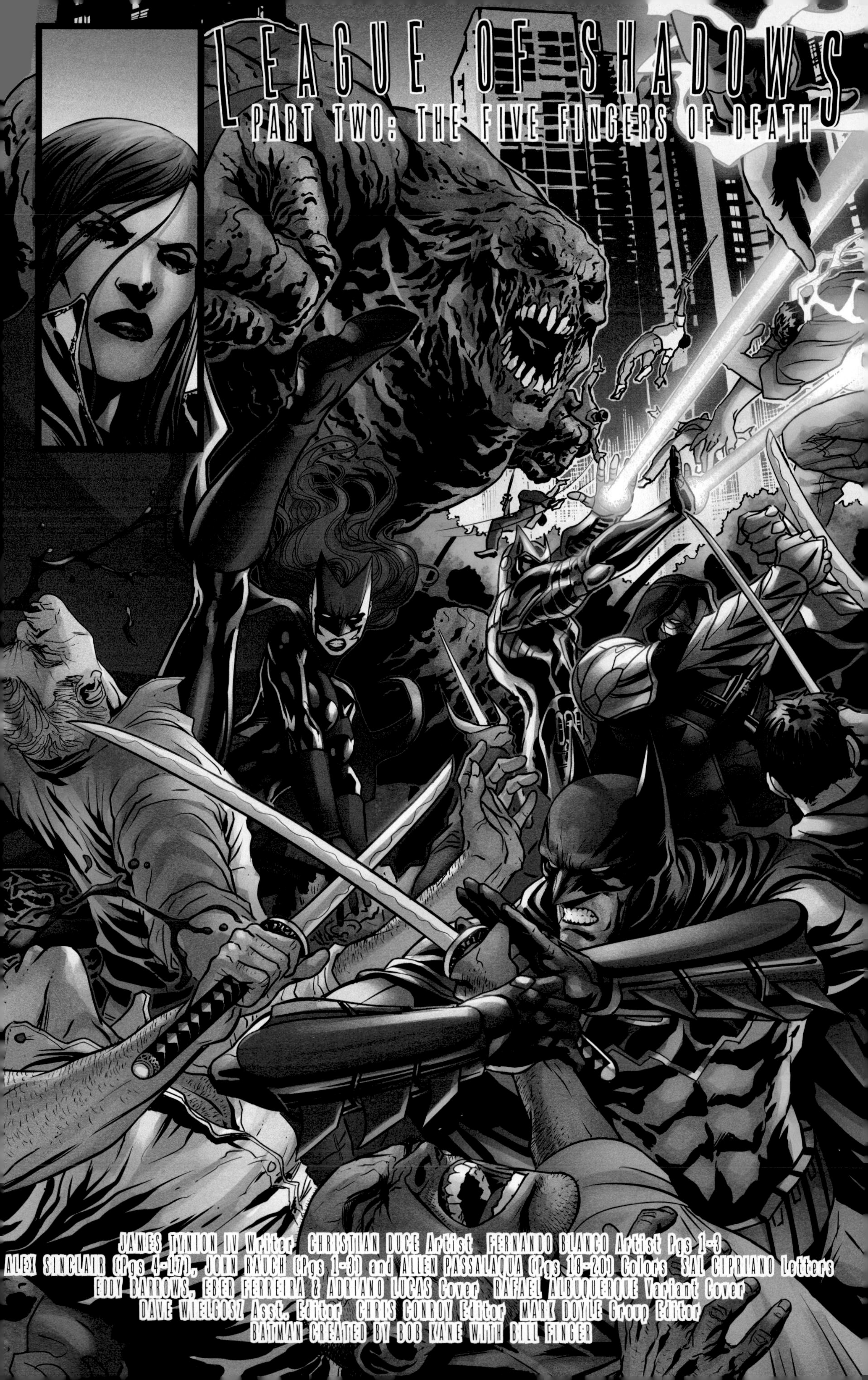
LEAGUE OF SHADOWS
PART TWO: THE FIVE FINGERS OF DEATH
JAMES TYNION IV Writer CHRISTIAN DUCE Artist FERNANDO BLANCO Artist Pgs 1-3
ALEX SINCLAIR (Pgs 4-17), JOHN RAUCH (Pgs 1-3) and ALLEN PASSALAQUA (Pgs 18-20) Colors SAL CIPRIANO Letters
EDDY BARROWS, EBER FERREIRA & ADRIANO LUCAS Cover RAFAEL ALBUQUERQUE Variant Cover
DAVE WIELGOSZ Asst. Editor CHRIS CONROY Editor MARK DOYLE Group Editor
BATMAN CREATED BY BOB KANE WITH BILL FINGER

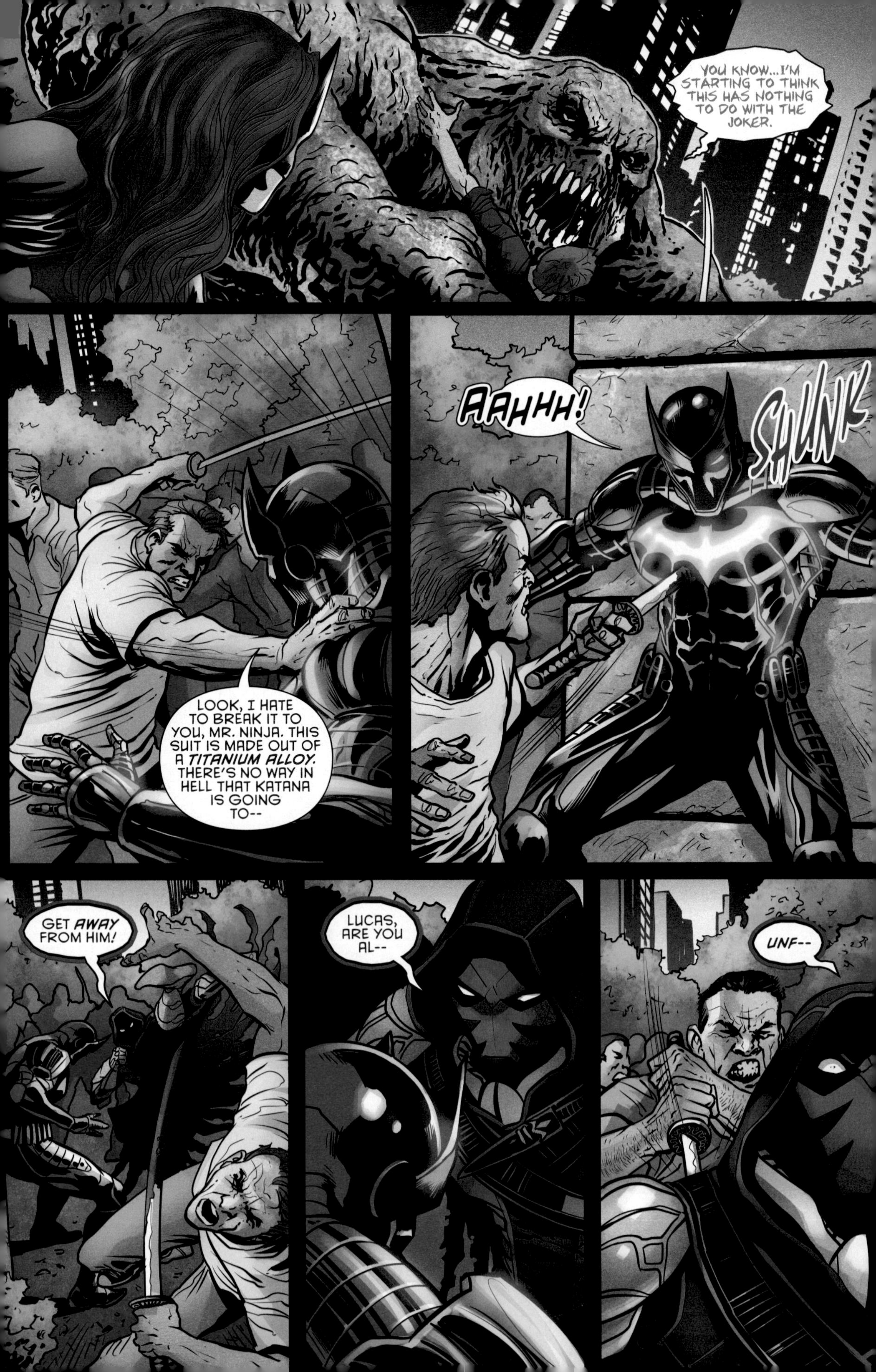
YOU KNOW...I'M STARTING TO THINK THIS HAS NOTHING TO DO WITH THE JOKER.
LOOK, I HATE TO BREAK IT TO YOU, MR. NINJA. THIS SUIT IS MADE OUT OF A *TITANIUM ALLOY.* THERE'S NO WAY IN HELL THAT KATANA IS GOING TO--
AAHHH!
SHUNK
GET **AWAY** FROM HIM!
LUCAS, ARE YOU AL--
UNF--

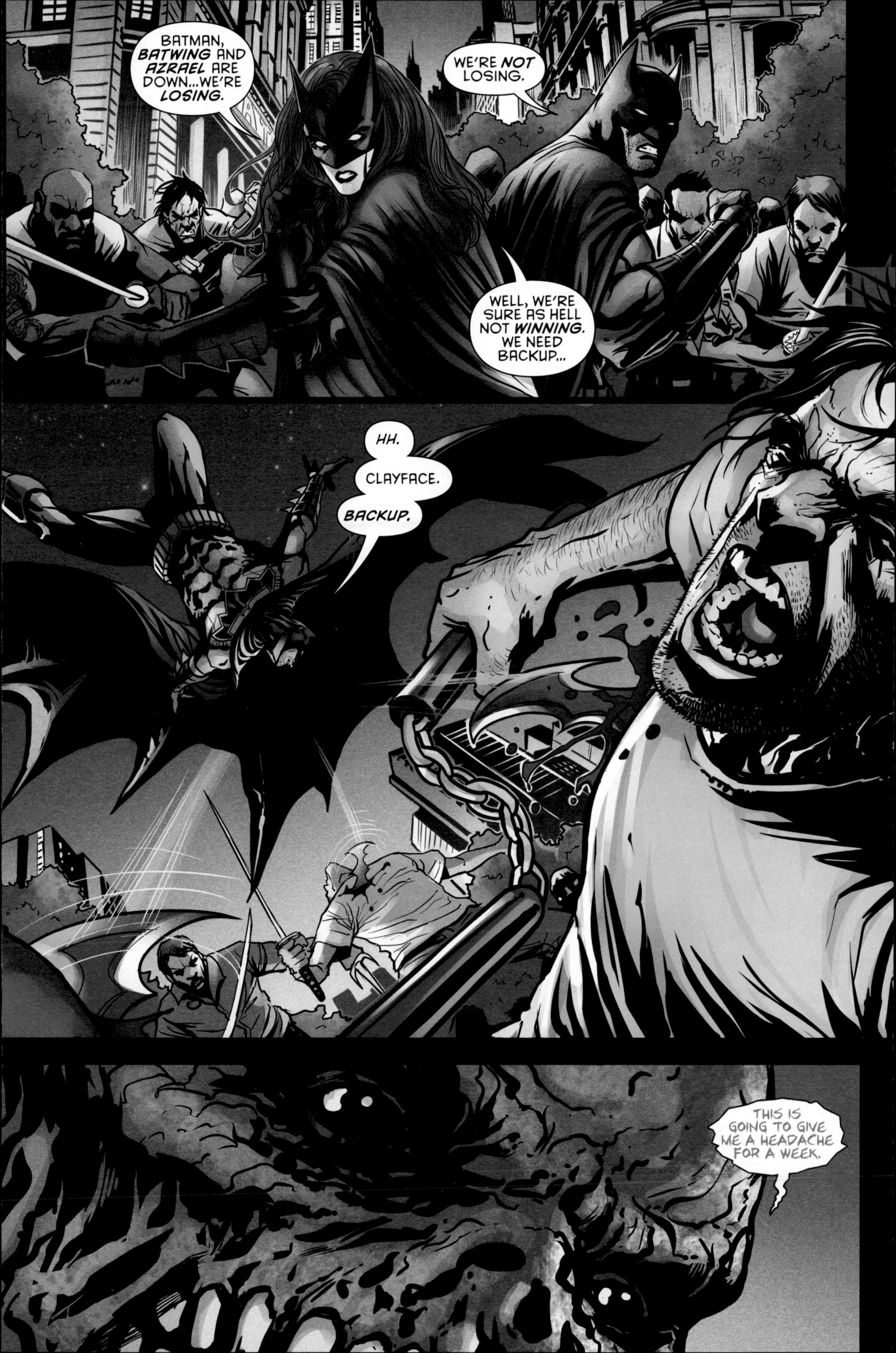
BATMAN, BATWING AND AZRAEL ARE DOWN...WE'RE LOSING.
WE'RE NOT LOSING.
WELL, WE'RE SURE AS HELL NOT WINNING. WE NEED BACKUP...
HH.
CLAYFACE.
BACKUP.
THIS IS GOING TO GIVE ME A HEADACHE FOR A WEEK.

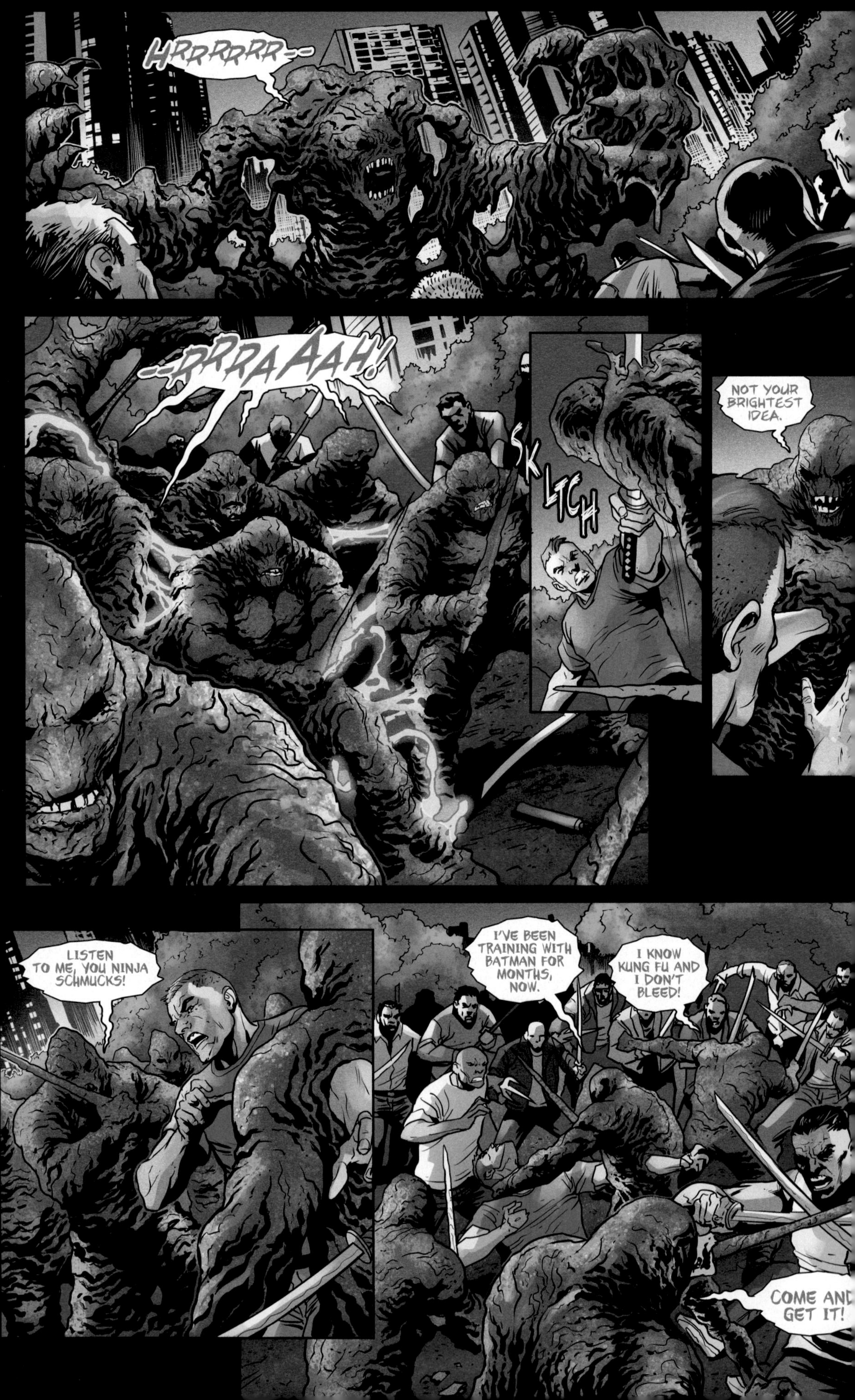
HRRRRRR--
--RRRAAAH!
SKLTCH
NOT YOUR BRIGHTEST IDEA.
LISTEN TO ME, YOU NINJA SCHMUCKS!
I'VE BEEN TRAINING WITH BATMAN FOR MONTHS, NOW.
I KNOW KUNG FU AND I DON'T BLEED!
COME AND GET IT!

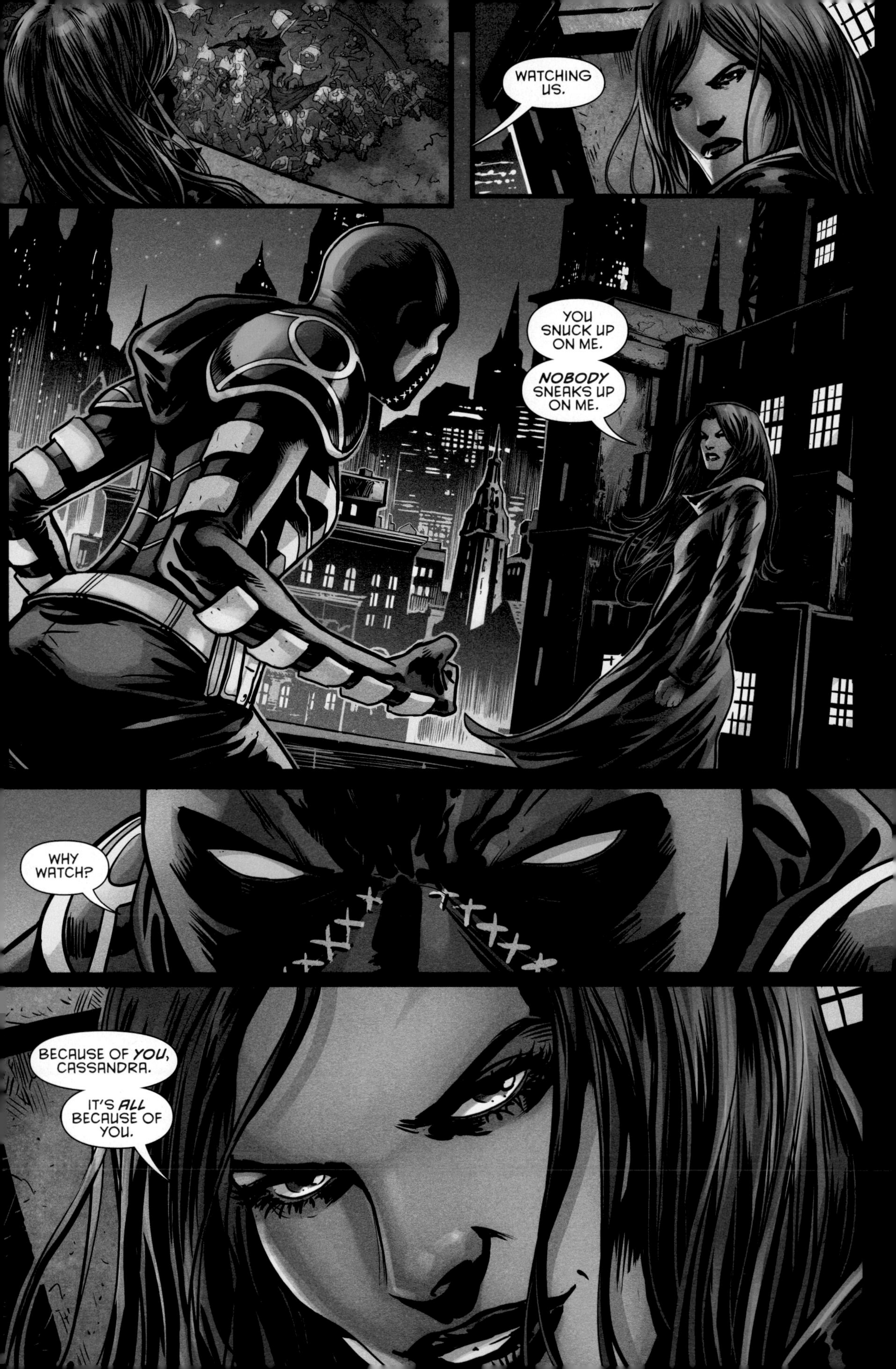
WATCHING US.
YOU SNUCK UP ON ME.
NOBODY SNEAKS UP ON ME.
WHY WATCH?
BECAUSE OF YOU, CASSANDRA.
IT'S ALL BECAUSE OF YOU.

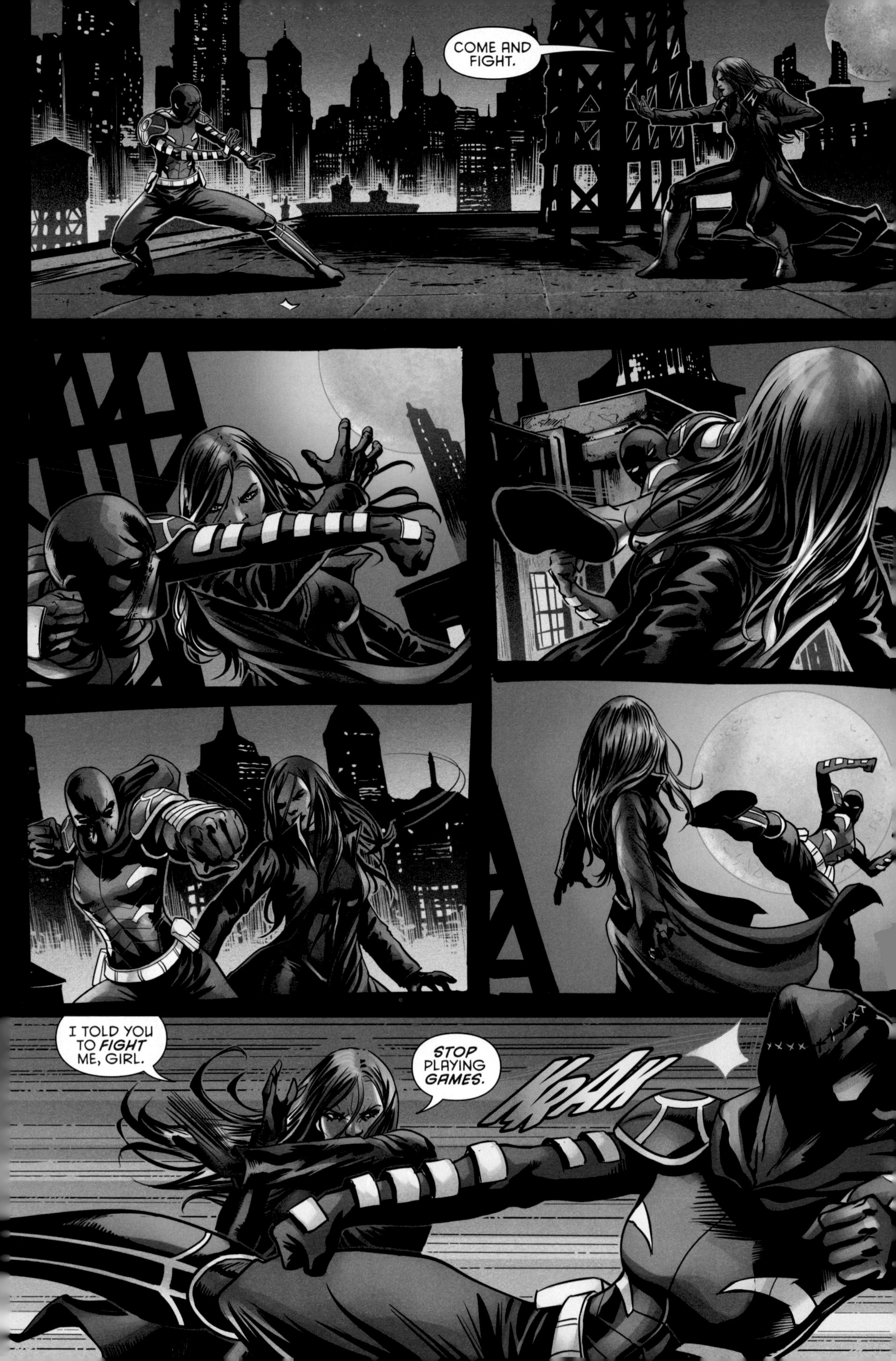
COME AND FIGHT.
I TOLD YOU TO FIGHT ME, GIRL.
STOP PLAYING GAMES.
WHAK

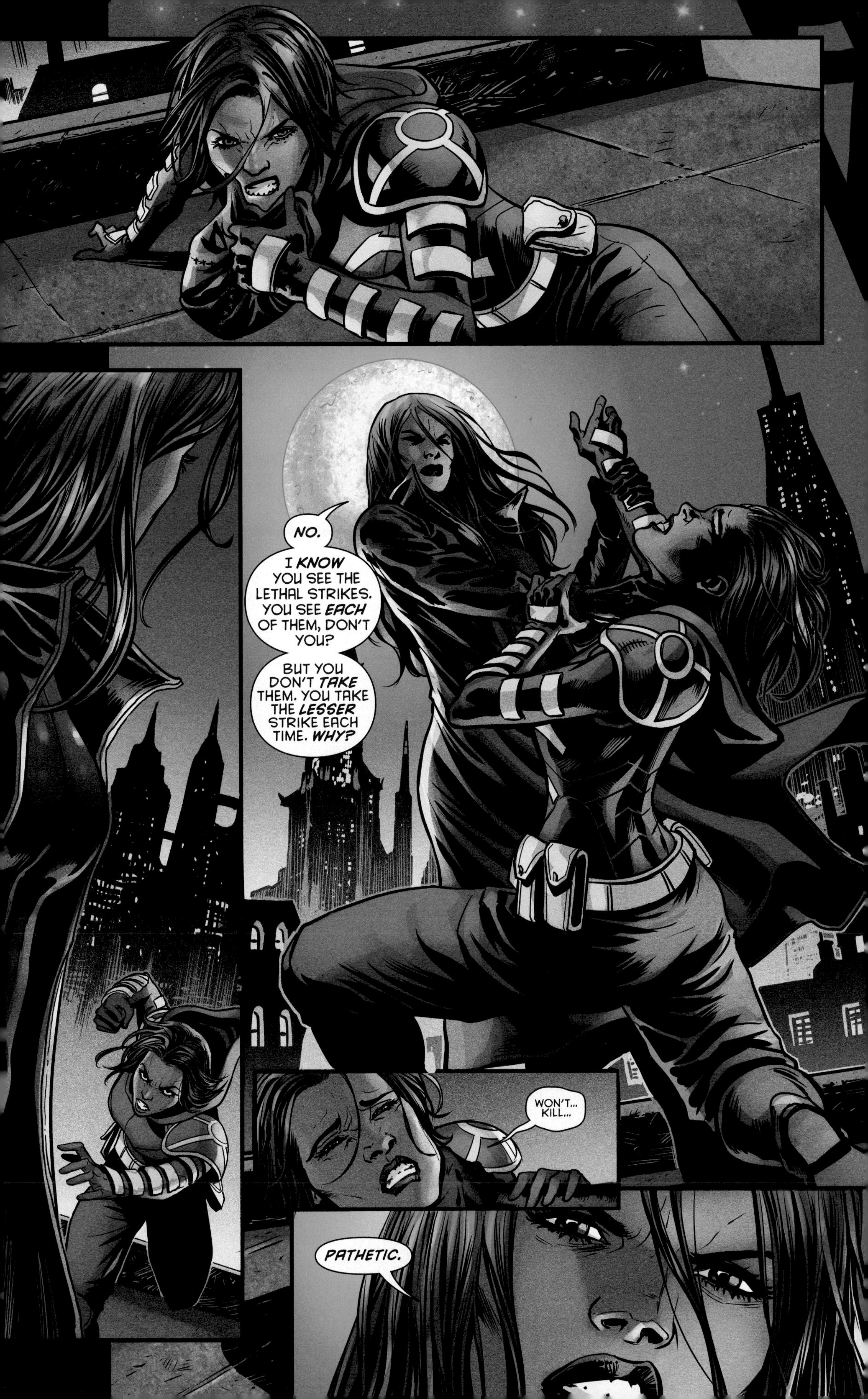
NO.
I KNOW YOU SEE THE LETHAL STRIKES. YOU SEE EACH OF THEM, DON'T YOU?
BUT YOU DON'T TAKE THEM. YOU TAKE THE LESSER STRIKE EACH TIME. WHY?
WON'T... KILL...
PATHETIC.

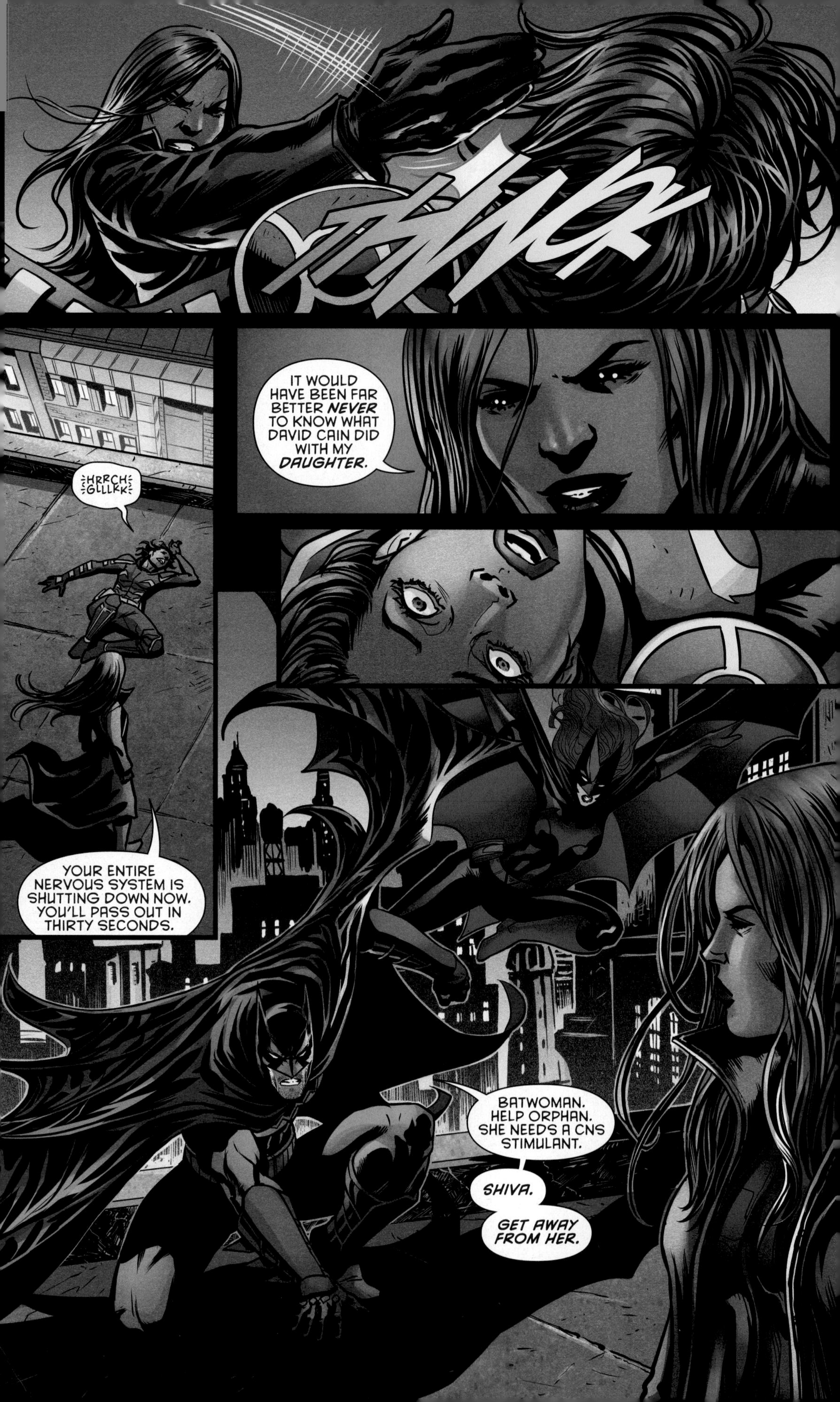
THWACK
IT WOULD HAVE BEEN FAR BETTER NEVER TO KNOW WHAT DAVID CAIN DID WITH MY DAUGHTER.
HRRCH GLLLKK
YOUR ENTIRE NERVOUS SYSTEM IS SHUTTING DOWN NOW. YOU'LL PASS OUT IN THIRTY SECONDS.
BATWOMAN. HELP ORPHAN. SHE NEEDS A CNS STIMULANT.
SHIVA.
GET AWAY FROM HER.

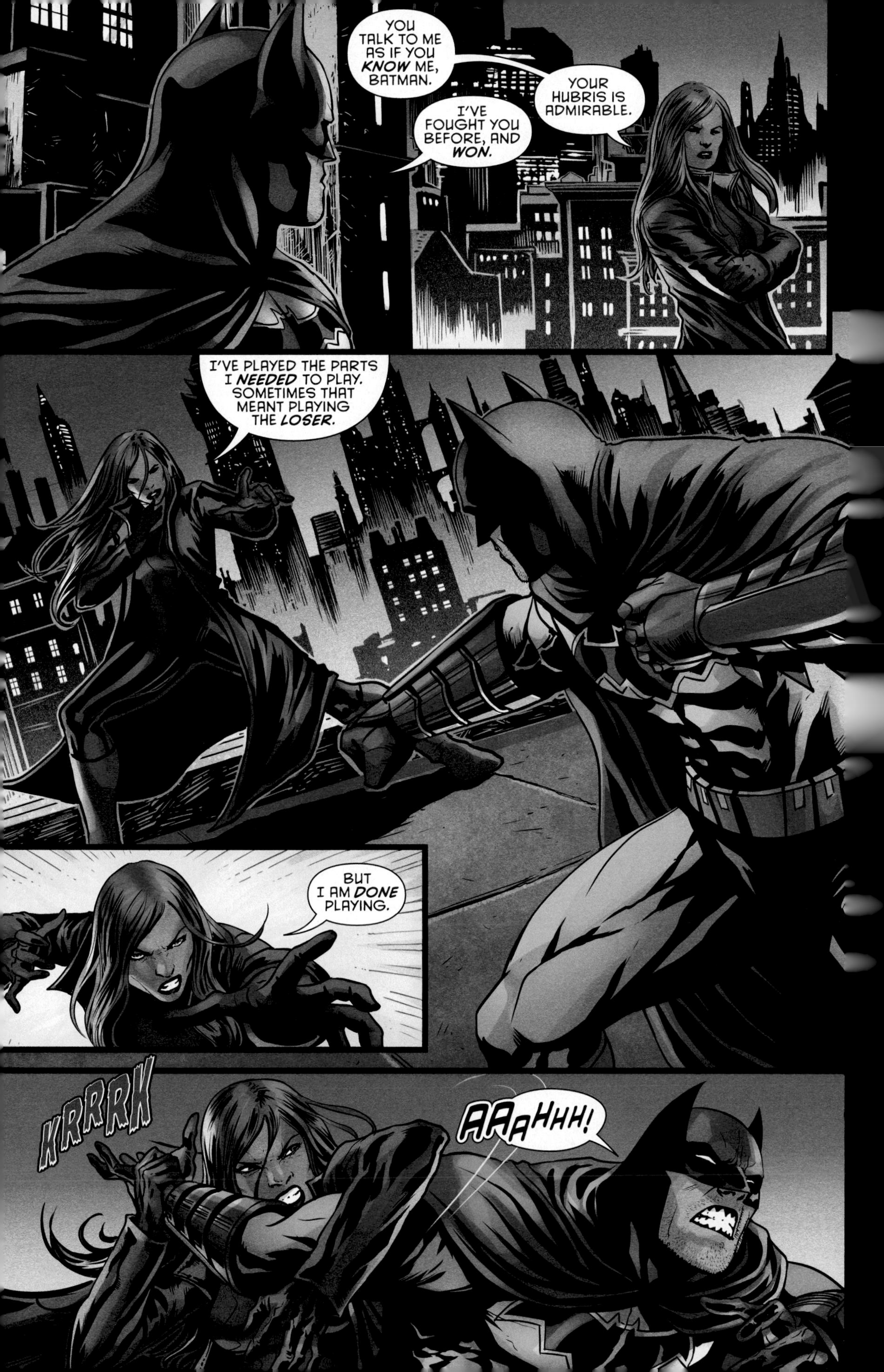
YOU TALK TO ME AS IF YOU KNOW ME, BATMAN.
YOUR HUBRIS IS ADMIRABLE.
I'VE FOUGHT YOU BEFORE, AND WON.
I'VE PLAYED THE PARTS I NEEDED TO PLAY. SOMETIMES THAT MEANT PLAYING THE LOSER.
BUT I AM DONE PLAYING.
KRRRK
AAAHHH!

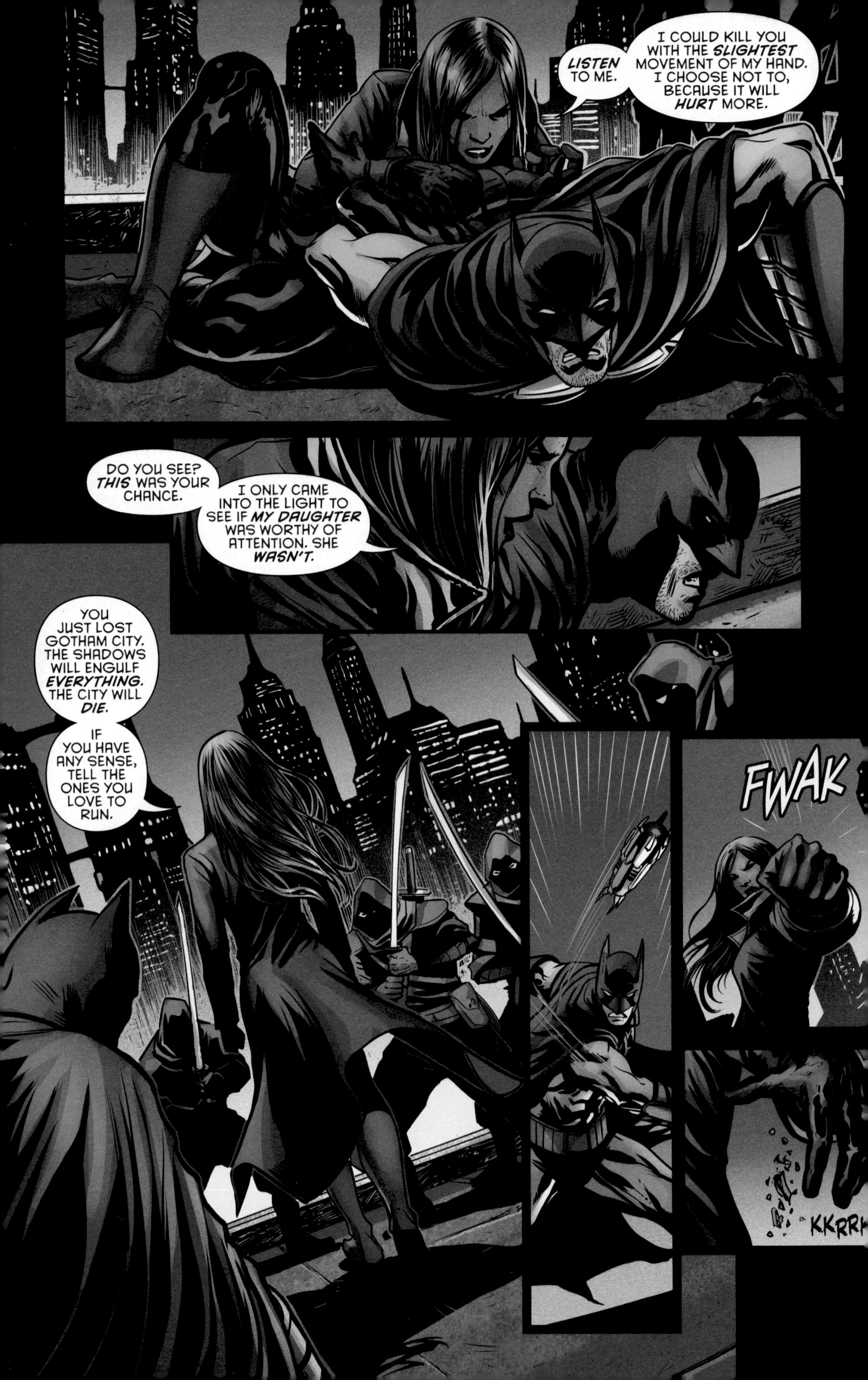
LISTEN TO ME.
I COULD KILL YOU WITH THE SLIGHTEST MOVEMENT OF MY HAND. I CHOOSE NOT TO, BECAUSE IT WILL HURT MORE.
DO YOU SEE? THIS WAS YOUR CHANCE.
I ONLY CAME INTO THE LIGHT TO SEE IF MY DAUGHTER WAS WORTHY OF ATTENTION. SHE WASN'T.
YOU JUST LOST GOTHAM CITY. THE SHADOWS WILL ENGULF EVERYTHING. THE CITY WILL DIE.
IF YOU HAVE ANY SENSE, TELL THE ONES YOU LOVE TO RUN.
FWAK
KKRRK

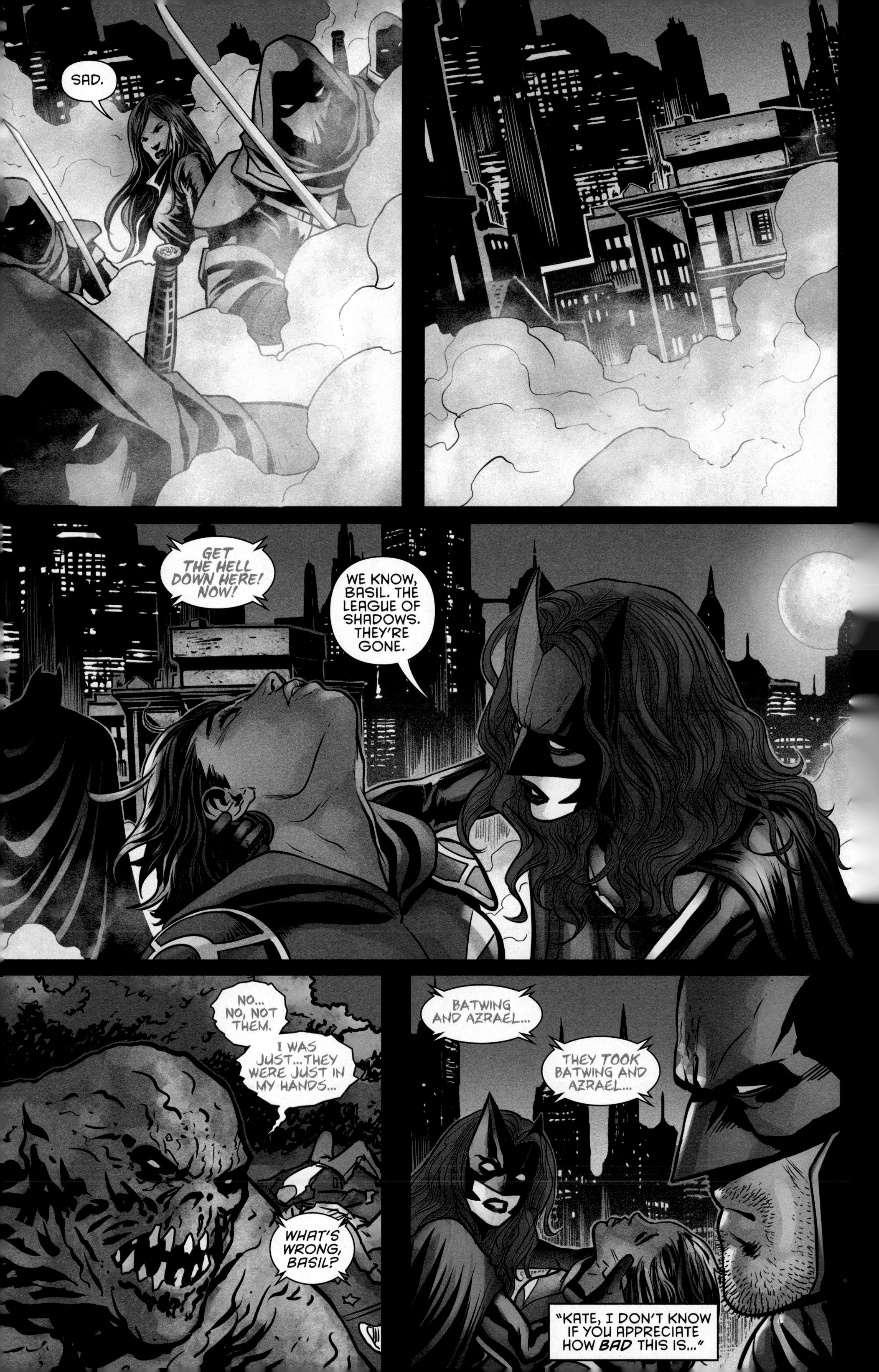
SAD.
GET THE HELL DOWN HERE! NOW!
WE KNOW, BASIL. THE LEAGUE OF SHADOWS. THEY'RE GONE.
NO... NO, NOT THEM.
I WAS JUST...THEY WERE JUST IN MY HANDS...
WHAT'S WRONG, BASIL?
BATWING AND AZRAEL...
THEY TOOK BATWING AND AZRAEL...
"KATE, I DON'T KNOW IF YOU APPRECIATE HOW BAD THIS IS..."

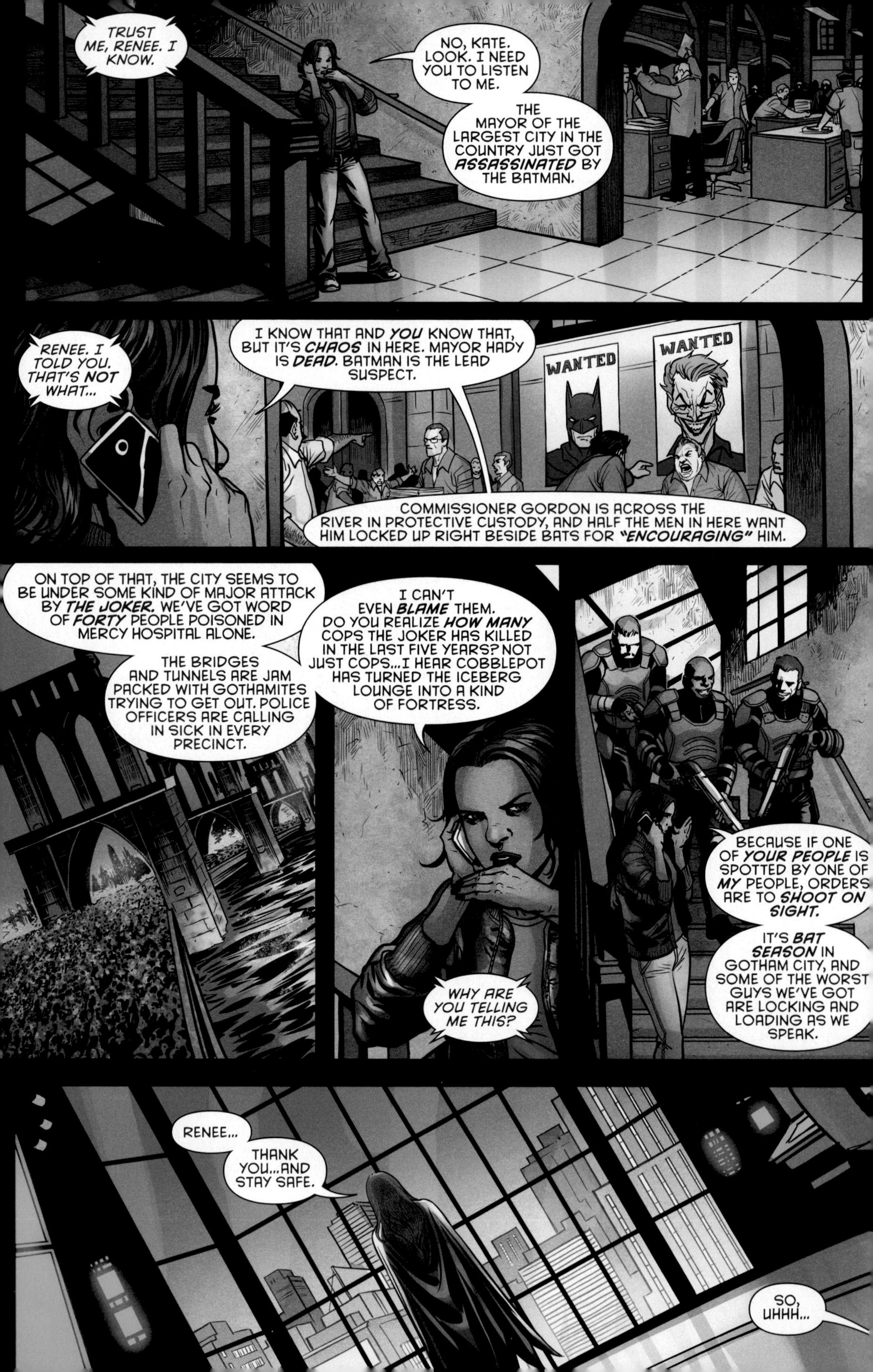
TRUST ME, RENEE. I KNOW.
NO, KATE. LOOK. I NEED YOU TO LISTEN TO ME.
THE MAYOR OF THE LARGEST CITY IN THE COUNTRY JUST GOT ASSASSINATED BY THE BATMAN.
RENEE. I TOLD YOU. THAT'S NOT WHAT...
I KNOW THAT AND YOU KNOW THAT, BUT IT'S CHAOS IN HERE. MAYOR HADY IS DEAD. BATMAN IS THE LEAD SUSPECT.
WANTED
WANTED
COMMISSIONER GORDON IS ACROSS THE RIVER IN PROTECTIVE CUSTODY, AND HALF THE MEN IN HERE WANT HIM LOCKED UP RIGHT BESIDE BATS FOR "ENCOURAGING" HIM.
ON TOP OF THAT, THE CITY SEEMS TO BE UNDER SOME KIND OF MAJOR ATTACK BY THE JOKER. WE'VE GOT WORD OF FORTY PEOPLE POISONED IN MERCY HOSPITAL ALONE.
THE BRIDGES AND TUNNELS ARE JAM PACKED WITH GOTHAMITES TRYING TO GET OUT. POLICE OFFICERS ARE CALLING IN SICK IN EVERY PRECINCT.
I CAN'T EVEN BLAME THEM. DO YOU REALIZE HOW MANY COPS THE JOKER HAS KILLED IN THE LAST FIVE YEARS? NOT JUST COPS...I HEAR COBBLEPOT HAS TURNED THE ICEBERG LOUNGE INTO A KIND OF FORTRESS.
WHY ARE YOU TELLING ME THIS?
BECAUSE IF ONE OF YOUR PEOPLE IS SPOTTED BY ONE OF MY PEOPLE, ORDERS ARE TO SHOOT ON SIGHT.
IT'S BAT SEASON IN GOTHAM CITY, AND SOME OF THE WORST GUYS WE'VE GOT ARE LOCKING AND LOADING AS WE SPEAK.
RENEE...
THANK YOU...AND STAY SAFE.
SO, UHHH...

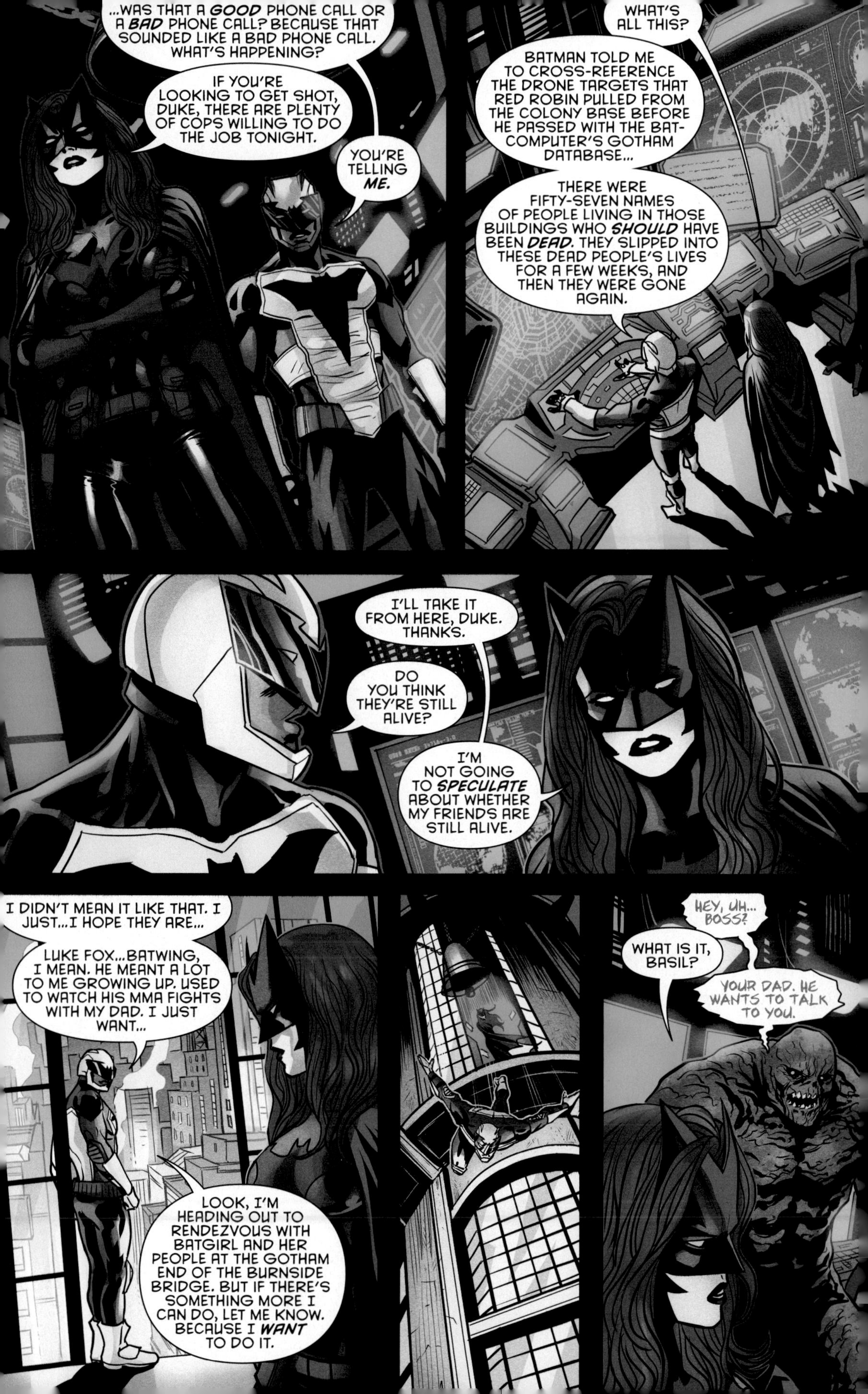

...WAS THAT A ***GOOD*** PHONE CALL OR A ***BAD*** PHONE CALL? BECAUSE THAT SOUNDED LIKE A BAD PHONE CALL. WHAT'S HAPPENING?
IF YOU'RE LOOKING TO GET SHOT, DUKE, THERE ARE PLENTY OF COPS WILLING TO DO THE JOB TONIGHT.
YOU'RE TELLING ***ME.***
WHAT'S ALL THIS?
BATMAN TOLD ME TO CROSS-REFERENCE THE DRONE TARGETS THAT RED ROBIN PULLED FROM THE COLONY BASE BEFORE HE PASSED WITH THE BAT-COMPUTER'S GOTHAM DATABASE...
THERE WERE FIFTY-SEVEN NAMES OF PEOPLE LIVING IN THOSE BUILDINGS WHO ***SHOULD*** HAVE BEEN ***DEAD***. THEY SLIPPED INTO THESE DEAD PEOPLE'S LIVES FOR A FEW WEEKS, AND THEN THEY WERE GONE AGAIN.
I'LL TAKE IT FROM HERE, DUKE. THANKS.
DO YOU THINK THEY'RE STILL ALIVE?
I'M NOT GOING TO ***SPECULATE*** ABOUT WHETHER MY FRIENDS ARE STILL ALIVE.
I DIDN'T MEAN IT LIKE THAT. I JUST...I HOPE THEY ARE...
LUKE FOX...BATWING, I MEAN. HE MEANT A LOT TO ME GROWING UP. USED TO WATCH HIS MMA FIGHTS WITH MY DAD. I JUST WANT...
LOOK, I'M HEADING OUT TO RENDEZVOUS WITH BATGIRL AND HER PEOPLE AT THE GOTHAM END OF THE BURNSIDE BRIDGE. BUT IF THERE'S SOMETHING MORE I CAN DO, LET ME KNOW. BECAUSE I ***WANT*** TO DO IT.
HEY, UH... BOSS?
WHAT IS IT, BASIL?
YOUR DAD. HE WANTS TO TALK TO YOU.

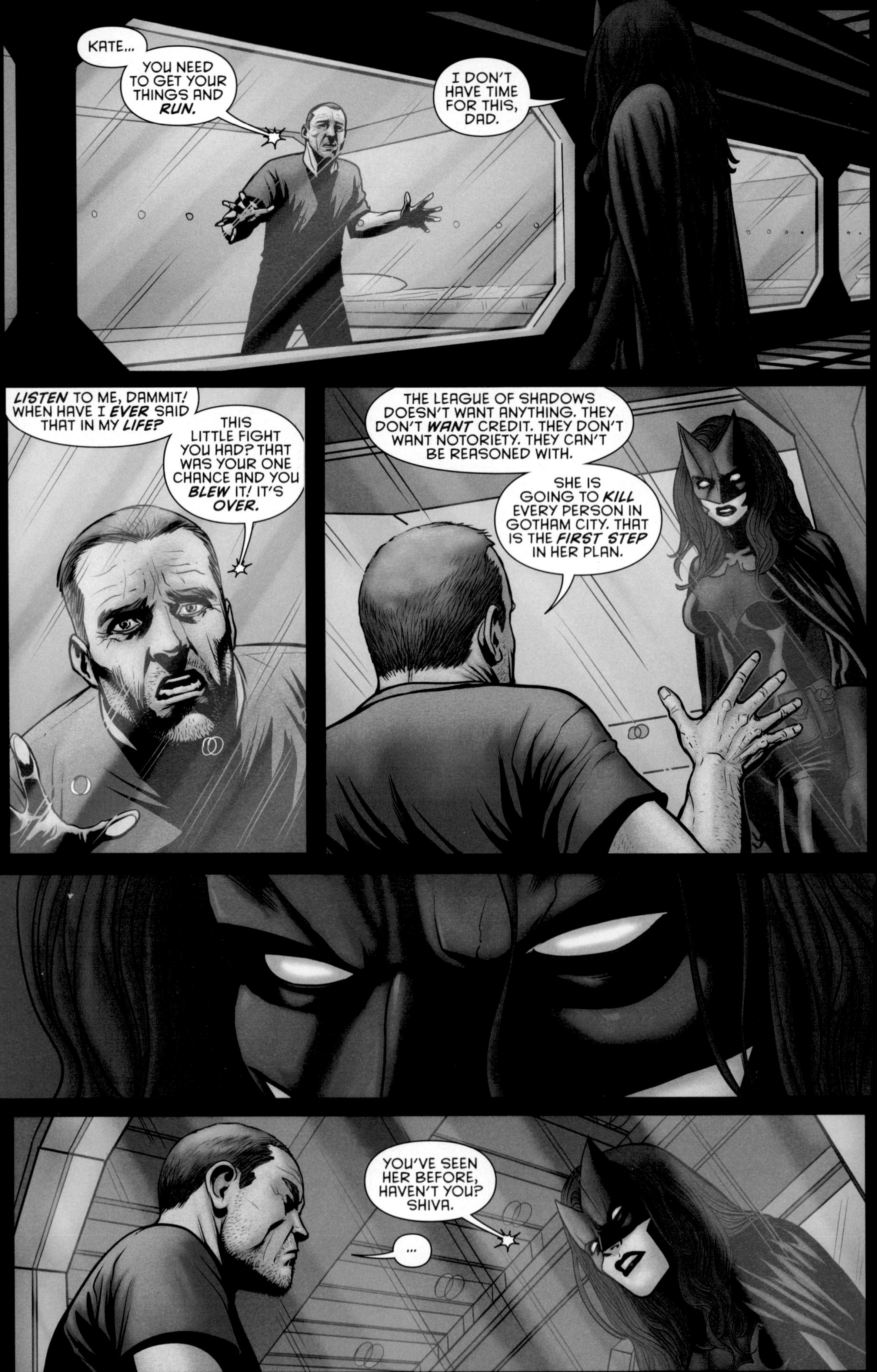
KATE...
YOU NEED TO GET YOUR THINGS AND RUN.
I DON'T HAVE TIME FOR THIS, DAD.
LISTEN TO ME, DAMMIT! WHEN HAVE I EVER SAID THAT IN MY LIFE?
THIS LITTLE FIGHT YOU HAD? THAT WAS YOUR ONE CHANCE AND YOU BLEW IT! IT'S OVER.
THE LEAGUE OF SHADOWS DOESN'T WANT ANYTHING. THEY DON'T WANT CREDIT. THEY DON'T WANT NOTORIETY. THEY CAN'T BE REASONED WITH.
SHE IS GOING TO KILL EVERY PERSON IN GOTHAM CITY. THAT IS THE FIRST STEP IN HER PLAN.
YOU'VE SEEN HER BEFORE, HAVEN'T YOU? SHIVA.
...

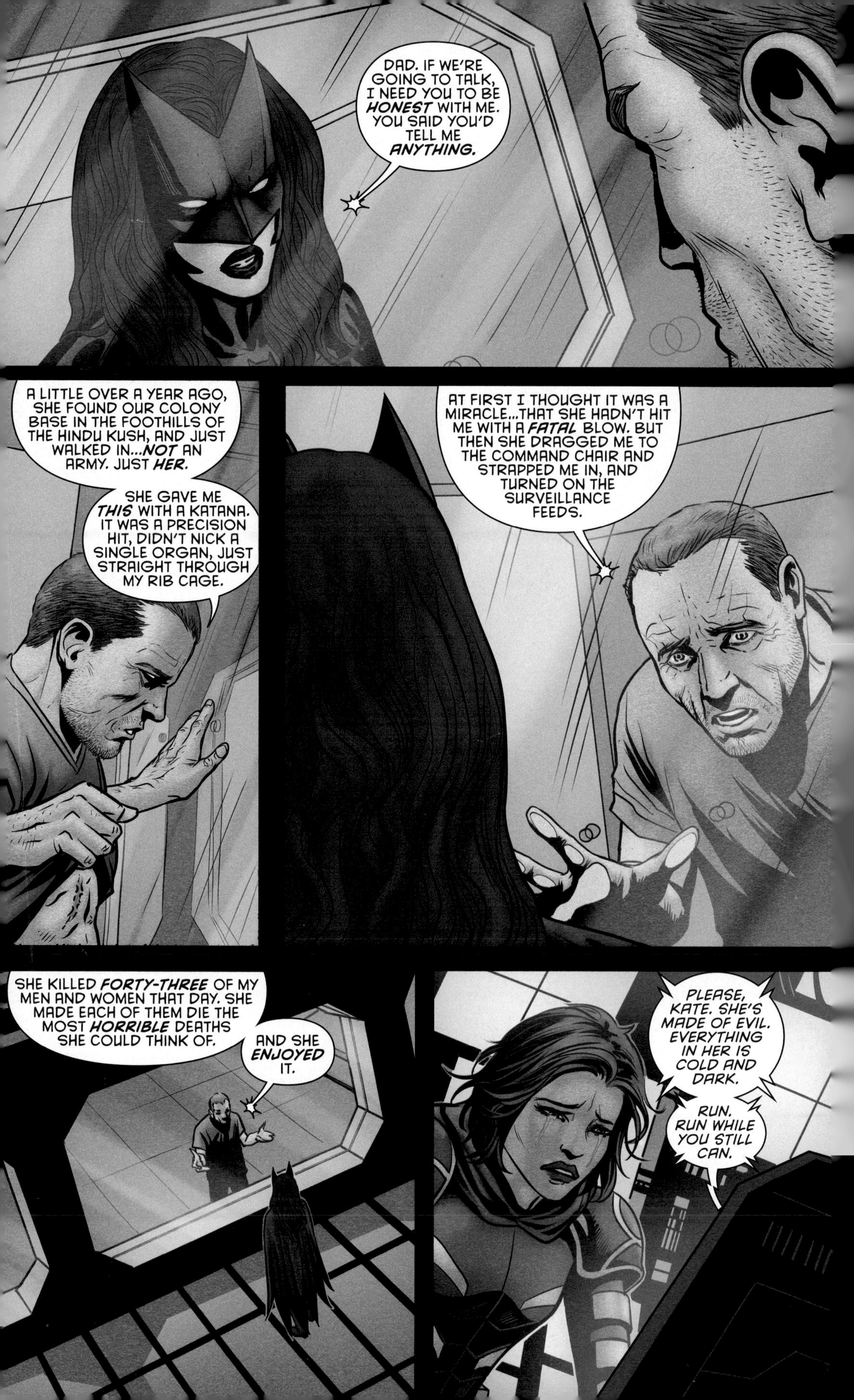
DAD. IF WE'RE GOING TO TALK, I NEED YOU TO BE HONEST WITH ME. YOU SAID YOU'D TELL ME ANYTHING.
A LITTLE OVER A YEAR AGO, SHE FOUND OUR COLONY BASE IN THE FOOTHILLS OF THE HINDU KUSH, AND JUST WALKED IN...NOT AN ARMY. JUST HER.
SHE GAVE ME THIS WITH A KATANA. IT WAS A PRECISION HIT, DIDN'T NICK A SINGLE ORGAN, JUST STRAIGHT THROUGH MY RIB CAGE.
AT FIRST I THOUGHT IT WAS A MIRACLE...THAT SHE HADN'T HIT ME WITH A FATAL BLOW. BUT THEN SHE DRAGGED ME TO THE COMMAND CHAIR AND STRAPPED ME IN, AND TURNED ON THE SURVEILLANCE FEEDS.
SHE KILLED FORTY-THREE OF MY MEN AND WOMEN THAT DAY. SHE MADE EACH OF THEM DIE THE MOST HORRIBLE DEATHS SHE COULD THINK OF.
AND SHE ENJOYED IT.
PLEASE, KATE. SHE'S MADE OF EVIL. EVERYTHING IN HER IS COLD AND DARK.
RUN. RUN WHILE YOU STILL CAN.

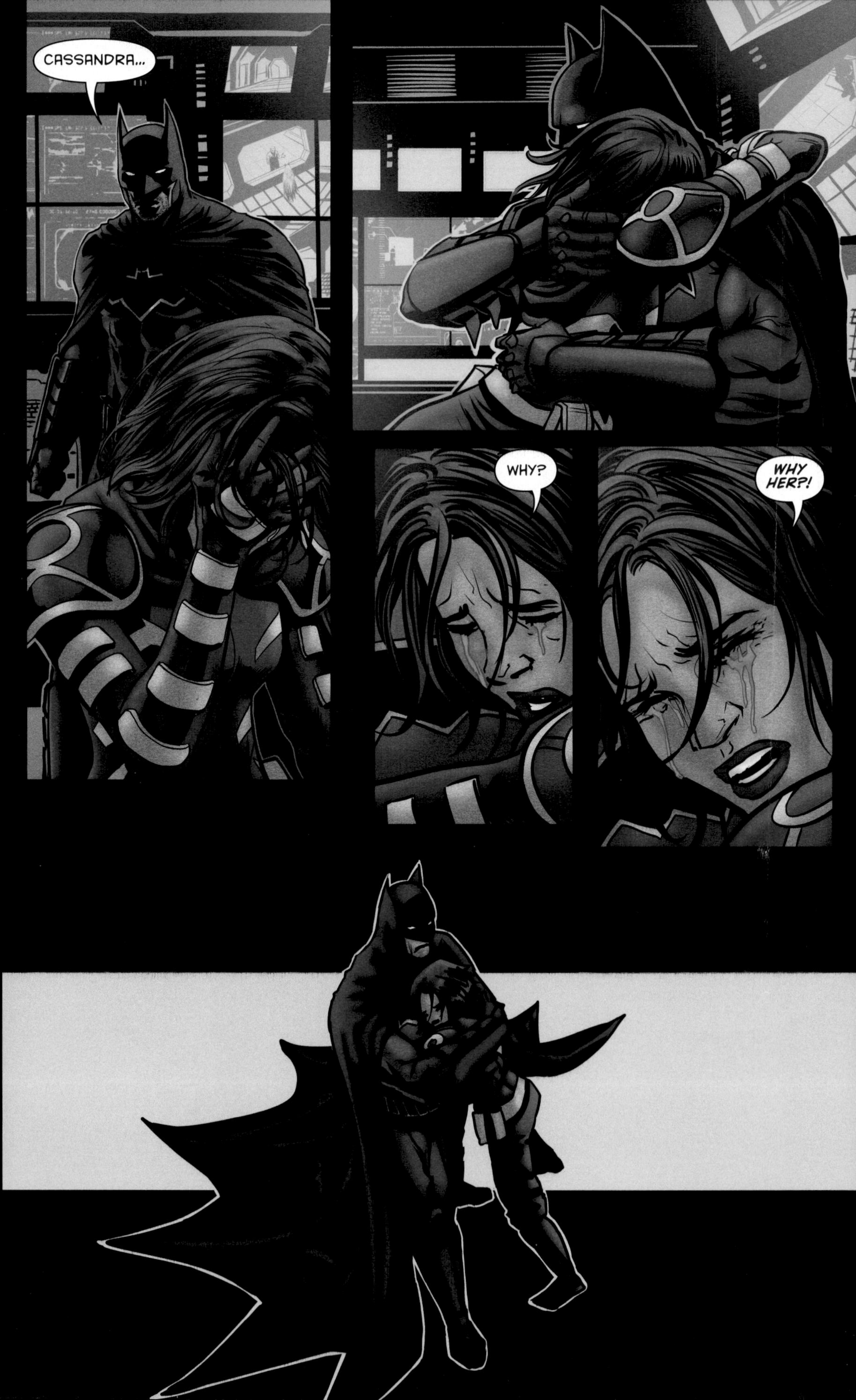
CASSANDRA...
WHY?
WHY HER?!

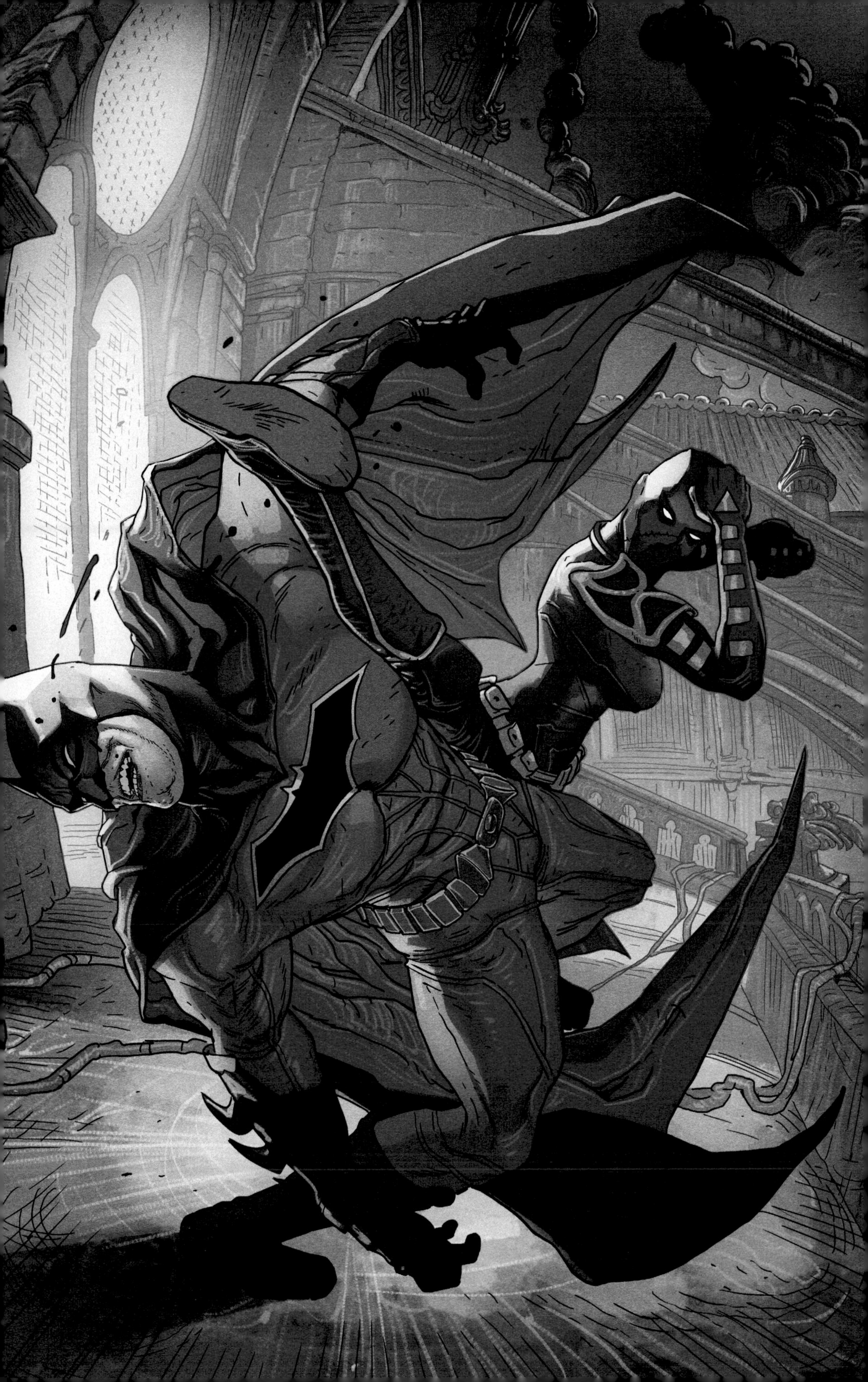

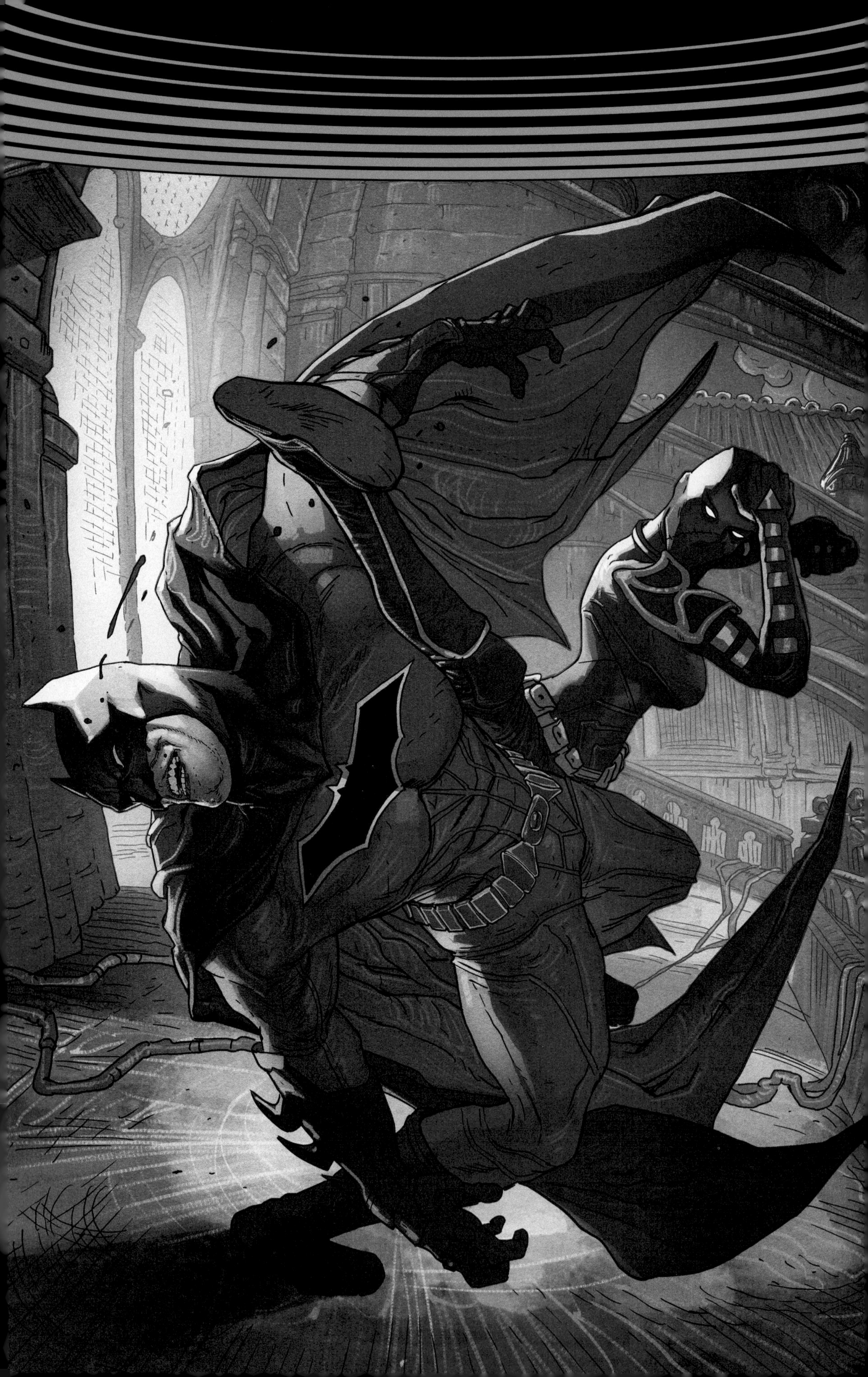

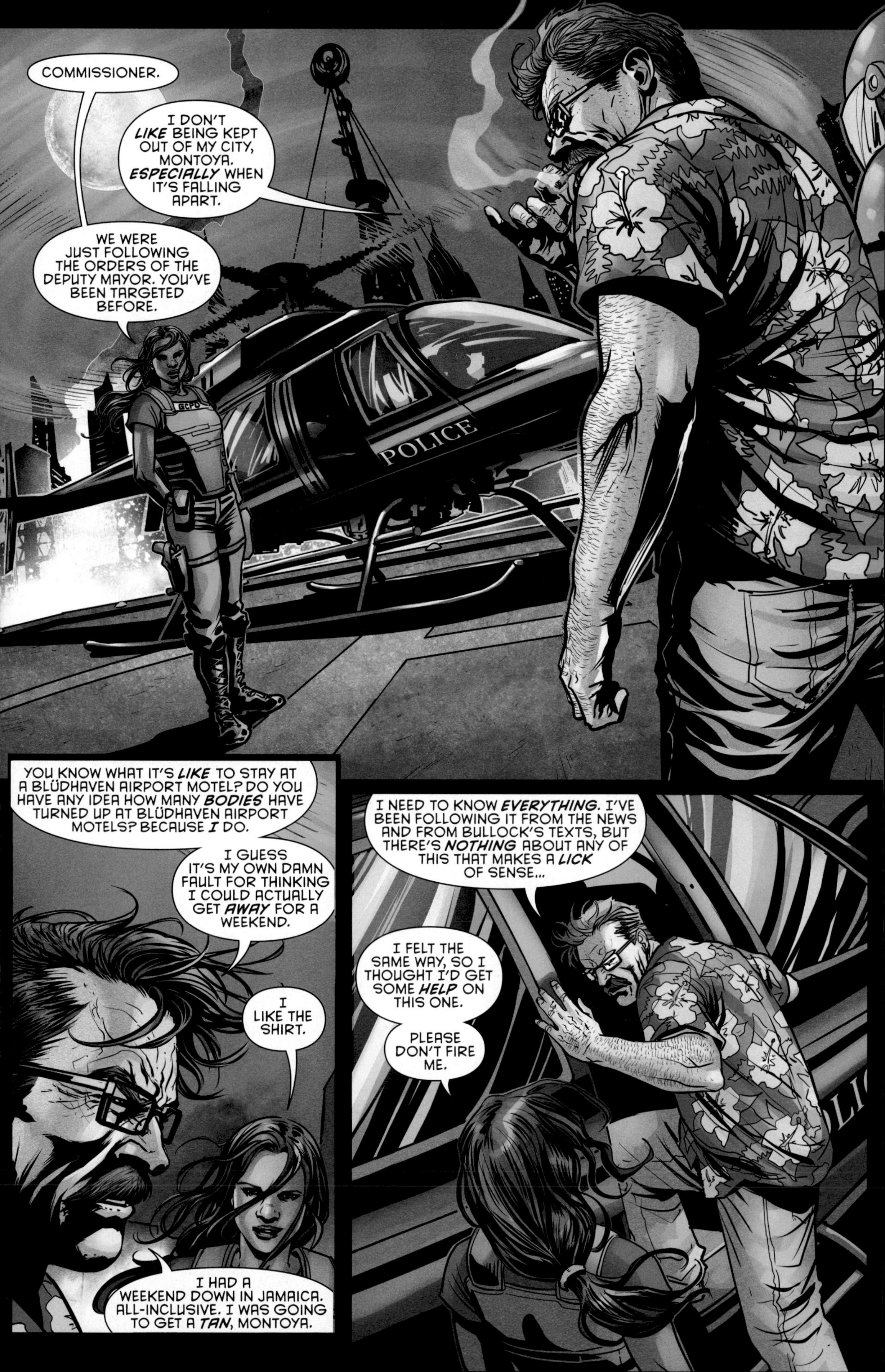
COMMISSIONER.
I DON'T LIKE BEING KEPT OUT OF MY CITY, MONTOYA. ESPECIALLY WHEN IT'S FALLING APART.
WE WERE JUST FOLLOWING THE ORDERS OF THE DEPUTY MAYOR. YOU'VE BEEN TARGETED BEFORE.
POLICE
GCPD
YOU KNOW WHAT IT'S LIKE TO STAY AT A BLÜDHAVEN AIRPORT MOTEL? DO YOU HAVE ANY IDEA HOW MANY BODIES HAVE TURNED UP AT BLÜDHAVEN AIRPORT MOTELS? BECAUSE I DO.
I GUESS IT'S MY OWN DAMN FAULT FOR THINKING I COULD ACTUALLY GET AWAY FOR A WEEKEND.
I LIKE THE SHIRT.
I HAD A WEEKEND DOWN IN JAMAICA. ALL-INCLUSIVE. I WAS GOING TO GET A TAN, MONTOYA.
I NEED TO KNOW EVERYTHING. I'VE BEEN FOLLOWING IT FROM THE NEWS AND FROM BULLOCK'S TEXTS, BUT THERE'S NOTHING ABOUT ANY OF THIS THAT MAKES A LICK OF SENSE...
I FELT THE SAME WAY, SO I THOUGHT I'D GET SOME HELP ON THIS ONE.
PLEASE DON'T FIRE ME.

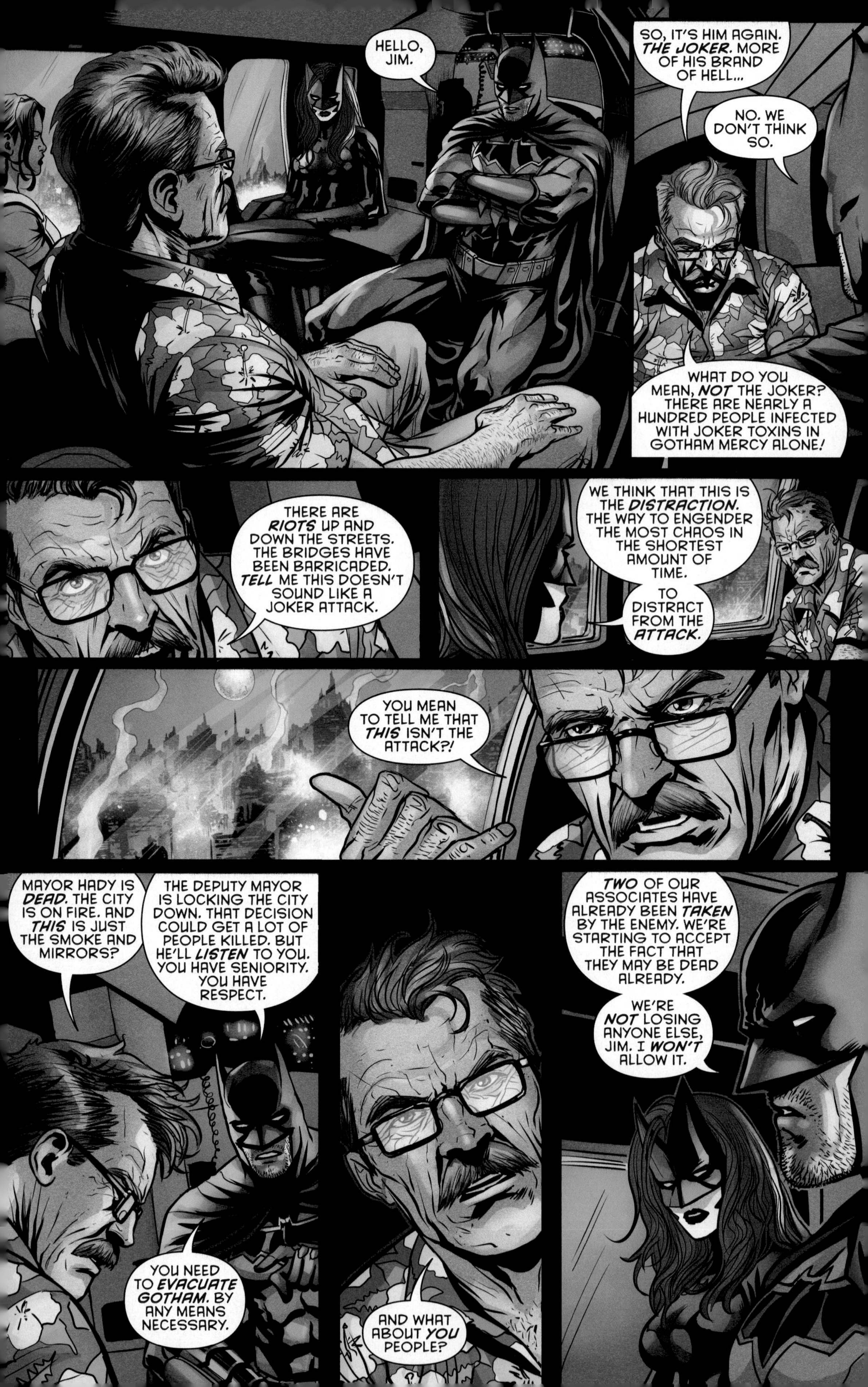
HELLO, JIM.
SO, IT'S HIM AGAIN. THE JOKER. MORE OF HIS BRAND OF HELL...
NO. WE DON'T THINK SO.
WHAT DO YOU MEAN, NOT THE JOKER? THERE ARE NEARLY A HUNDRED PEOPLE INFECTED WITH JOKER TOXINS IN GOTHAM MERCY ALONE!
THERE ARE RIOTS UP AND DOWN THE STREETS. THE BRIDGES HAVE BEEN BARRICADED. TELL ME THIS DOESN'T SOUND LIKE A JOKER ATTACK.
WE THINK THAT THIS IS THE DISTRACTION. THE WAY TO ENGENDER THE MOST CHAOS IN THE SHORTEST AMOUNT OF TIME.
TO DISTRACT FROM THE ATTACK.
YOU MEAN TO TELL ME THAT THIS ISN'T THE ATTACK?!
MAYOR HADY IS DEAD. THE CITY IS ON FIRE. AND THIS IS JUST THE SMOKE AND MIRRORS?
THE DEPUTY MAYOR IS LOCKING THE CITY DOWN. THAT DECISION COULD GET A LOT OF PEOPLE KILLED. BUT HE'LL LISTEN TO YOU. YOU HAVE SENIORITY. YOU HAVE RESPECT.
YOU NEED TO EVACUATE GOTHAM. BY ANY MEANS NECESSARY.
AND WHAT ABOUT YOU PEOPLE?
TWO OF OUR ASSOCIATES HAVE ALREADY BEEN TAKEN BY THE ENEMY. WE'RE STARTING TO ACCEPT THE FACT THAT THEY MAY BE DEAD ALREADY.
WE'RE NOT LOSING ANYONE ELSE, JIM. I WON'T ALLOW IT.

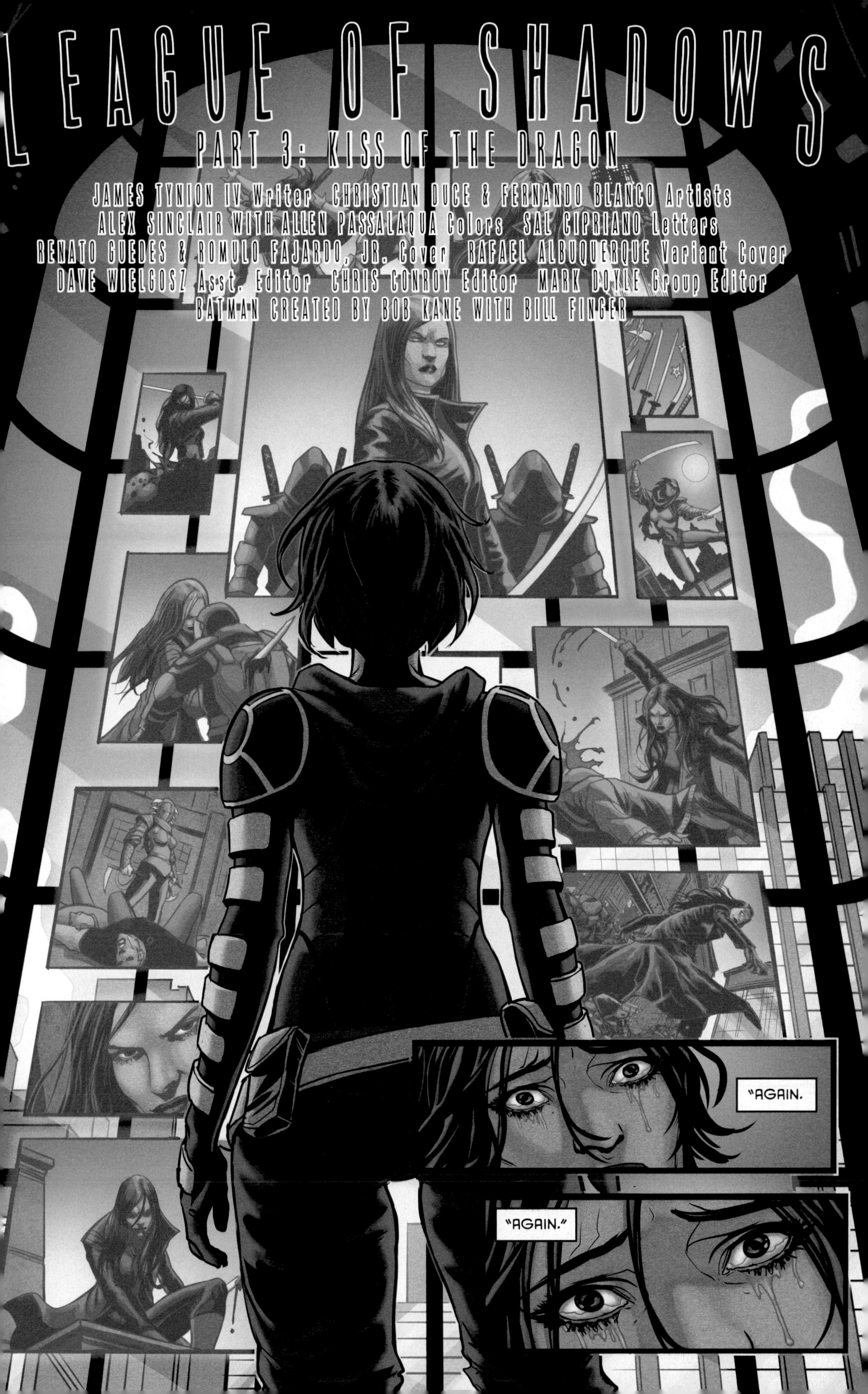
LEAGUE OF SHADOWS
PART 3: KISS OF THE DRAGON
JAMES TYNION IV Writer CHRISTIAN DUCE & FERNANDO BLANCO Artists
ALEX SINCLAIR WITH ALLEN PASSALAQUA Colors SAL CIPRIANO Letters
RENATO GUEDES & ROMULO FAJARDO, JR. Cover RAFAEL ALBUQUERQUE Variant Cover
DAVE WIELGOSZ Asst. Editor CHRIS CONROY Editor MARK DOYLE Group Editor
BATMAN CREATED BY BOB KANE WITH BILL FINGER
"AGAIN.
"AGAIN."

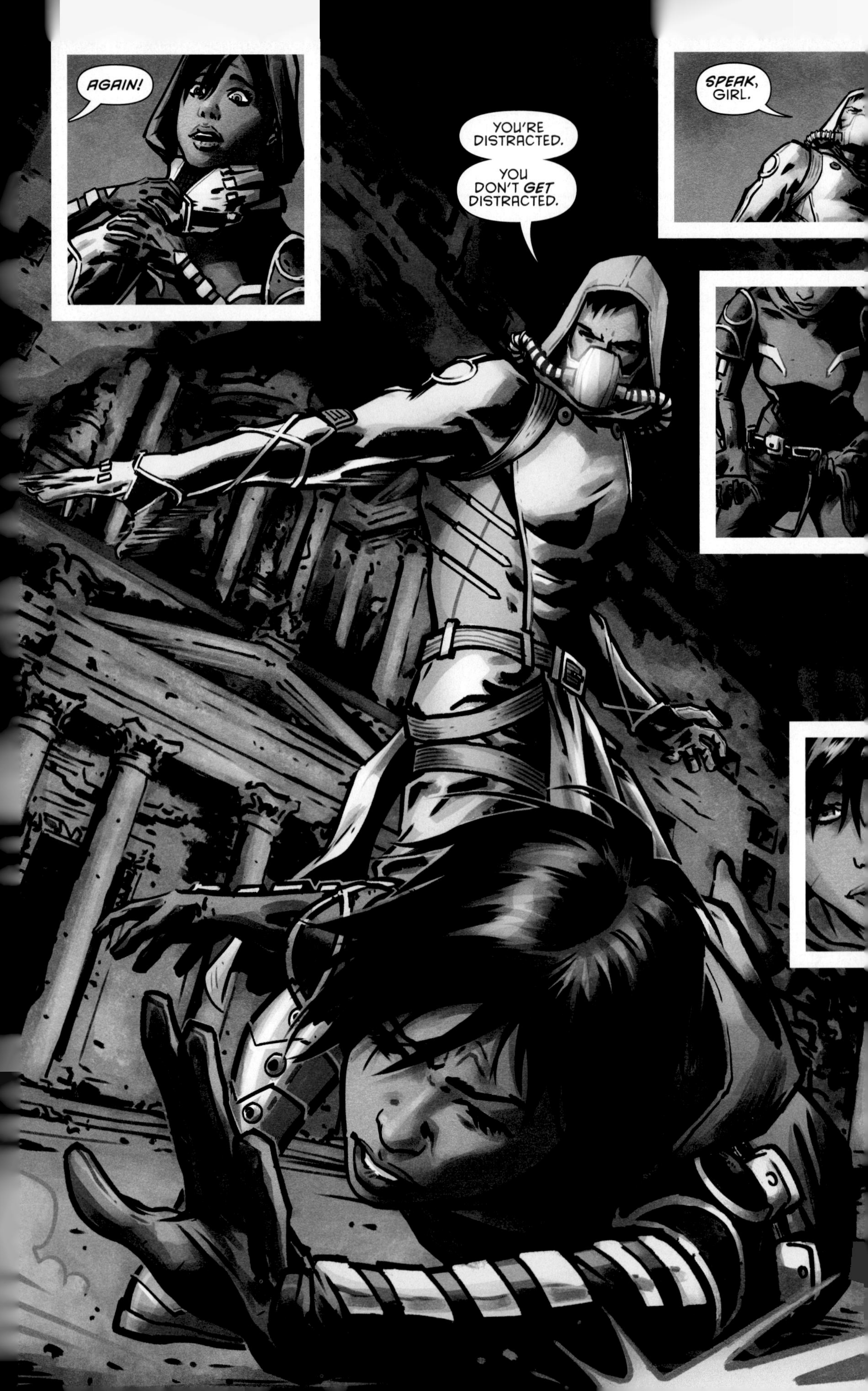
AGAIN!
YOU'RE DISTRACTED.
YOU DON'T GET DISTRACTED.
SPEAK, GIRL.

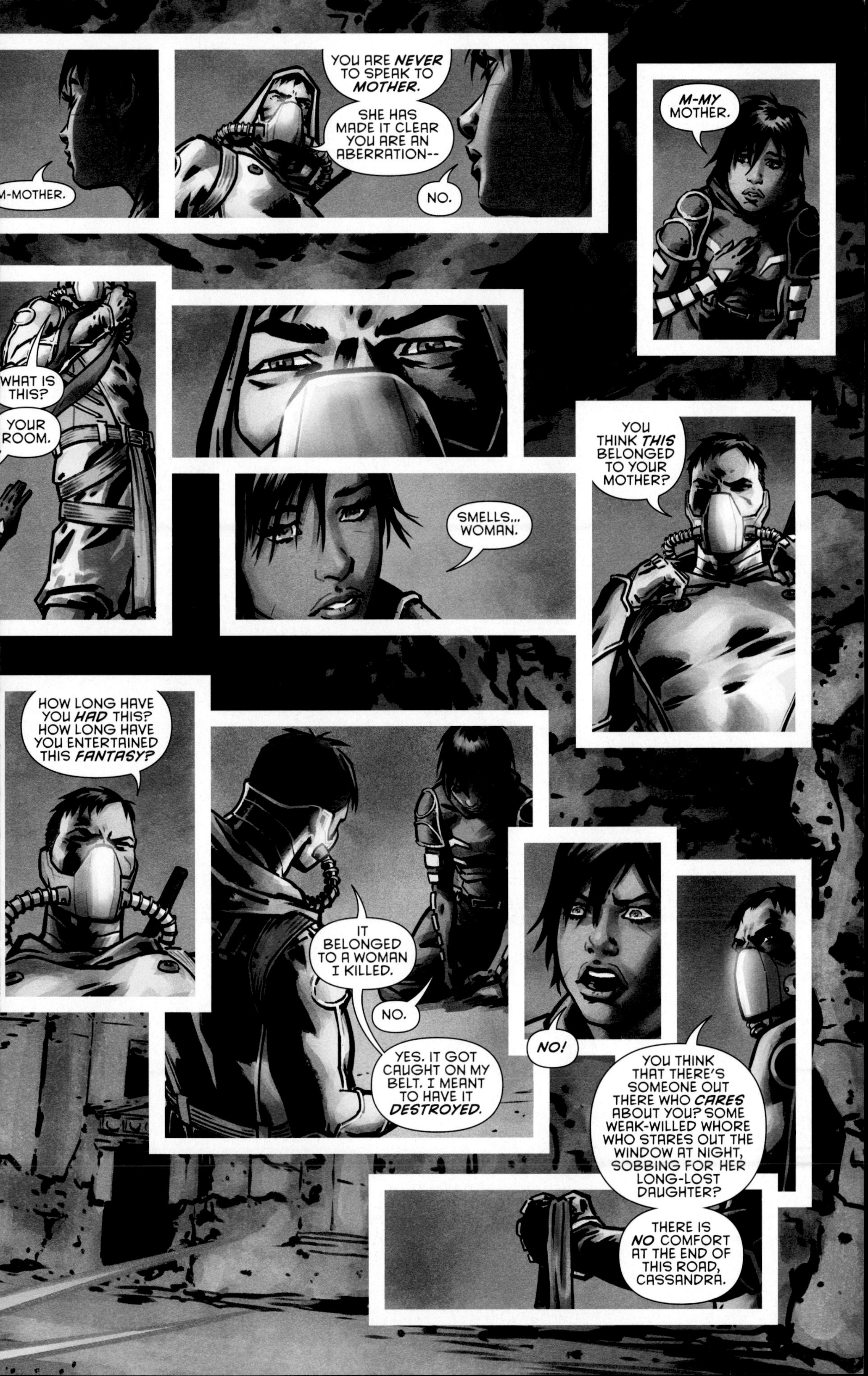
M-MOTHER.
YOU ARE NEVER TO SPEAK TO MOTHER.
SHE HAS MADE IT CLEAR YOU ARE AN ABERRATION--
NO.
M-MY MOTHER.
WHAT IS THIS?
YOUR ROOM.
SMELLS... WOMAN.
YOU THINK THIS BELONGED TO YOUR MOTHER?
HOW LONG HAVE YOU HAD THIS? HOW LONG HAVE YOU ENTERTAINED THIS FANTASY?
IT BELONGED TO A WOMAN I KILLED.
NO.
YES. IT GOT CAUGHT ON MY BELT. I MEANT TO HAVE IT DESTROYED.
NO!
YOU THINK THAT THERE'S SOMEONE OUT THERE WHO CARES ABOUT YOU? SOME WEAK-WILLED WHORE WHO STARES OUT THE WINDOW AT NIGHT, SOBBING FOR HER LONG-LOST DAUGHTER?
THERE IS NO COMFORT AT THE END OF THIS ROAD, CASSANDRA.

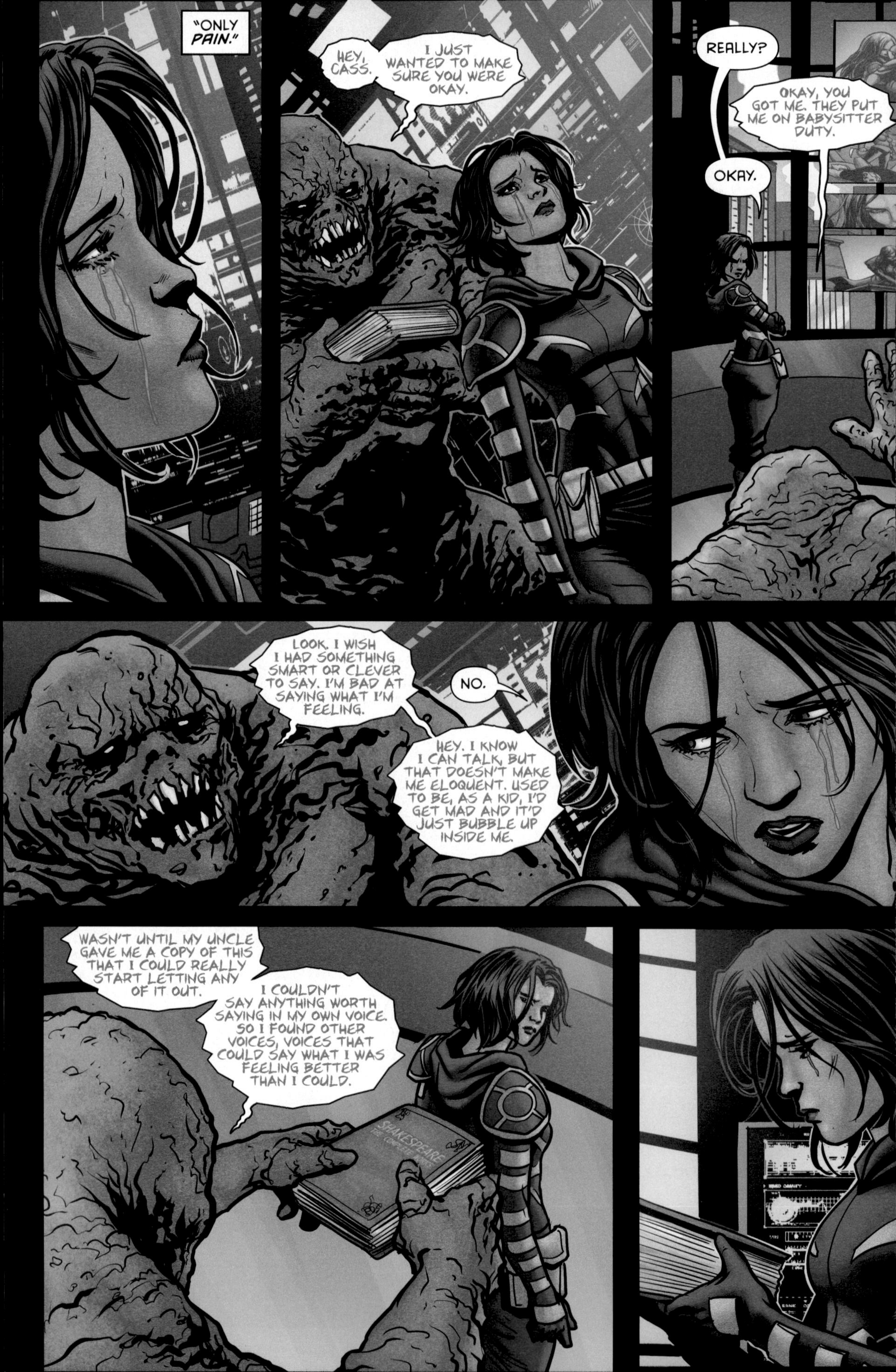
"ONLY PAIN."
HEY, CASS.
I JUST WANTED TO MAKE SURE YOU WERE OKAY.
REALLY?
OKAY, YOU GOT ME. THEY PUT ME ON BABYSITTER DUTY.
OKAY.
LOOK. I WISH I HAD SOMETHING SMART OR CLEVER TO SAY. I'M BAD AT SAYING WHAT I'M FEELING.
NO.
HEY. I KNOW I CAN TALK, BUT THAT DOESN'T MAKE ME ELOQUENT. USED TO BE, AS A KID, I'D GET MAD AND IT'D JUST BUBBLE UP INSIDE ME.
WASN'T UNTIL MY UNCLE GAVE ME A COPY OF THIS THAT I COULD REALLY START LETTING ANY OF IT OUT.
I COULDN'T SAY ANYTHING WORTH SAYING IN MY OWN VOICE. SO I FOUND OTHER VOICES, VOICES THAT COULD SAY WHAT I WAS FEELING BETTER THAN I COULD.
SHAKESPEARE
THE COMPLETE WORKS

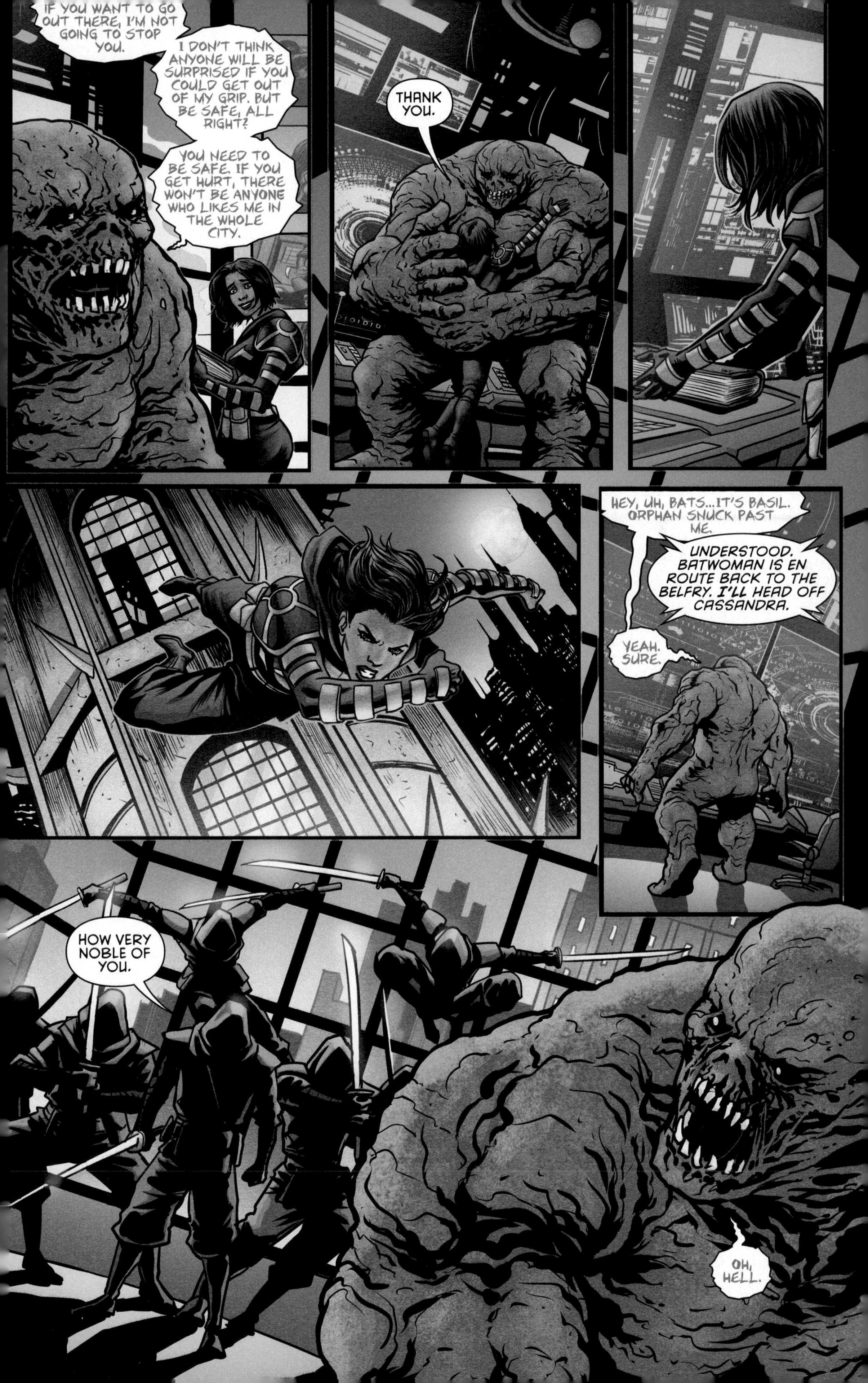
IF YOU WANT TO GO OUT THERE, I'M NOT GOING TO STOP YOU.
I DON'T THINK ANYONE WILL BE SURPRISED IF YOU COULD GET OUT OF MY GRIP. BUT BE SAFE, ALL RIGHT?
YOU NEED TO BE SAFE. IF YOU GET HURT, THERE WON'T BE ANYONE WHO LIKES ME IN THE WHOLE CITY.
THANK YOU.
HEY, UH, BATS...IT'S BASIL. ORPHAN SNUCK PAST ME.
UNDERSTOOD. BATWOMAN IS EN ROUTE BACK TO THE BELFRY. I'LL HEAD OFF CASSANDRA.
YEAH. SURE.
HOW VERY NOBLE OF YOU.
OH, HELL.

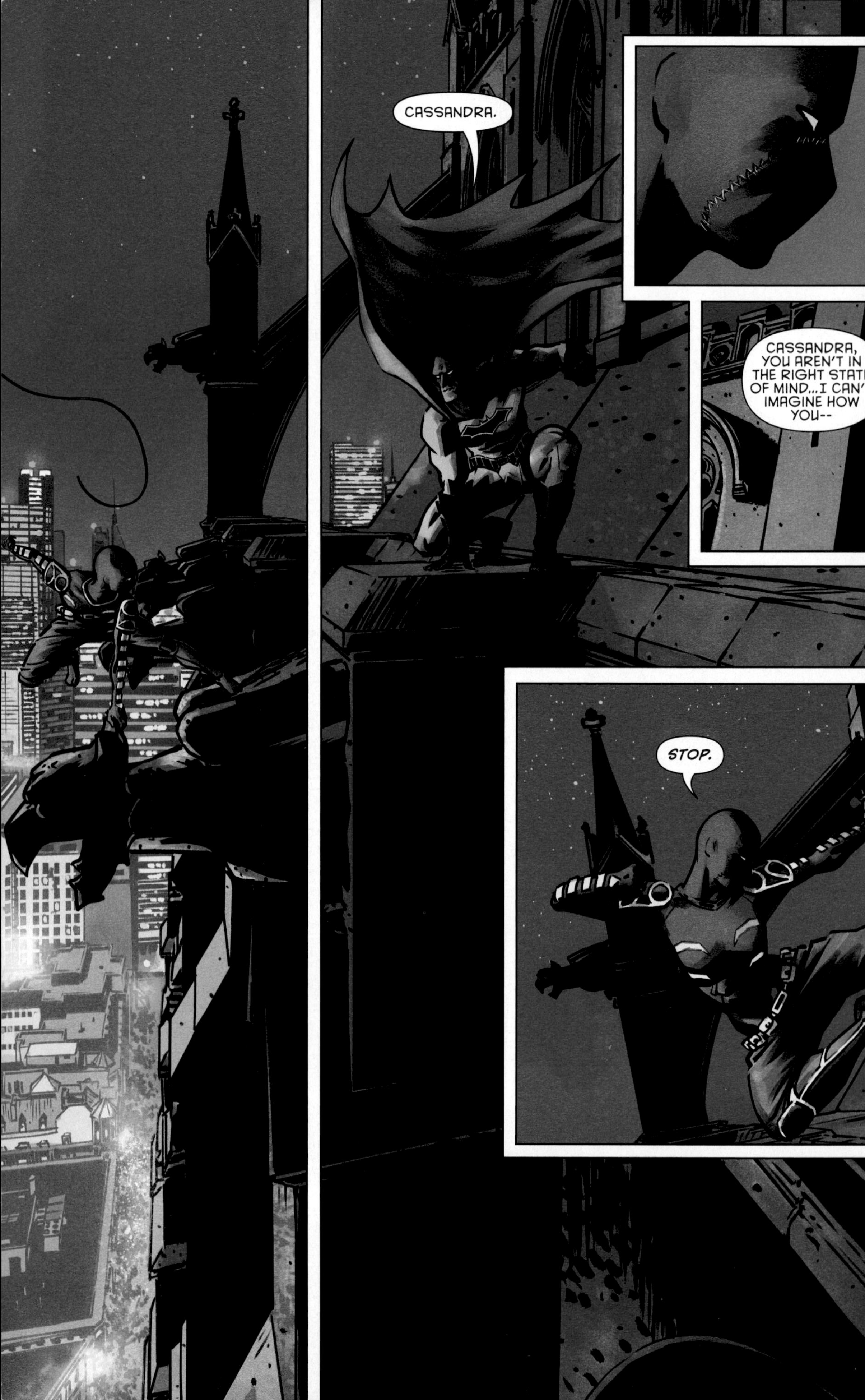
CASSANDRA.
CASSANDRA, YOU AREN'T IN THE RIGHT STATE OF MIND...I CAN'T IMAGINE HOW YOU--
STOP.

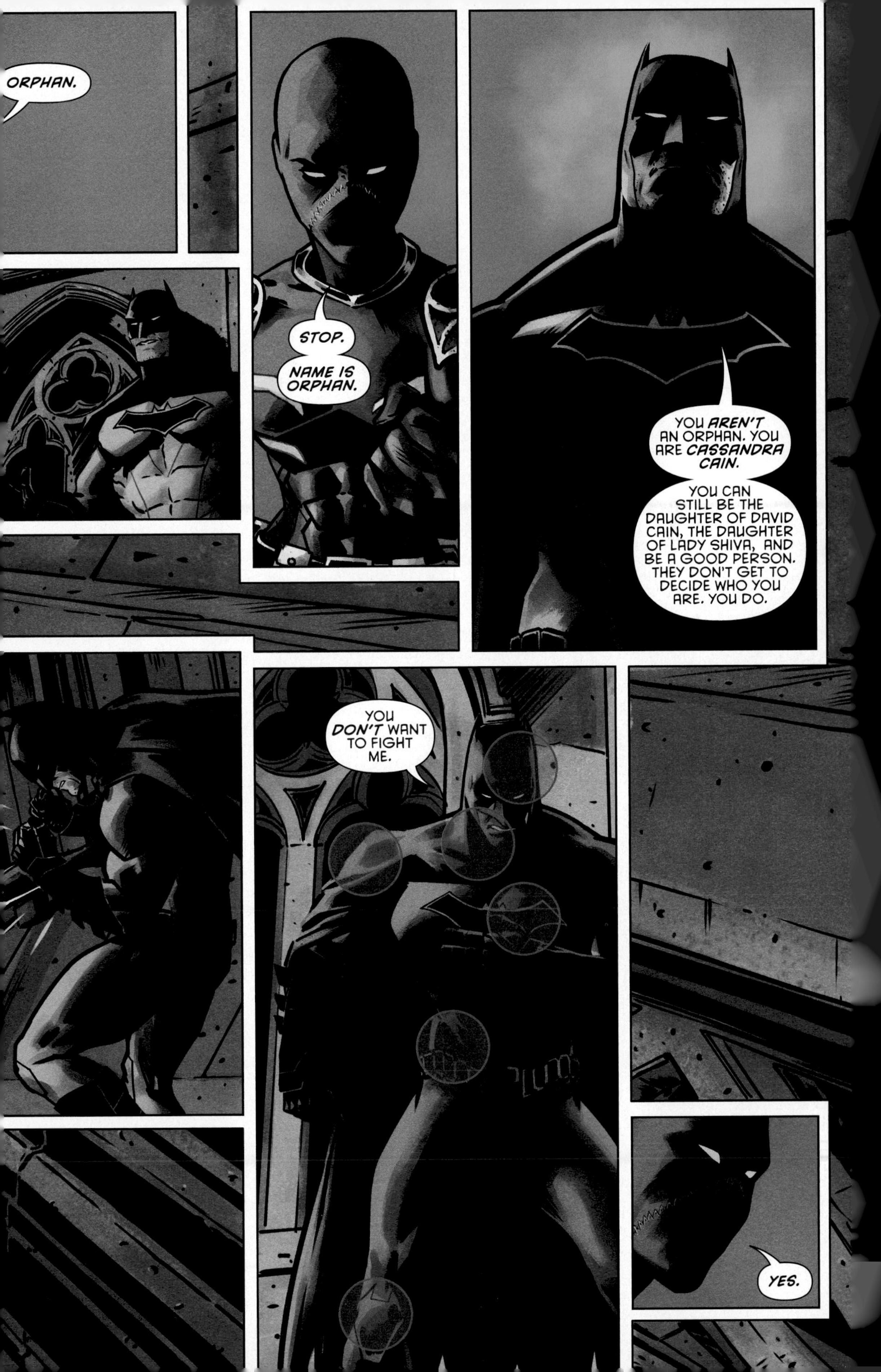
ORPHAN.
STOP.
NAME IS ORPHAN.
YOU AREN'T AN ORPHAN. YOU ARE CASSANDRA CAIN.
YOU CAN STILL BE THE DAUGHTER OF DAVID CAIN, THE DAUGHTER OF LADY SHIVA, AND BE A GOOD PERSON. THEY DON'T GET TO DECIDE WHO YOU ARE. YOU DO.
YOU DON'T WANT TO FIGHT ME.
YES.

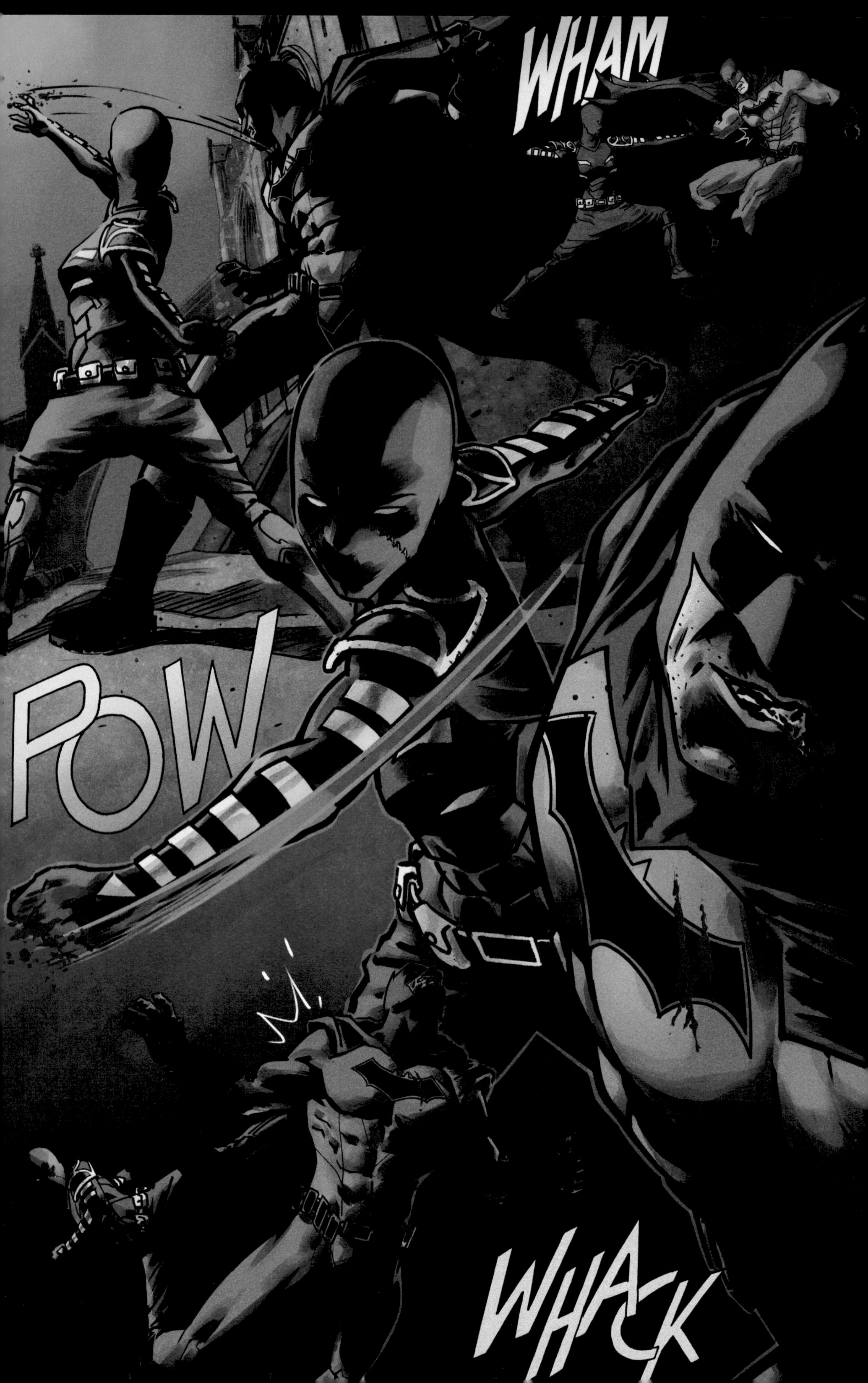
WHAM
POW
WHACK

I WON'T FIGHT YOU. YOU CAN HURT ME ALL YOU WANT, I WON'T DO IT. BUT I WANT YOU TO *LISTEN* TO ME...

I *BELIEVE* IN YOU. I BELIEVE IN CASSANDRA C--

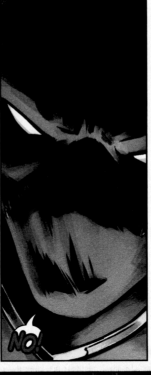

NO!

KRAK

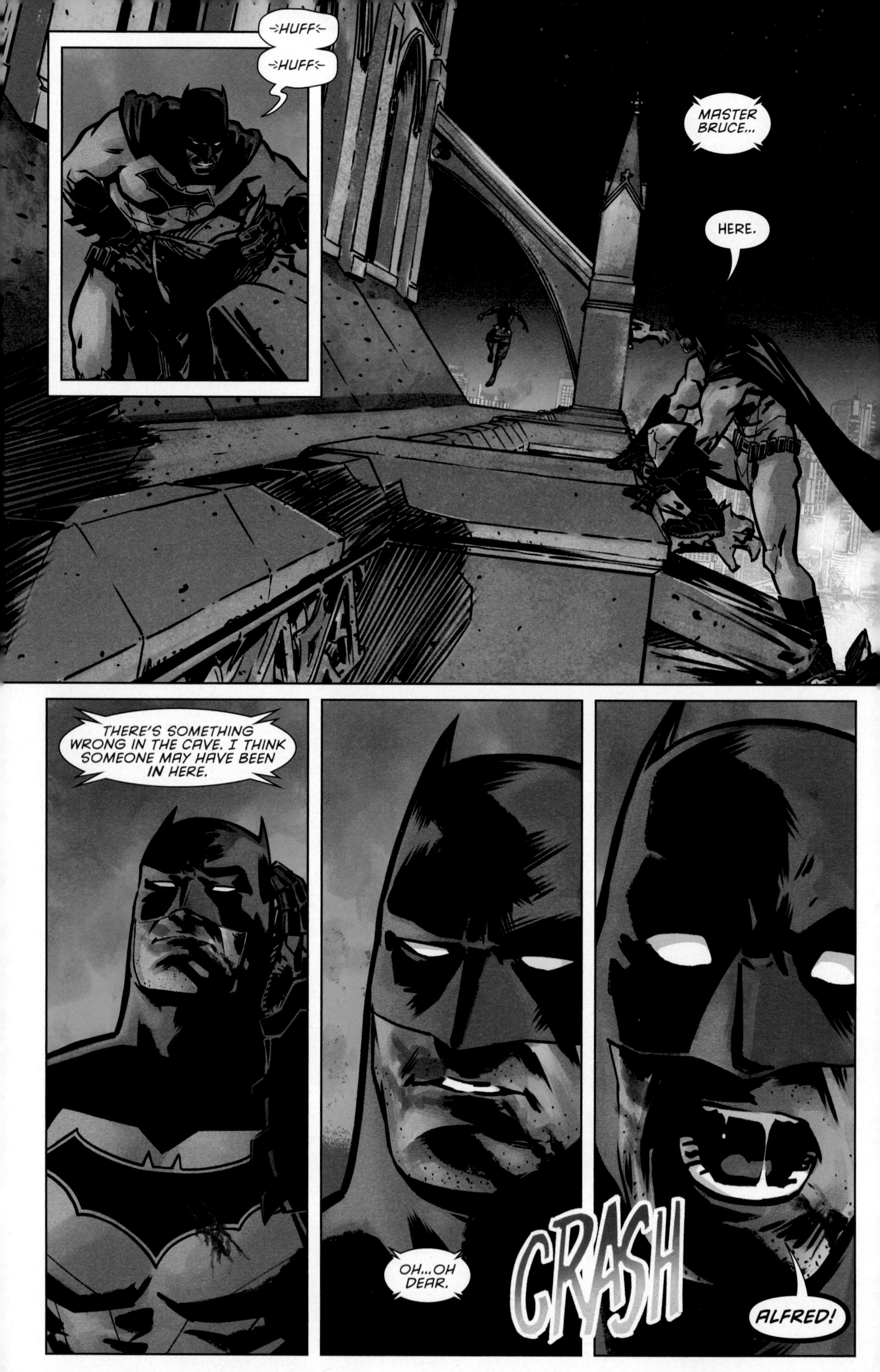
HUFF
HUFF
MASTER BRUCE...
HERE.
THERE'S SOMETHING WRONG IN THE CAVE. I THINK SOMEONE MAY HAVE BEEN IN HERE.
OH...OH DEAR.
CRASH
ALFRED!

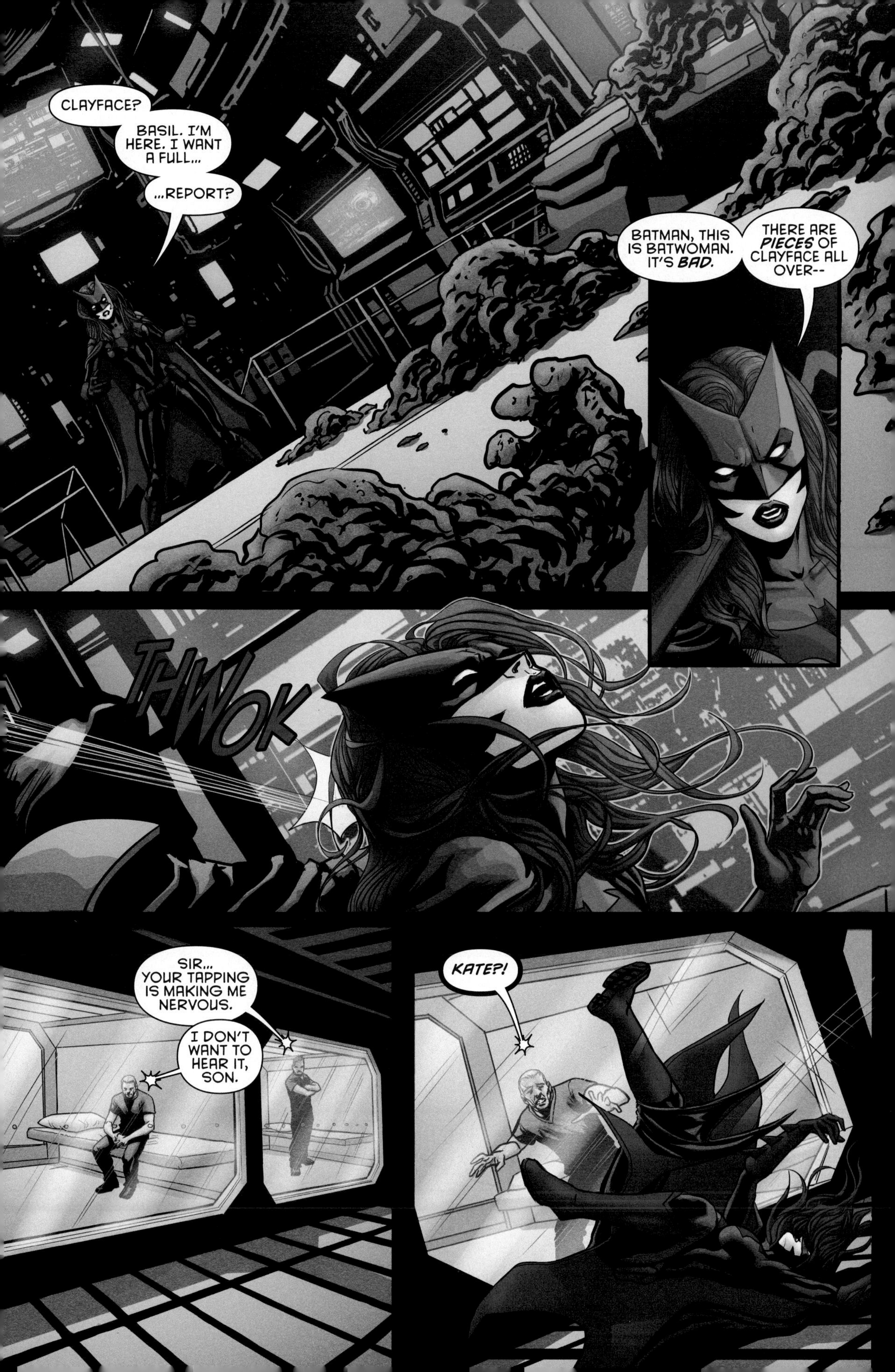
CLAYFACE?
BASIL. I'M HERE. I WANT A FULL...
...REPORT?
BATMAN, THIS IS BATWOMAN. IT'S BAD.
THERE ARE PIECES OF CLAYFACE ALL OVER--
THWOK
SIR... YOUR TAPPING IS MAKING ME NERVOUS.
I DON'T WANT TO HEAR IT, SON.
KATE?!

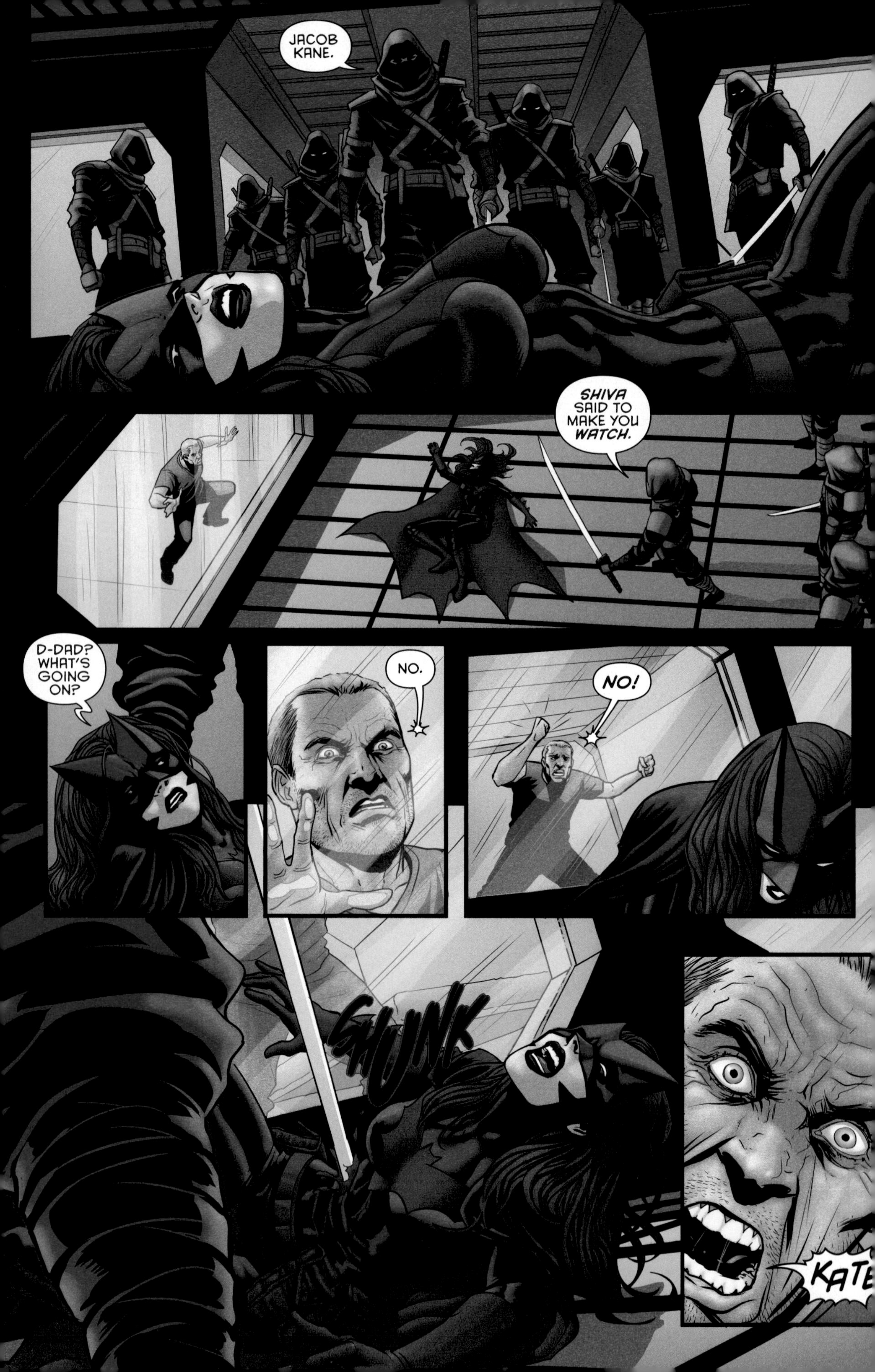
JACOB KANE.
SHIVA SAID TO MAKE YOU WATCH.
D-DAD? WHAT'S GOING ON?
NO.
NO!
SHUNK
KATE

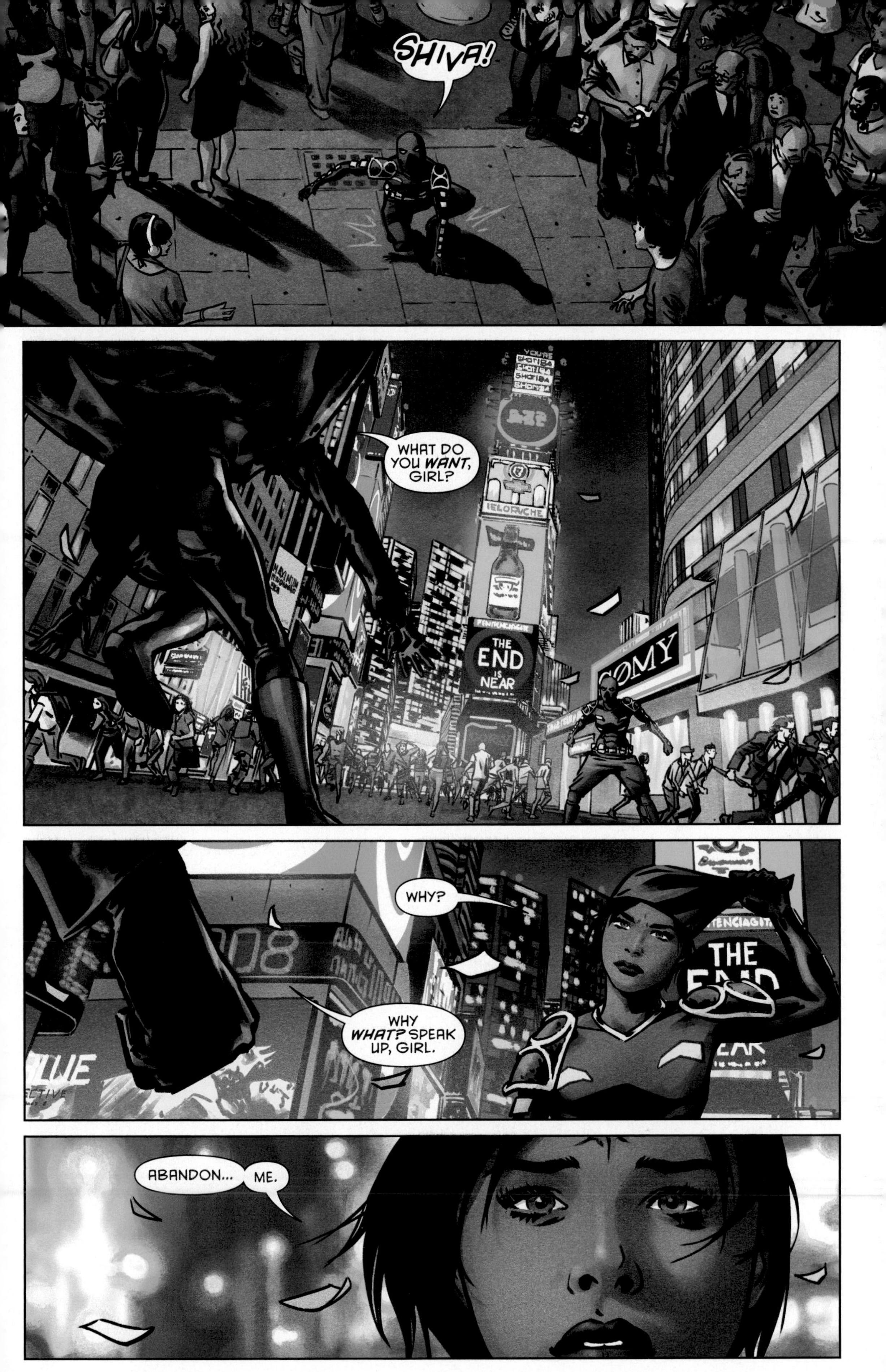
SHIVA!
WHAT DO YOU WANT, GIRL?
THE END IS NEAR
WHY?
WHY WHAT? SPEAK UP, GIRL.
ABANDON...
ME.

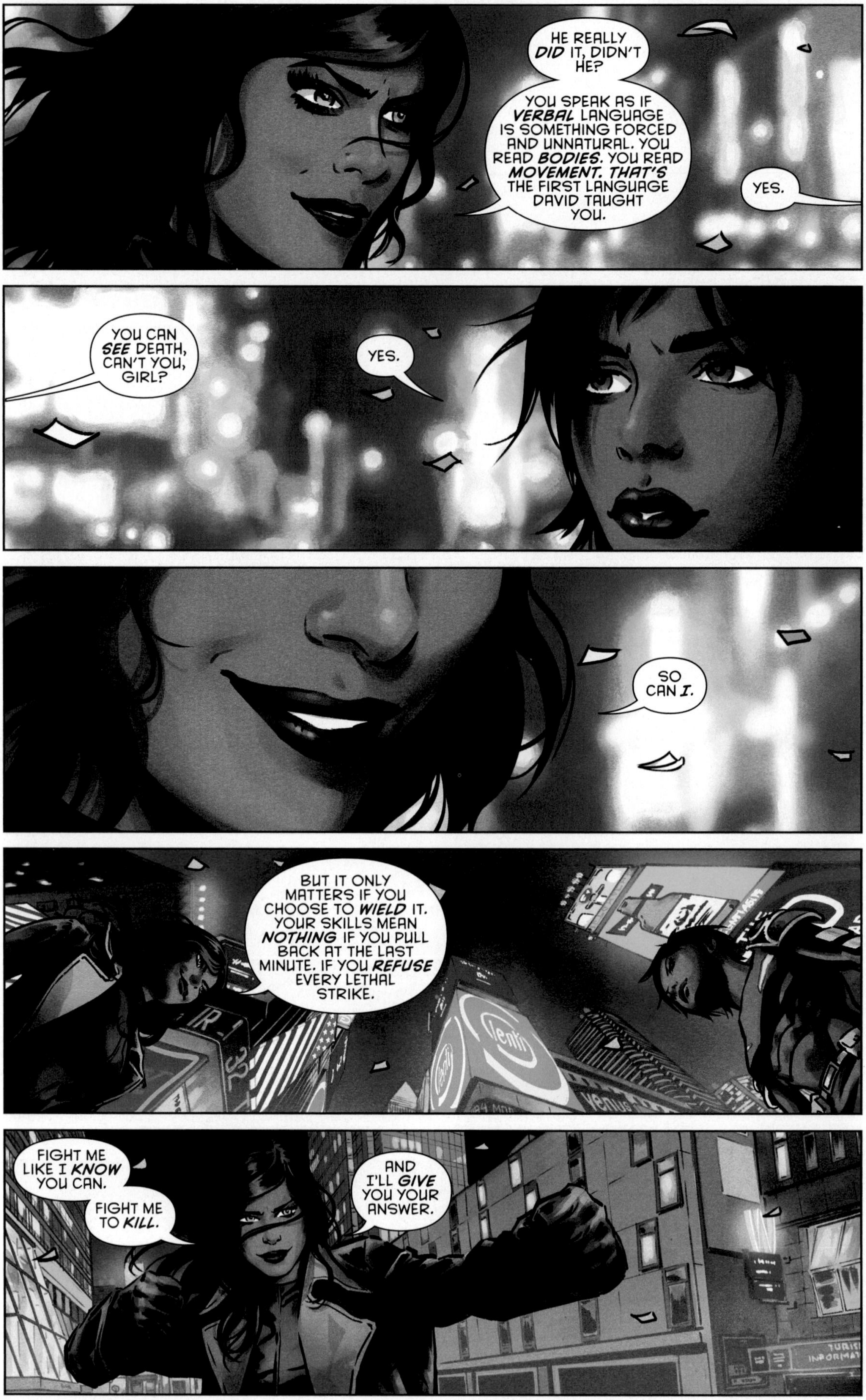
HE REALLY *DID* IT, DIDN'T HE?
YOU SPEAK AS IF *VERBAL* LANGUAGE IS SOMETHING FORCED AND UNNATURAL. YOU READ *BODIES*. YOU READ *MOVEMENT. THAT'S* THE FIRST LANGUAGE DAVID TAUGHT YOU.
YES.
YOU CAN *SEE* DEATH, CAN'T YOU, GIRL?
YES.
SO CAN *I*.
BUT IT ONLY MATTERS IF YOU CHOOSE TO *WIELD* IT. YOUR SKILLS MEAN *NOTHING* IF YOU PULL BACK AT THE LAST MINUTE. IF YOU *REFUSE* EVERY LETHAL STRIKE.
FIGHT ME LIKE I *KNOW* YOU CAN.
FIGHT ME TO *KILL*.
AND I'LL *GIVE* YOU YOUR ANSWER.

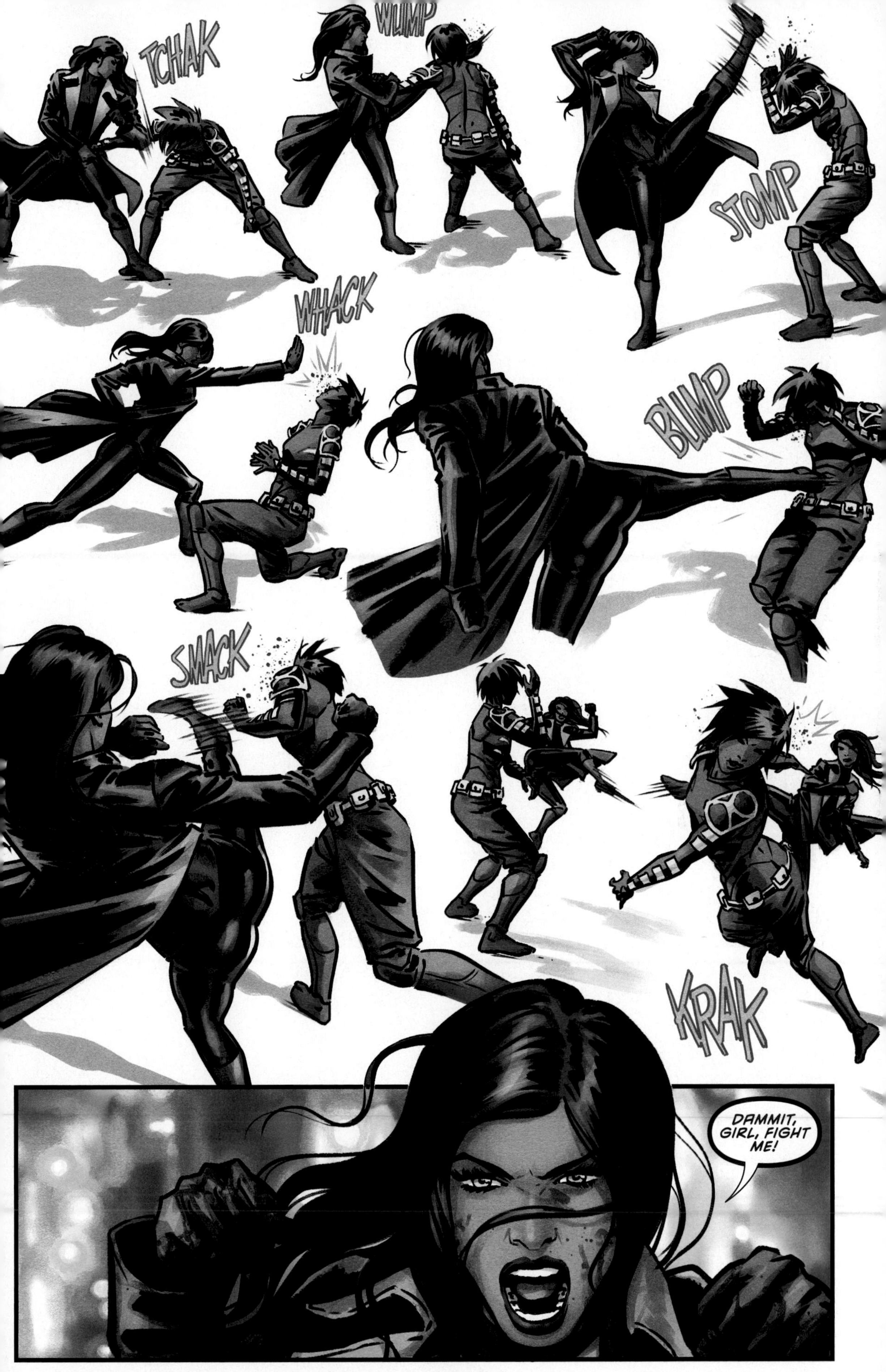
TCHAK
WUMP
STOMP
WHACK
BUMP
SMACK
KRAK
DAMMIT, GIRL, FIGHT ME!

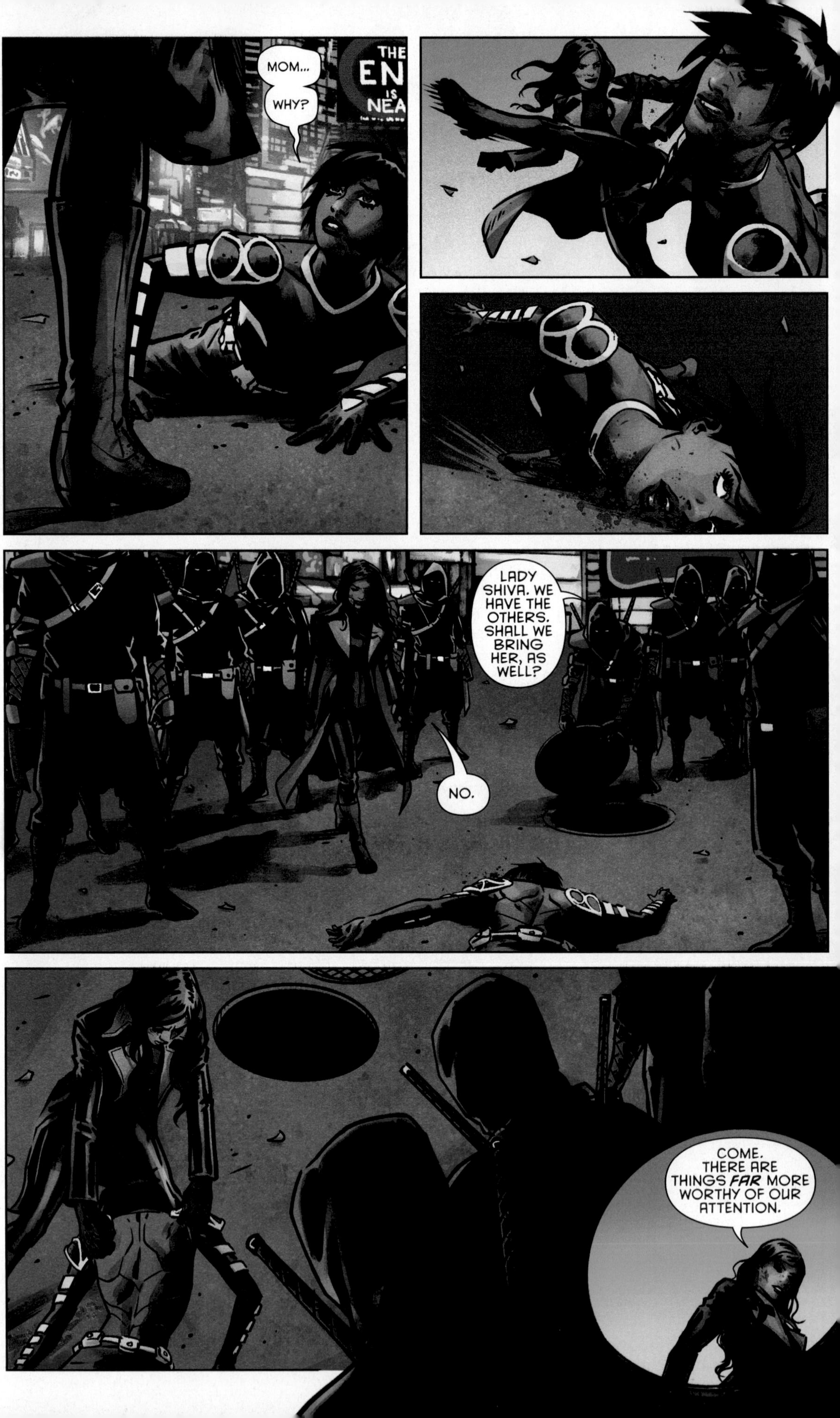
THE END IS NEAR
MOM...
WHY?
LADY SHIVA. WE HAVE THE OTHERS. SHALL WE BRING HER, AS WELL?
NO.
COME. THERE ARE THINGS *FAR* MORE WORTHY OF OUR ATTENTION.

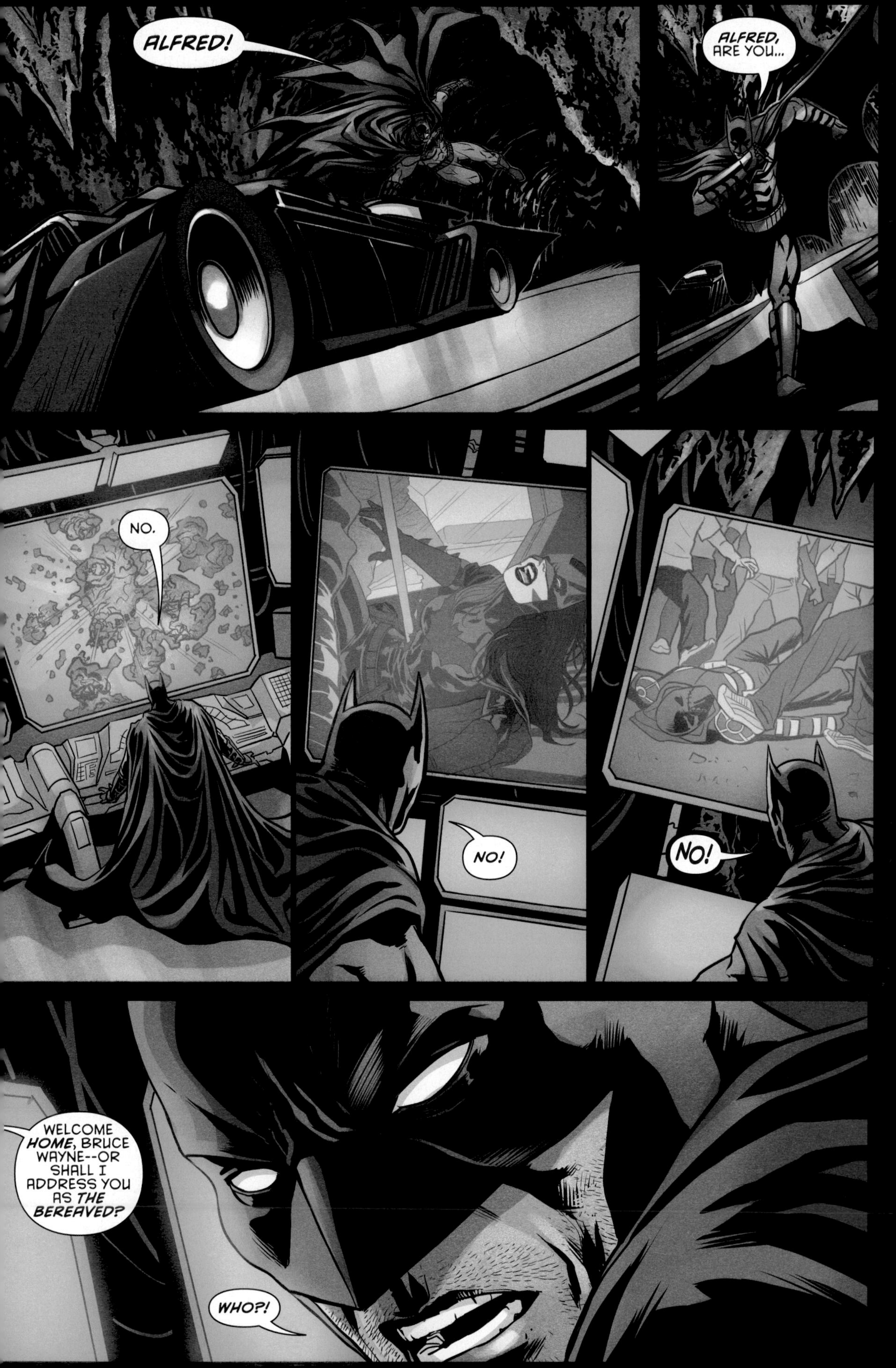
ALFRED!
ALFRED, ARE YOU...
NO.
NO!
NO!
WELCOME HOME, BRUCE WAYNE--OR SHALL I ADDRESS YOU AS THE BEREAVED?
WHO?!

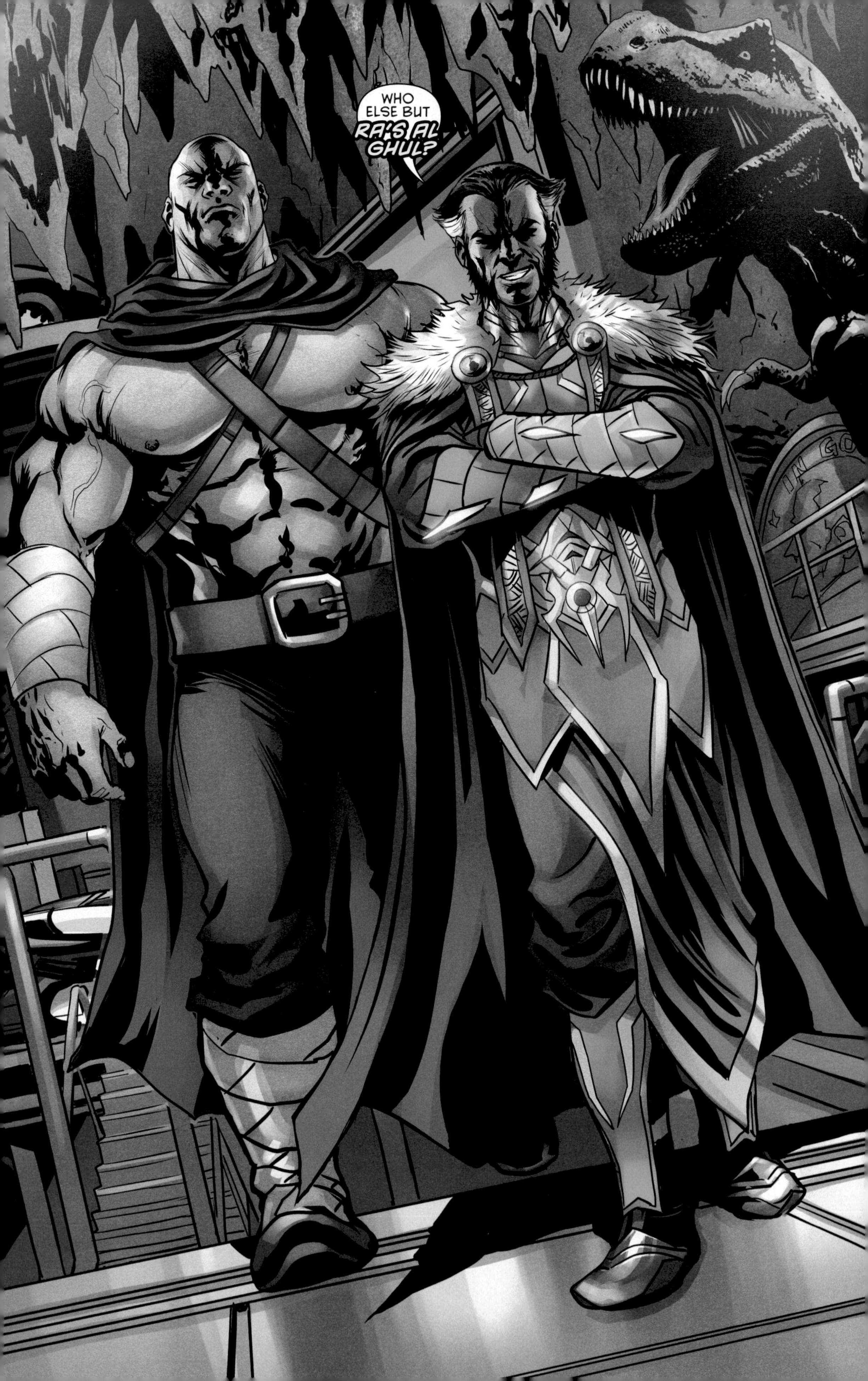
WHO ELSE BUT RA'S AL GHUL?

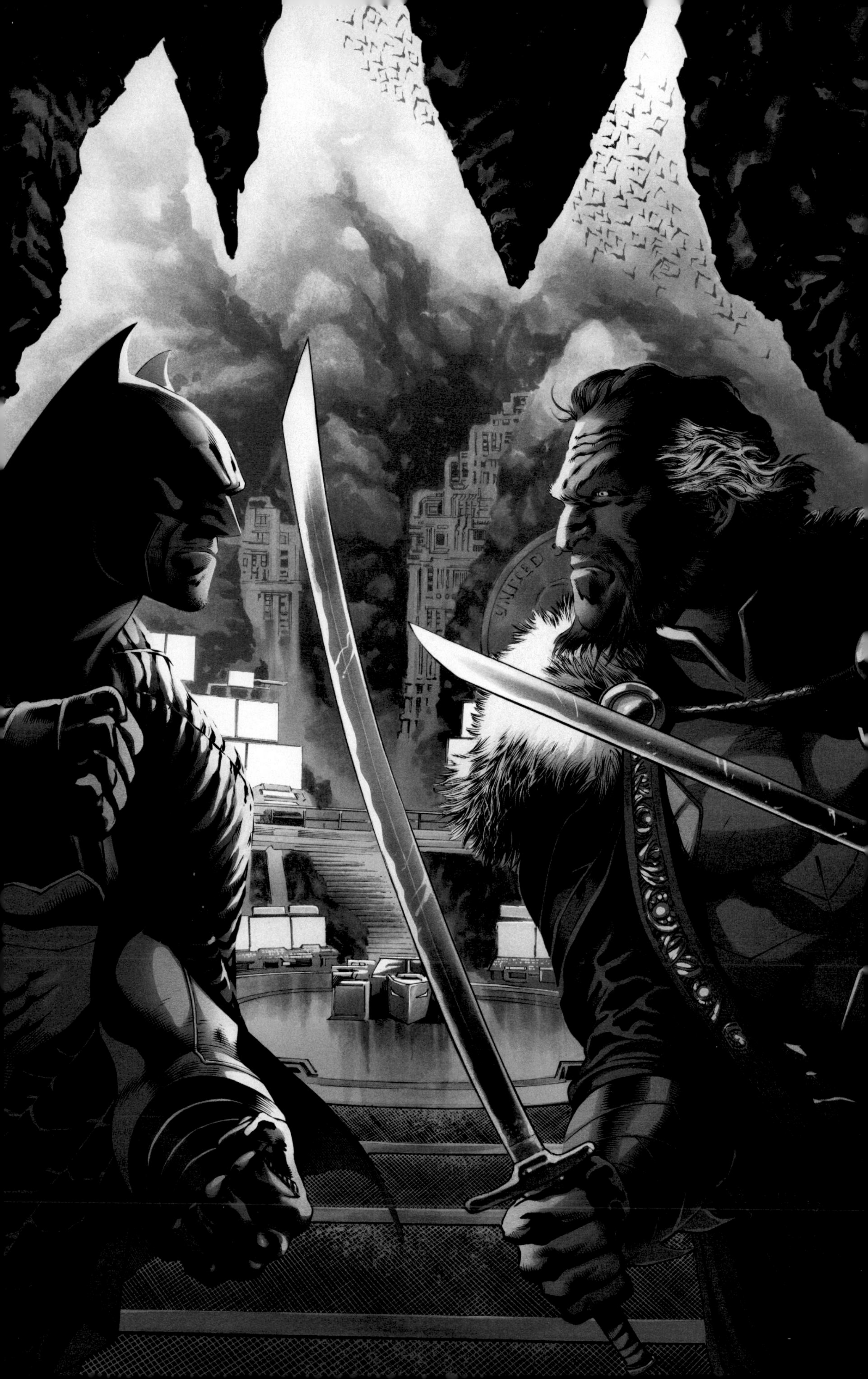
UNITED

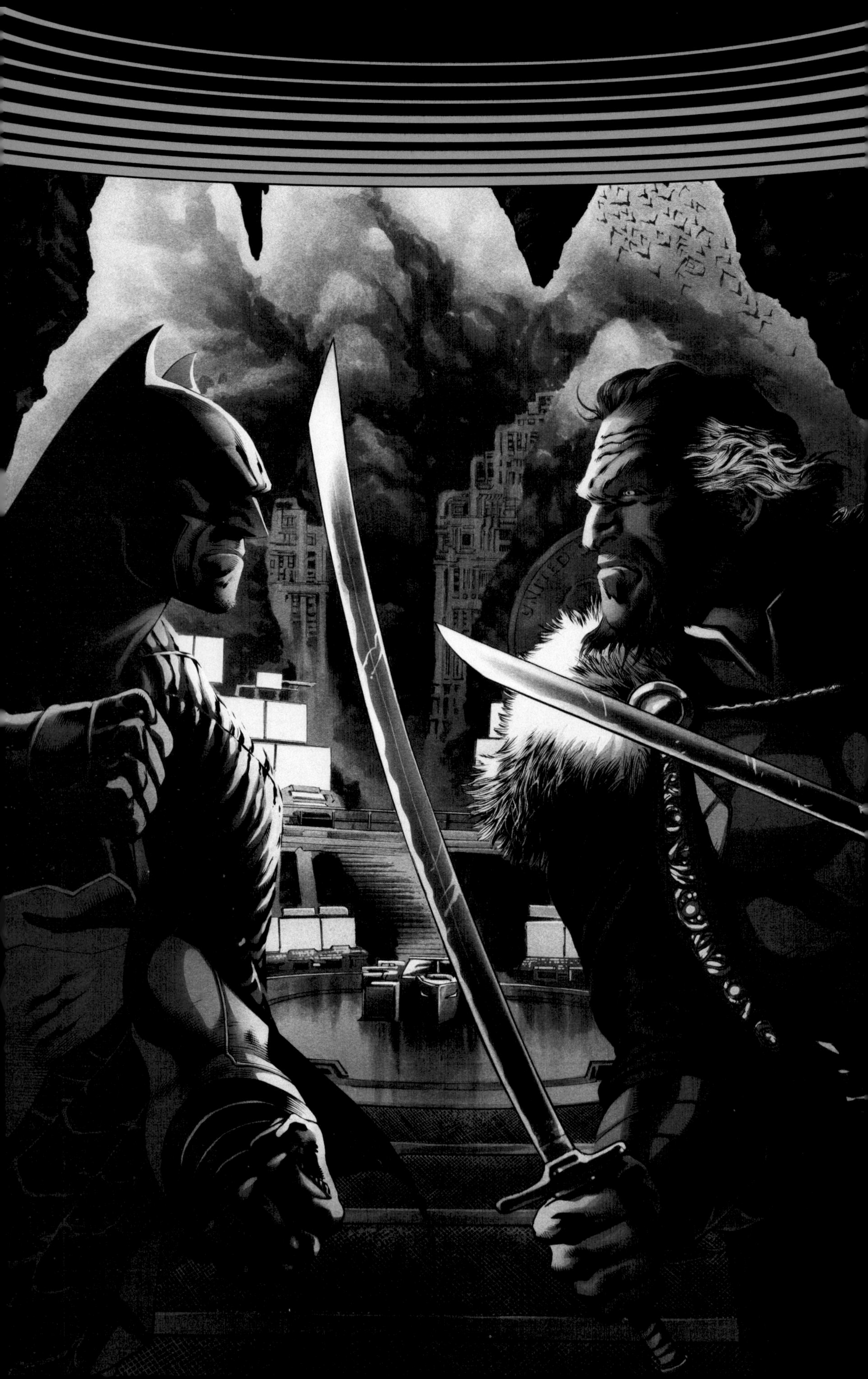

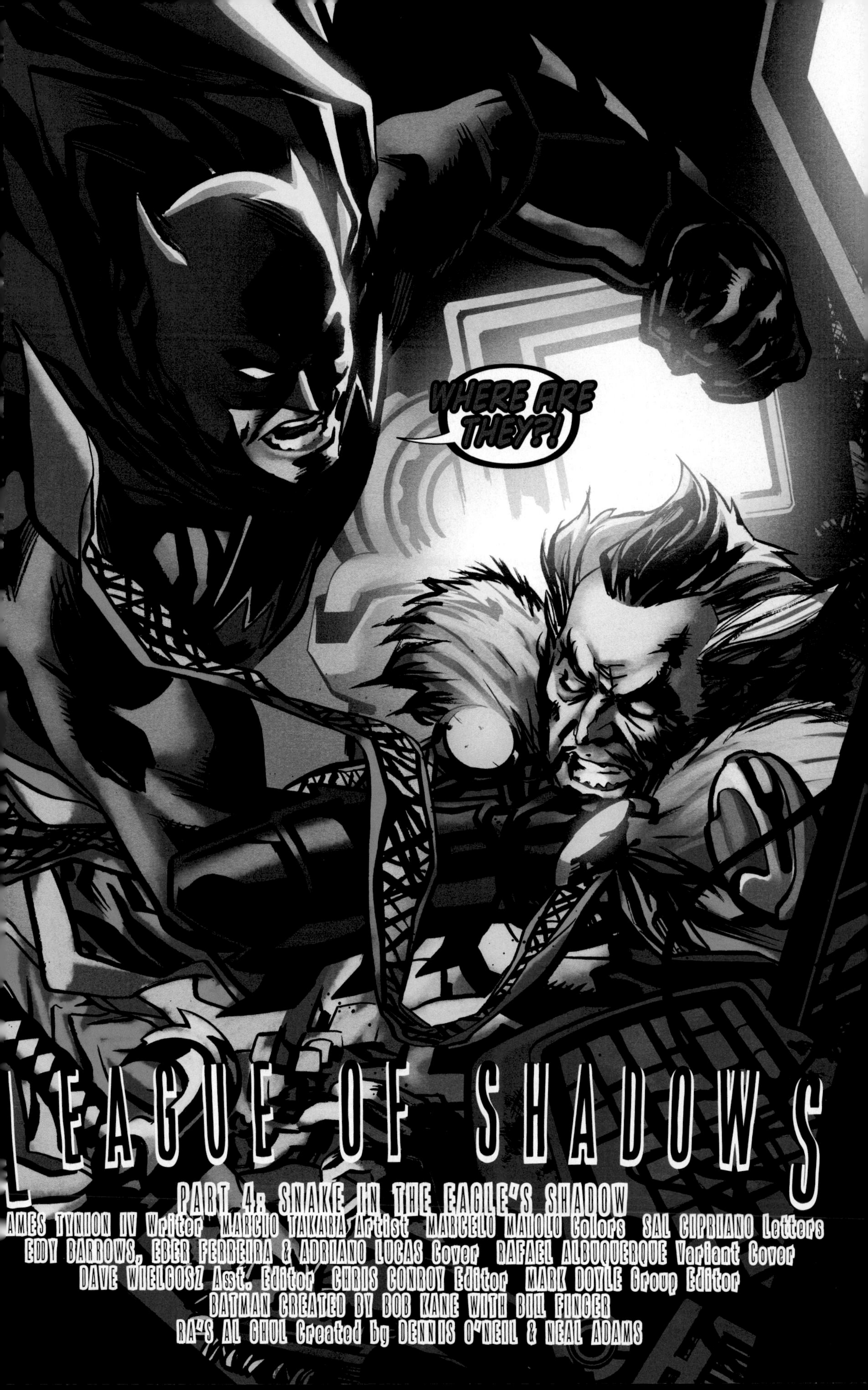
WHERE ARE THEY?!
LEAGUE OF SHADOWS
PART 4: SNAKE IN THE EAGLE'S SHADOW
AMES TYNION IV Writer MARCIO TAKARA Artist MARCELO MAIOLO Colors SAL CIPRIANO Letters
EDDY BARROWS, EBER FERREIRA & ADRIANO LUCAS Cover RAFAEL ALBUQUERQUE Variant Cover
DAVE WIELGOSZ Asst. Editor CHRIS CONROY Editor MARK DOYLE Group Editor
BATMAN CREATED BY BOB KANE WITH BILL FINGER
RA'S AL GHUL Created by DENNIS O'NEIL & NEAL ADAMS

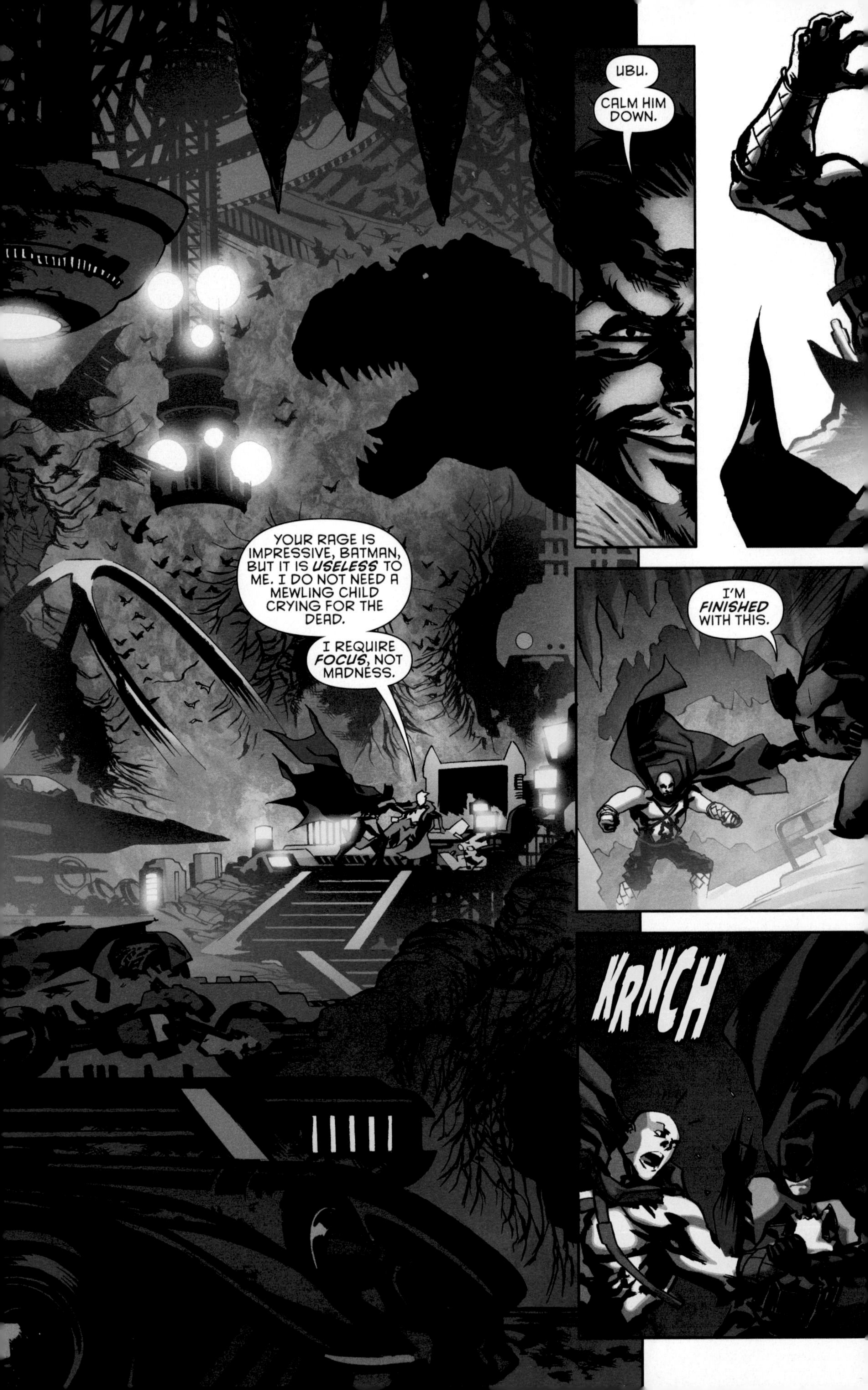
YOUR RAGE IS IMPRESSIVE, BATMAN, BUT IT IS USELESS TO ME. I DO NOT NEED A MEWLING CHILD CRYING FOR THE DEAD.
I REQUIRE FOCUS, NOT MADNESS.
UBU.
CALM HIM DOWN.
I'M FINISHED WITH THIS.
KRNCH

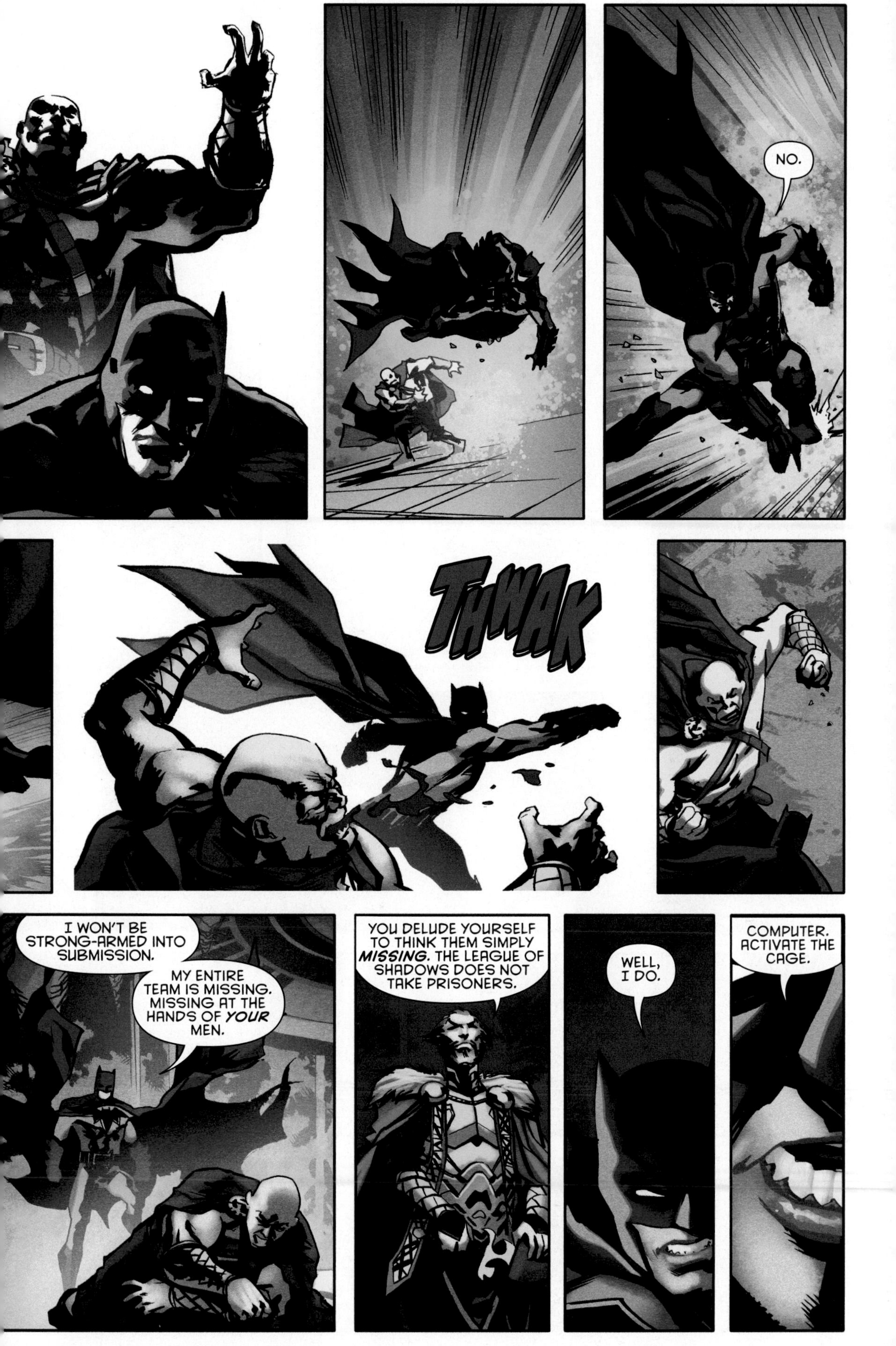
NO.
THWAK
I WON'T BE STRONG-ARMED INTO SUBMISSION.
MY ENTIRE TEAM IS MISSING. MISSING AT THE HANDS OF *YOUR* MEN.
YOU DELUDE YOURSELF TO THINK THEM SIMPLY *MISSING*. THE LEAGUE OF SHADOWS DOES NOT TAKE PRISONERS.
WELL, I DO.
COMPUTER. ACTIVATE THE CAGE.

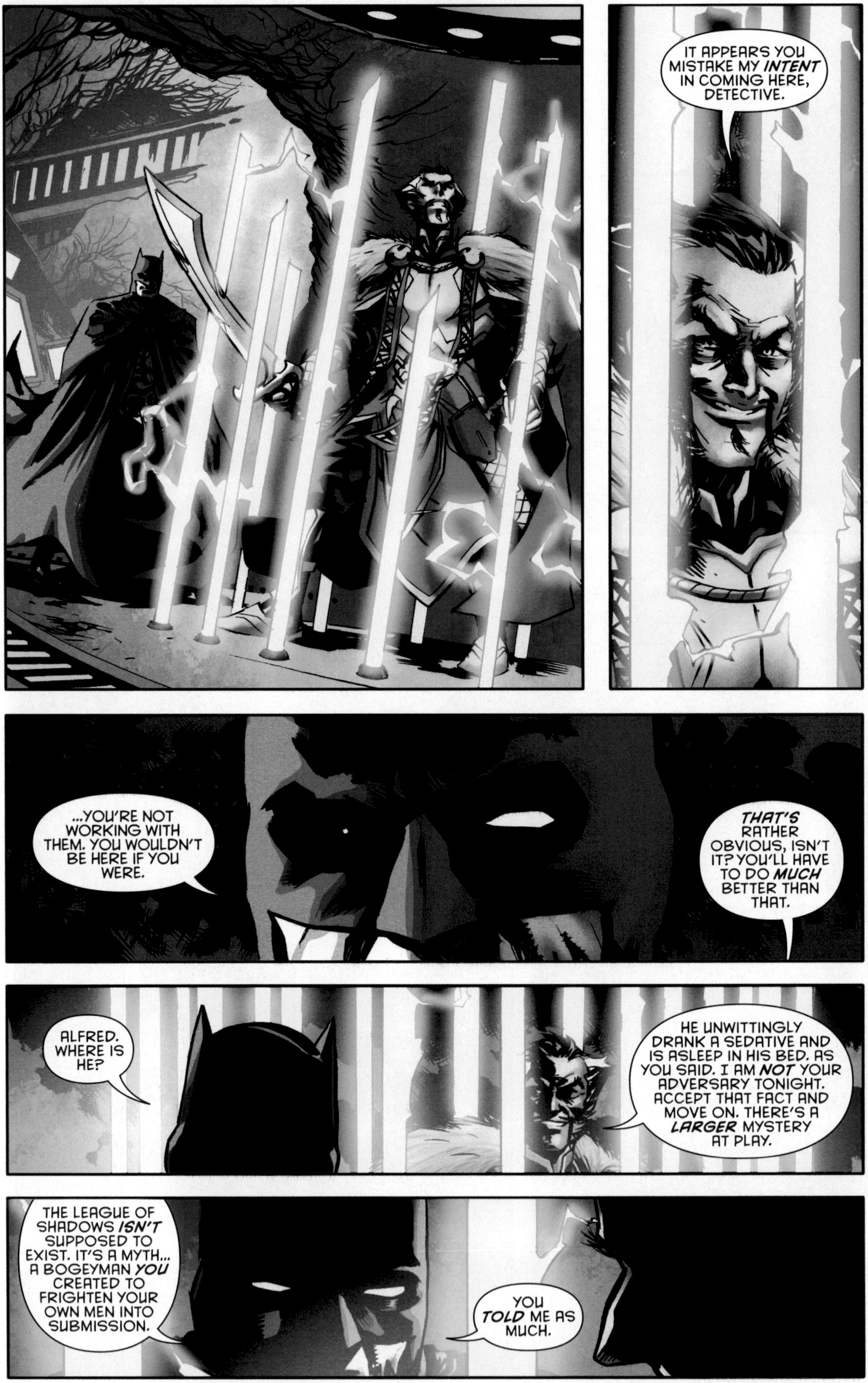
IT APPEARS YOU MISTAKE MY INTENT IN COMING HERE, DETECTIVE.
...YOU'RE NOT WORKING WITH THEM. YOU WOULDN'T BE HERE IF YOU WERE.
THAT'S RATHER OBVIOUS, ISN'T IT? YOU'LL HAVE TO DO MUCH BETTER THAN THAT.
ALFRED. WHERE IS HE?
HE UNWITTINGLY DRANK A SEDATIVE AND IS ASLEEP IN HIS BED. AS YOU SAID. I AM NOT YOUR ADVERSARY TONIGHT. ACCEPT THAT FACT AND MOVE ON. THERE'S A LARGER MYSTERY AT PLAY.
THE LEAGUE OF SHADOWS ISN'T SUPPOSED TO EXIST. IT'S A MYTH... A BOGEYMAN YOU CREATED TO FRIGHTEN YOUR OWN MEN INTO SUBMISSION.
YOU TOLD ME AS MUCH.

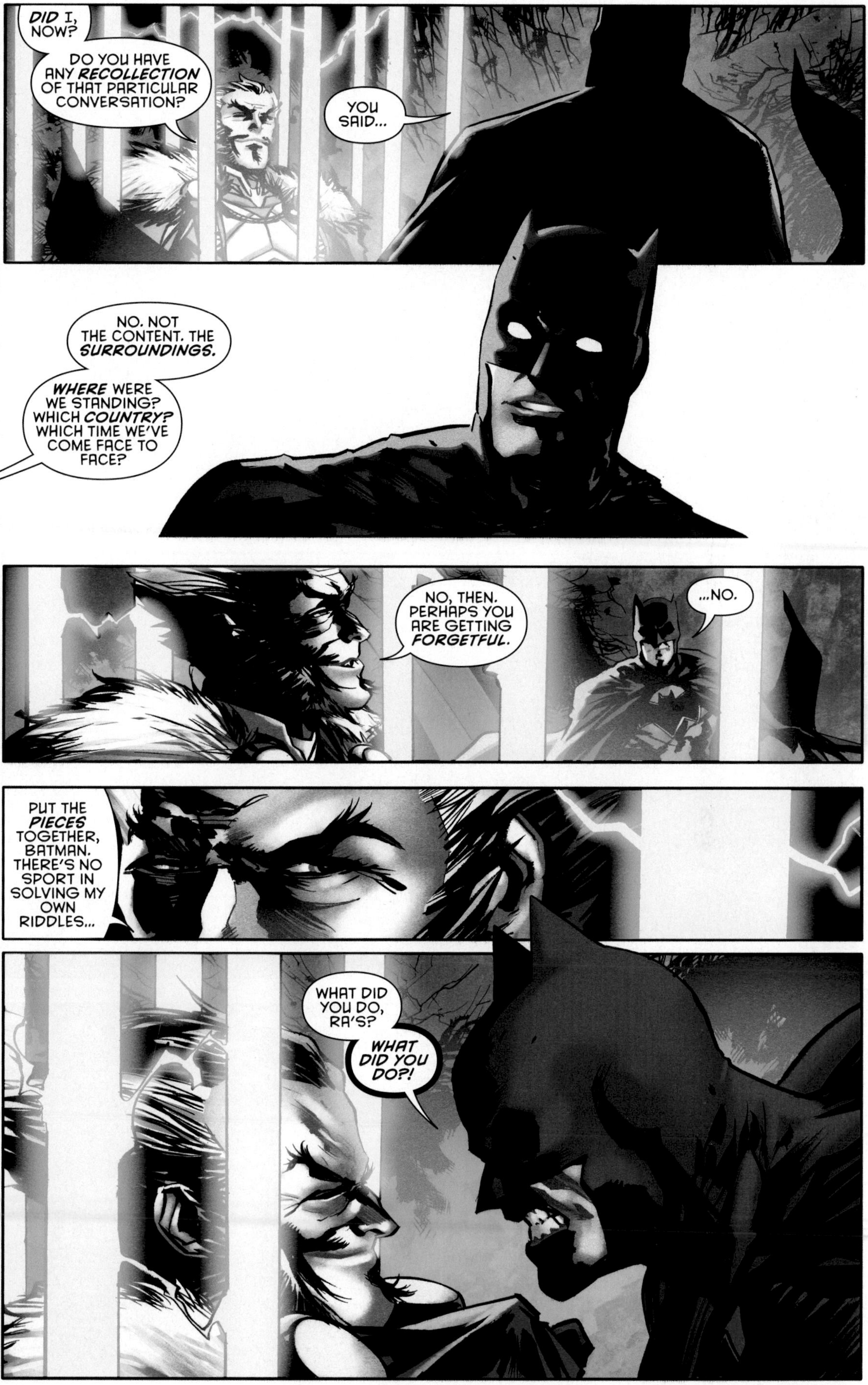
DID I, NOW?
DO YOU HAVE ANY RECOLLECTION OF THAT PARTICULAR CONVERSATION?
YOU SAID...
NO. NOT THE CONTENT. THE SURROUNDINGS.
WHERE WERE WE STANDING? WHICH COUNTRY? WHICH TIME WE'VE COME FACE TO FACE?
NO, THEN. PERHAPS YOU ARE GETTING FORGETFUL.
...NO.
PUT THE PIECES TOGETHER, BATMAN. THERE'S NO SPORT IN SOLVING MY OWN RIDDLES...
WHAT DID YOU DO, RA'S?
WHAT DID YOU DO?!

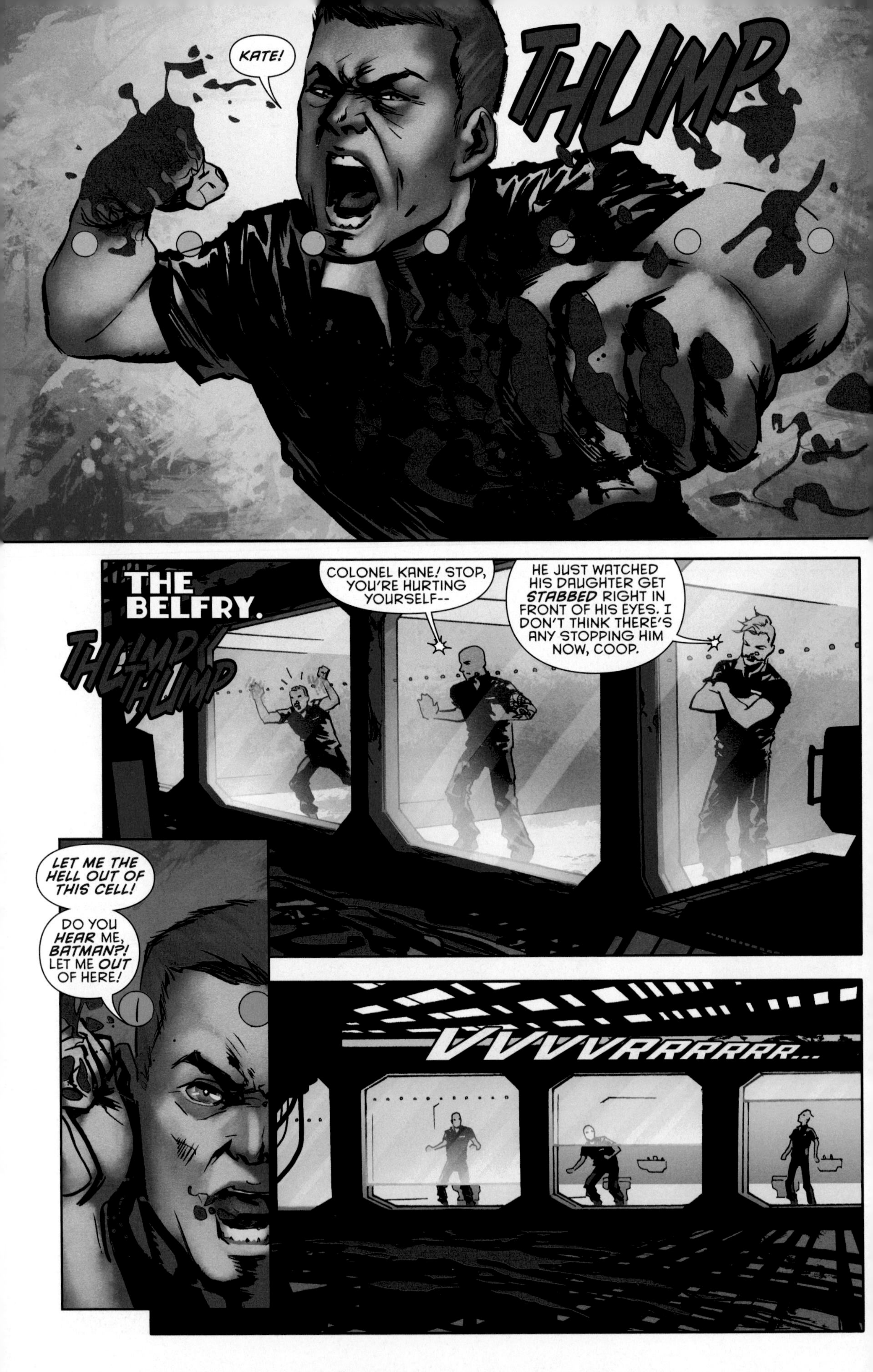
KATE!
THUMP
THE BELFRY.
THUMP THUMP
COLONEL KANE! STOP, YOU'RE HURTING YOURSELF--
HE JUST WATCHED HIS DAUGHTER GET STABBED RIGHT IN FRONT OF HIS EYES. I DON'T THINK THERE'S ANY STOPPING HIM NOW, COOP.
LET ME THE HELL OUT OF THIS CELL!
DO YOU HEAR ME, BATMAN?! LET ME OUT OF HERE!
VVVVRRRRRRR...

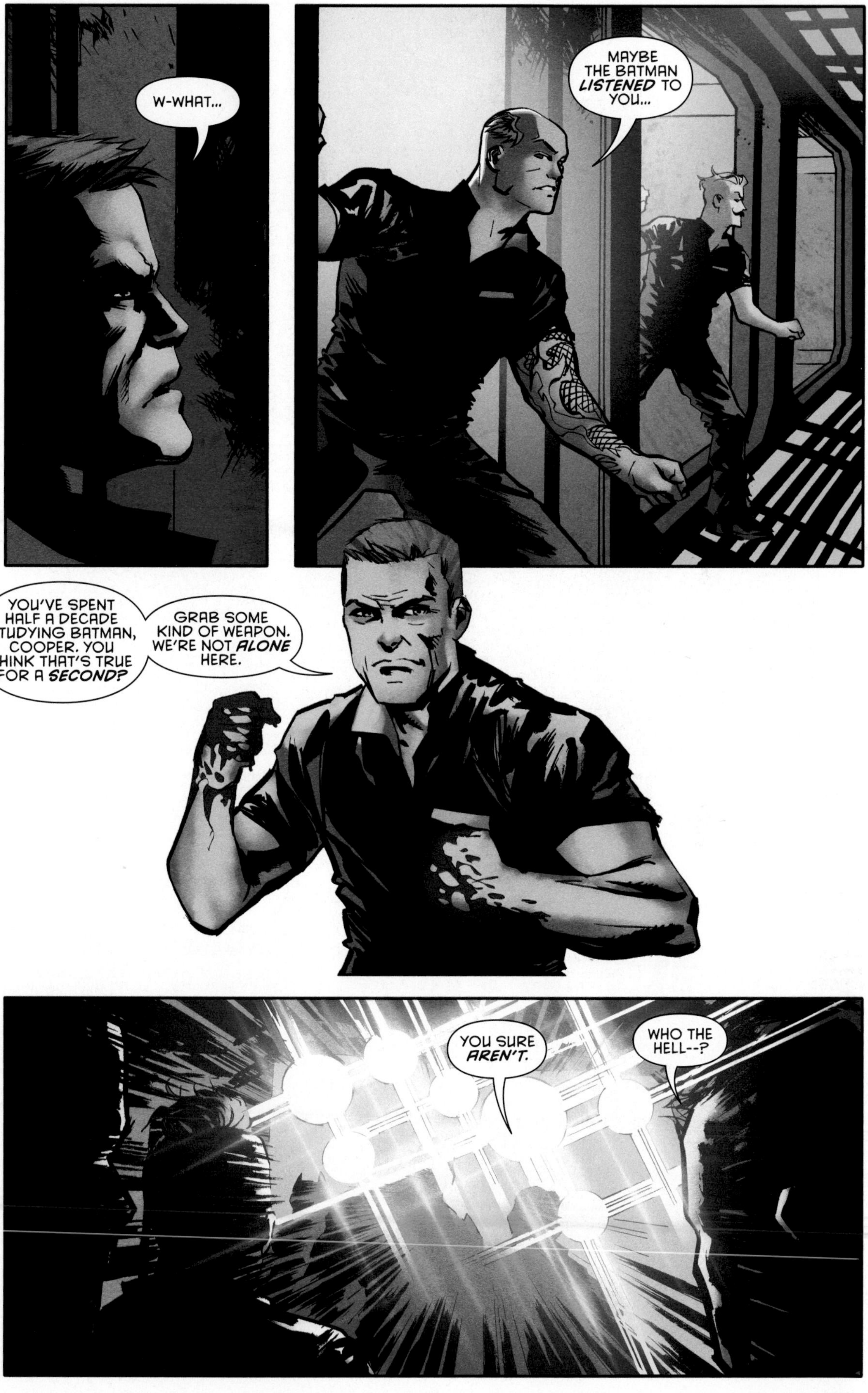
W-WHAT...
MAYBE THE BATMAN *LISTENED* TO YOU...
YOU'VE SPENT HALF A DECADE STUDYING BATMAN, COOPER. YOU THINK THAT'S TRUE FOR A *SECOND?*
GRAB SOME KIND OF WEAPON. WE'RE NOT *ALONE* HERE.
YOU SURE *AREN'T.*
WHO THE HELL--?

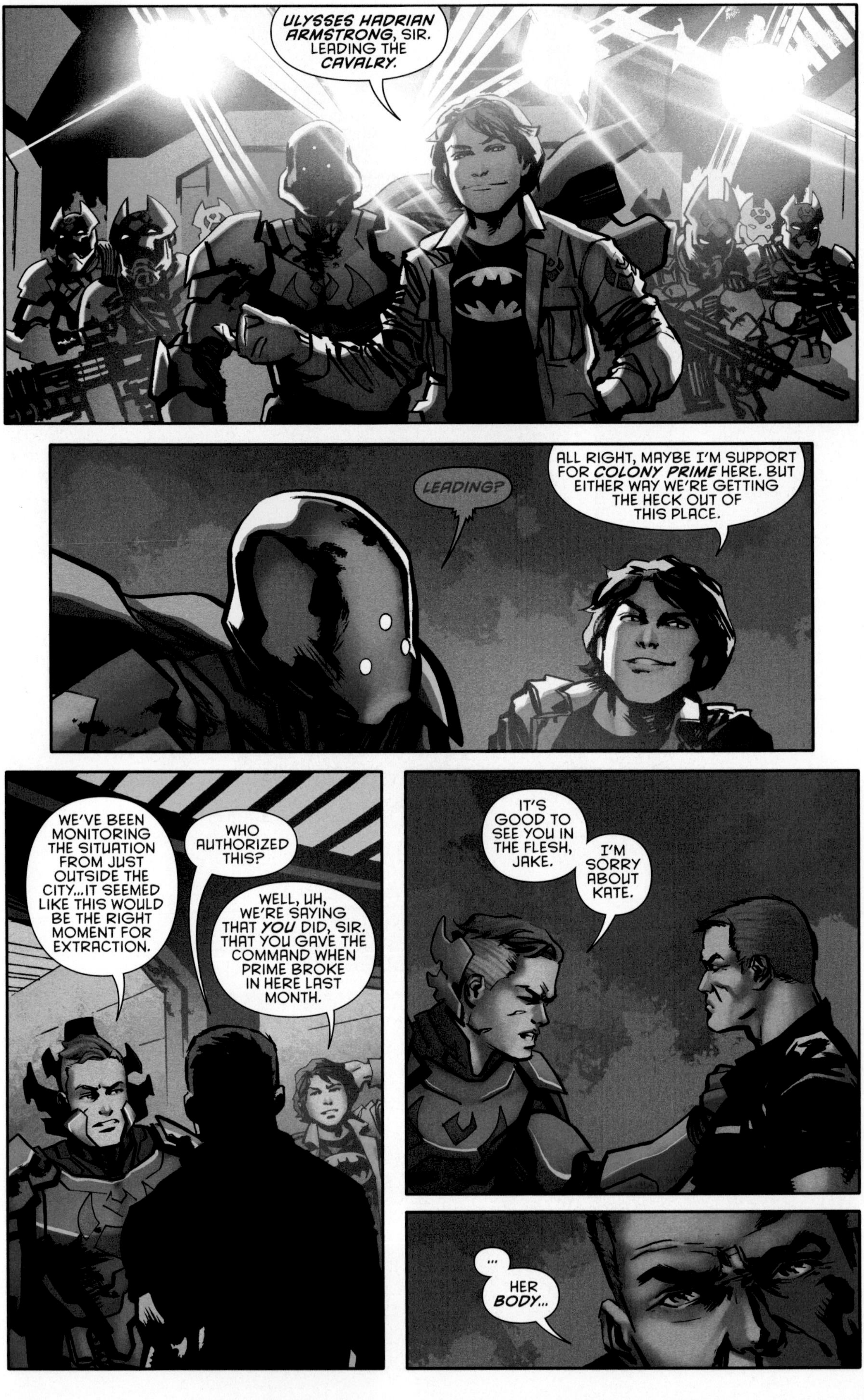
ULYSSES HADRIAN ARMSTRONG, SIR. LEADING THE CAVALRY.
LEADING?
ALL RIGHT, MAYBE I'M SUPPORT FOR COLONY PRIME HERE. BUT EITHER WAY WE'RE GETTING THE HECK OUT OF THIS PLACE.
WE'VE BEEN MONITORING THE SITUATION FROM JUST OUTSIDE THE CITY...IT SEEMED LIKE THIS WOULD BE THE RIGHT MOMENT FOR EXTRACTION.
WHO AUTHORIZED THIS?
WELL, UH, WE'RE SAYING THAT YOU DID, SIR. THAT YOU GAVE THE COMMAND WHEN PRIME BROKE IN HERE LAST MONTH.
IT'S GOOD TO SEE YOU IN THE FLESH, JAKE.
I'M SORRY ABOUT KATE.
...
HER BODY...

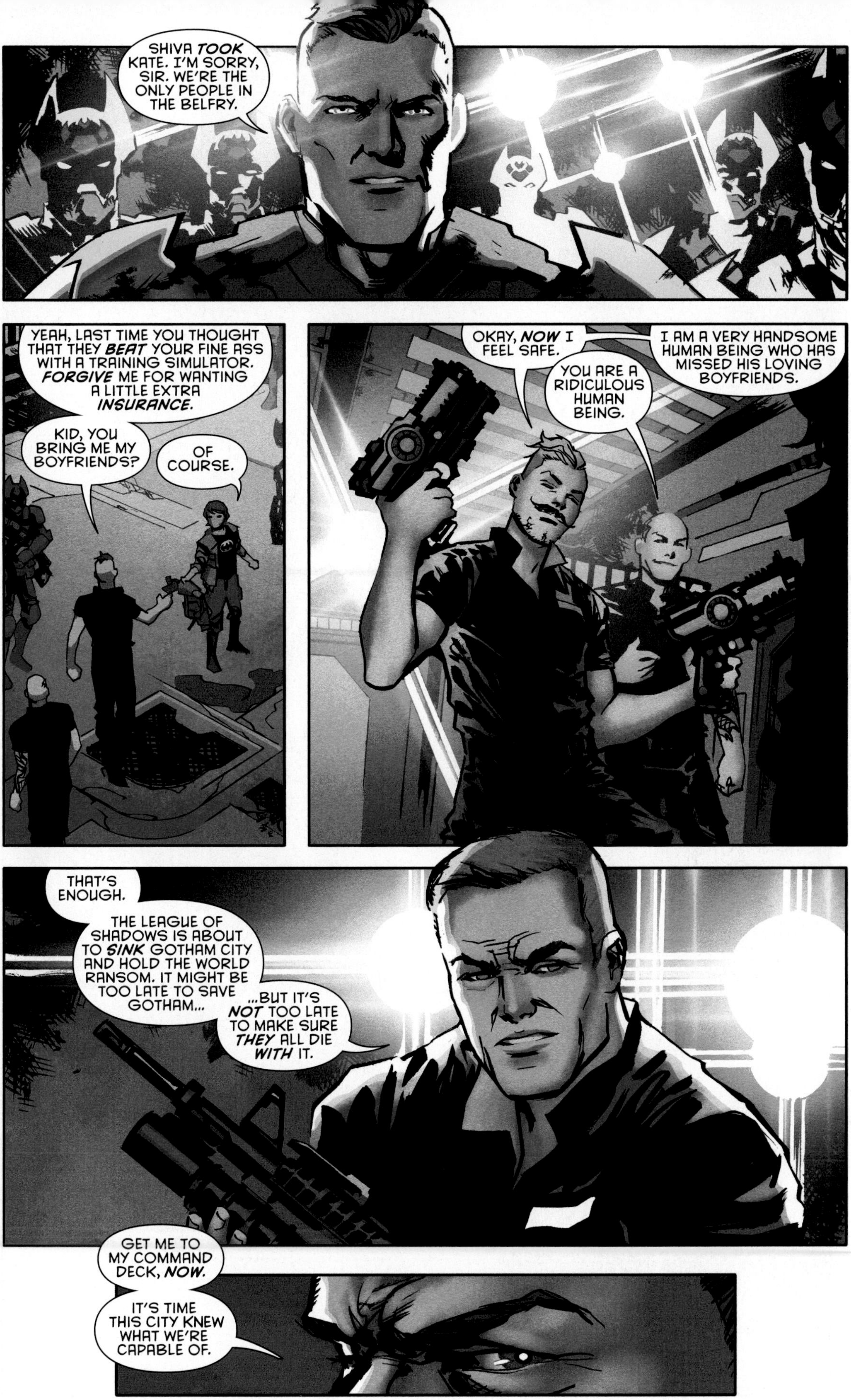
SHIVA *TOOK* KATE. I'M SORRY, SIR. WE'RE THE ONLY PEOPLE IN THE BELFRY.
YEAH, LAST TIME YOU THOUGHT THAT THEY *BEAT* YOUR FINE ASS WITH A TRAINING SIMULATOR. *FORGIVE* ME FOR WANTING A LITTLE EXTRA *INSURANCE*.
KID, YOU BRING ME MY BOYFRIENDS?
OF COURSE.
OKAY, *NOW* I FEEL SAFE.
YOU ARE A RIDICULOUS HUMAN BEING.
I AM A VERY HANDSOME HUMAN BEING WHO HAS MISSED HIS LOVING BOYFRIENDS.
THAT'S ENOUGH.
THE LEAGUE OF SHADOWS IS ABOUT TO *SINK* GOTHAM CITY AND HOLD THE WORLD RANSOM. IT MIGHT BE TOO LATE TO SAVE GOTHAM...
...BUT IT'S *NOT* TOO LATE TO MAKE SURE *THEY* ALL DIE *WITH* IT.
GET ME TO MY COMMAND DECK, *NOW*.
IT'S TIME THIS CITY KNEW WHAT WE'RE CAPABLE OF.

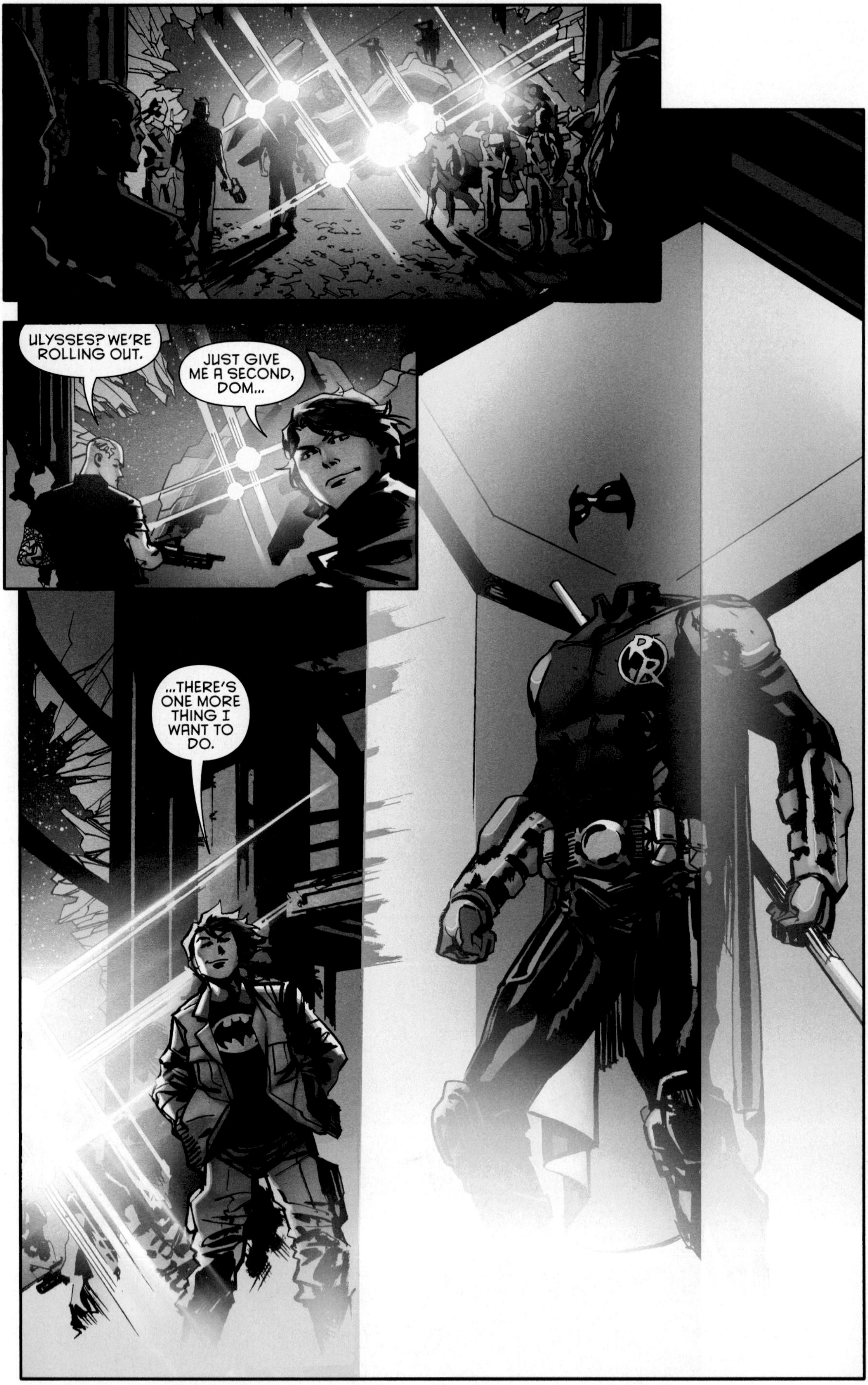
ULYSSES? WE'RE ROLLING OUT.
JUST GIVE ME A SECOND, DOM...
...THERE'S ONE MORE THING I WANT TO DO.

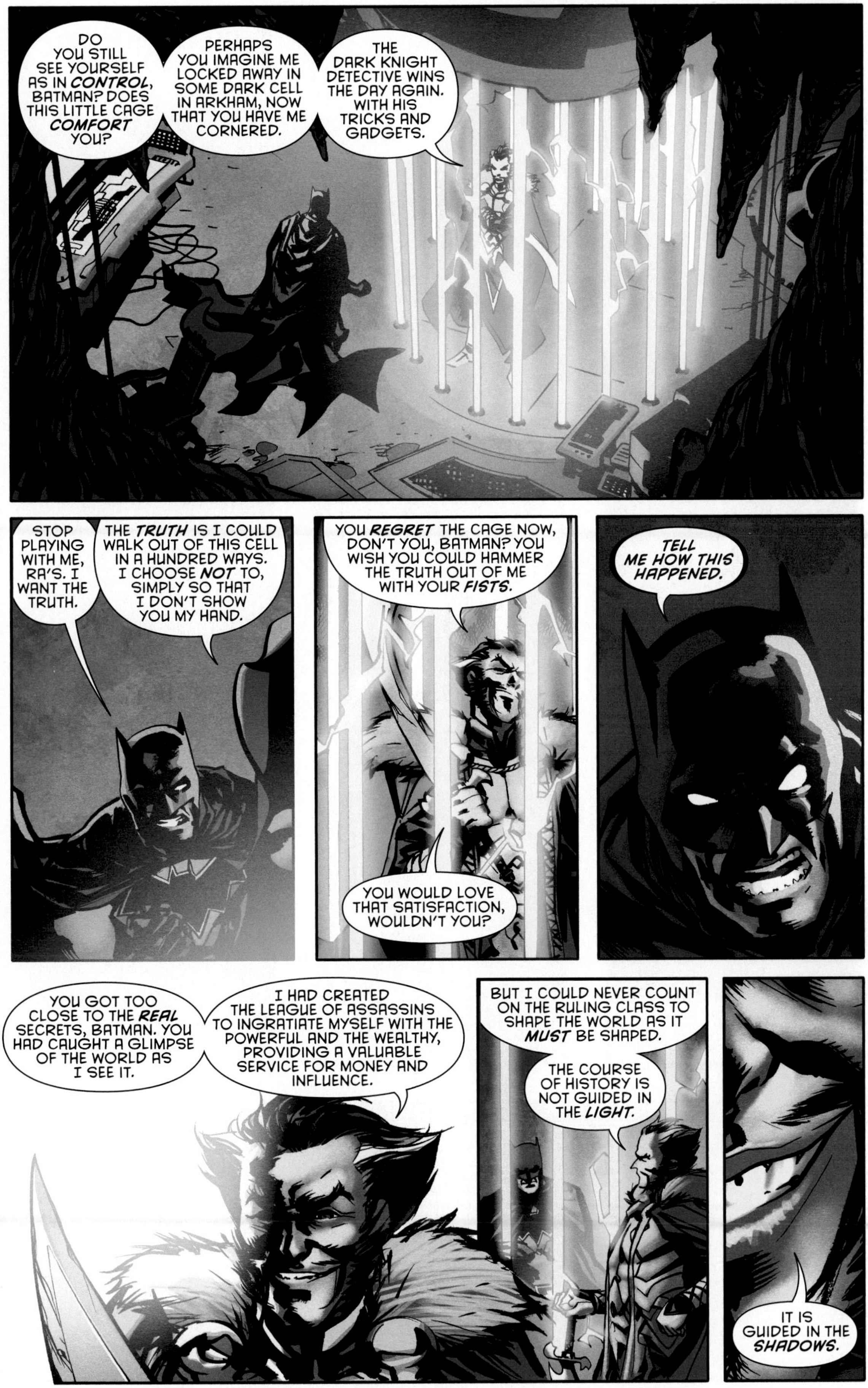
DO YOU STILL SEE YOURSELF AS IN CONTROL, BATMAN? DOES THIS LITTLE CAGE COMFORT YOU?
PERHAPS YOU IMAGINE ME LOCKED AWAY IN SOME DARK CELL IN ARKHAM, NOW THAT YOU HAVE ME CORNERED.
THE DARK KNIGHT DETECTIVE WINS THE DAY AGAIN. WITH HIS TRICKS AND GADGETS.
STOP PLAYING WITH ME, RA'S. I WANT THE TRUTH.
THE TRUTH IS I COULD WALK OUT OF THIS CELL IN A HUNDRED WAYS. I CHOOSE NOT TO, SIMPLY SO THAT I DON'T SHOW YOU MY HAND.
YOU REGRET THE CAGE NOW, DON'T YOU, BATMAN? YOU WISH YOU COULD HAMMER THE TRUTH OUT OF ME WITH YOUR FISTS.
YOU WOULD LOVE THAT SATISFACTION, WOULDN'T YOU?
TELL ME HOW THIS HAPPENED.
YOU GOT TOO CLOSE TO THE REAL SECRETS, BATMAN. YOU HAD CAUGHT A GLIMPSE OF THE WORLD AS I SEE IT.
I HAD CREATED THE LEAGUE OF ASSASSINS TO INGRATIATE MYSELF WITH THE POWERFUL AND THE WEALTHY, PROVIDING A VALUABLE SERVICE FOR MONEY AND INFLUENCE.
BUT I COULD NEVER COUNT ON THE RULING CLASS TO SHAPE THE WORLD AS IT MUST BE SHAPED.
THE COURSE OF HISTORY IS NOT GUIDED IN THE LIGHT.
IT IS GUIDED IN THE SHADOWS.

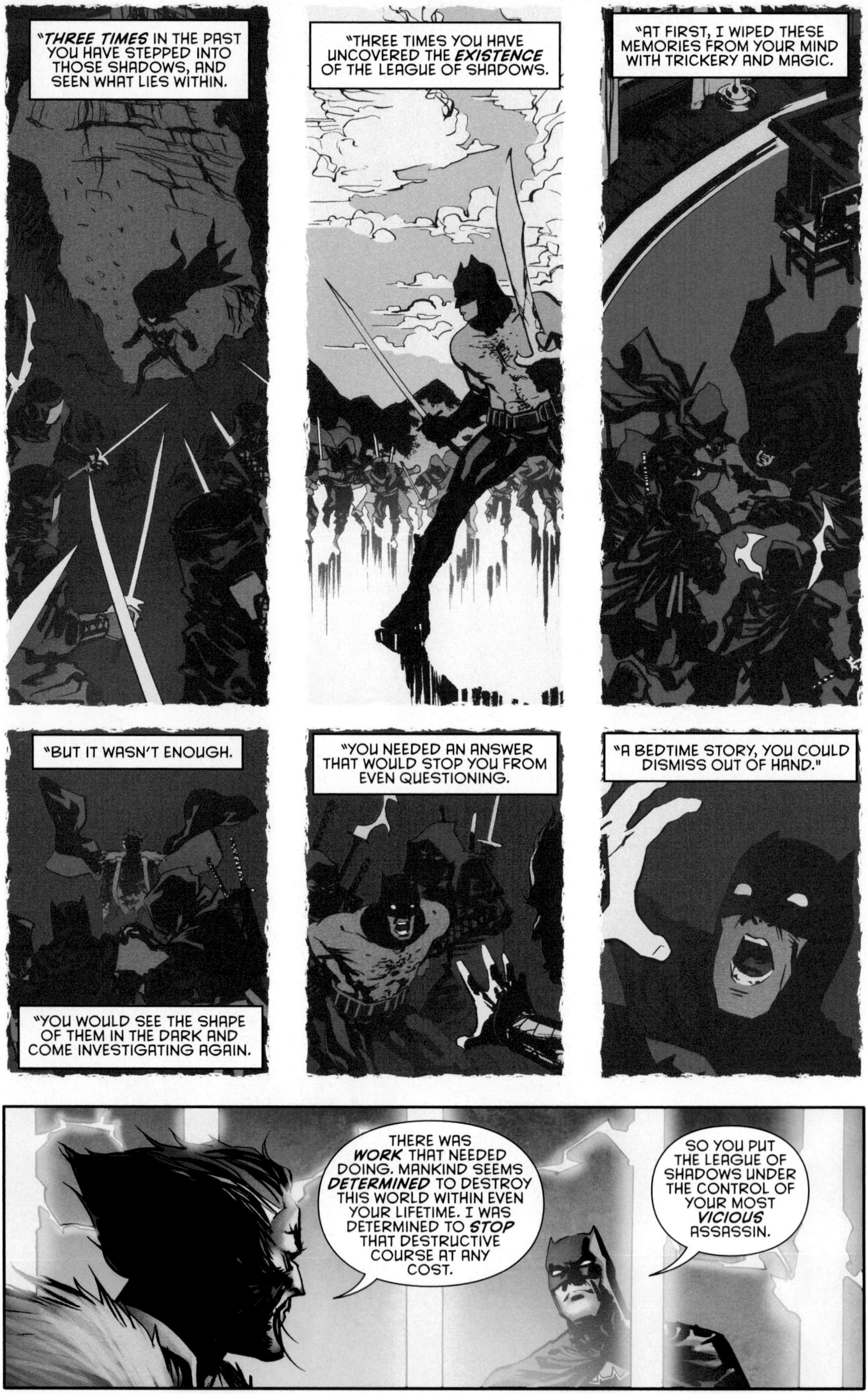
"THREE TIMES IN THE PAST YOU HAVE STEPPED INTO THOSE SHADOWS, AND SEEN WHAT LIES WITHIN.
"THREE TIMES YOU HAVE UNCOVERED THE EXISTENCE OF THE LEAGUE OF SHADOWS.
"AT FIRST, I WIPED THESE MEMORIES FROM YOUR MIND WITH TRICKERY AND MAGIC.
"BUT IT WASN'T ENOUGH.
"YOU WOULD SEE THE SHAPE OF THEM IN THE DARK AND COME INVESTIGATING AGAIN.
"YOU NEEDED AN ANSWER THAT WOULD STOP YOU FROM EVEN QUESTIONING.
"A BEDTIME STORY, YOU COULD DISMISS OUT OF HAND."
THERE WAS WORK THAT NEEDED DOING. MANKIND SEEMS DETERMINED TO DESTROY THIS WORLD WITHIN EVEN YOUR LIFETIME. I WAS DETERMINED TO STOP THAT DESTRUCTIVE COURSE AT ANY COST.
SO YOU PUT THE LEAGUE OF SHADOWS UNDER THE CONTROL OF YOUR MOST VICIOUS ASSASSIN.

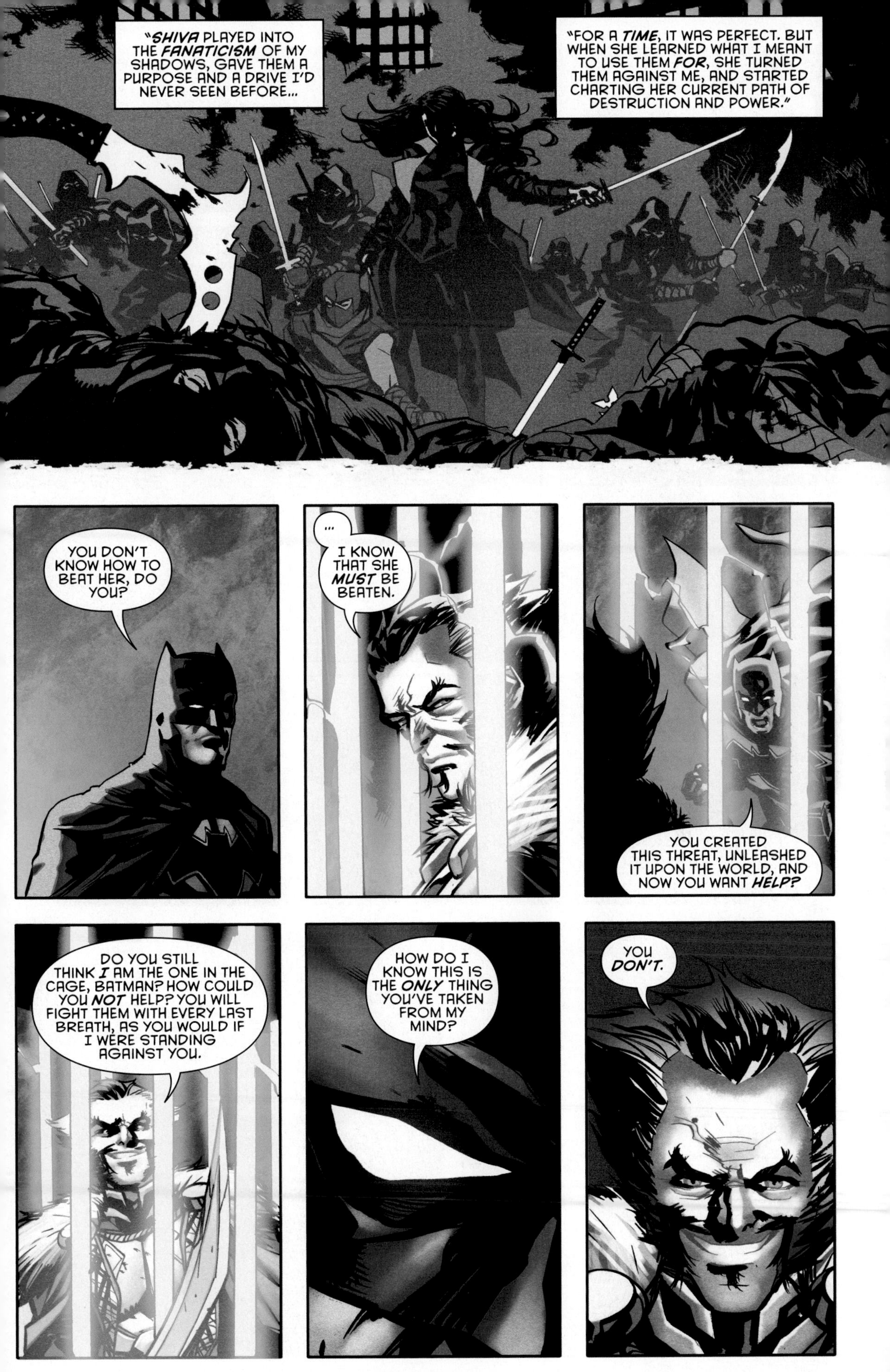
"SHIVA PLAYED INTO THE FANATICISM OF MY SHADOWS, GAVE THEM A PURPOSE AND A DRIVE I'D NEVER SEEN BEFORE...
"FOR A TIME, IT WAS PERFECT. BUT WHEN SHE LEARNED WHAT I MEANT TO USE THEM FOR, SHE TURNED THEM AGAINST ME, AND STARTED CHARTING HER CURRENT PATH OF DESTRUCTION AND POWER."
YOU DON'T KNOW HOW TO BEAT HER, DO YOU?
...
I KNOW THAT SHE MUST BE BEATEN.
YOU CREATED THIS THREAT, UNLEASHED IT UPON THE WORLD, AND NOW YOU WANT HELP?
DO YOU STILL THINK I AM THE ONE IN THE CAGE, BATMAN? HOW COULD YOU NOT HELP? YOU WILL FIGHT THEM WITH EVERY LAST BREATH, AS YOU WOULD IF I WERE STANDING AGAINST YOU.
HOW DO I KNOW THIS IS THE ONLY THING YOU'VE TAKEN FROM MY MIND?
YOU DON'T.

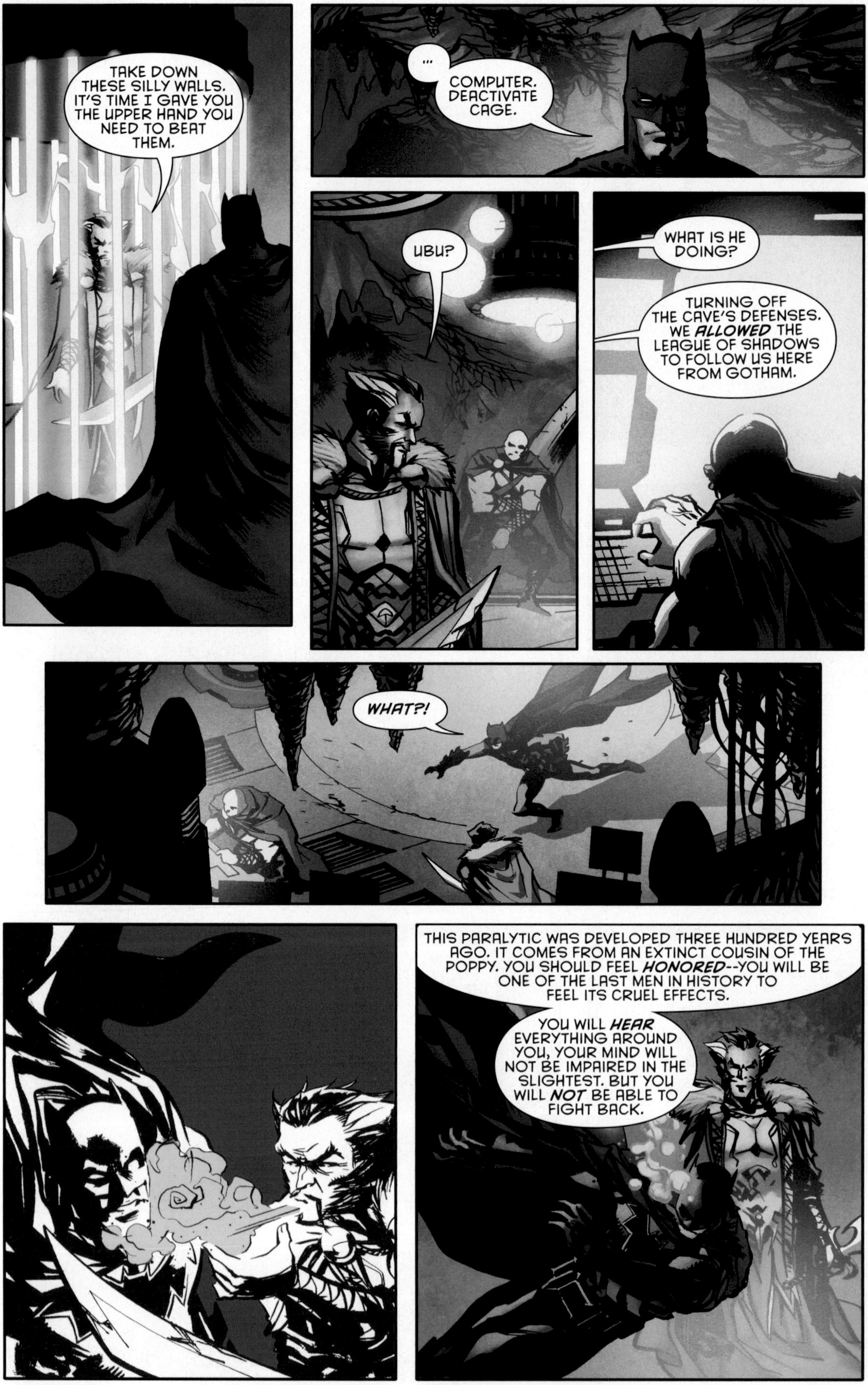
TAKE DOWN THESE SILLY WALLS. IT'S TIME I GAVE YOU THE UPPER HAND YOU NEED TO BEAT THEM.
...
COMPUTER. DEACTIVATE CAGE.
UBU?
WHAT IS HE DOING?
TURNING OFF THE CAVE'S DEFENSES. WE ALLOWED THE LEAGUE OF SHADOWS TO FOLLOW US HERE FROM GOTHAM.
WHAT?!
THIS PARALYTIC WAS DEVELOPED THREE HUNDRED YEARS AGO. IT COMES FROM AN EXTINCT COUSIN OF THE POPPY. YOU SHOULD FEEL HONORED--YOU WILL BE ONE OF THE LAST MEN IN HISTORY TO FEEL ITS CRUEL EFFECTS.
YOU WILL HEAR EVERYTHING AROUND YOU, YOUR MIND WILL NOT BE IMPAIRED IN THE SLIGHTEST. BUT YOU WILL NOT BE ABLE TO FIGHT BACK.

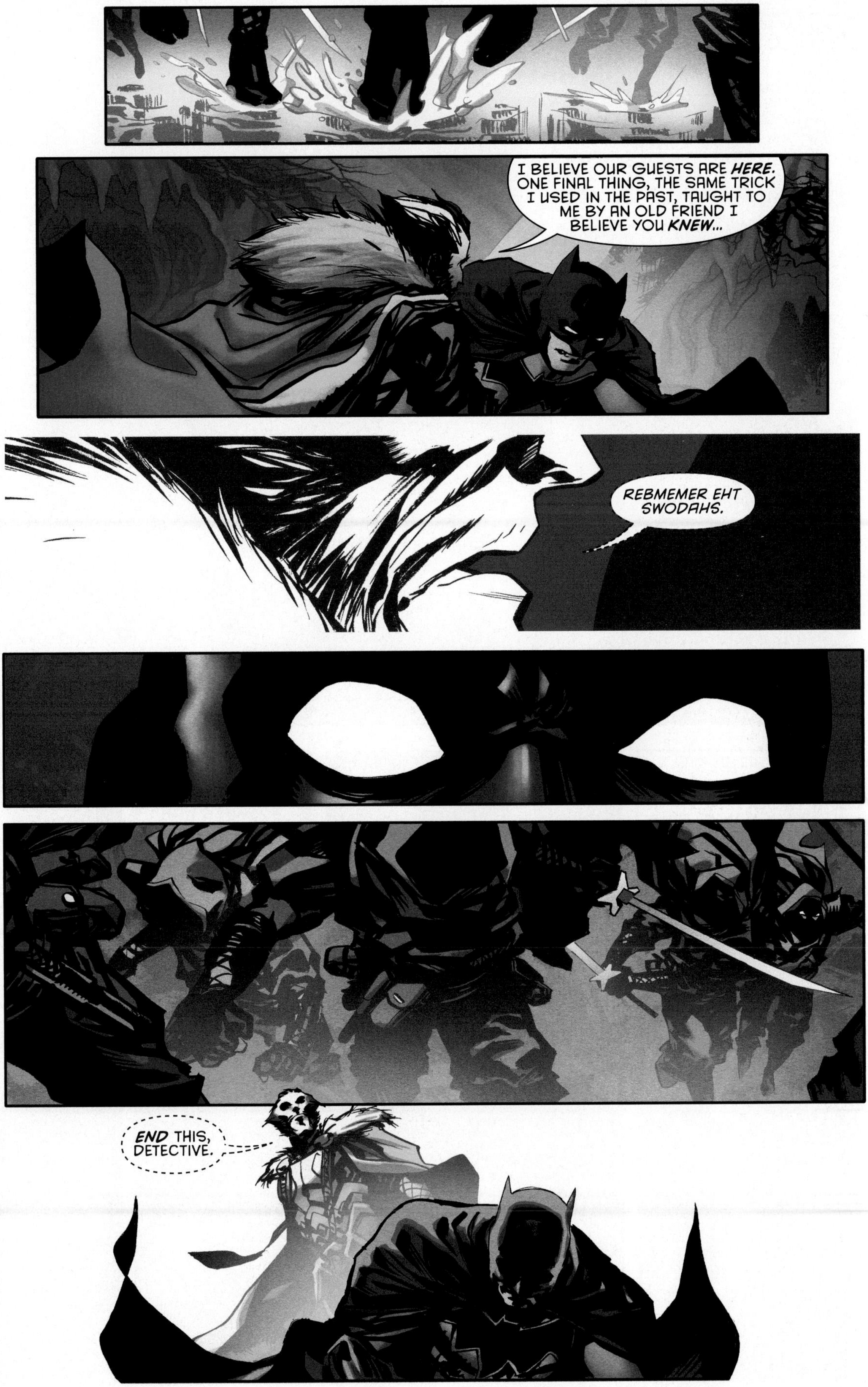
I BELIEVE OUR GUESTS ARE HERE. ONE FINAL THING, THE SAME TRICK I USED IN THE PAST, TAUGHT TO ME BY AN OLD FRIEND I BELIEVE YOU KNEW...
REBMEMER EHT SWODAHS.
END THIS, DETECTIVE.

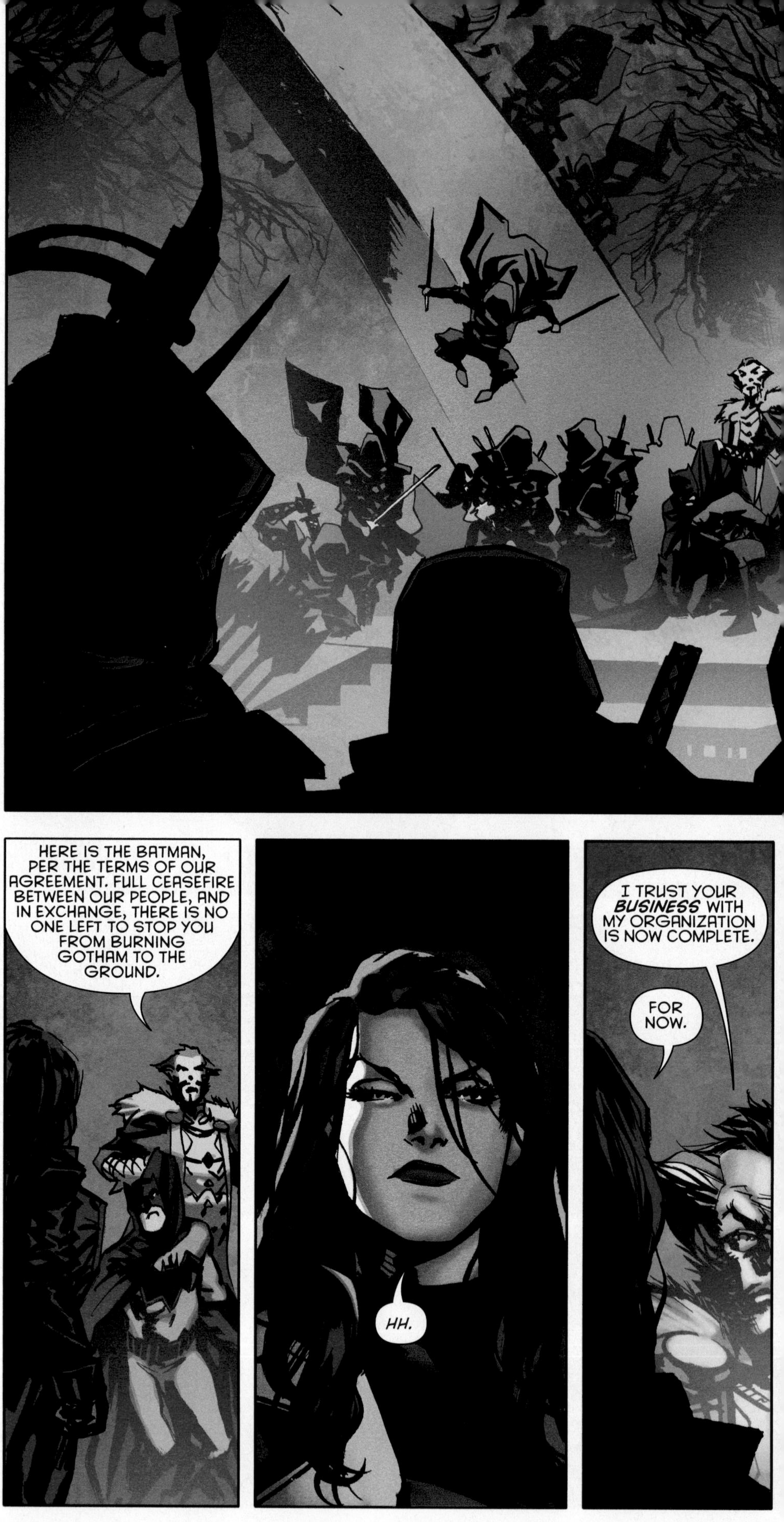
HERE IS THE BATMAN, PER THE TERMS OF OUR AGREEMENT. FULL CEASEFIRE BETWEEN OUR PEOPLE, AND IN EXCHANGE, THERE IS NO ONE LEFT TO STOP YOU FROM BURNING GOTHAM TO THE GROUND.
HH.
I TRUST YOUR *BUSINESS* WITH MY ORGANIZATION IS NOW COMPLETE.
FOR NOW.

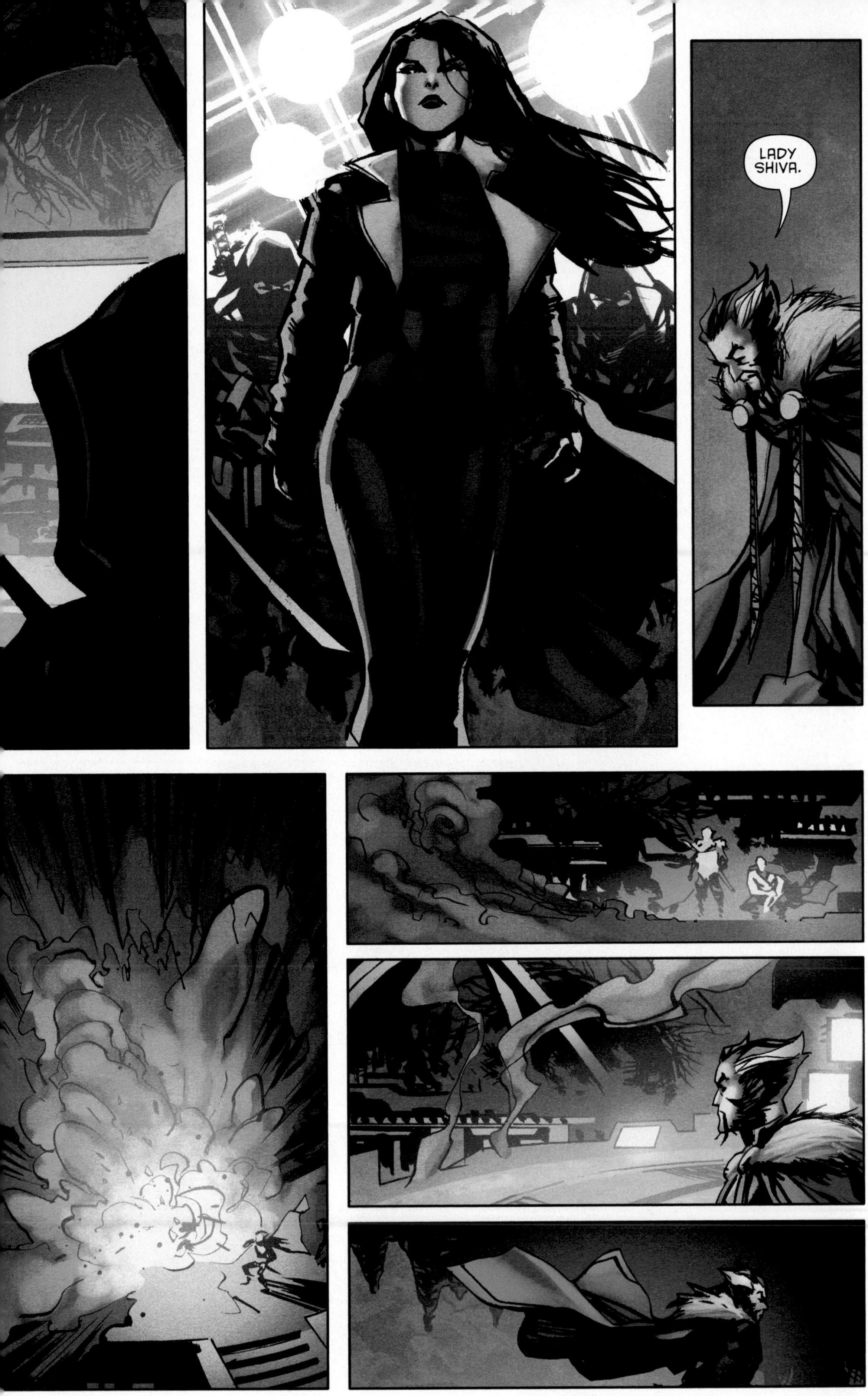
LADY SHIVA.

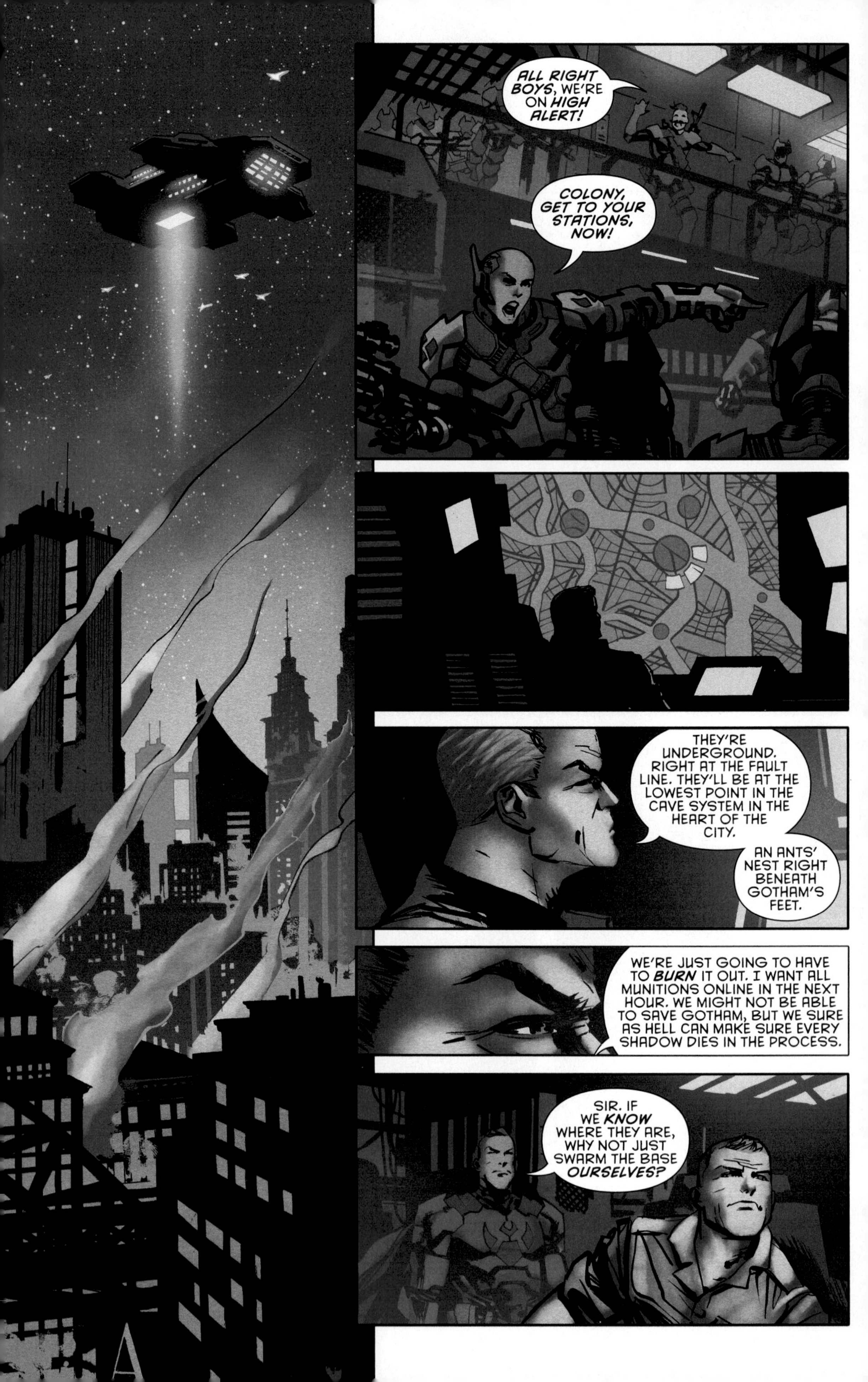
ALL RIGHT BOYS, WE'RE ON HIGH ALERT!
COLONY, GET TO YOUR STATIONS, NOW!
THEY'RE UNDERGROUND. RIGHT AT THE FAULT LINE. THEY'LL BE AT THE LOWEST POINT IN THE CAVE SYSTEM IN THE HEART OF THE CITY.
AN ANTS' NEST RIGHT BENEATH GOTHAM'S FEET.
WE'RE JUST GOING TO HAVE TO BURN IT OUT. I WANT ALL MUNITIONS ONLINE IN THE NEXT HOUR. WE MIGHT NOT BE ABLE TO SAVE GOTHAM, BUT WE SURE AS HELL CAN MAKE SURE EVERY SHADOW DIES IN THE PROCESS.
SIR. IF WE KNOW WHERE THEY ARE, WHY NOT JUST SWARM THE BASE OURSELVES?

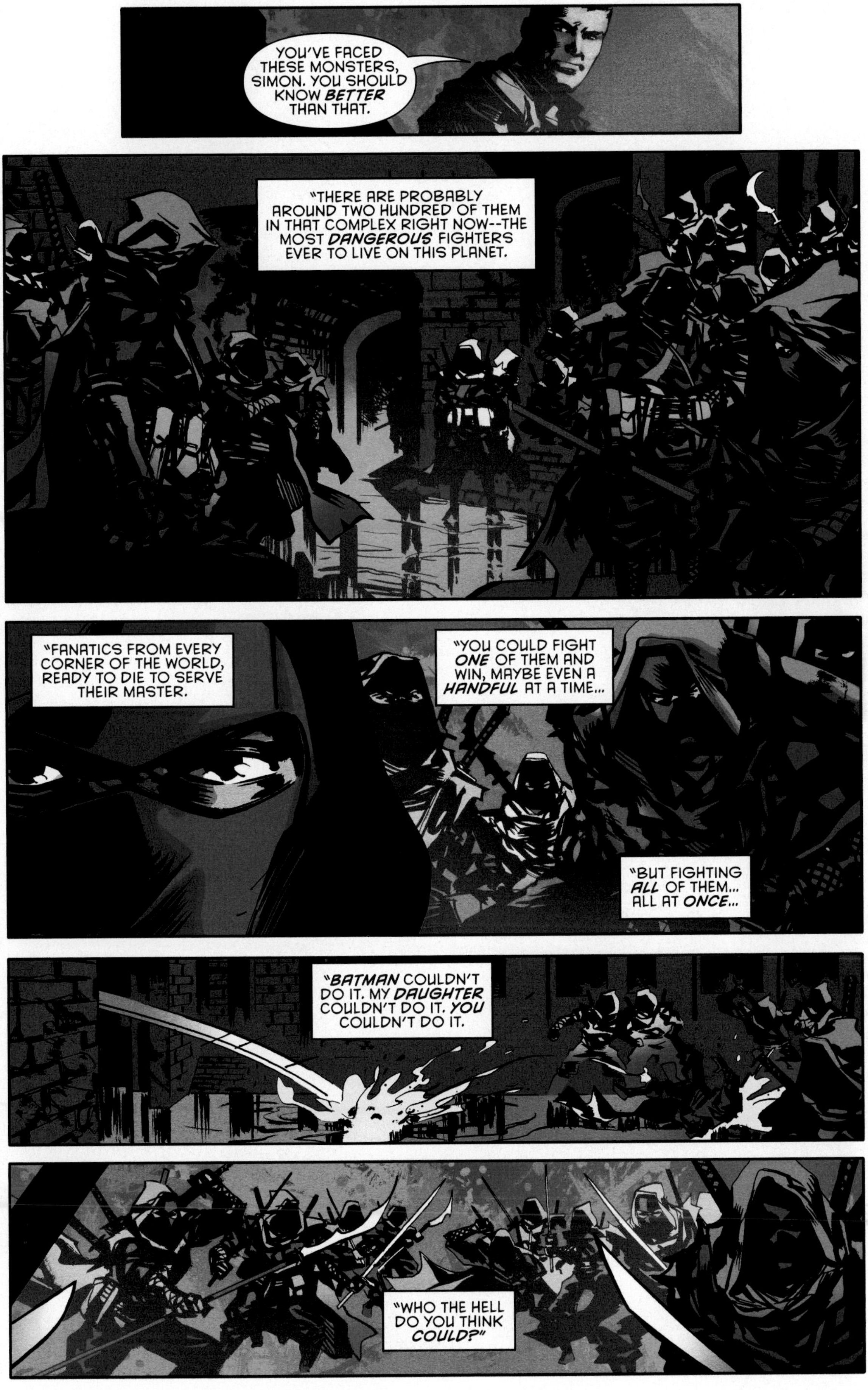
YOU'VE FACED THESE MONSTERS, SIMON. YOU SHOULD KNOW *BETTER* THAN THAT.
"THERE ARE PROBABLY AROUND TWO HUNDRED OF THEM IN THAT COMPLEX RIGHT NOW--THE MOST *DANGEROUS* FIGHTERS EVER TO LIVE ON THIS PLANET.
"FANATICS FROM EVERY CORNER OF THE WORLD, READY TO DIE TO SERVE THEIR MASTER.
"YOU COULD FIGHT *ONE* OF THEM AND WIN, MAYBE EVEN A *HANDFUL* AT A TIME...
"BUT FIGHTING *ALL* OF THEM... ALL AT *ONCE*...
"*BATMAN* COULDN'T DO IT. MY *DAUGHTER* COULDN'T DO IT. *YOU* COULDN'T DO IT.
"WHO THE HELL DO YOU THINK *COULD*?"

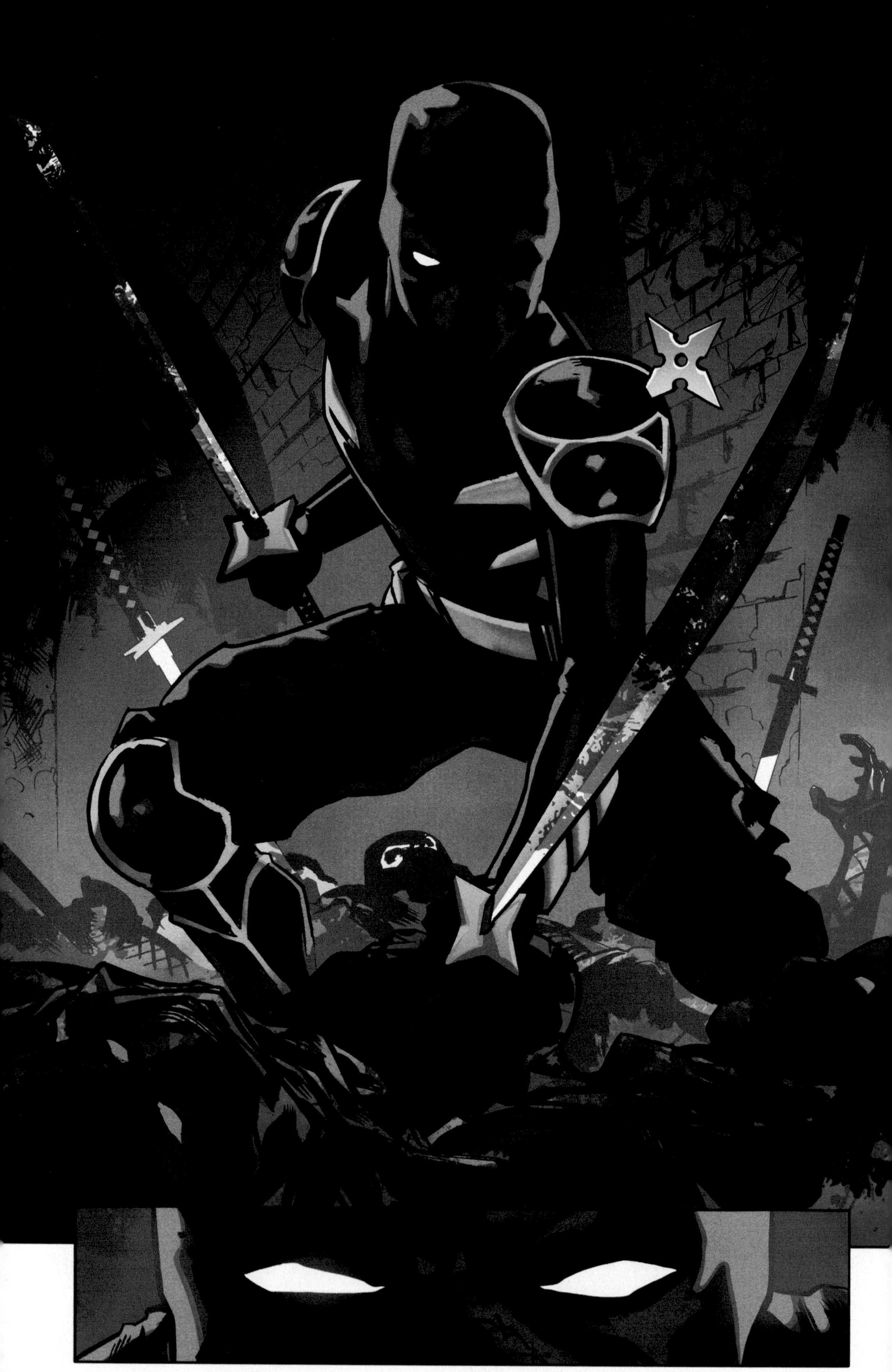

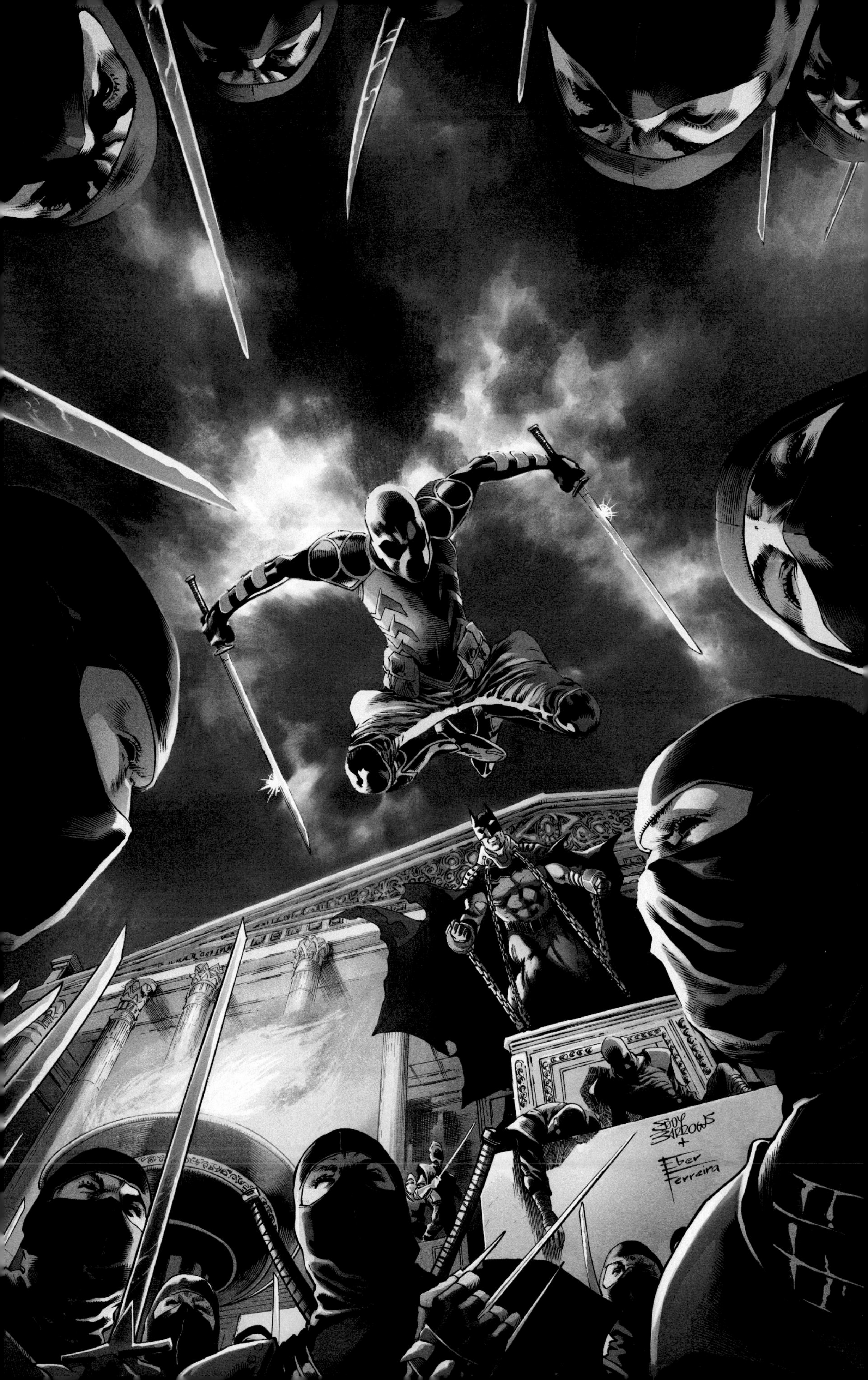
EDDY BARROWS
+
Eber Ferreira

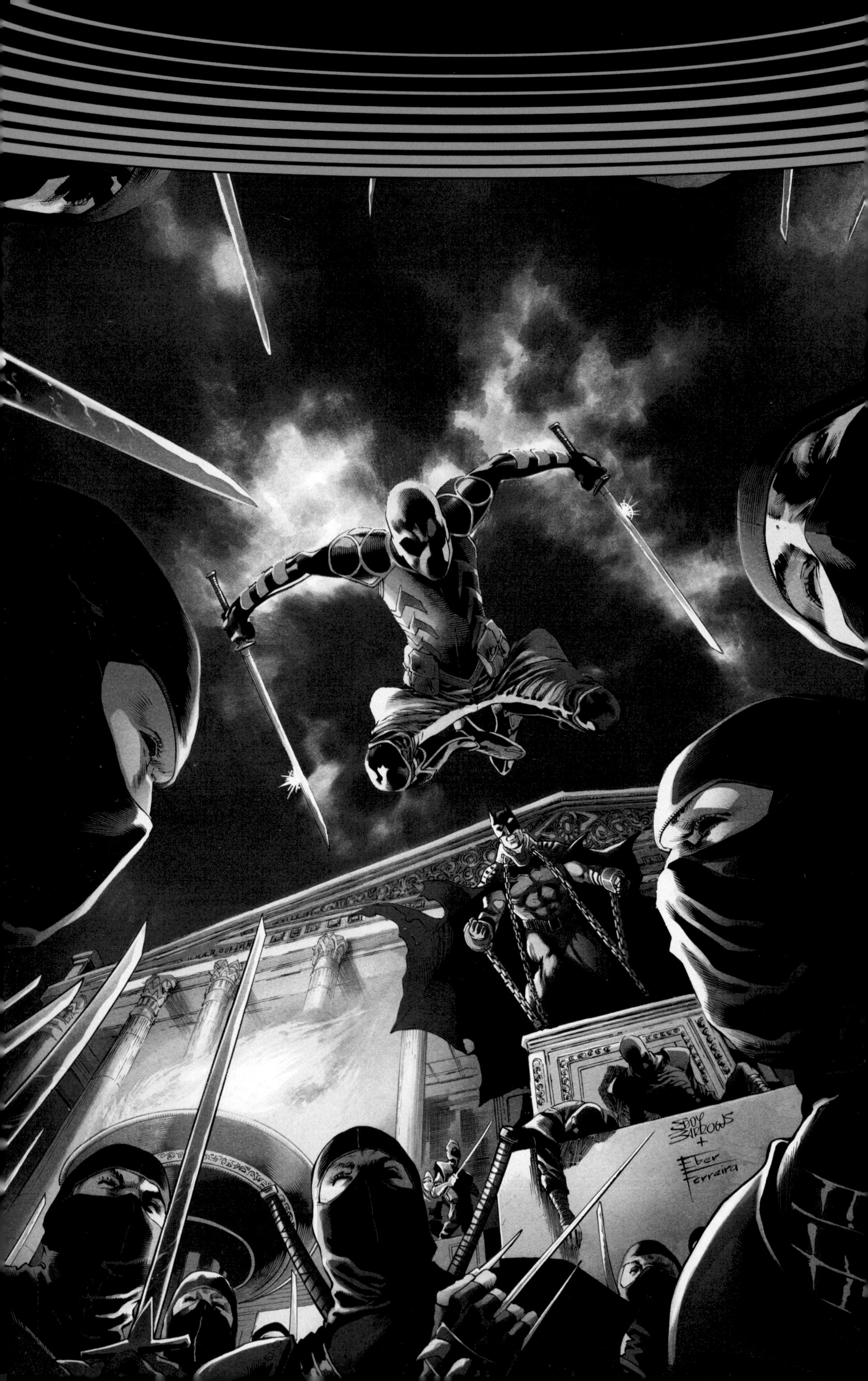
EDDY BARROWS
+
Eber Ferreira

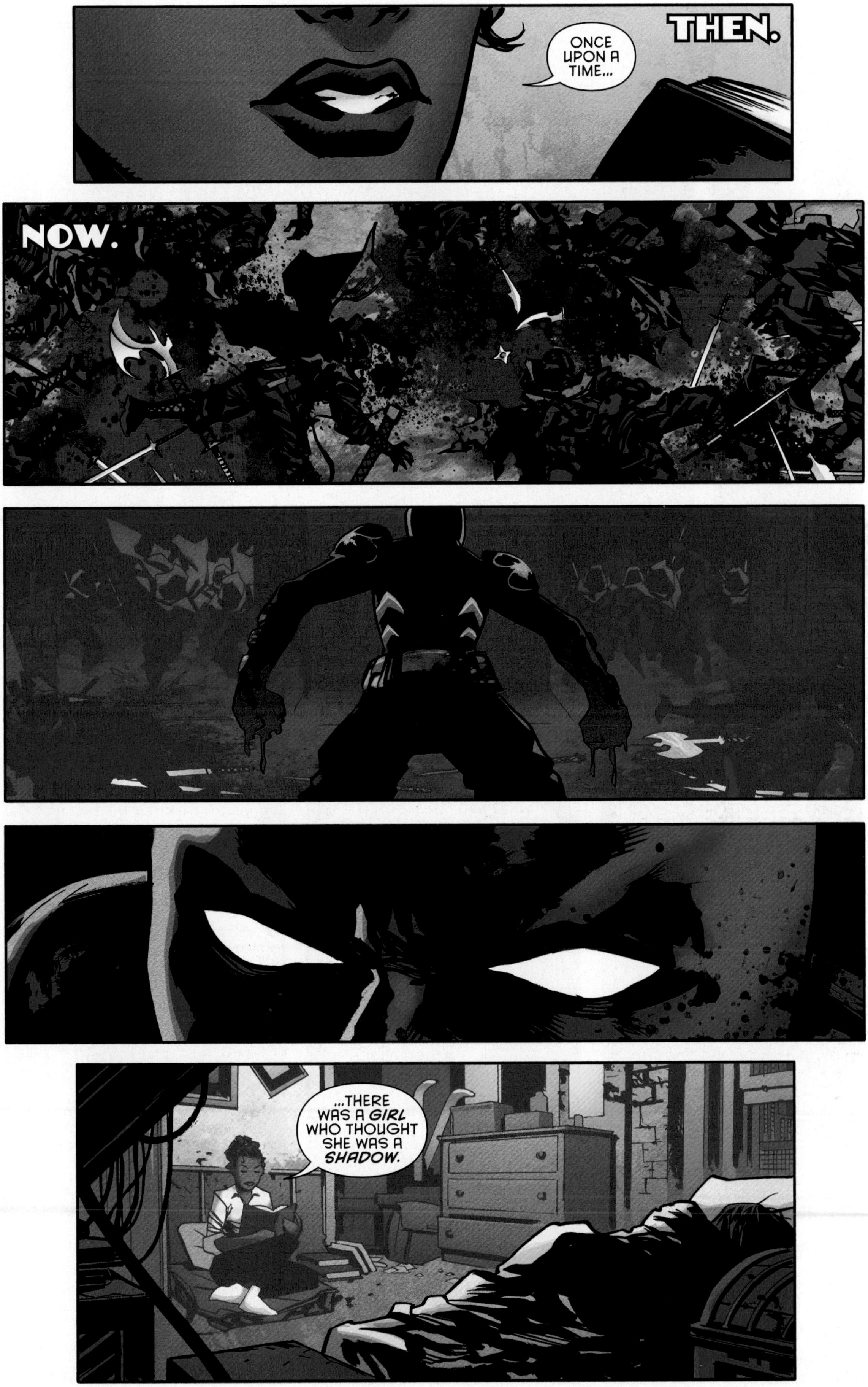
THEN.
ONCE UPON A TIME...
NOW.
...THERE WAS A GIRL WHO THOUGHT SHE WAS A SHADOW.

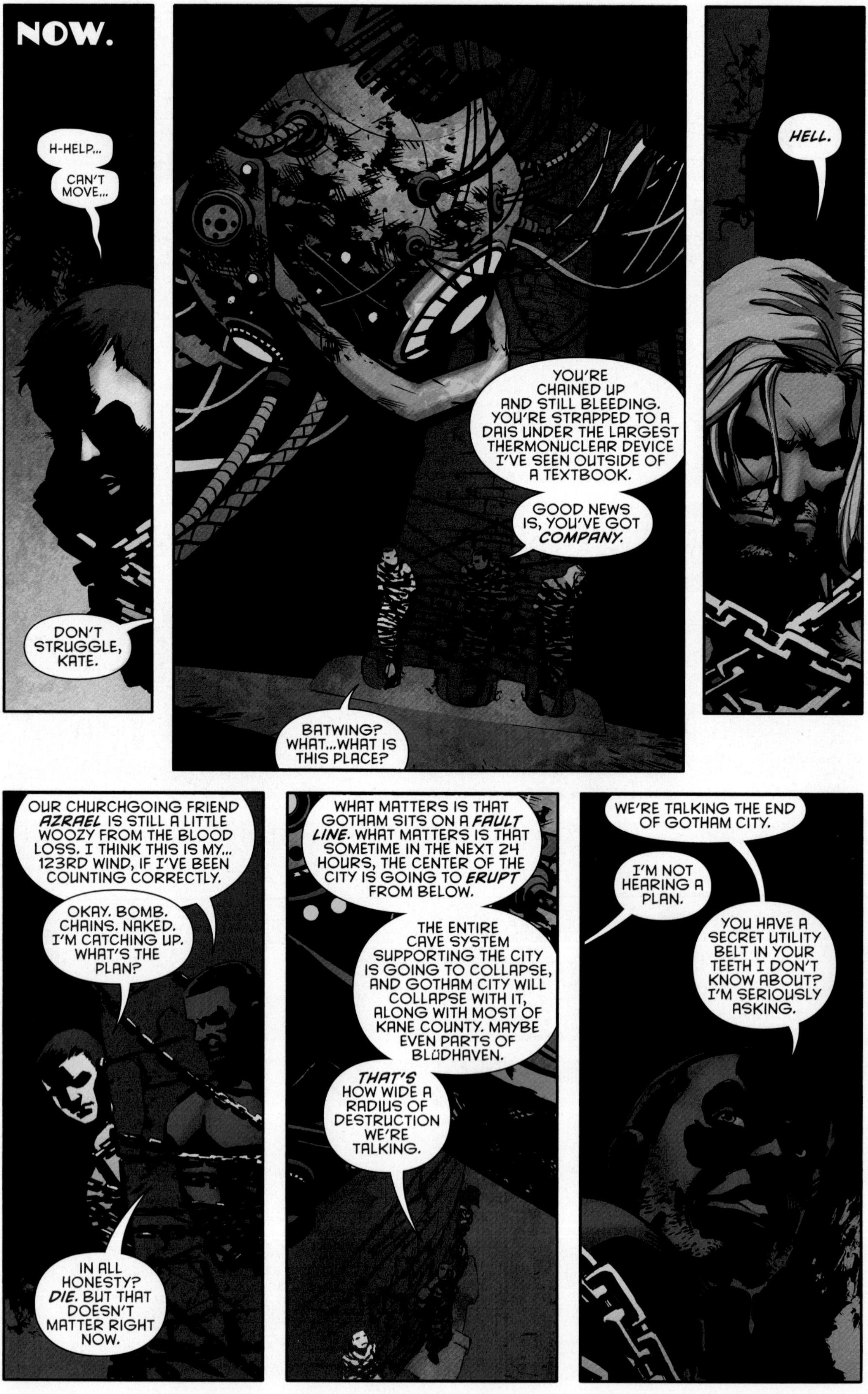
NOW.
H-HELP...
CAN'T MOVE...
DON'T STRUGGLE, KATE.
YOU'RE CHAINED UP AND STILL BLEEDING. YOU'RE STRAPPED TO A DAIS UNDER THE LARGEST THERMONUCLEAR DEVICE I'VE SEEN OUTSIDE OF A TEXTBOOK.
GOOD NEWS IS, YOU'VE GOT COMPANY.
BATWING? WHAT...WHAT IS THIS PLACE?
HELL.
OUR CHURCHGOING FRIEND AZRAEL IS STILL A LITTLE WOOZY FROM THE BLOOD LOSS. I THINK THIS IS MY... 123RD WIND, IF I'VE BEEN COUNTING CORRECTLY.
OKAY. BOMB. CHAINS. NAKED. I'M CATCHING UP. WHAT'S THE PLAN?
IN ALL HONESTY? DIE. BUT THAT DOESN'T MATTER RIGHT NOW.
WHAT MATTERS IS THAT GOTHAM SITS ON A FAULT LINE. WHAT MATTERS IS THAT SOMETIME IN THE NEXT 24 HOURS, THE CENTER OF THE CITY IS GOING TO ERUPT FROM BELOW.
THE ENTIRE CAVE SYSTEM SUPPORTING THE CITY IS GOING TO COLLAPSE, AND GOTHAM CITY WILL COLLAPSE WITH IT, ALONG WITH MOST OF KANE COUNTY. MAYBE EVEN PARTS OF BLÜDHAVEN.
THAT'S HOW WIDE A RADIUS OF DESTRUCTION WE'RE TALKING.
WE'RE TALKING THE END OF GOTHAM CITY.
I'M NOT HEARING A PLAN.
YOU HAVE A SECRET UTILITY BELT IN YOUR TEETH I DON'T KNOW ABOUT? I'M SERIOUSLY ASKING.

CLAYFACE...?

YOU SEE THOSE CANISTERS THERE, ALONG THE WALL? HE'S SPREAD BETWEEN A DOZEN OF THEM.

DAMMIT.

WHY ARE WE *ALONE?*

WE AREN'T.

WHAT DO YOU MEAN?

FOCUS ON THE SHADOWS. LET YOUR EYES ADJUST.

UNLESS YOU HAVE THAT BELT OR SOME SECRET SUPER-STRENGTH YOU'VE BEEN WAITING FOR A SPECIAL OCCASION TO TROT OUT...I THINK ALL WE CAN DO IS *WAIT.*

FOR WHAT?

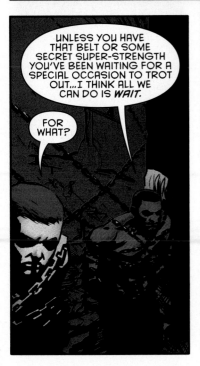

BATMAN.

I MEAN, END OF THE DAY, HE'S STILL BATMAN. HE'S NOT GOING TO LET THIS HAPPEN.

LUCAS...

I WOULDN'T BE TOO SURE OF THAT.

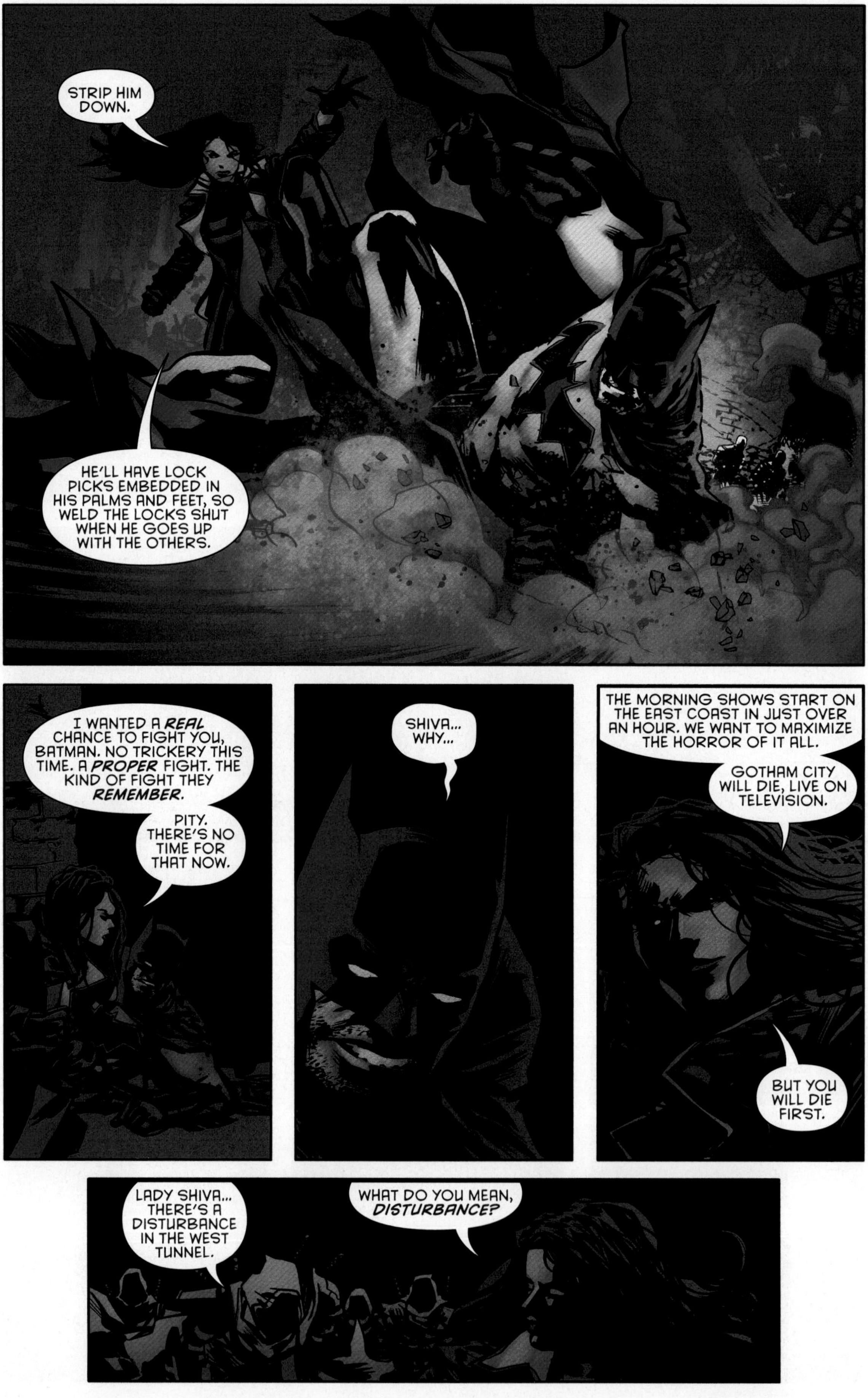
STRIP HIM DOWN.
HE'LL HAVE LOCK PICKS EMBEDDED IN HIS PALMS AND FEET, SO WELD THE LOCKS SHUT WHEN HE GOES UP WITH THE OTHERS.
I WANTED A REAL CHANCE TO FIGHT YOU, BATMAN. NO TRICKERY THIS TIME. A PROPER FIGHT. THE KIND OF FIGHT THEY REMEMBER.
PITY. THERE'S NO TIME FOR THAT NOW.
SHIVA... WHY...
THE MORNING SHOWS START ON THE EAST COAST IN JUST OVER AN HOUR. WE WANT TO MAXIMIZE THE HORROR OF IT ALL.
GOTHAM CITY WILL DIE, LIVE ON TELEVISION.
BUT YOU WILL DIE FIRST.
LADY SHIVA... THERE'S A DISTURBANCE IN THE WEST TUNNEL.
WHAT DO YOU MEAN, DISTURBANCE?

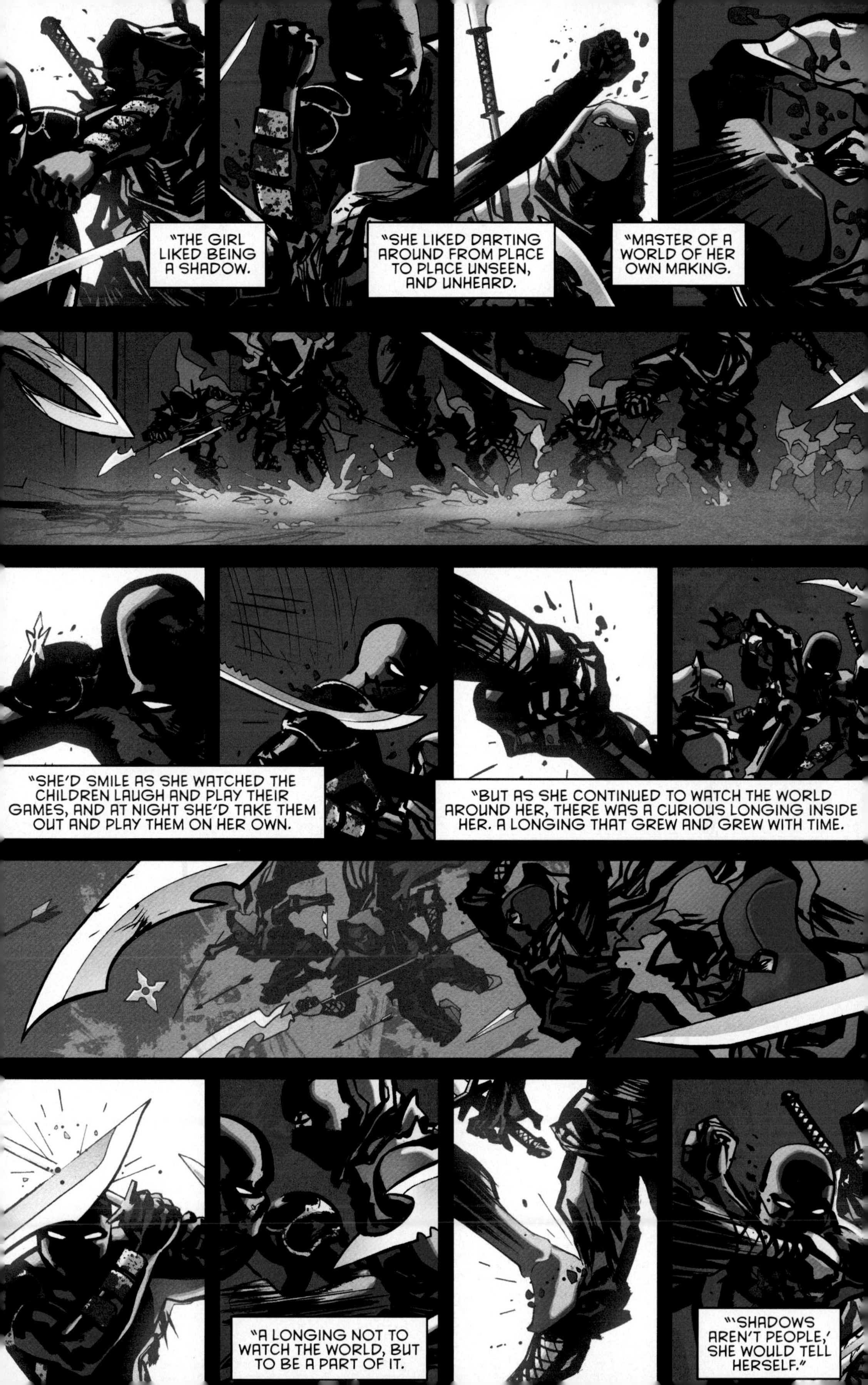
"THE GIRL LIKED BEING A SHADOW.
"SHE LIKED DARTING AROUND FROM PLACE TO PLACE UNSEEN, AND UNHEARD.
"MASTER OF A WORLD OF HER OWN MAKING.
"SHE'D SMILE AS SHE WATCHED THE CHILDREN LAUGH AND PLAY THEIR GAMES, AND AT NIGHT SHE'D TAKE THEM OUT AND PLAY THEM ON HER OWN.
"BUT AS SHE CONTINUED TO WATCH THE WORLD AROUND HER, THERE WAS A CURIOUS LONGING INSIDE HER. A LONGING THAT GREW AND GREW WITH TIME.
"A LONGING NOT TO WATCH THE WORLD, BUT TO BE A PART OF IT.
"'SHADOWS AREN'T PEOPLE,' SHE WOULD TELL HERSELF."

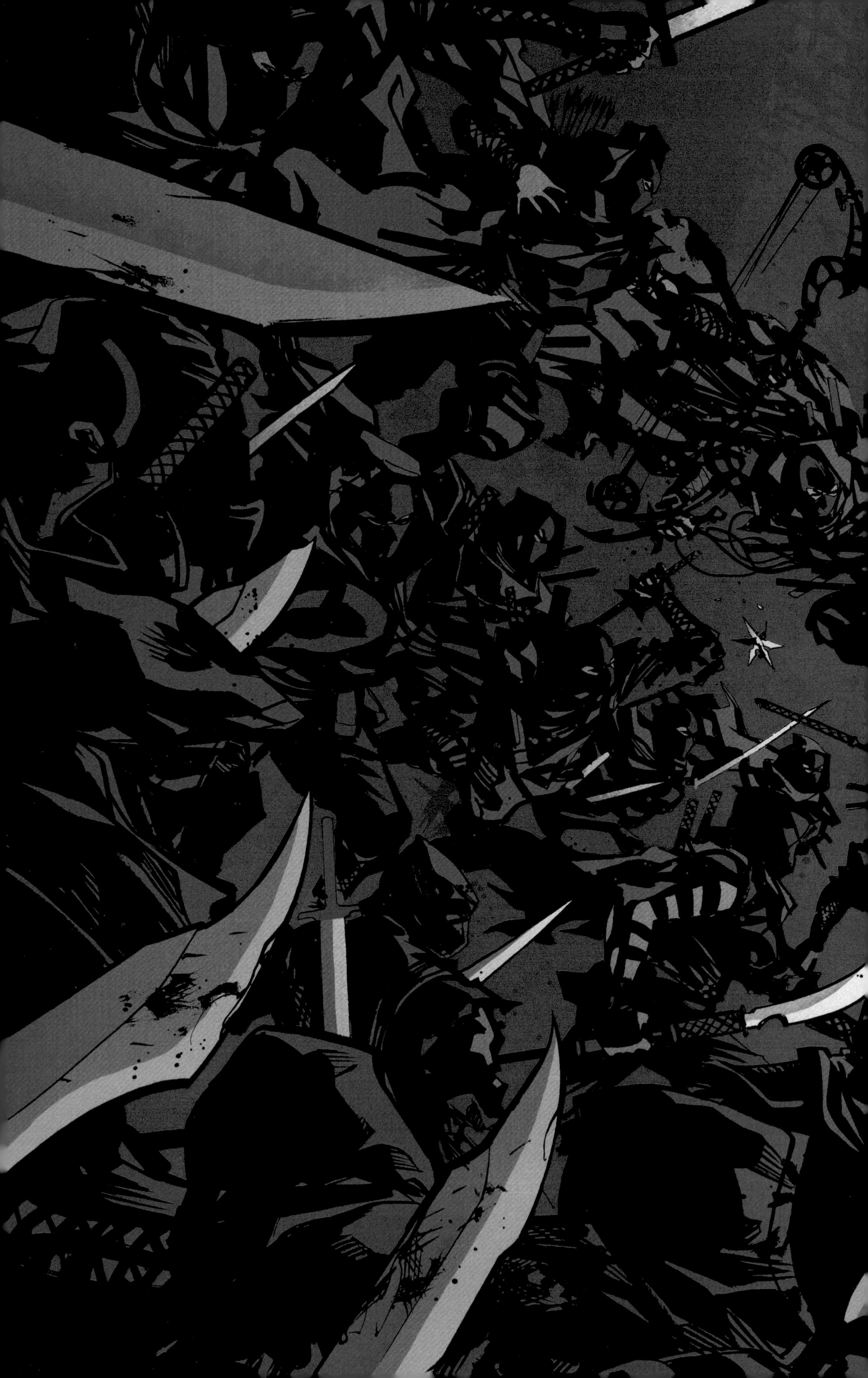

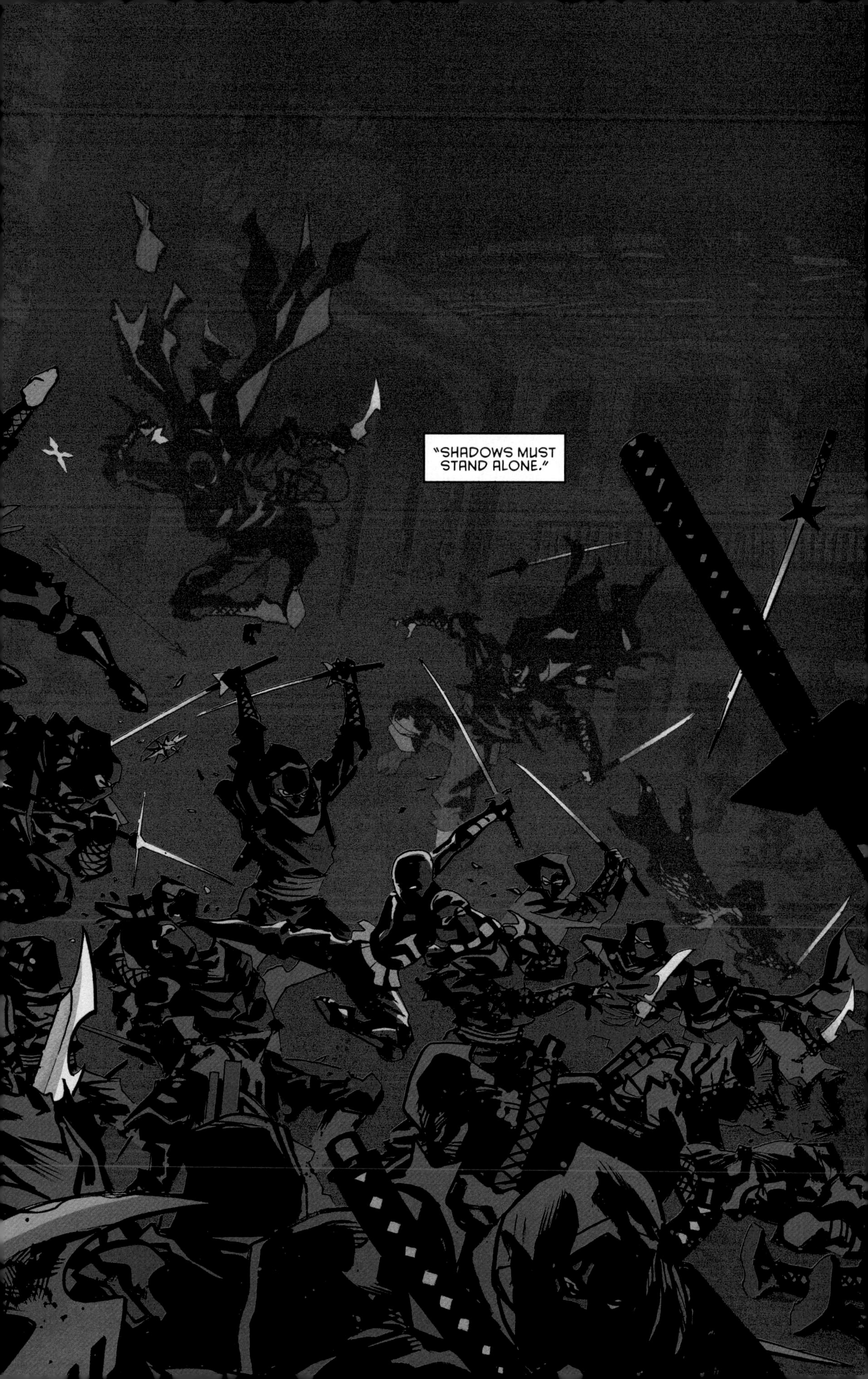
"SHADOWS MUST STAND ALONE."

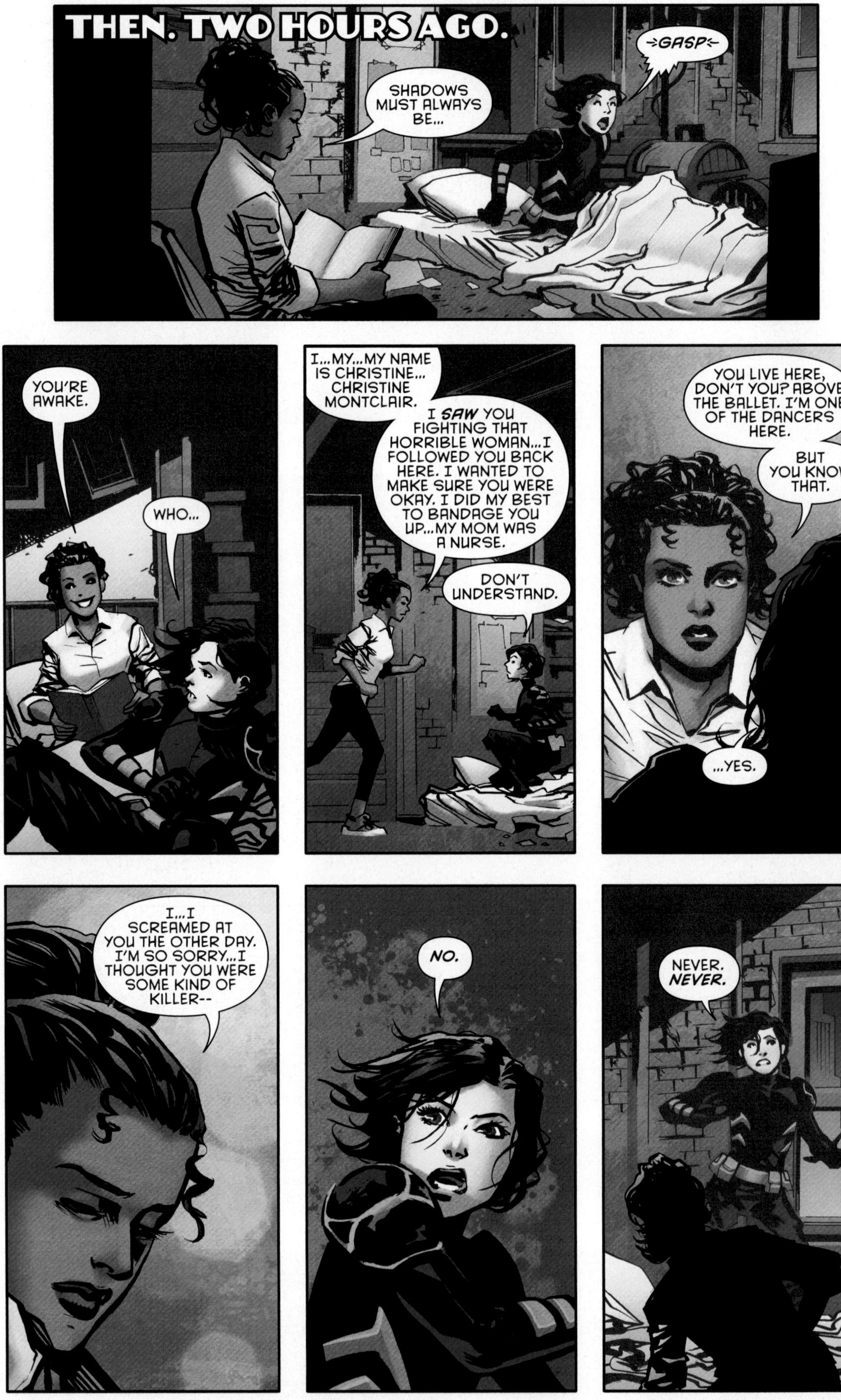
THEN. TWO HOURS AGO.
SHADOWS MUST ALWAYS BE...
GASP
YOU'RE AWAKE.
WHO...
I...MY...MY NAME IS CHRISTINE... CHRISTINE MONTCLAIR.
I SAW YOU FIGHTING THAT HORRIBLE WOMAN...I FOLLOWED YOU BACK HERE. I WANTED TO MAKE SURE YOU WERE OKAY. I DID MY BEST TO BANDAGE YOU UP...MY MOM WAS A NURSE.
DON'T UNDERSTAND.
YOU LIVE HERE, DON'T YOU? ABOVE THE BALLET. I'M ONE OF THE DANCERS HERE.
BUT YOU KNOW THAT.
...YES.
I...I SCREAMED AT YOU THE OTHER DAY. I'M SO SORRY...I THOUGHT YOU WERE SOME KIND OF KILLER--
NO.
NEVER. NEVER.

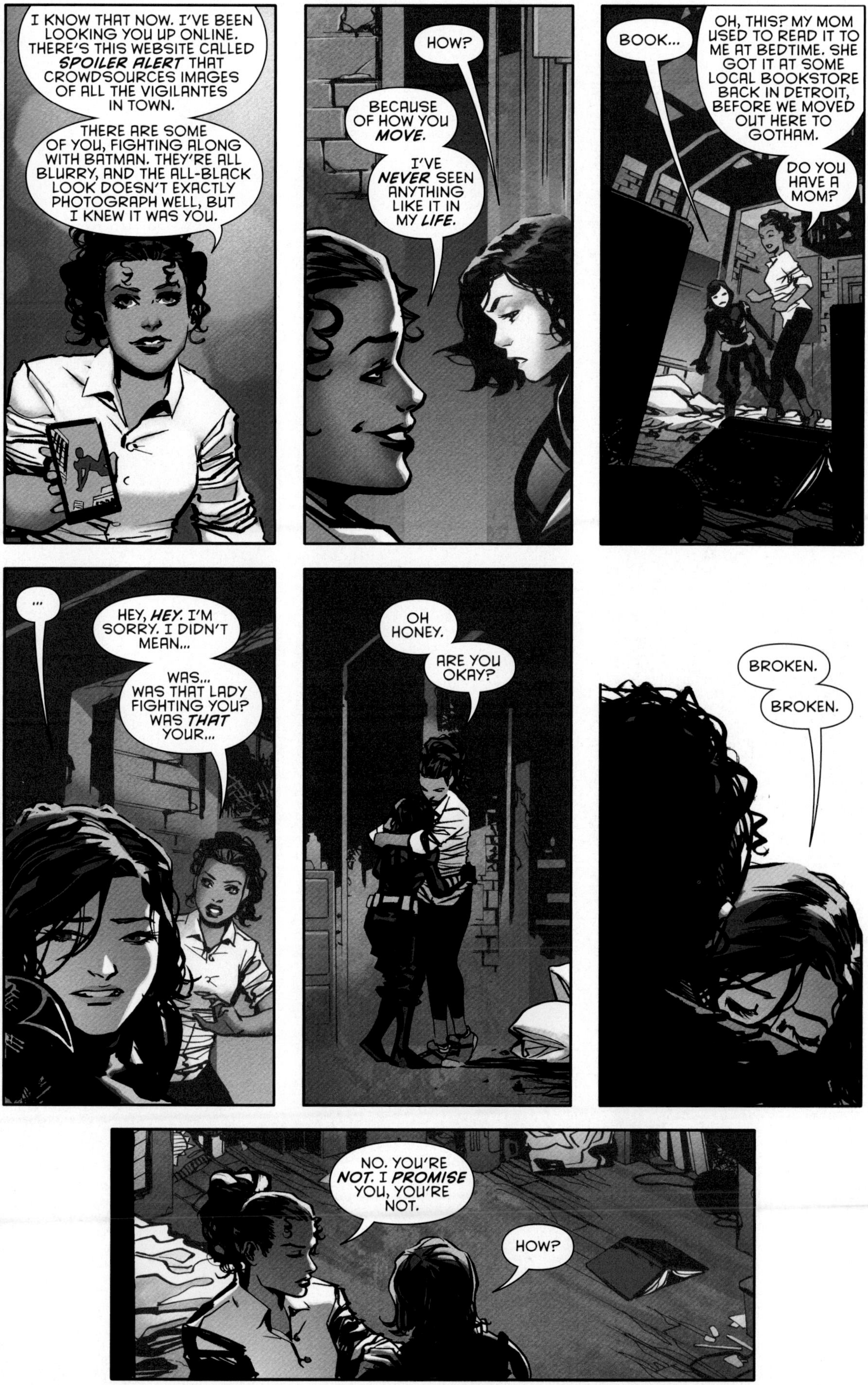
I KNOW THAT NOW. I'VE BEEN LOOKING YOU UP ONLINE. THERE'S THIS WEBSITE CALLED ***SPOILER ALERT*** THAT CROWDSOURCES IMAGES OF ALL THE VIGILANTES IN TOWN.
THERE ARE SOME OF YOU, FIGHTING ALONG WITH BATMAN. THEY'RE ALL BLURRY, AND THE ALL-BLACK LOOK DOESN'T EXACTLY PHOTOGRAPH WELL, BUT I KNEW IT WAS YOU.
HOW?
BECAUSE OF HOW YOU ***MOVE***.
I'VE ***NEVER*** SEEN ANYTHING LIKE IT IN MY ***LIFE***.
BOOK...
OH, THIS? MY MOM USED TO READ IT TO ME AT BEDTIME. SHE GOT IT AT SOME LOCAL BOOKSTORE BACK IN DETROIT, BEFORE WE MOVED OUT HERE TO GOTHAM.
DO YOU HAVE A MOM?
...
HEY, ***HEY***. I'M SORRY. I DIDN'T MEAN...
WAS... WAS THAT LADY FIGHTING YOU? WAS ***THAT*** YOUR...
OH HONEY.
ARE YOU OKAY?
BROKEN.
BROKEN.
NO. YOU'RE ***NOT***. I ***PROMISE*** YOU, YOU'RE NOT.
HOW?

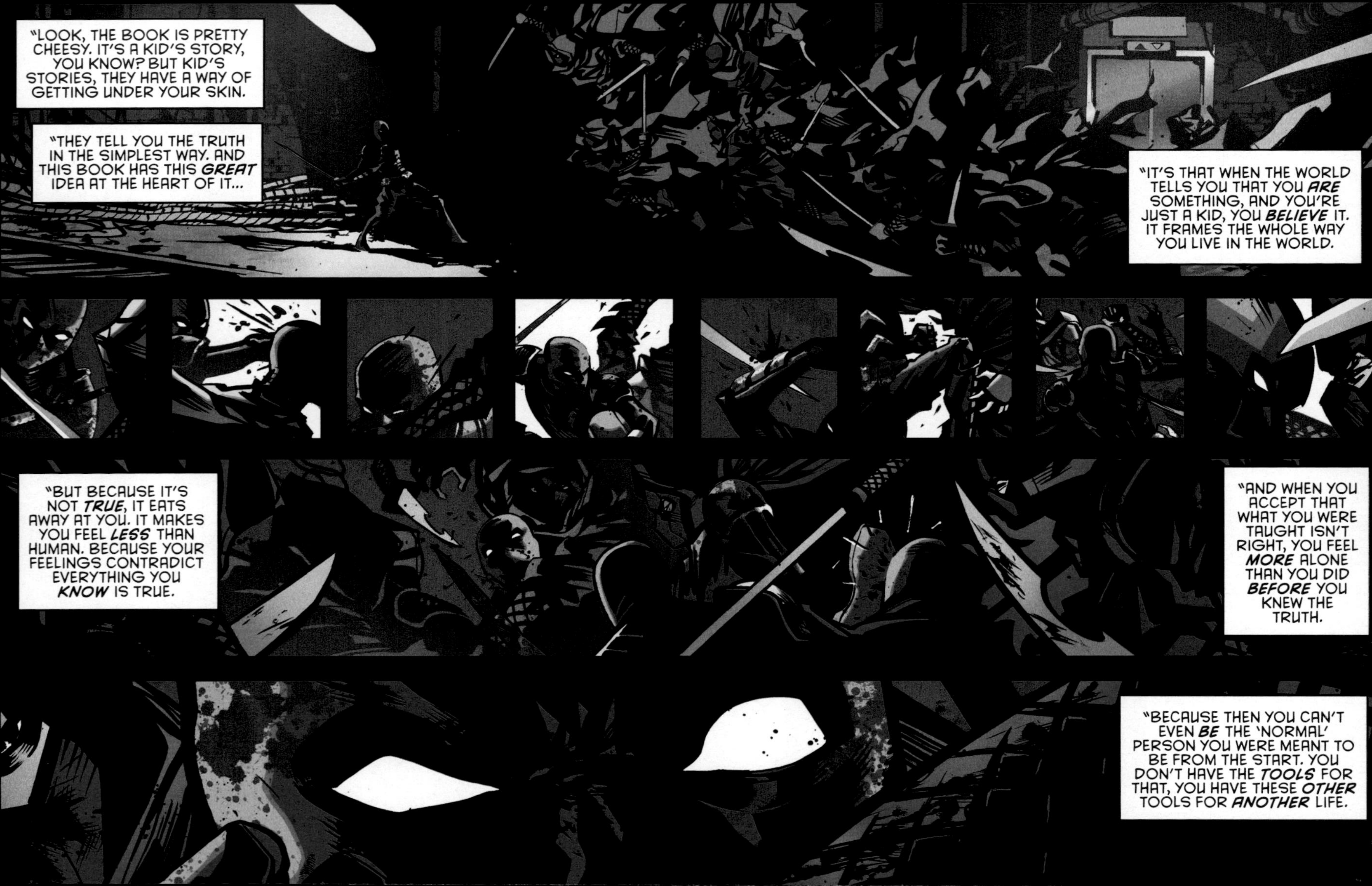
"LOOK, THE BOOK IS PRETTY CHEESY. IT'S A KID'S STORY, YOU KNOW? BUT KID'S STORIES, THEY HAVE A WAY OF GETTING UNDER YOUR SKIN.
"THEY TELL YOU THE TRUTH IN THE SIMPLEST WAY. AND THIS BOOK HAS THIS *GREAT* IDEA AT THE HEART OF IT...
"IT'S THAT WHEN THE WORLD TELLS YOU THAT YOU *ARE* SOMETHING, AND YOU'RE JUST A KID, YOU *BELIEVE* IT. IT FRAMES THE WHOLE WAY YOU LIVE IN THE WORLD.
"BUT BECAUSE IT'S NOT *TRUE*, IT EATS AWAY AT YOU. IT MAKES YOU FEEL *LESS* THAN HUMAN. BECAUSE YOUR FEELINGS CONTRADICT EVERYTHING YOU *KNOW* IS TRUE.
"AND WHEN YOU ACCEPT THAT WHAT YOU WERE TAUGHT ISN'T RIGHT, YOU FEEL *MORE* ALONE THAN YOU DID *BEFORE* YOU KNEW THE TRUTH.
"BECAUSE THEN YOU CAN'T EVEN *BE* THE 'NORMAL' PERSON YOU WERE MEANT TO BE FROM THE START. YOU DON'T HAVE THE *TOOLS* FOR THAT, YOU HAVE THESE *OTHER* TOOLS FOR *ANOTHER* LIFE.

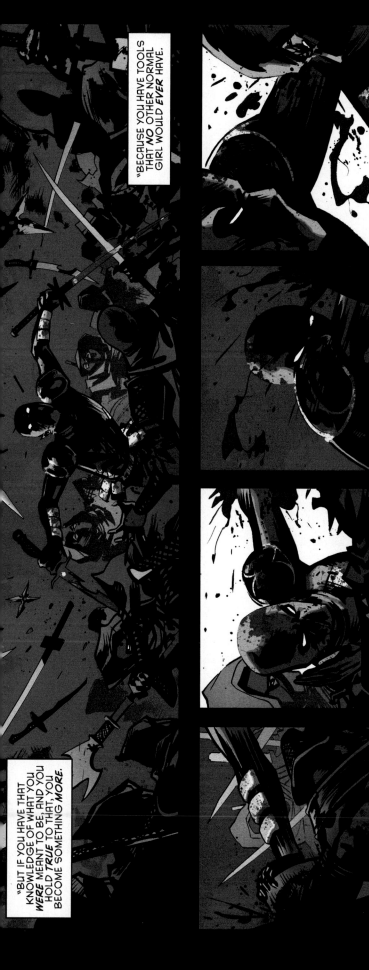

"BECAUSE YOU HAVE TOOLS THAT *NO* OTHER NORMAL GIRL WOULD *EVER* HAVE.

"YOU HAVE THE TOOLS TO FINALLY, TRULY *KNOW* YOURSELF."

"BUT IF YOU HAVE THAT KNOWLEDGE OF WHAT YOU *WERE* MEANT TO BE, AND YOU HOLD *TRUE* TO THAT, YOU BECOME SOMETHING *MORE.*

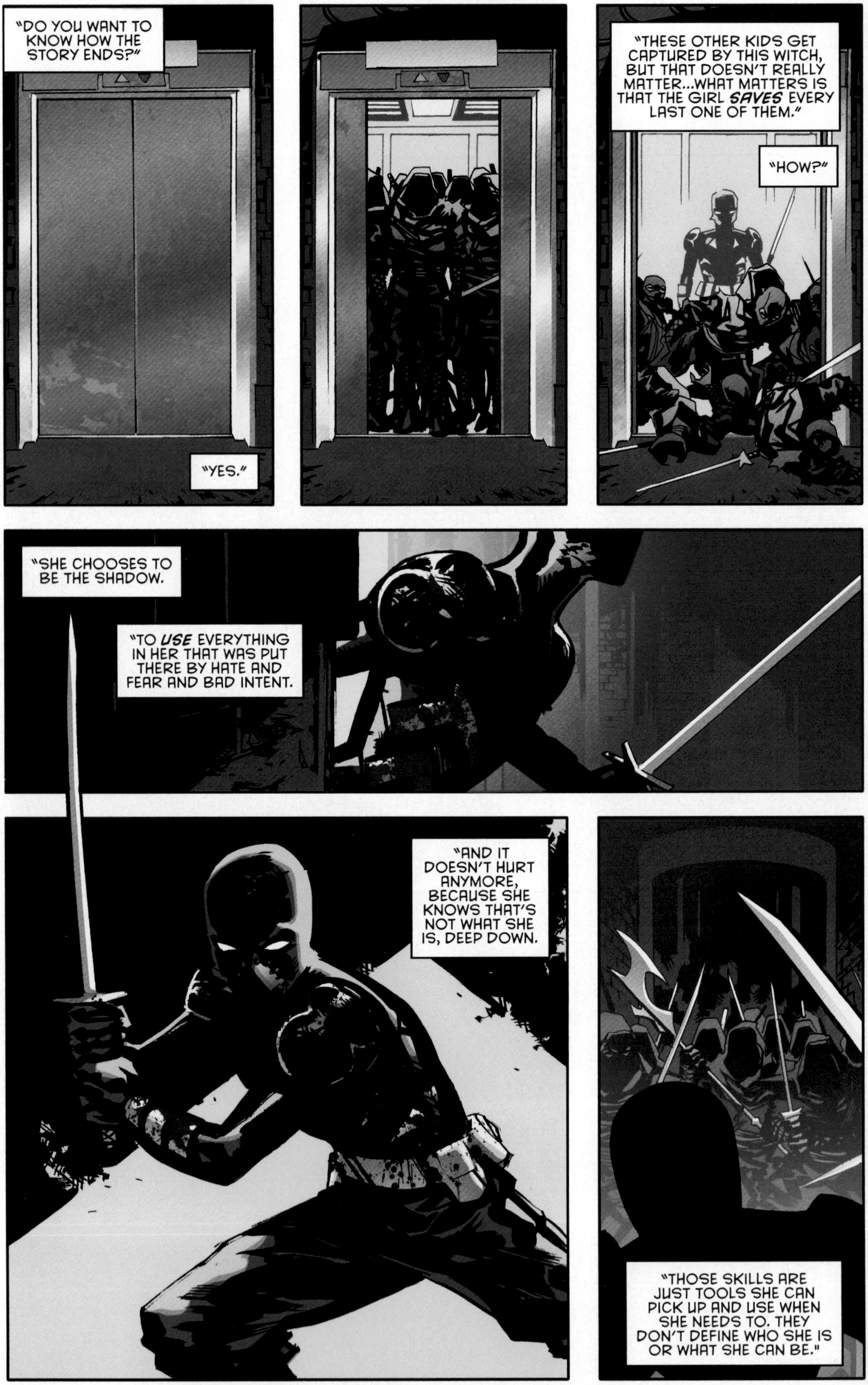
"DO YOU WANT TO KNOW HOW THE STORY ENDS?"
"YES."
"THESE OTHER KIDS GET CAPTURED BY THIS WITCH, BUT THAT DOESN'T REALLY MATTER...WHAT MATTERS IS THAT THE GIRL SAVES EVERY LAST ONE OF THEM."
"HOW?"
"SHE CHOOSES TO BE THE SHADOW.
"TO USE EVERYTHING IN HER THAT WAS PUT THERE BY HATE AND FEAR AND BAD INTENT.
"AND IT DOESN'T HURT ANYMORE, BECAUSE SHE KNOWS THAT'S NOT WHAT SHE IS, DEEP DOWN.
"THOSE SKILLS ARE JUST TOOLS SHE CAN PICK UP AND USE WHEN SHE NEEDS TO. THEY DON'T DEFINE WHO SHE IS OR WHAT SHE CAN BE."

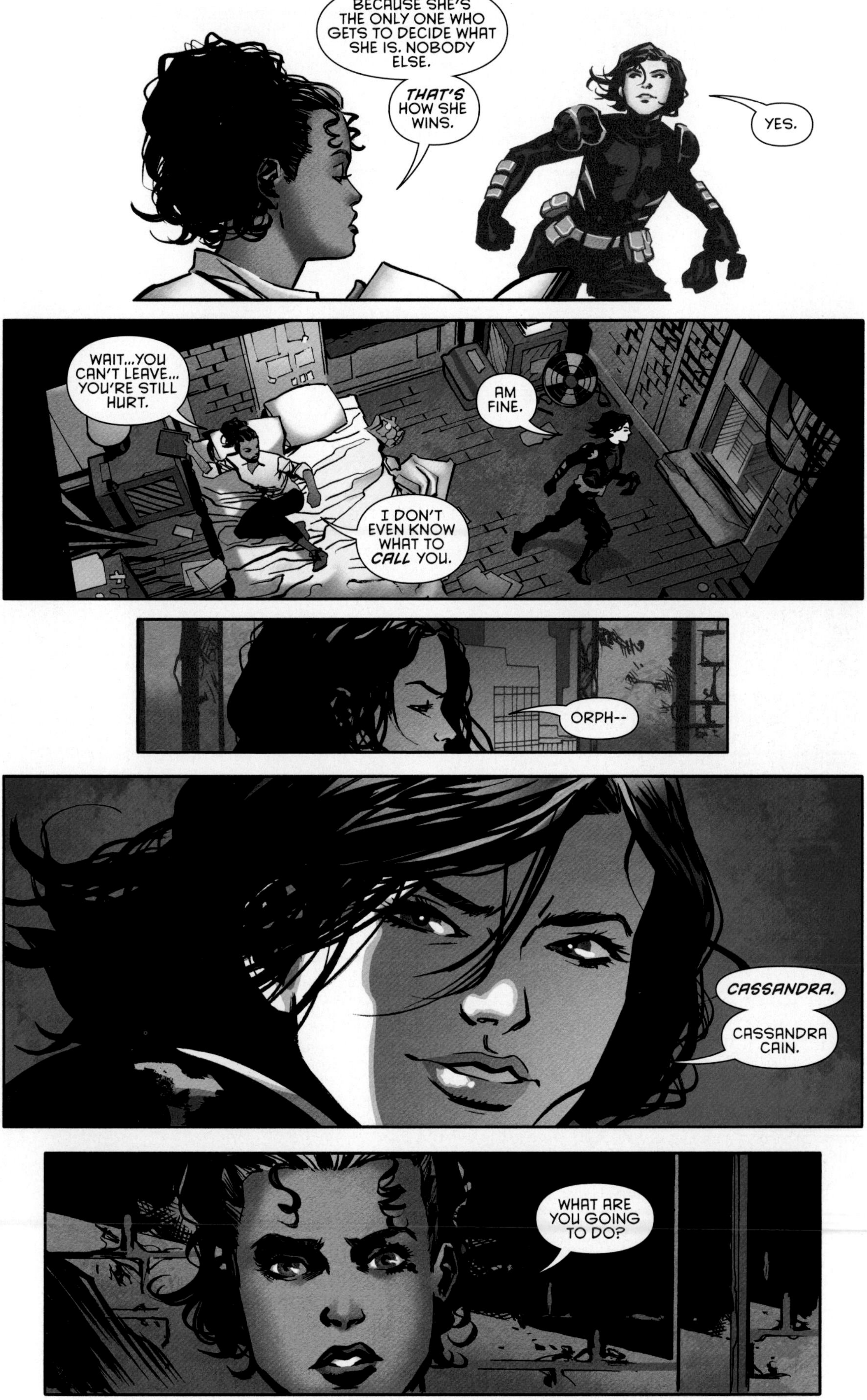
BECAUSE SHE'S THE ONLY ONE WHO GETS TO DECIDE WHAT SHE IS. NOBODY ELSE.
THAT'S HOW SHE WINS.
YES.
WAIT...YOU CAN'T LEAVE... YOU'RE STILL HURT.
AM FINE.
I DON'T EVEN KNOW WHAT TO CALL YOU.
ORPH--
CASSANDRA.
CASSANDRA CAIN.
WHAT ARE YOU GOING TO DO?

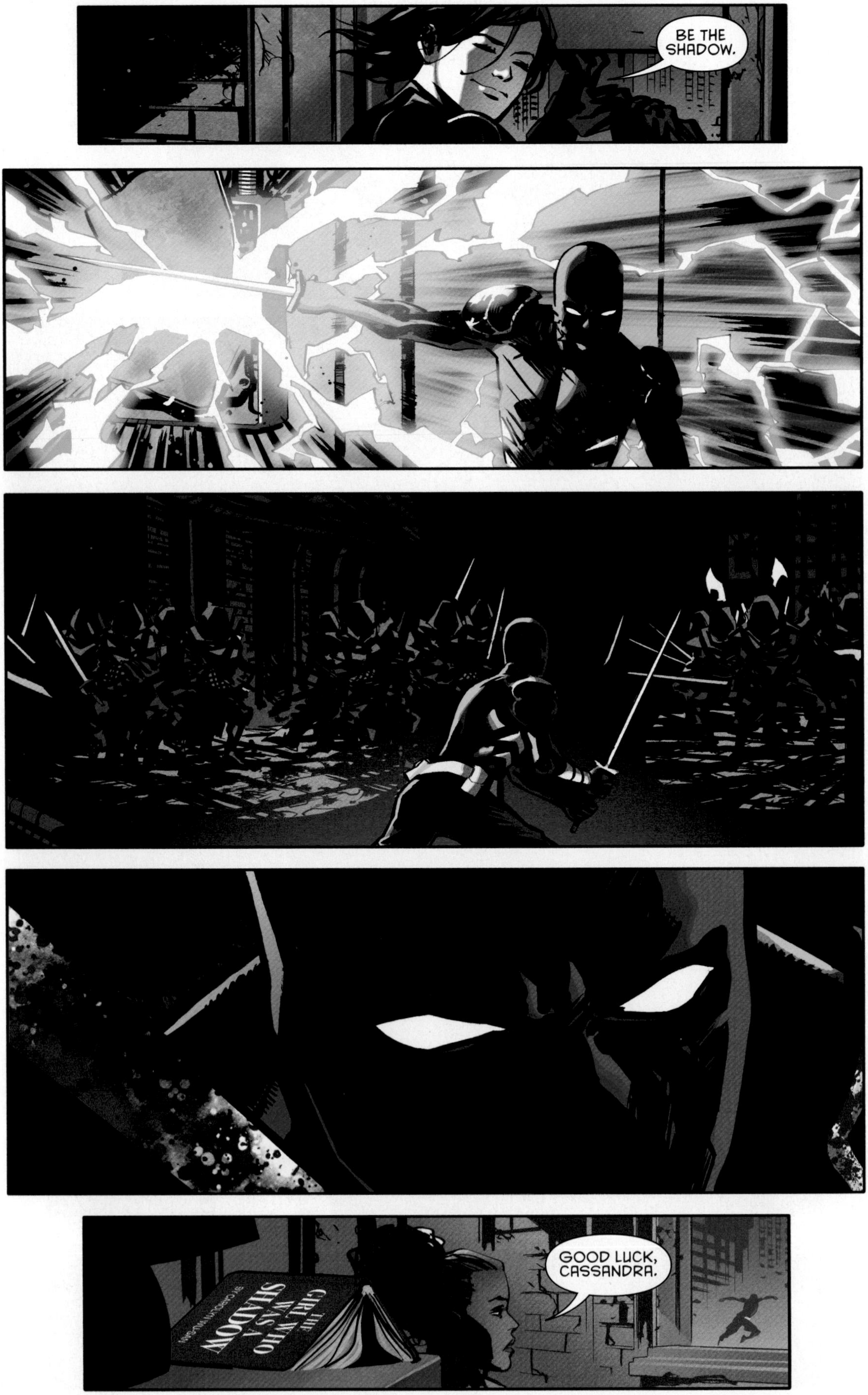
BE THE SHADOW.
GOOD LUCK, CASSANDRA.
THE GIRL WHO WAS A SHADOW

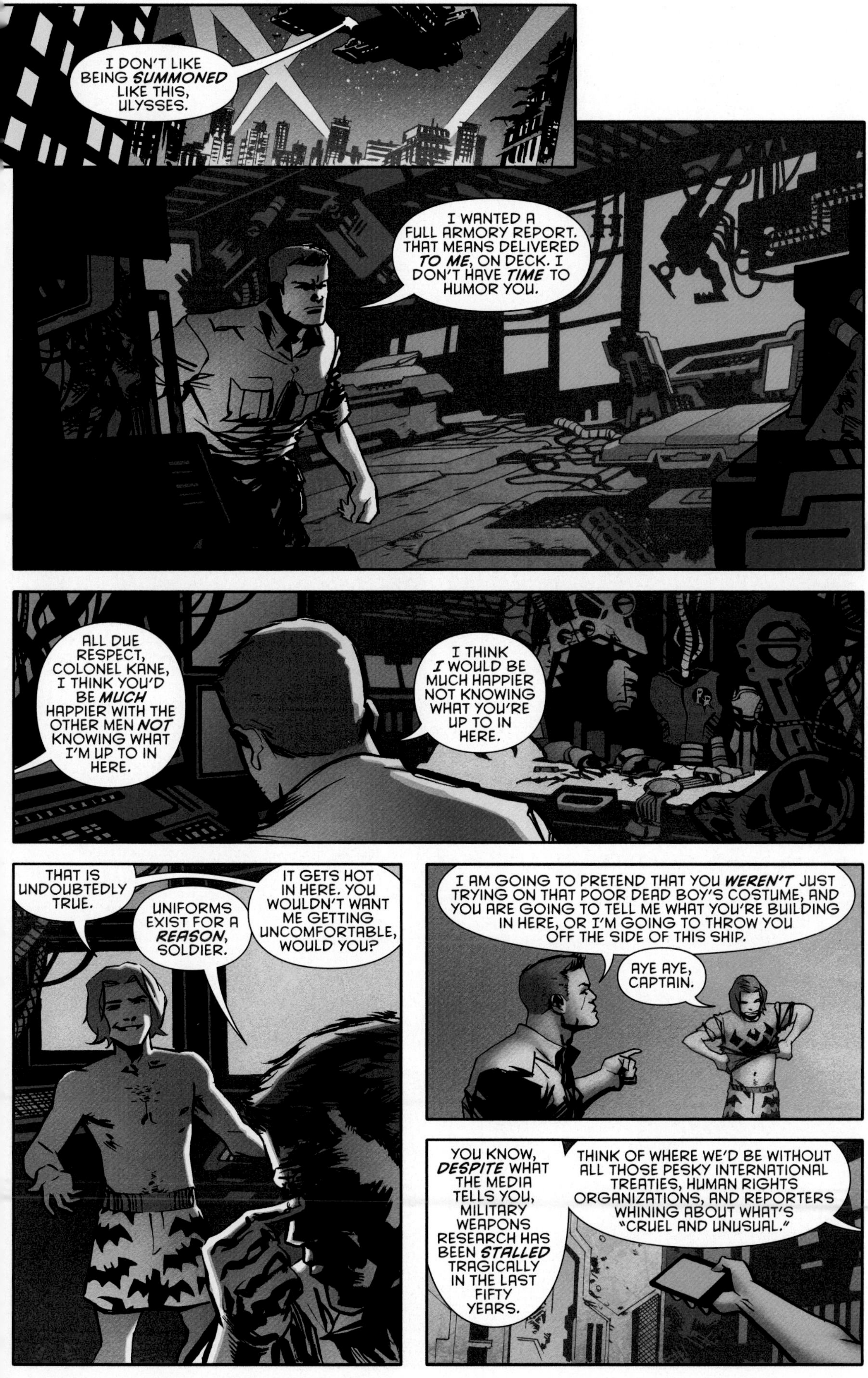
I DON'T LIKE BEING *SUMMONED* LIKE THIS, ULYSSES.
I WANTED A FULL ARMORY REPORT. THAT MEANS DELIVERED *TO ME*, ON DECK. I DON'T HAVE *TIME* TO HUMOR YOU.
ALL DUE RESPECT, COLONEL KANE, I THINK YOU'D BE *MUCH* HAPPIER WITH THE OTHER MEN *NOT* KNOWING WHAT I'M UP TO IN HERE.
I THINK *I* WOULD BE MUCH HAPPIER NOT KNOWING WHAT YOU'RE UP TO IN HERE.
IT GETS HOT IN HERE. YOU WOULDN'T WANT ME GETTING UNCOMFORTABLE, WOULD YOU?
UNIFORMS EXIST FOR A *REASON*, SOLDIER.
THAT IS UNDOUBTEDLY TRUE.
I AM GOING TO PRETEND THAT YOU *WEREN'T* JUST TRYING ON THAT POOR DEAD BOY'S COSTUME, AND YOU ARE GOING TO TELL ME WHAT YOU'RE BUILDING IN HERE, OR I'M GOING TO THROW YOU OFF THE SIDE OF THIS SHIP.
AYE AYE, CAPTAIN.
YOU KNOW, *DESPITE* WHAT THE MEDIA TELLS YOU, MILITARY WEAPONS RESEARCH HAS BEEN *STALLED* TRAGICALLY IN THE LAST FIFTY YEARS.
THINK OF WHERE WE'D BE WITHOUT ALL THOSE PESKY INTERNATIONAL TREATIES, HUMAN RIGHTS ORGANIZATIONS, AND REPORTERS WHINING ABOUT WHAT'S "CRUEL AND UNUSUAL."

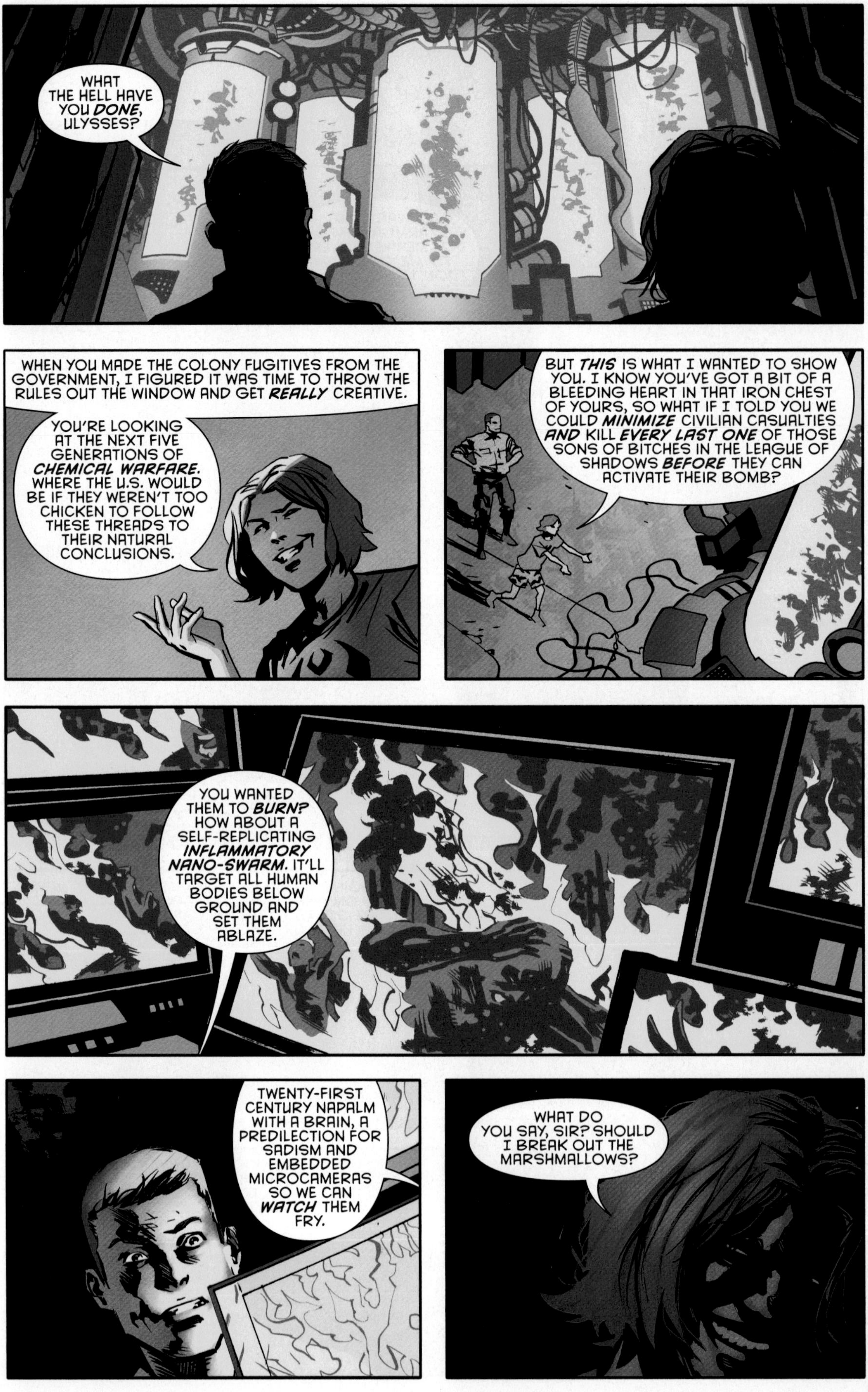
WHAT THE HELL HAVE YOU DONE, ULYSSES?
WHEN YOU MADE THE COLONY FUGITIVES FROM THE GOVERNMENT, I FIGURED IT WAS TIME TO THROW THE RULES OUT THE WINDOW AND GET REALLY CREATIVE.
YOU'RE LOOKING AT THE NEXT FIVE GENERATIONS OF CHEMICAL WARFARE. WHERE THE U.S. WOULD BE IF THEY WEREN'T TOO CHICKEN TO FOLLOW THESE THREADS TO THEIR NATURAL CONCLUSIONS.
BUT THIS IS WHAT I WANTED TO SHOW YOU. I KNOW YOU'VE GOT A BIT OF A BLEEDING HEART IN THAT IRON CHEST OF YOURS, SO WHAT IF I TOLD YOU WE COULD MINIMIZE CIVILIAN CASUALTIES AND KILL EVERY LAST ONE OF THOSE SONS OF BITCHES IN THE LEAGUE OF SHADOWS BEFORE THEY CAN ACTIVATE THEIR BOMB?
YOU WANTED THEM TO BURN? HOW ABOUT A SELF-REPLICATING INFLAMMATORY NANO-SWARM. IT'LL TARGET ALL HUMAN BODIES BELOW GROUND AND SET THEM ABLAZE.
TWENTY-FIRST CENTURY NAPALM WITH A BRAIN, A PREDILECTION FOR SADISM AND EMBEDDED MICROCAMERAS SO WE CAN WATCH THEM FRY.
WHAT DO YOU SAY, SIR? SHOULD I BREAK OUT THE MARSHMALLOWS?

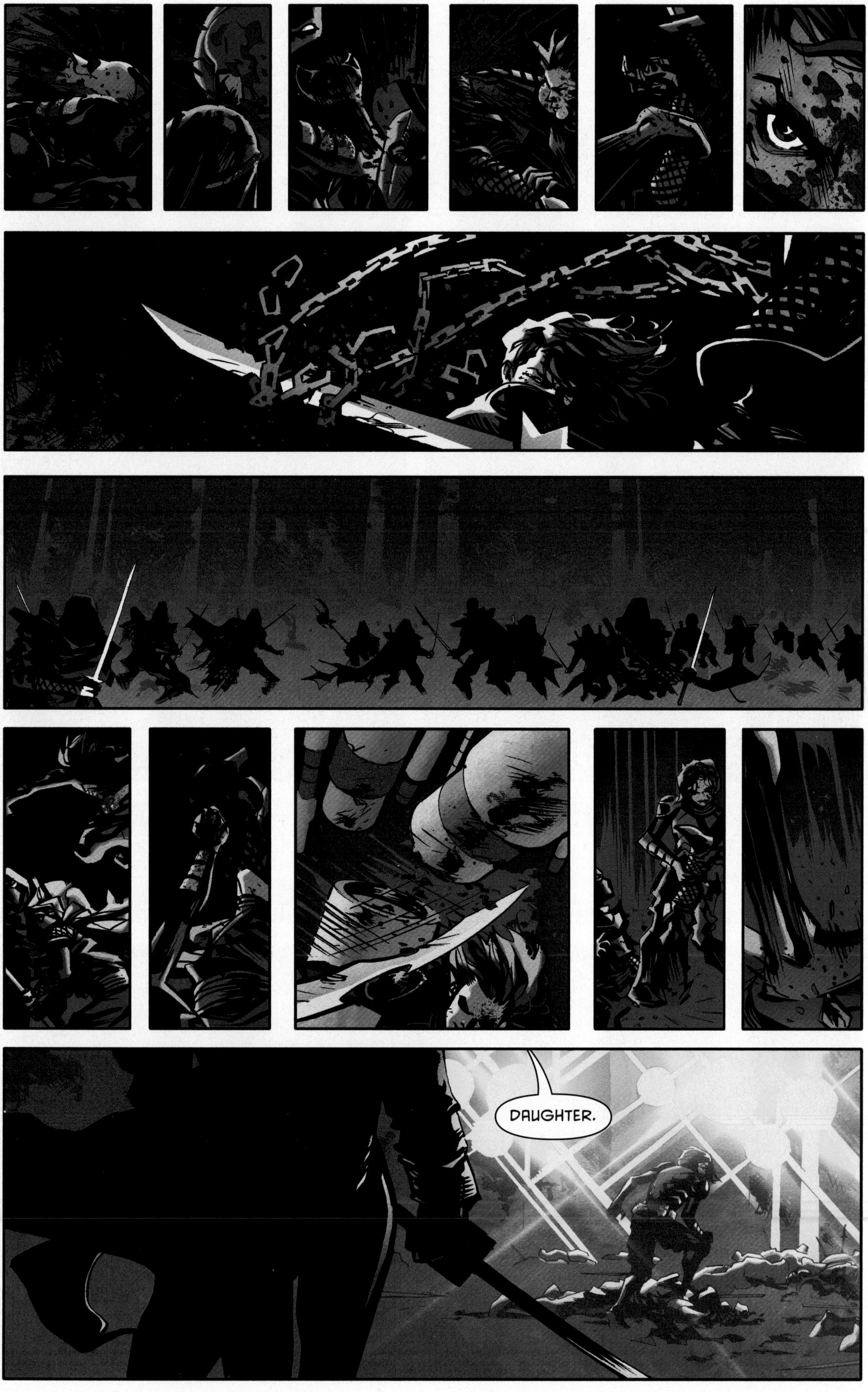
DAUGHTER.

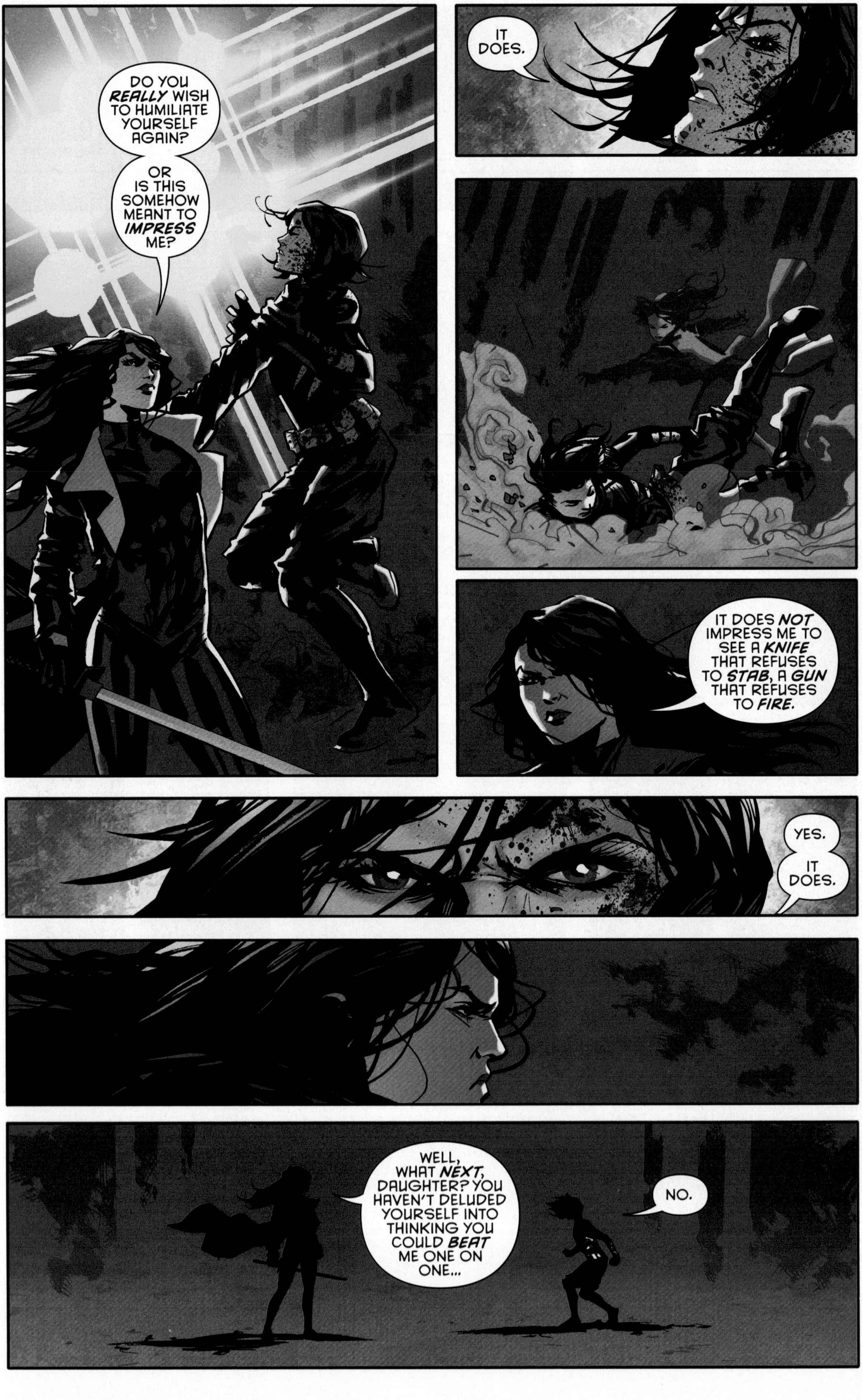
DO YOU REALLY WISH TO HUMILIATE YOURSELF AGAIN?
OR IS THIS SOMEHOW MEANT TO IMPRESS ME?
IT DOES.
IT DOES NOT IMPRESS ME TO SEE A KNIFE THAT REFUSES TO STAB, A GUN THAT REFUSES TO FIRE.
YES.
IT DOES.
WELL, WHAT NEXT, DAUGHTER? YOU HAVEN'T DELUDED YOURSELF INTO THINKING YOU COULD BEAT ME ONE ON ONE...
NO.

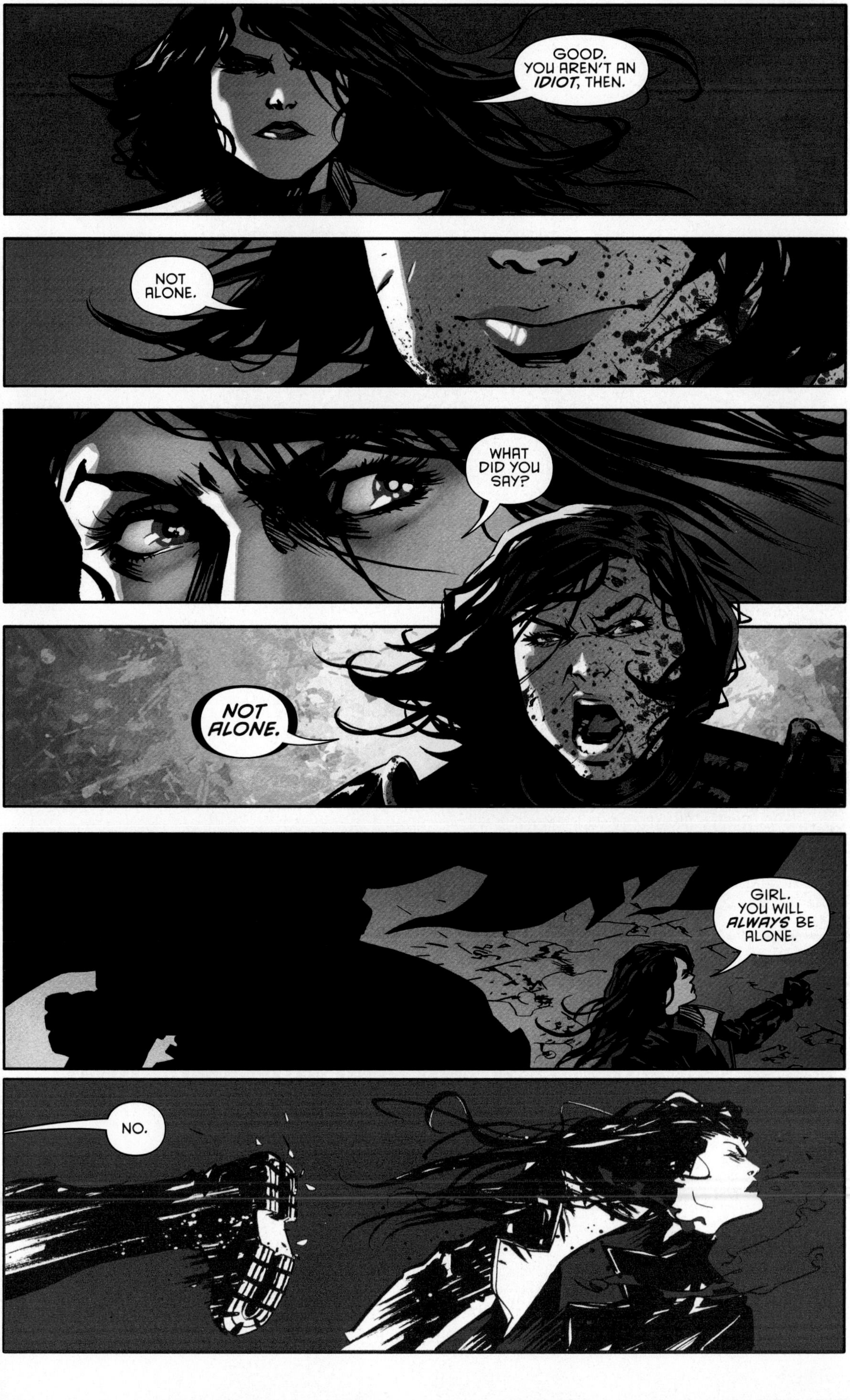
GOOD. YOU AREN'T AN *IDIOT*, THEN.
NOT ALONE.
WHAT DID YOU SAY?
NOT ALONE.
GIRL. YOU WILL *ALWAYS* BE ALONE.
NO.

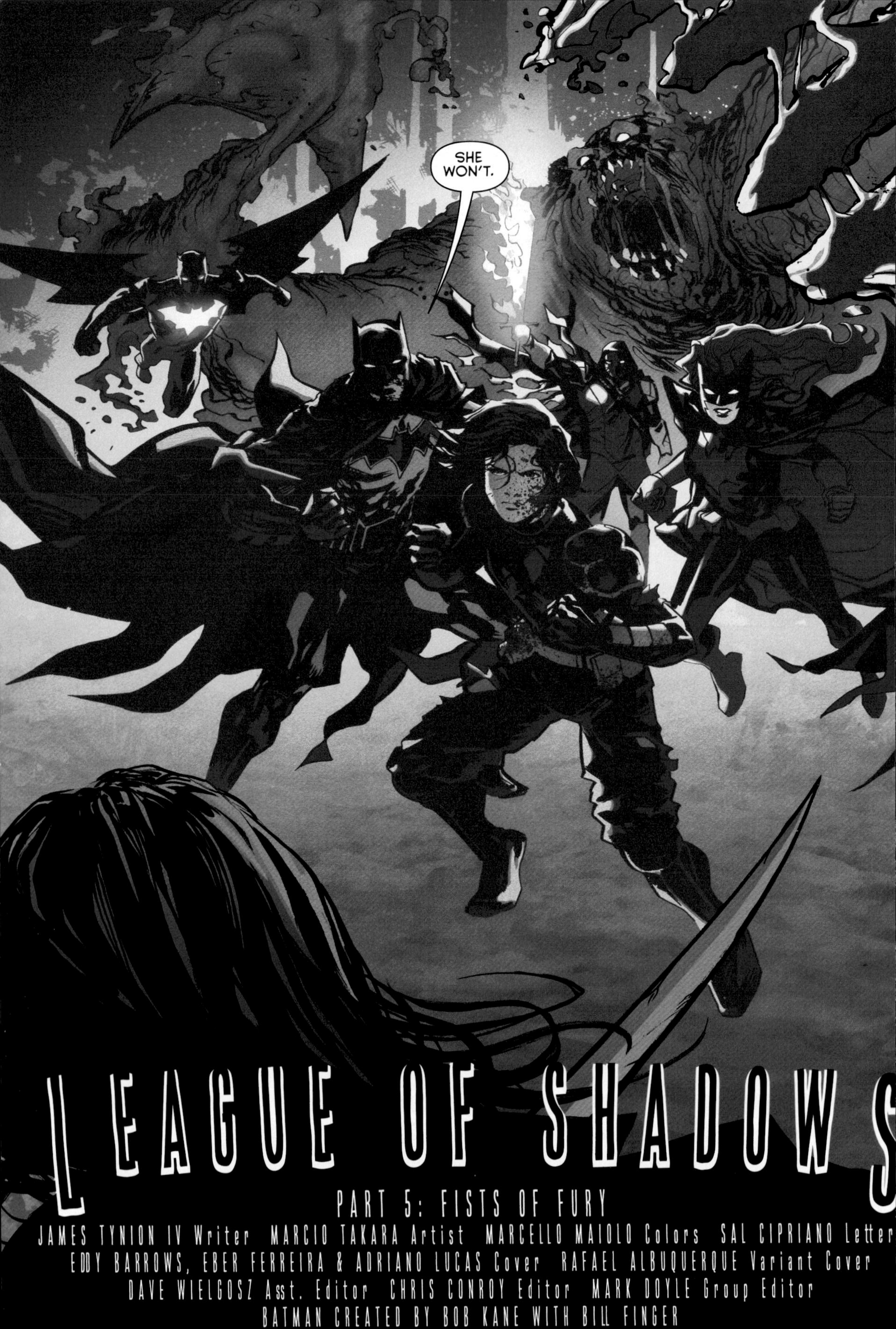
SHE WON'T.
LEAGUE OF SHADOWS
PART 5: FISTS OF FURY
JAMES TYNION IV Writer MARCIO TAKARA Artist MARCELLO MAIOLO Colors SAL CIPRIANO Letter
EDDY BARROWS, EBER FERREIRA & ADRIANO LUCAS Cover RAFAEL ALBUQUERQUE Variant Cover
DAVE WIELGOSZ Asst. Editor CHRIS CONROY Editor MARK DOYLE Group Editor
BATMAN CREATED BY BOB KANE WITH BILL FINGER

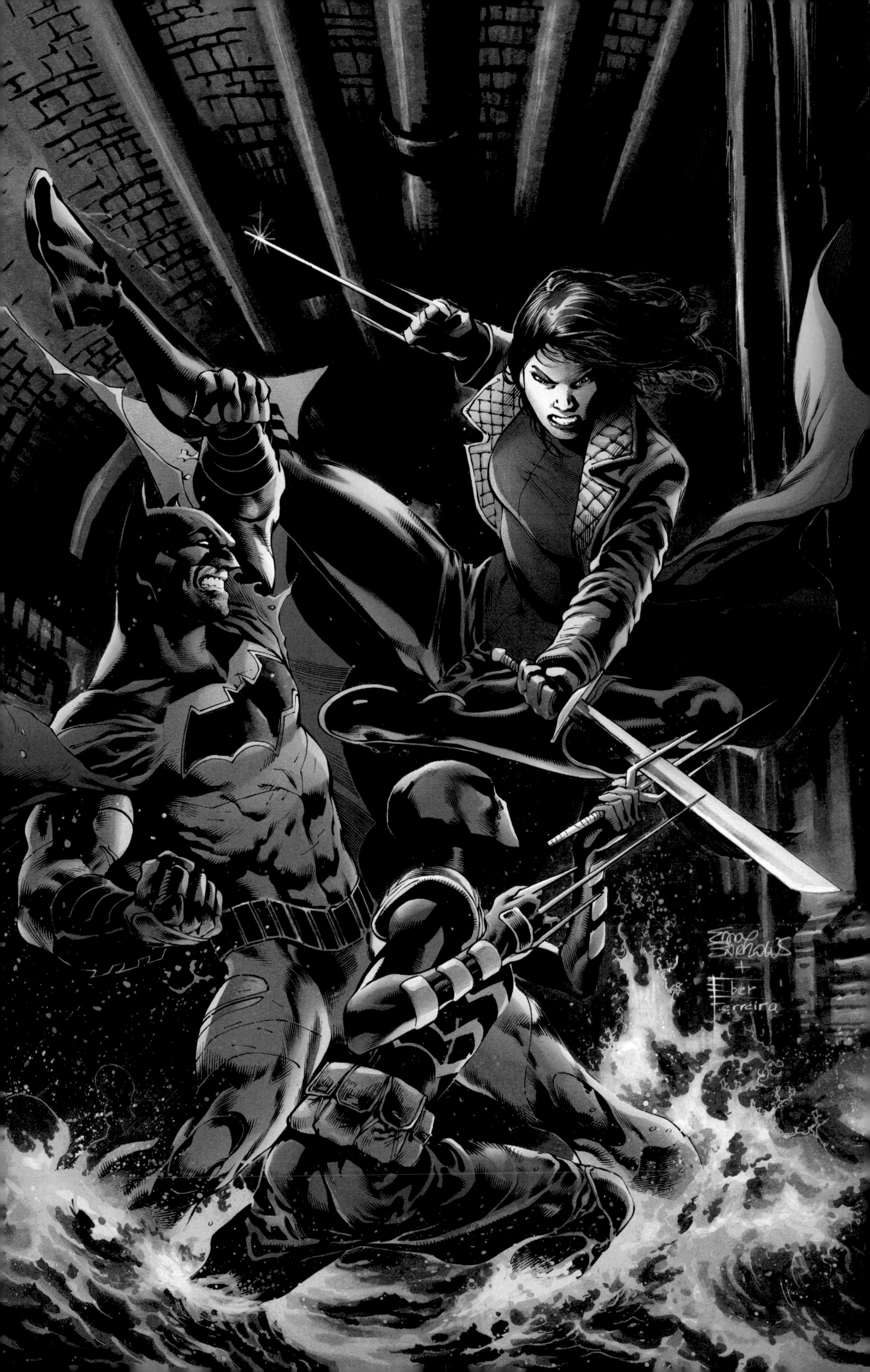

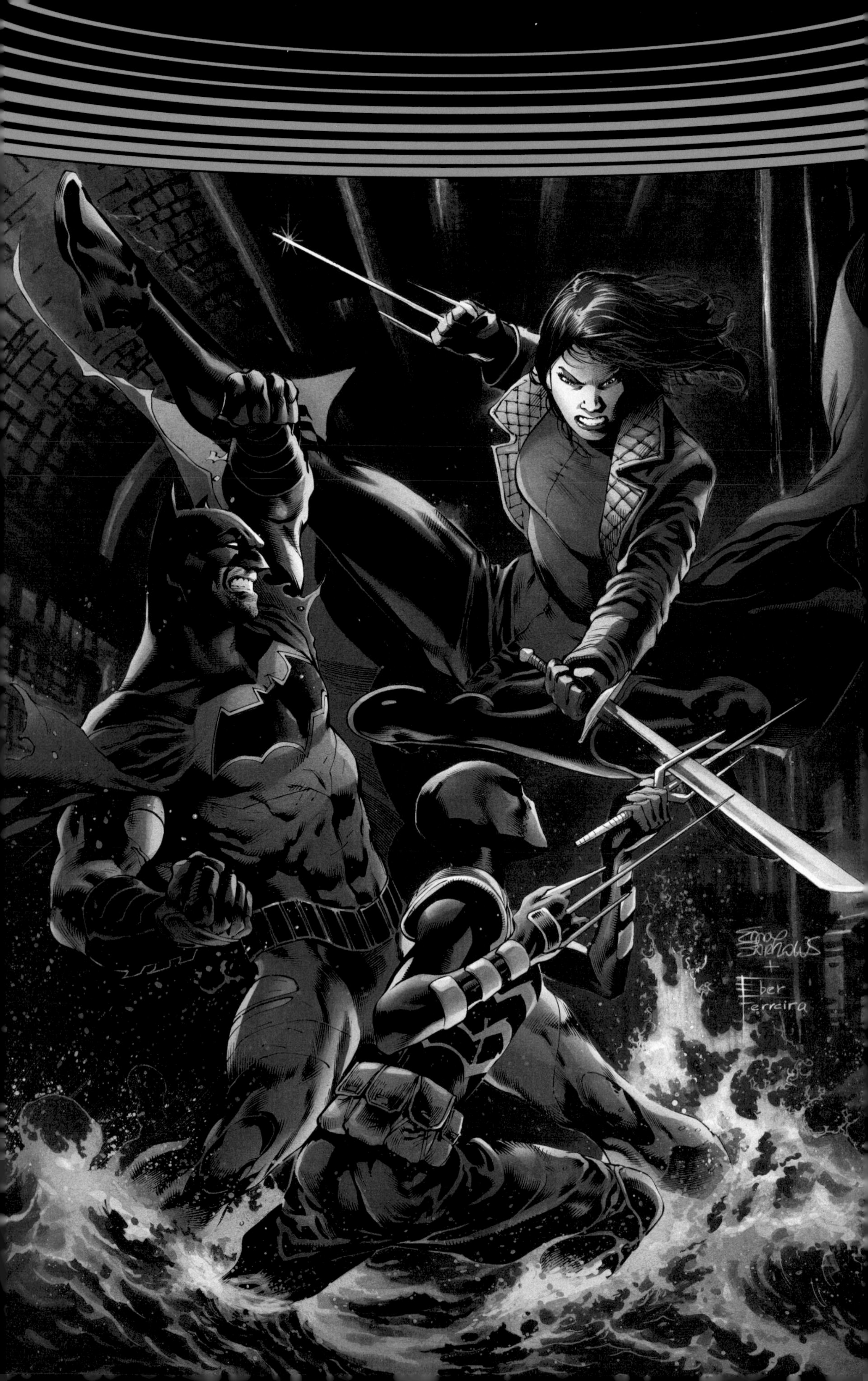
Eber
Ferreira

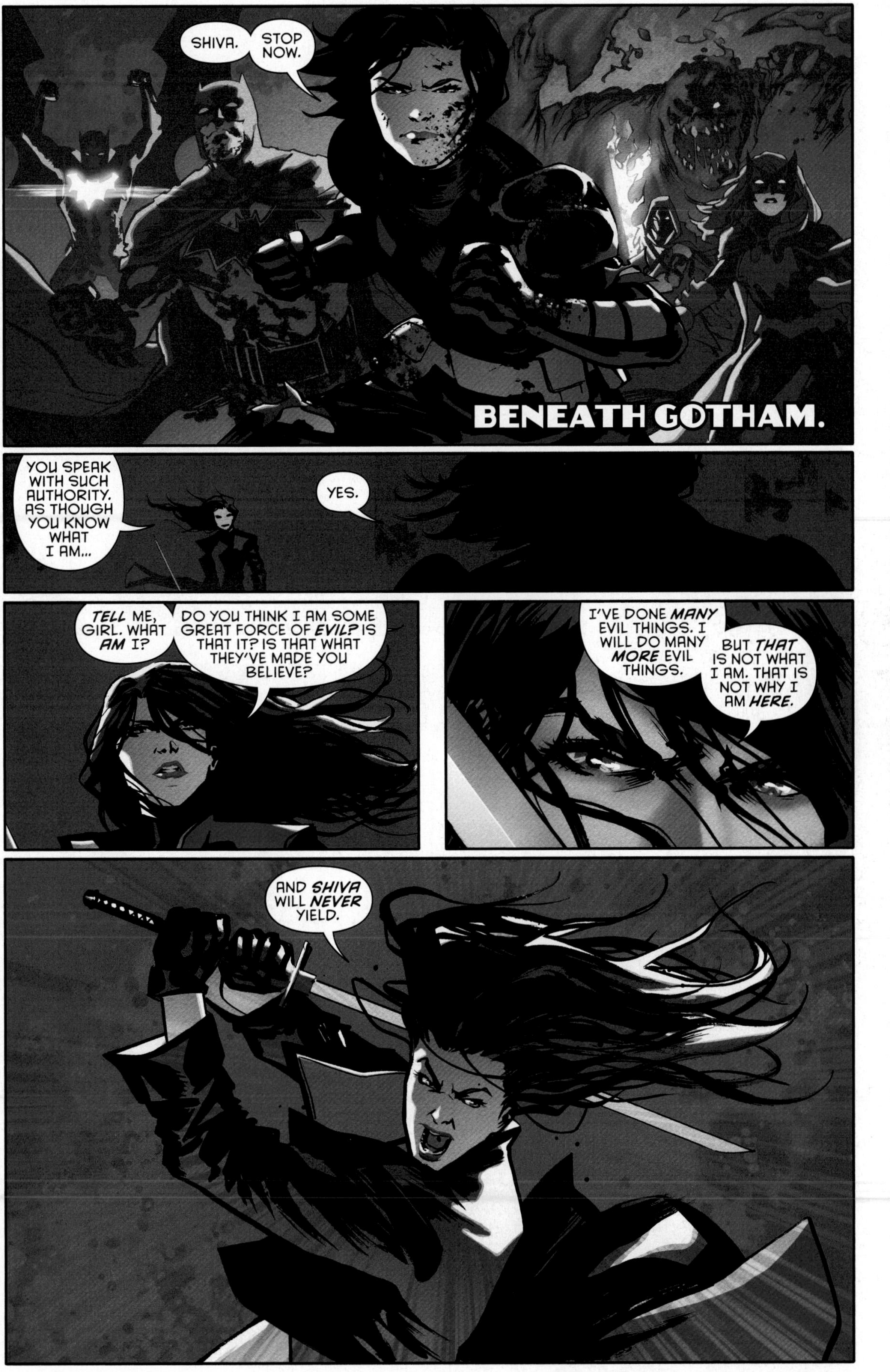
SHIVA.
STOP NOW.
BENEATH GOTHAM.
YOU SPEAK WITH SUCH AUTHORITY. AS THOUGH YOU KNOW WHAT I AM...
YES.
TELL ME, GIRL. WHAT AM I?
DO YOU THINK I AM SOME GREAT FORCE OF EVIL? IS THAT IT? IS THAT WHAT THEY'VE MADE YOU BELIEVE?
I'VE DONE MANY EVIL THINGS. I WILL DO MANY MORE EVIL THINGS.
BUT THAT IS NOT WHAT I AM. THAT IS NOT WHY I AM HERE.
AND SHIVA WILL NEVER YIELD.

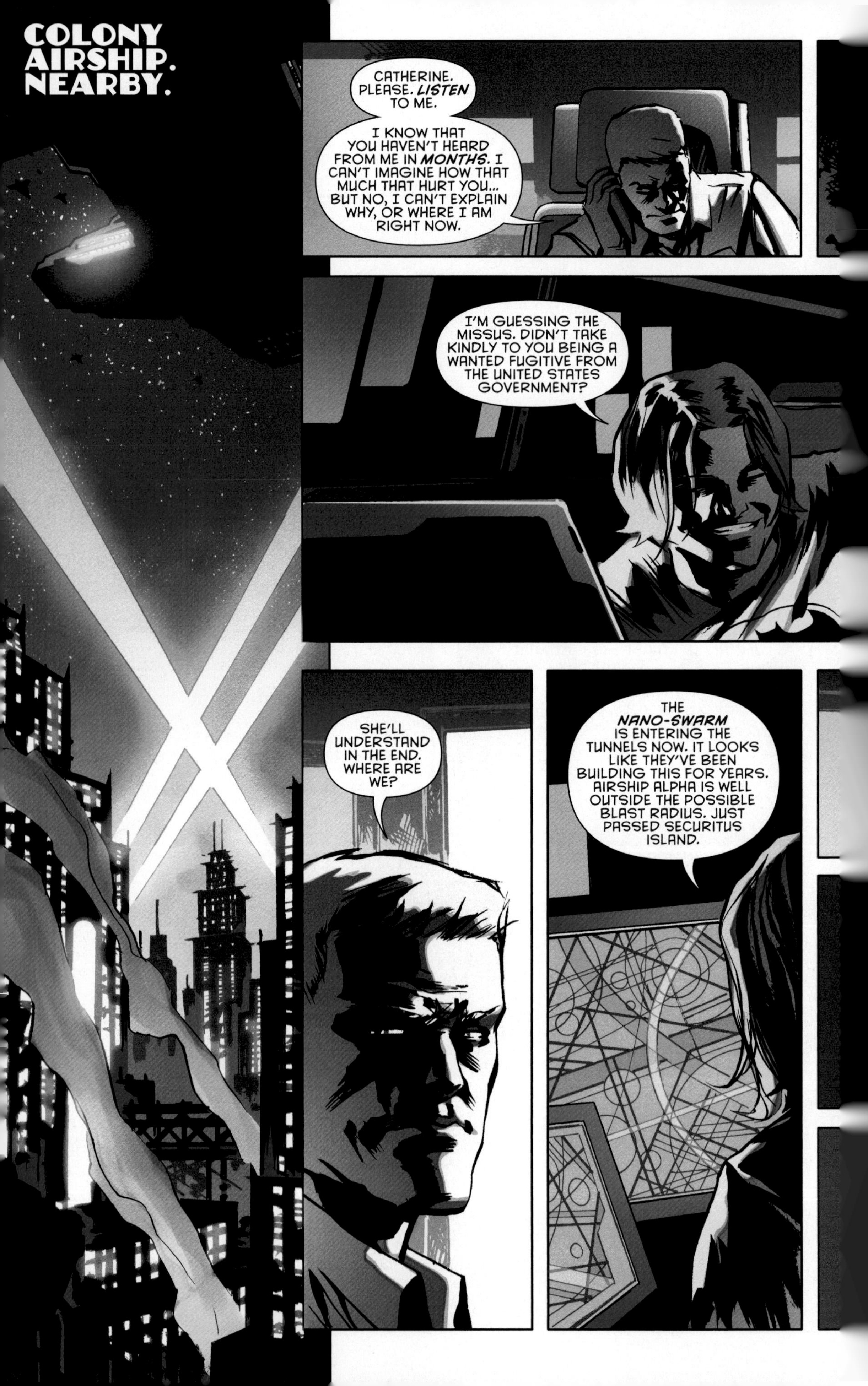
COLONY AIRSHIP. NEARBY.
CATHERINE. PLEASE. LISTEN TO ME.
I KNOW THAT YOU HAVEN'T HEARD FROM ME IN MONTHS. I CAN'T IMAGINE HOW THAT MUCH THAT HURT YOU... BUT NO, I CAN'T EXPLAIN WHY, OR WHERE I AM RIGHT NOW.
I'M GUESSING THE MISSUS. DIDN'T TAKE KINDLY TO YOU BEING A WANTED FUGITIVE FROM THE UNITED STATES GOVERNMENT?
SHE'LL UNDERSTAND IN THE END. WHERE ARE WE?
THE NANO-SWARM IS ENTERING THE TUNNELS NOW. IT LOOKS LIKE THEY'VE BEEN BUILDING THIS FOR YEARS. AIRSHIP ALPHA IS WELL OUTSIDE THE POSSIBLE BLAST RADIUS. JUST PASSED SECURITUS ISLAND.

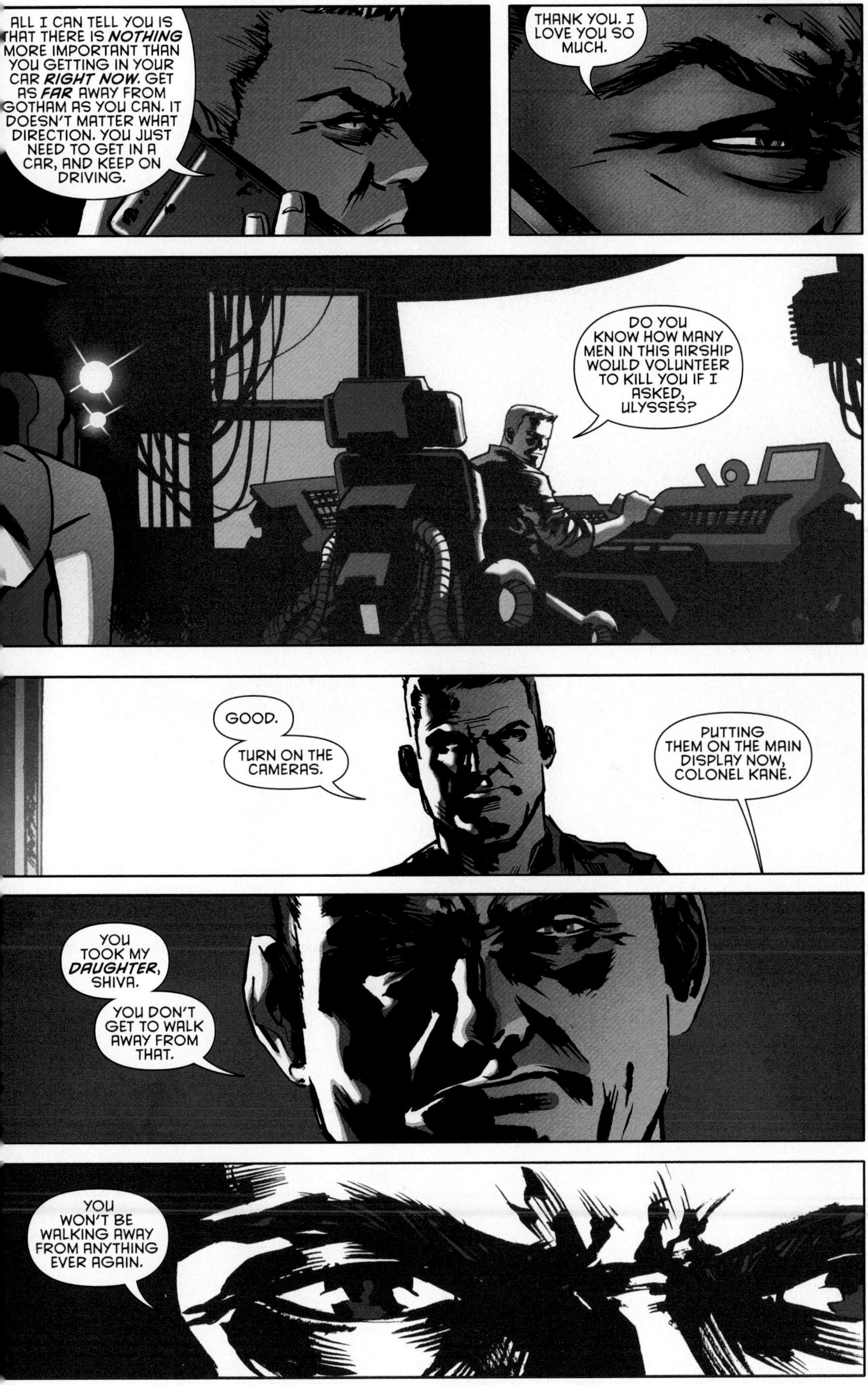
ALL I CAN TELL YOU IS THAT THERE IS *NOTHING* MORE IMPORTANT THAN YOU GETTING IN YOUR CAR *RIGHT NOW*. GET AS *FAR* AWAY FROM GOTHAM AS YOU CAN. IT DOESN'T MATTER WHAT DIRECTION. YOU JUST NEED TO GET IN A CAR, AND KEEP ON DRIVING.
THANK YOU. I LOVE YOU SO MUCH.
DO YOU KNOW HOW MANY MEN IN THIS AIRSHIP WOULD VOLUNTEER TO KILL YOU IF I ASKED, ULYSSES?
GOOD.
TURN ON THE CAMERAS.
PUTTING THEM ON THE MAIN DISPLAY NOW, COLONEL KANE.
YOU TOOK MY *DAUGHTER*, SHIVA.
YOU DON'T GET TO WALK AWAY FROM THAT.
YOU WON'T BE WALKING AWAY FROM ANYTHING EVER AGAIN.

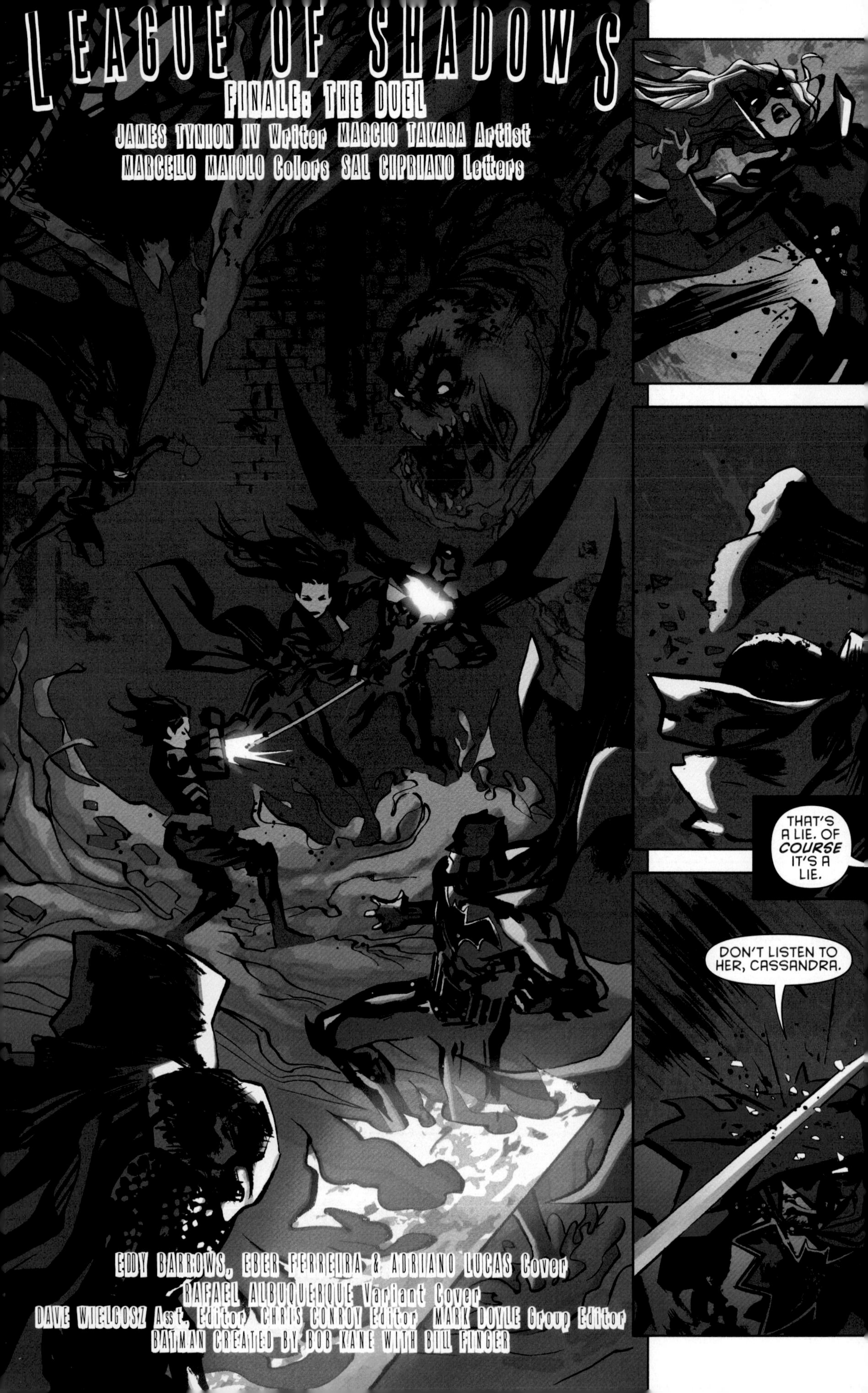
LEAGUE OF SHADOWS
FINALE: THE DUEL
JAMES TYNION IV Writer MARCIO TAKARA Artist
MARCELLO MAIOLO Colors SAL CIPRIANO Letters
EDDY BARROWS, EBER FERREIRA & ADRIANO LUCAS Cover
RAFAEL ALBUQUERQUE Variant Cover
DAVE WIELGOSZ Asst. Editor CHRIS CONROY Editor MARK DOYLE Group Editor
BATMAN CREATED BY BOB KANE WITH BILL FINGER
THAT'S A LIE. OF COURSE IT'S A LIE.
DON'T LISTEN TO HER, CASSANDRA.

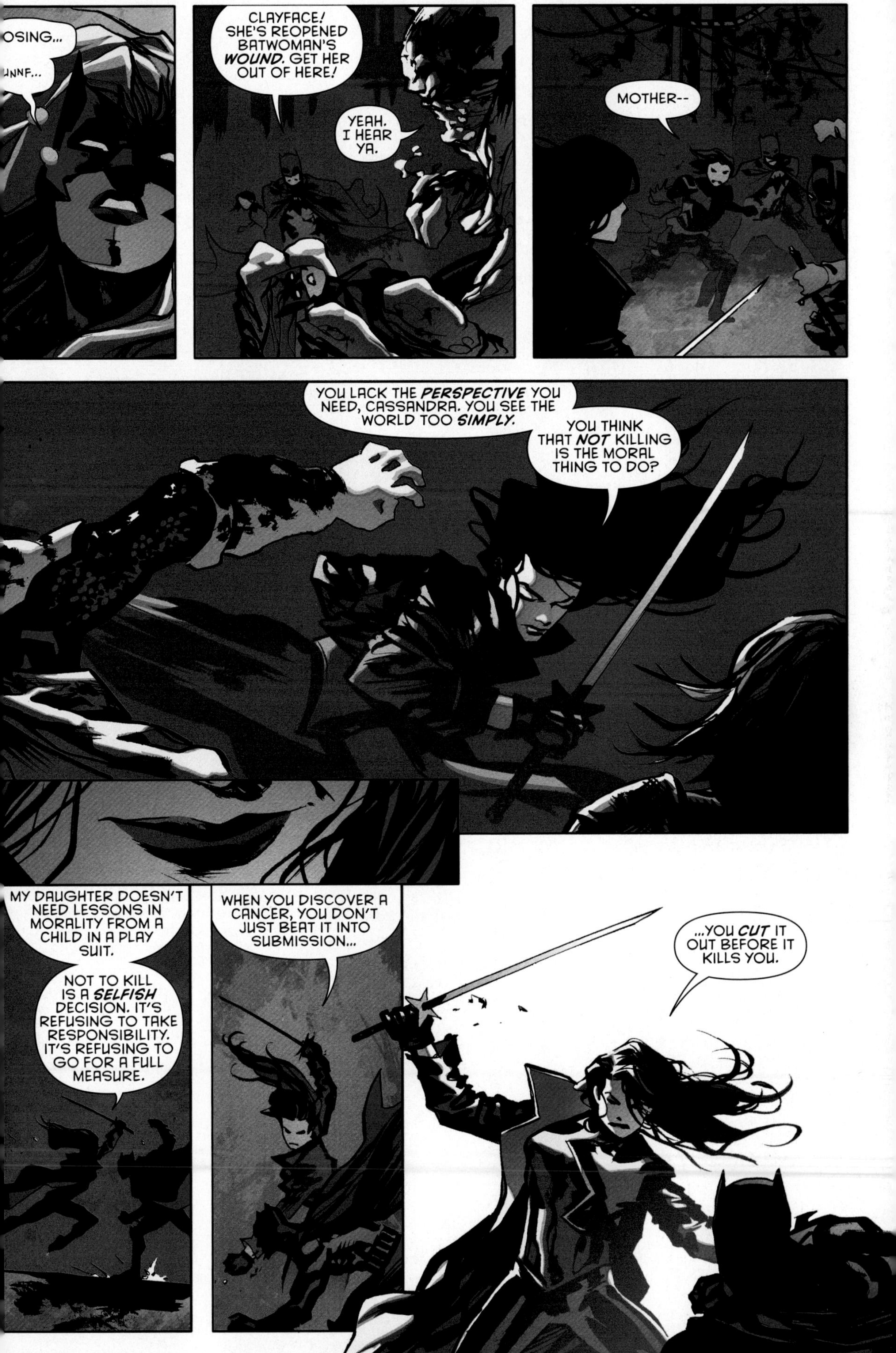
OSING...
UNNF...
CLAYFACE! SHE'S REOPENED BATWOMAN'S WOUND. GET HER OUT OF HERE!
YEAH. I HEAR YA.
MOTHER--
YOU LACK THE PERSPECTIVE YOU NEED, CASSANDRA. YOU SEE THE WORLD TOO SIMPLY.
YOU THINK THAT NOT KILLING IS THE MORAL THING TO DO?
MY DAUGHTER DOESN'T NEED LESSONS IN MORALITY FROM A CHILD IN A PLAY SUIT.
NOT TO KILL IS A SELFISH DECISION. IT'S REFUSING TO TAKE RESPONSIBILITY. IT'S REFUSING TO GO FOR A FULL MEASURE.
WHEN YOU DISCOVER A CANCER, YOU DON'T JUST BEAT IT INTO SUBMISSION...
...YOU CUT IT OUT BEFORE IT KILLS YOU.

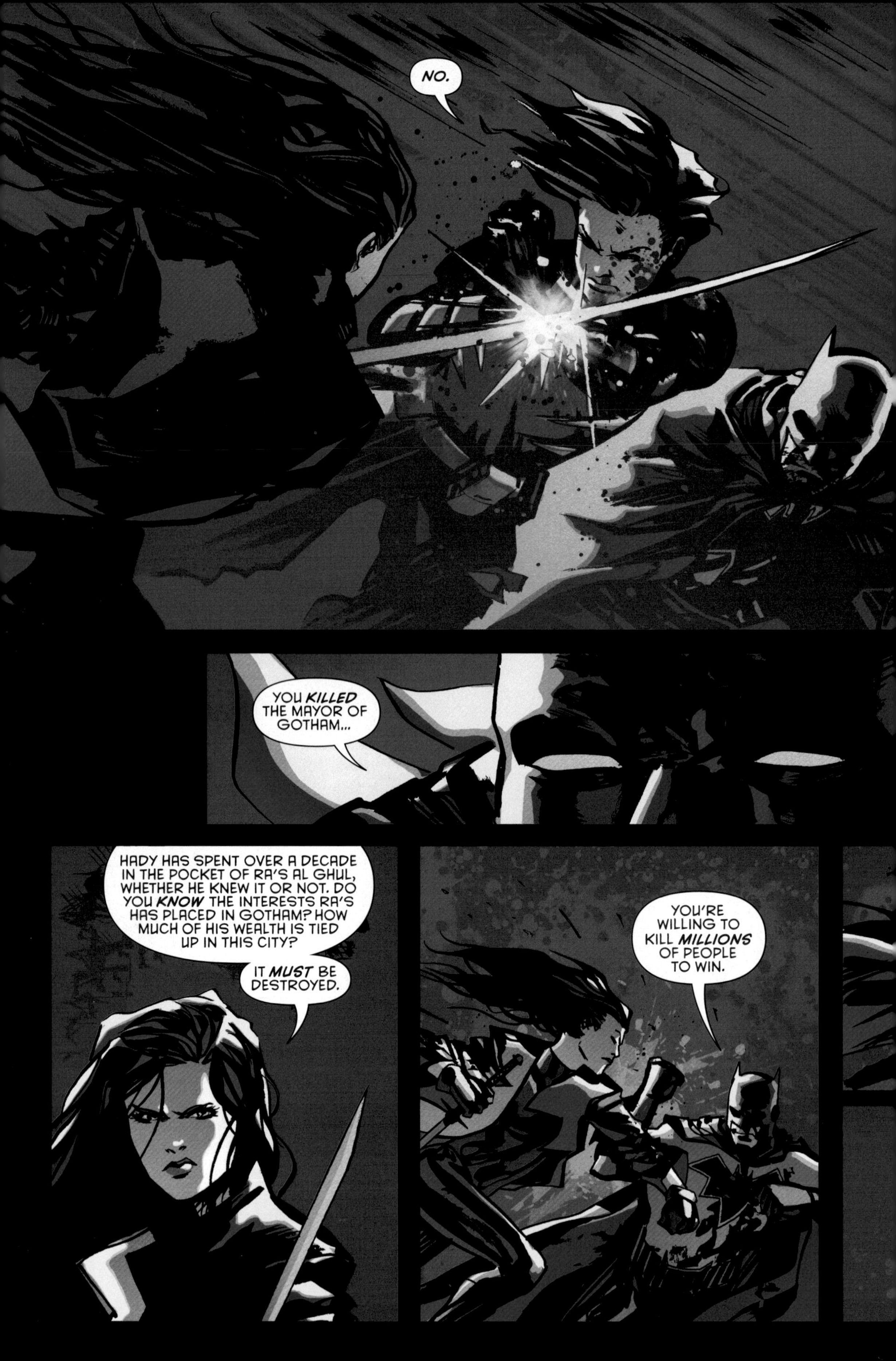
NO.
YOU **KILLED** THE MAYOR OF GOTHAM...
HADY HAS SPENT OVER A DECADE IN THE POCKET OF RA'S AL GHUL, WHETHER HE KNEW IT OR NOT. DO YOU **KNOW** THE INTERESTS RA'S HAS PLACED IN GOTHAM? HOW MUCH OF HIS WEALTH IS TIED UP IN THIS CITY?
IT **MUST** BE DESTROYED.
YOU'RE WILLING TO KILL **MILLIONS** OF PEOPLE TO WIN.

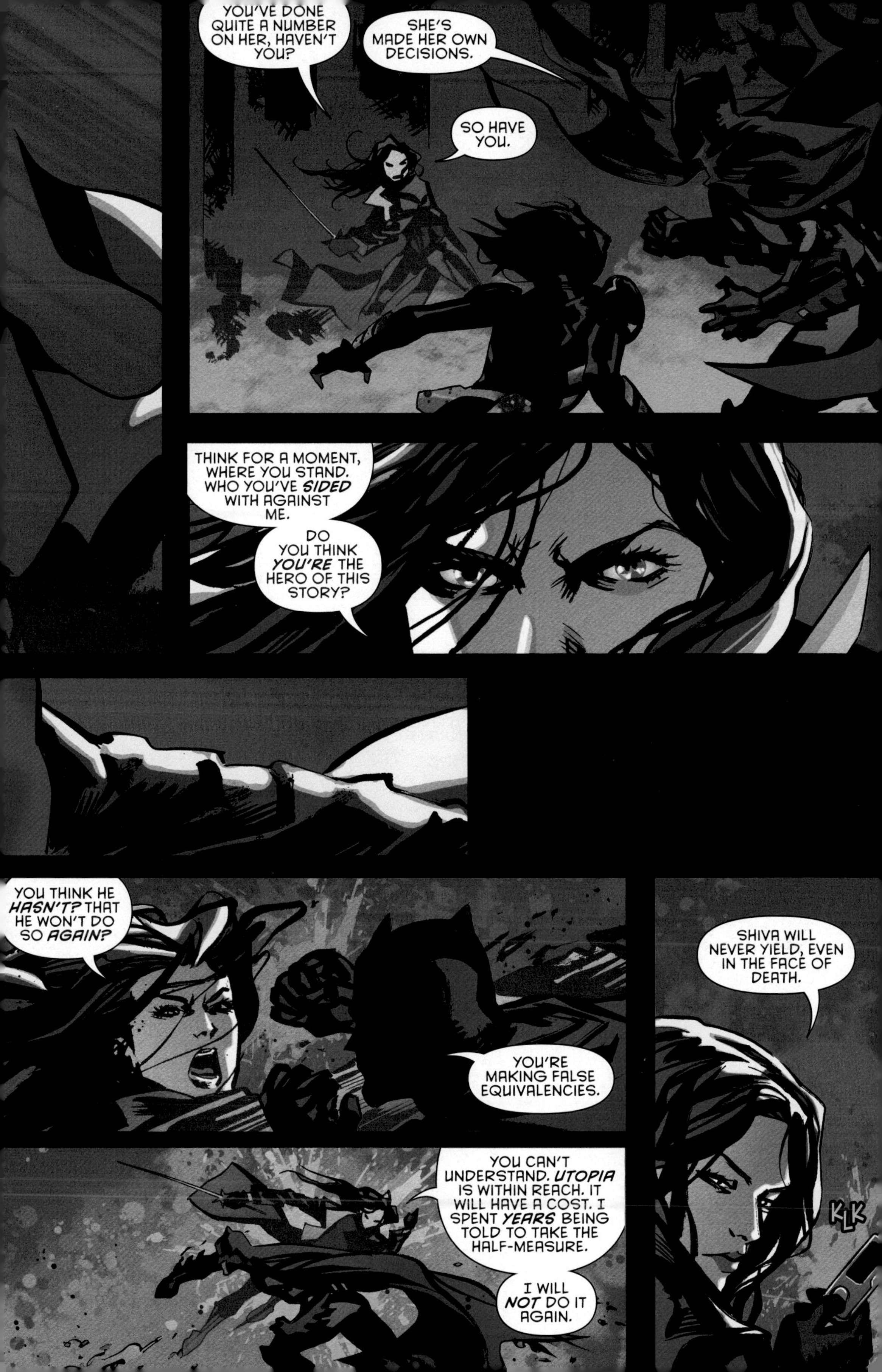
YOU'VE DONE QUITE A NUMBER ON HER, HAVEN'T YOU?
SHE'S MADE HER OWN DECISIONS.
SO HAVE YOU.
THINK FOR A MOMENT, WHERE YOU STAND. WHO YOU'VE SIDED WITH AGAINST ME.
DO YOU THINK YOU'RE THE HERO OF THIS STORY?
YOU THINK HE HASN'T? THAT HE WON'T DO SO AGAIN?
YOU'RE MAKING FALSE EQUIVALENCIES.
YOU CAN'T UNDERSTAND. UTOPIA IS WITHIN REACH. IT WILL HAVE A COST. I SPENT YEARS BEING TOLD TO TAKE THE HALF-MEASURE.
I WILL NOT DO IT AGAIN.
SHIVA WILL NEVER YIELD, EVEN IN THE FACE OF DEATH.
KLK

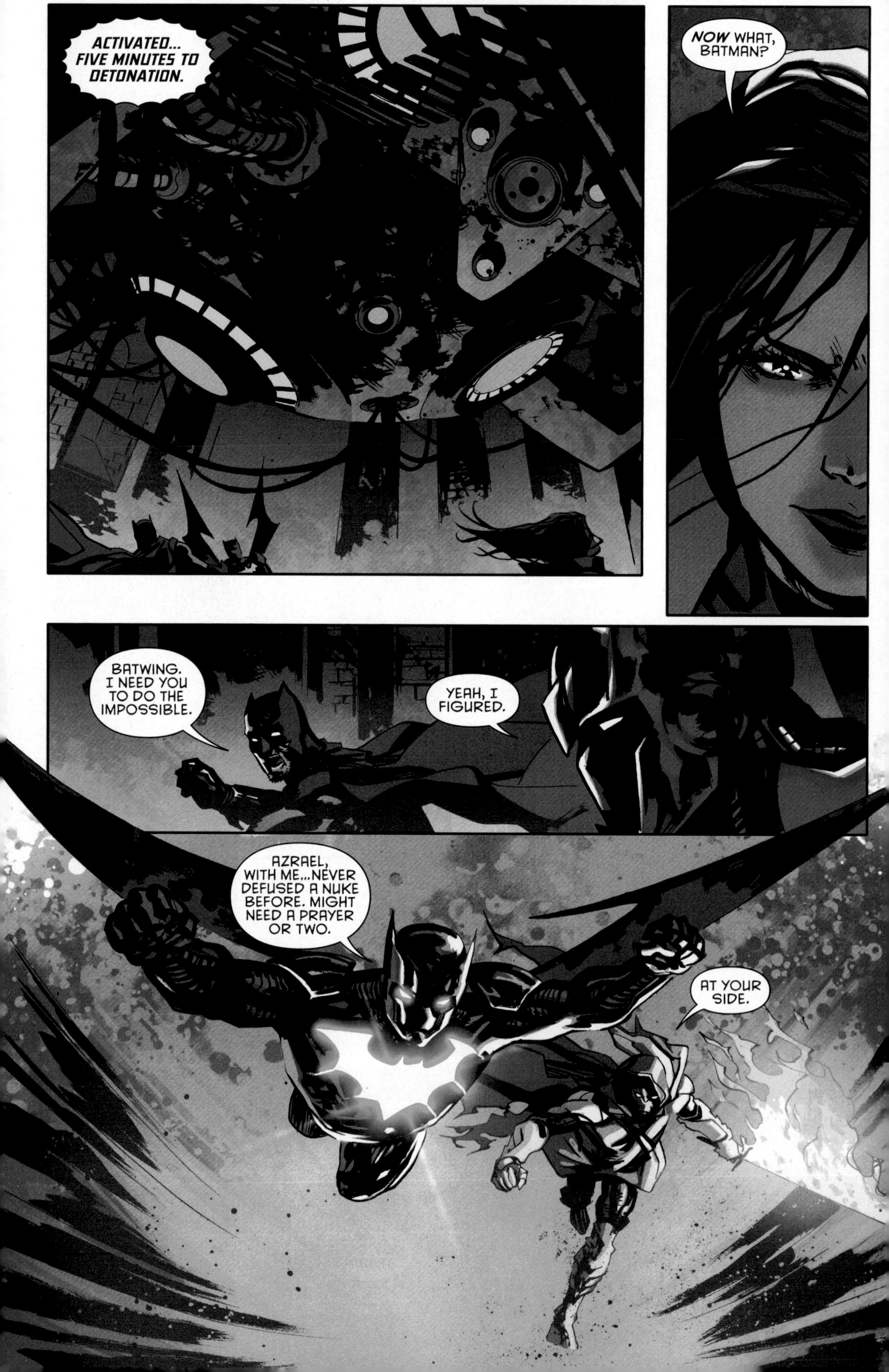
ACTIVATED... FIVE MINUTES TO DETONATION.
NOW WHAT, BATMAN?
BATWING. I NEED YOU TO DO THE IMPOSSIBLE.
YEAH, I FIGURED.
AZRAEL, WITH ME...NEVER DEFUSED A NUKE BEFORE. MIGHT NEED A PRAYER OR TWO.
AT YOUR SIDE.

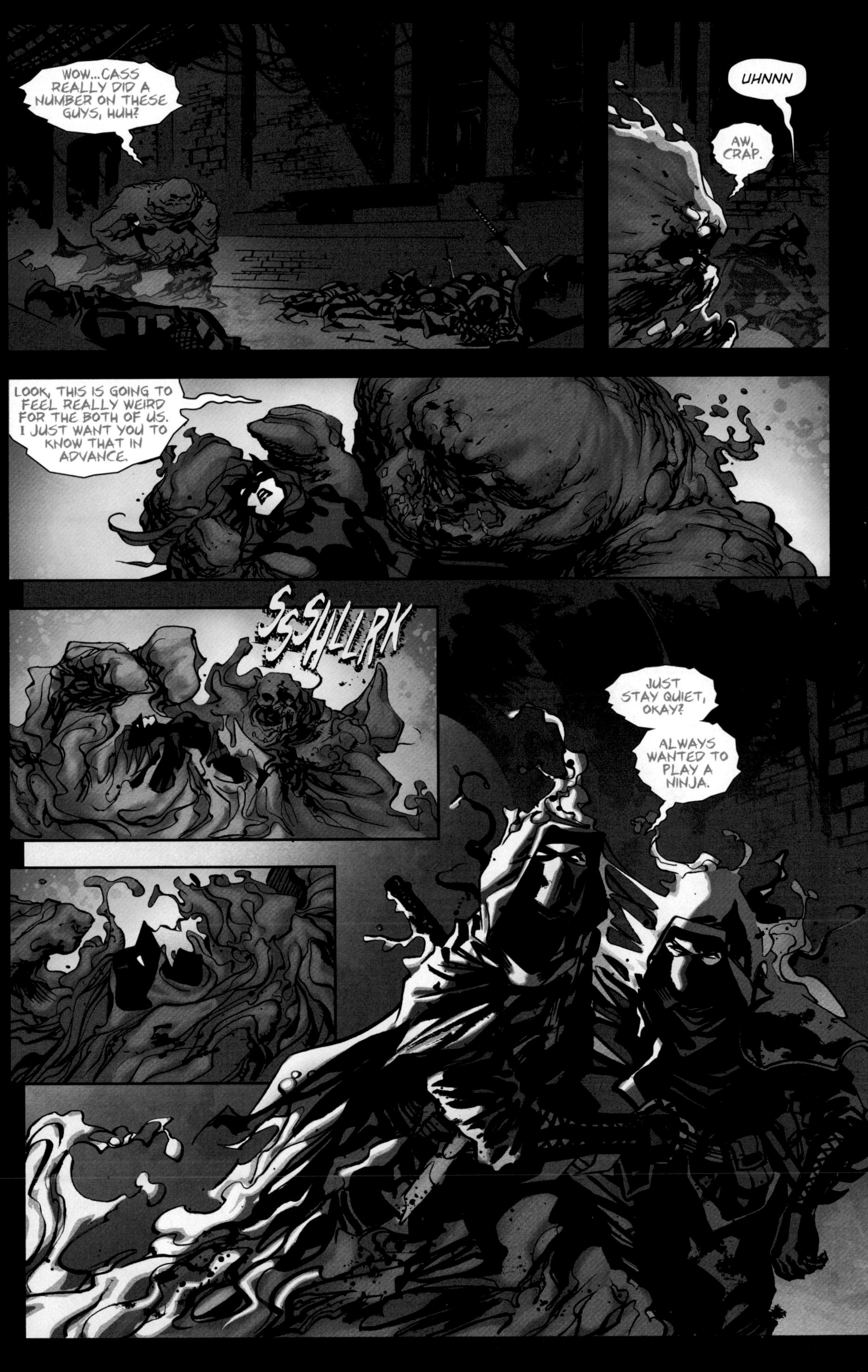
WOW...CASS REALLY DID A NUMBER ON THESE GUYS, HUH?
UHNNN
AW, CRAP.
LOOK, THIS IS GOING TO FEEL REALLY WEIRD FOR THE BOTH OF US. I JUST WANT YOU TO KNOW THAT IN ADVANCE.
SSSHLLRK
JUST STAY QUIET, OKAY?
ALWAYS WANTED TO PLAY A NINJA.

COLONEL KANE?

WE'RE GETTING SOME STRANGE READINGS...

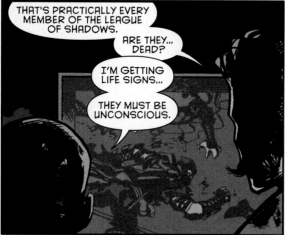

THAT'S PRACTICALLY EVERY MEMBER OF THE LEAGUE OF SHADOWS.

ARE THEY... DEAD?

I'M GETTING LIFE SIGNS...

THEY MUST BE UNCONSCIOUS.

WELL... THEY'LL BURN UP JUST THE SAME...THINK OF THEM AS *KINDLING.*

WHO THE HELL WOULD LEAVE THEM *ALIVE...*

PULLING THE TRIGGER NOW.

STOP, ULYSSES...

SEND THE SWARM DEEPER INTO THE CAVES.

THERE'S SOMETHING OFF HERE.

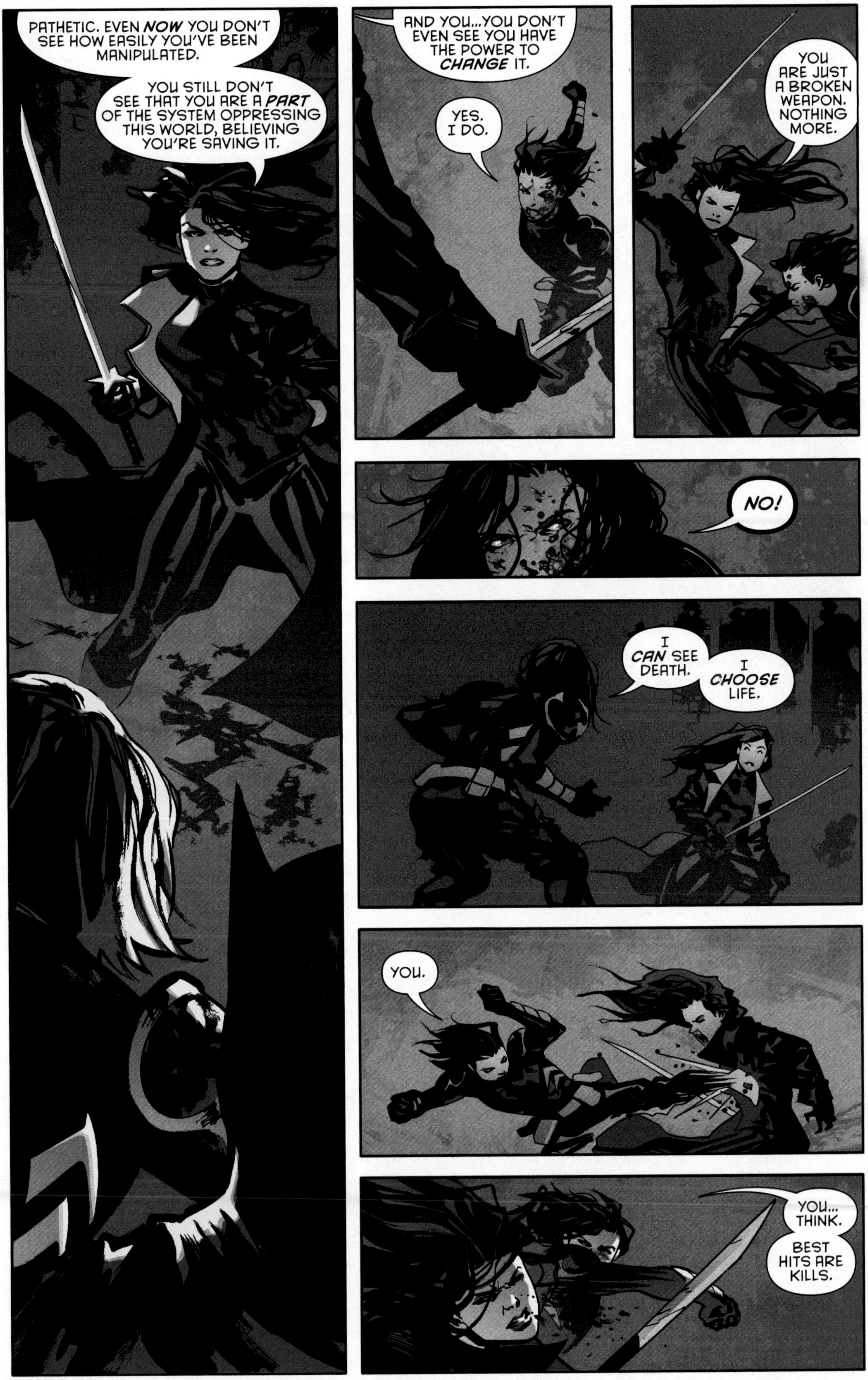
PATHETIC. EVEN NOW YOU DON'T SEE HOW EASILY YOU'VE BEEN MANIPULATED.
YOU STILL DON'T SEE THAT YOU ARE A PART OF THE SYSTEM OPPRESSING THIS WORLD, BELIEVING YOU'RE SAVING IT.
AND YOU...YOU DON'T EVEN SEE YOU HAVE THE POWER TO CHANGE IT.
YES. I DO.
YOU ARE JUST A BROKEN WEAPON. NOTHING MORE.
NO!
I CAN SEE DEATH.
I CHOOSE LIFE.
YOU.
YOU... THINK.
BEST HITS ARE KILLS.

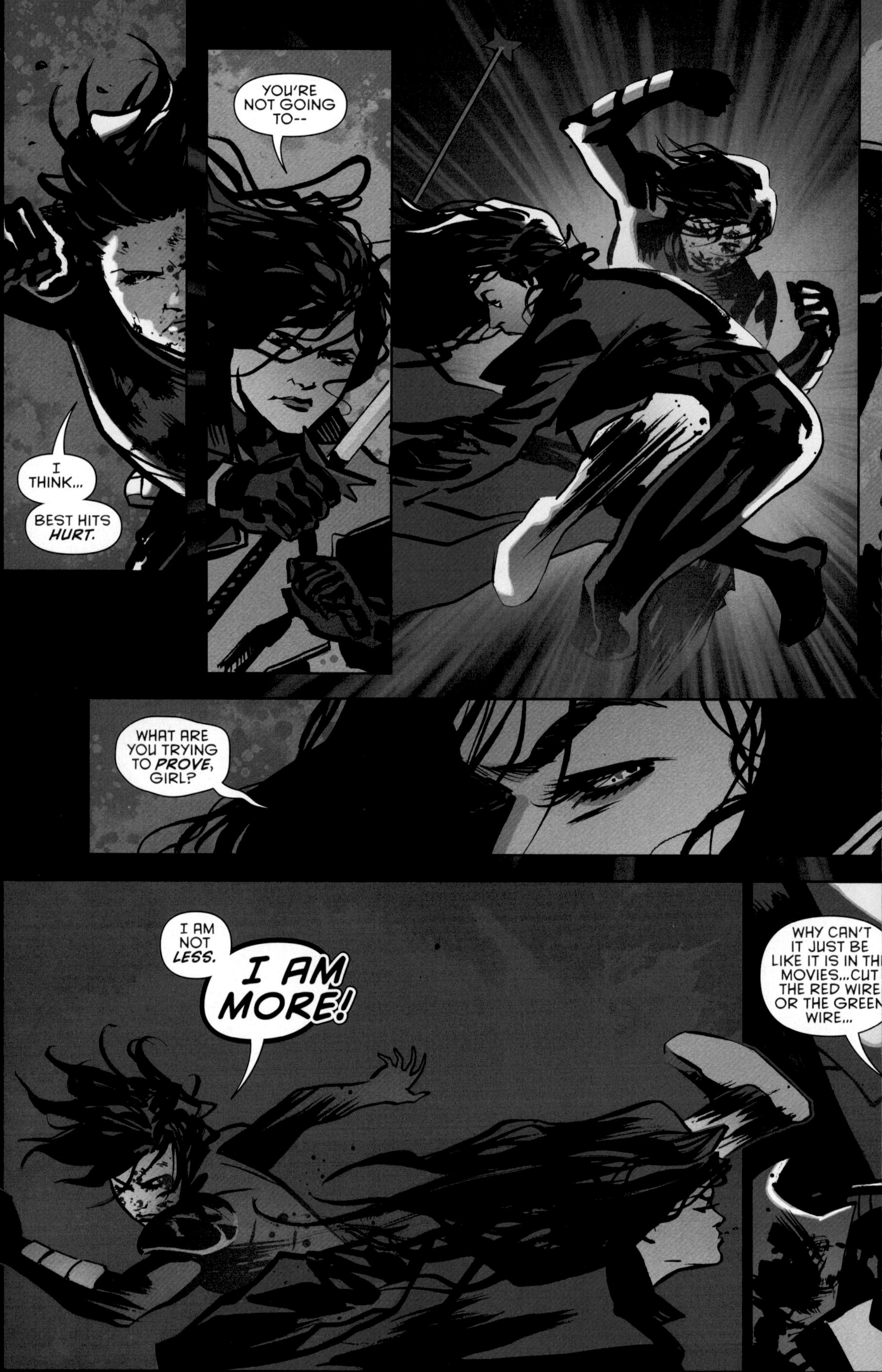
I THINK...
BEST HITS *HURT*.
YOU'RE NOT GOING TO--
WHAT ARE YOU TRYING TO *PROVE*, GIRL?
I AM NOT *LESS*.
I AM MORE!
WHY CAN'T IT JUST BE LIKE IT IS IN TH MOVIES...CUT THE RED WIRE OR THE GREEN WIRE...

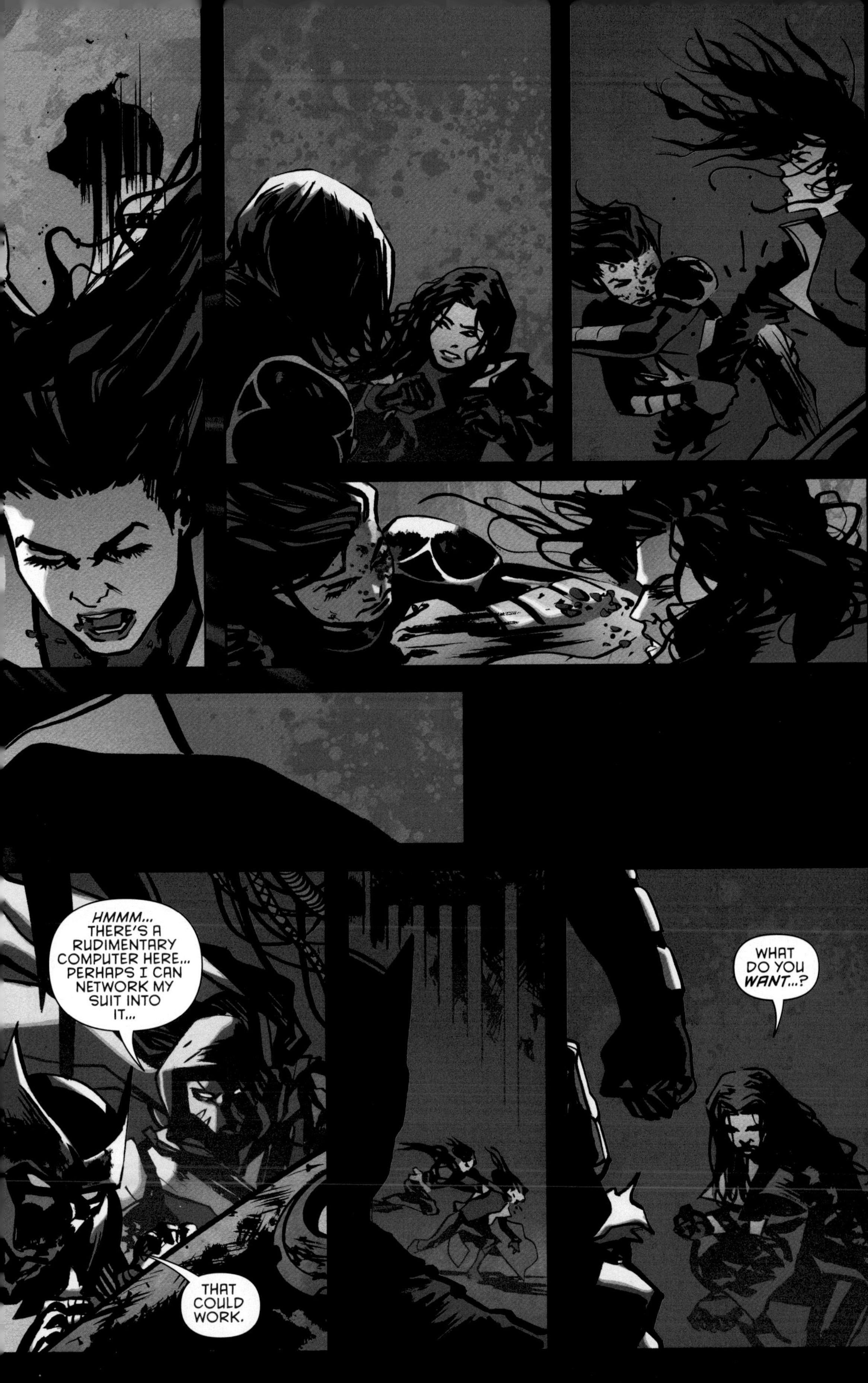
HMMM... THERE'S A RUDIMENTARY COMPUTER HERE... PERHAPS I CAN NETWORK MY SUIT INTO IT...
THAT COULD WORK.
WHAT DO YOU WANT...?

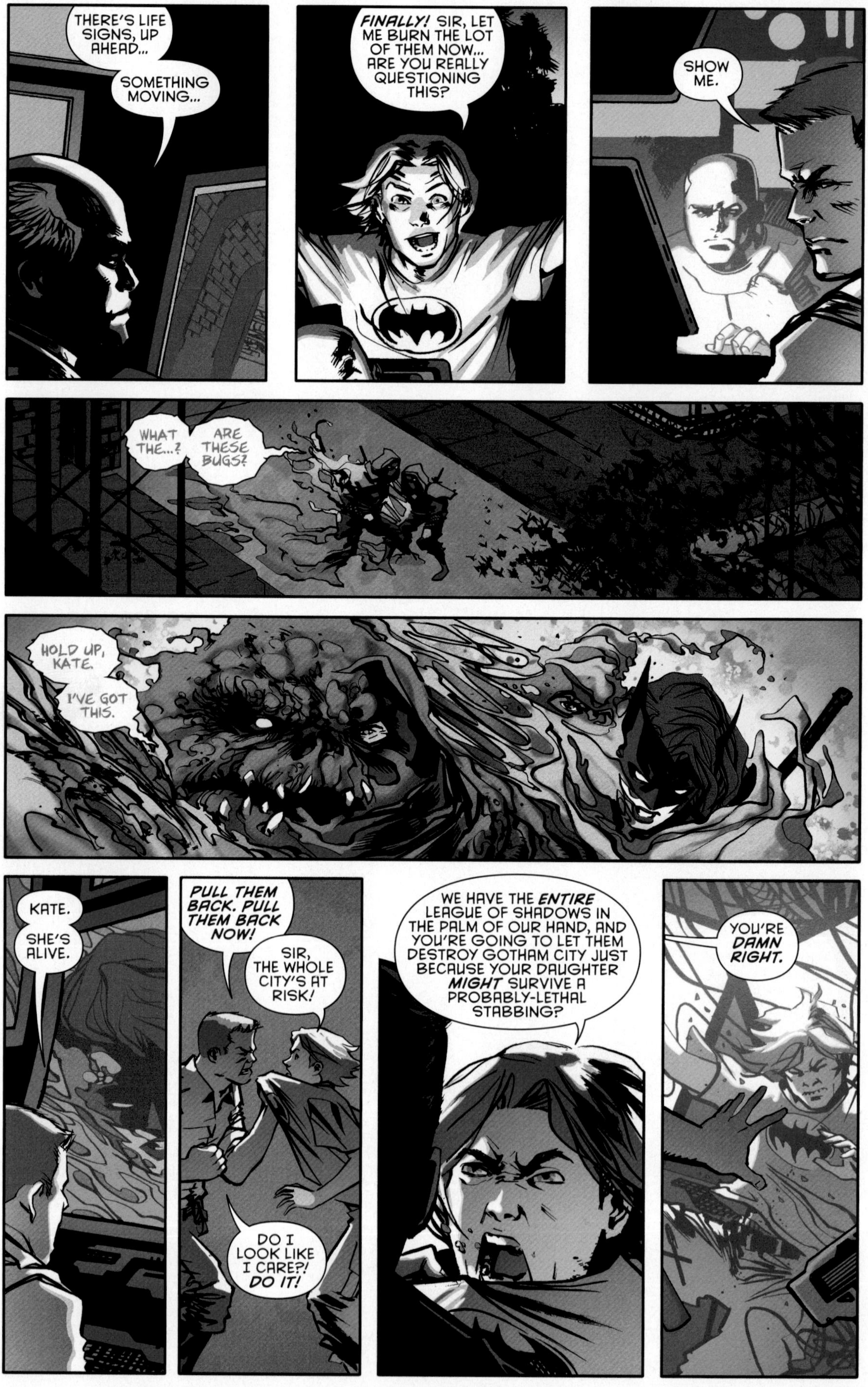
THERE'S LIFE SIGNS, UP AHEAD...
SOMETHING MOVING...
FINALLY! SIR, LET ME BURN THE LOT OF THEM NOW... ARE YOU REALLY QUESTIONING THIS?
SHOW ME.
WHAT THE...?
ARE THESE BUGS?
HOLD UP, KATE.
I'VE GOT THIS.
KATE.
SHE'S ALIVE.
PULL THEM BACK. PULL THEM BACK NOW!
SIR, THE WHOLE CITY'S AT RISK!
DO I LOOK LIKE I CARE?! DO IT!
WE HAVE THE ENTIRE LEAGUE OF SHADOWS IN THE PALM OF OUR HAND, AND YOU'RE GOING TO LET THEM DESTROY GOTHAM CITY JUST BECAUSE YOUR DAUGHTER MIGHT SURVIVE A PROBABLY-LETHAL STABBING?
YOU'RE DAMN RIGHT.

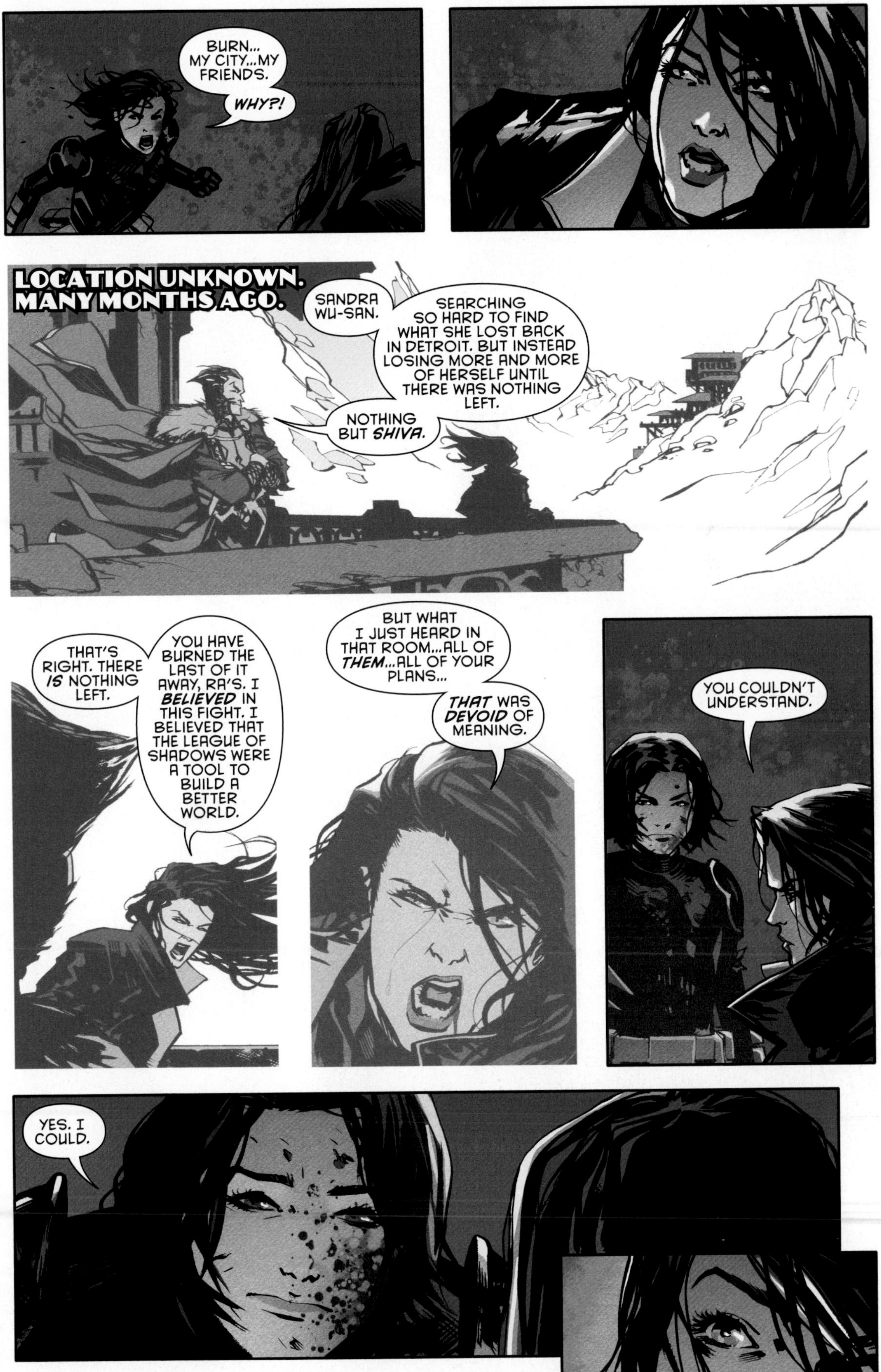
BURN... MY CITY...MY FRIENDS.
WHY?!
LOCATION UNKNOWN. MANY MONTHS AGO.
SANDRA WU-SAN.
SEARCHING SO HARD TO FIND WHAT SHE LOST BACK IN DETROIT. BUT INSTEAD LOSING MORE AND MORE OF HERSELF UNTIL THERE WAS NOTHING LEFT.
NOTHING BUT SHIVA.
THAT'S RIGHT. THERE IS NOTHING LEFT.
YOU HAVE BURNED THE LAST OF IT AWAY, RA'S. I BELIEVED IN THIS FIGHT. I BELIEVED THAT THE LEAGUE OF SHADOWS WERE A TOOL TO BUILD A BETTER WORLD.
BUT WHAT I JUST HEARD IN THAT ROOM...ALL OF THEM...ALL OF YOUR PLANS...
THAT WAS DEVOID OF MEANING.
YOU COULDN'T UNDERSTAND.
YES. I COULD.

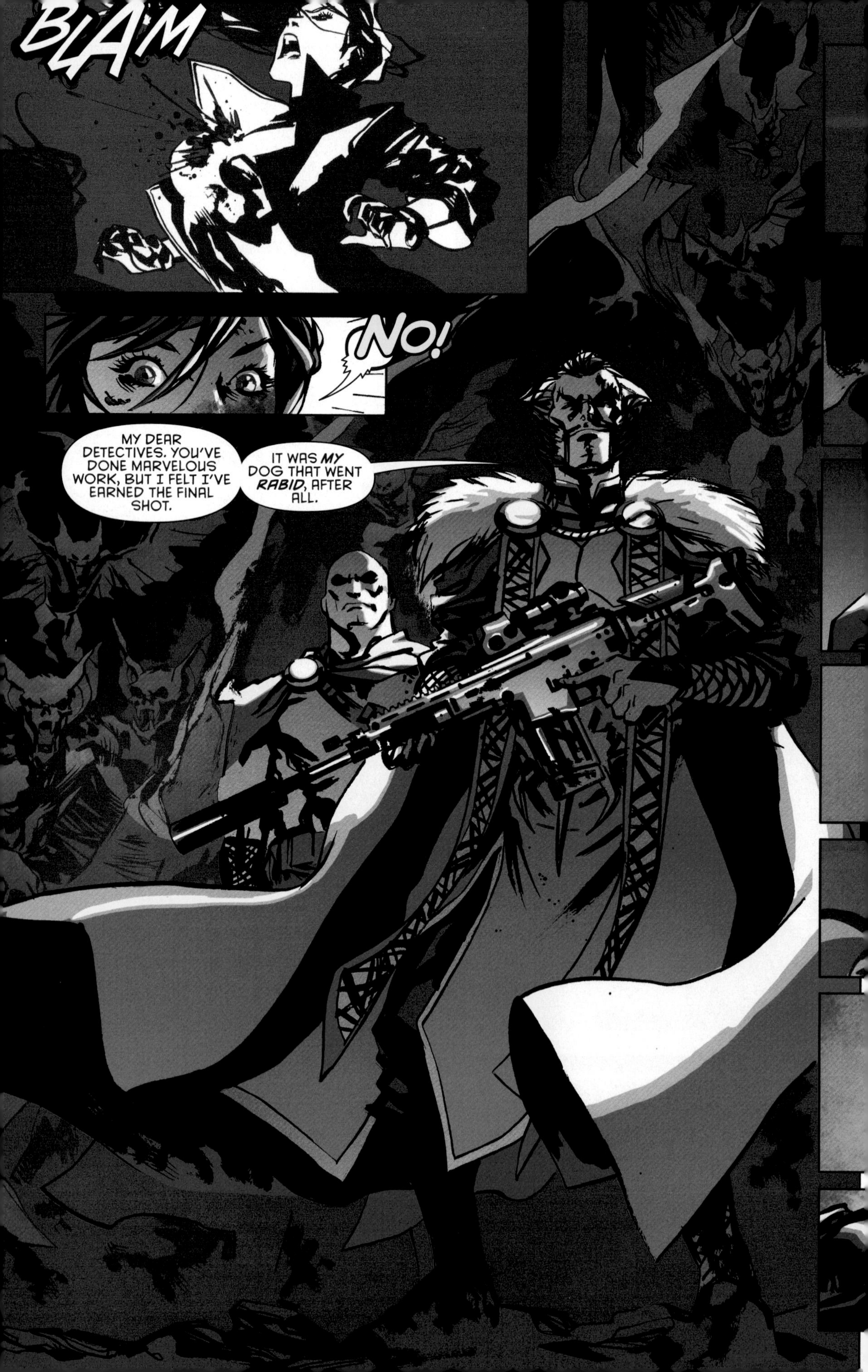
BLAM
NO!
MY DEAR DETECTIVES. YOU'VE DONE MARVELOUS WORK, BUT I FELT I'VE EARNED THE FINAL SHOT.
IT WAS MY DOG THAT WENT RABID, AFTER ALL.

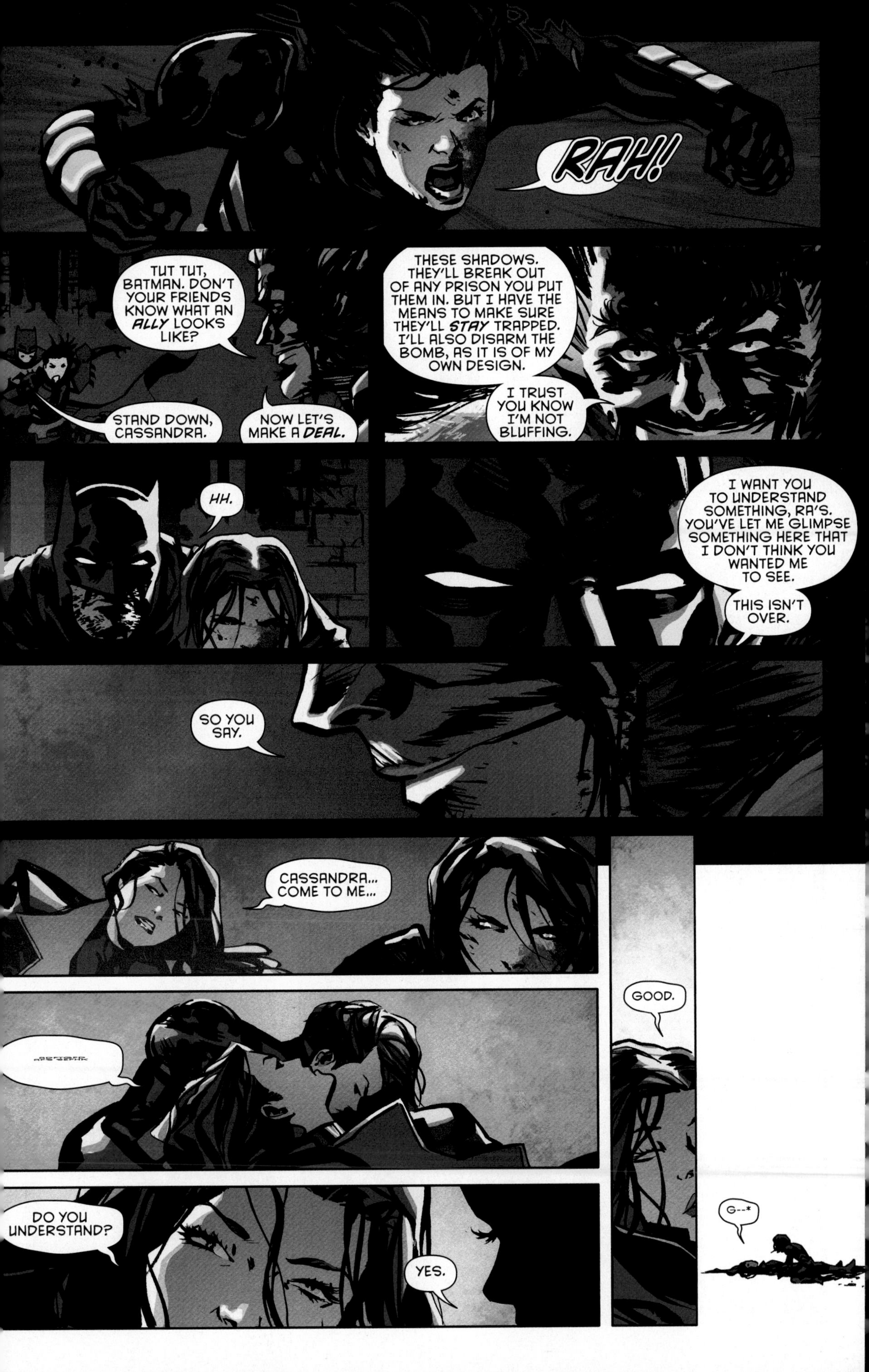
RAH!
TUT TUT, BATMAN. DON'T YOUR FRIENDS KNOW WHAT AN ALLY LOOKS LIKE?
STAND DOWN, CASSANDRA.
NOW LET'S MAKE A DEAL.
THESE SHADOWS. THEY'LL BREAK OUT OF ANY PRISON YOU PUT THEM IN. BUT I HAVE THE MEANS TO MAKE SURE THEY'LL STAY TRAPPED. I'LL ALSO DISARM THE BOMB, AS IT IS OF MY OWN DESIGN.
I TRUST YOU KNOW I'M NOT BLUFFING.
HH.
I WANT YOU TO UNDERSTAND SOMETHING, RA'S. YOU'VE LET ME GLIMPSE SOMETHING HERE THAT I DON'T THINK YOU WANTED ME TO SEE.
THIS ISN'T OVER.
SO YOU SAY.
CASSANDRA... COME TO ME...
DO YOU UNDERSTAND?
YES.
GOOD.
G--*

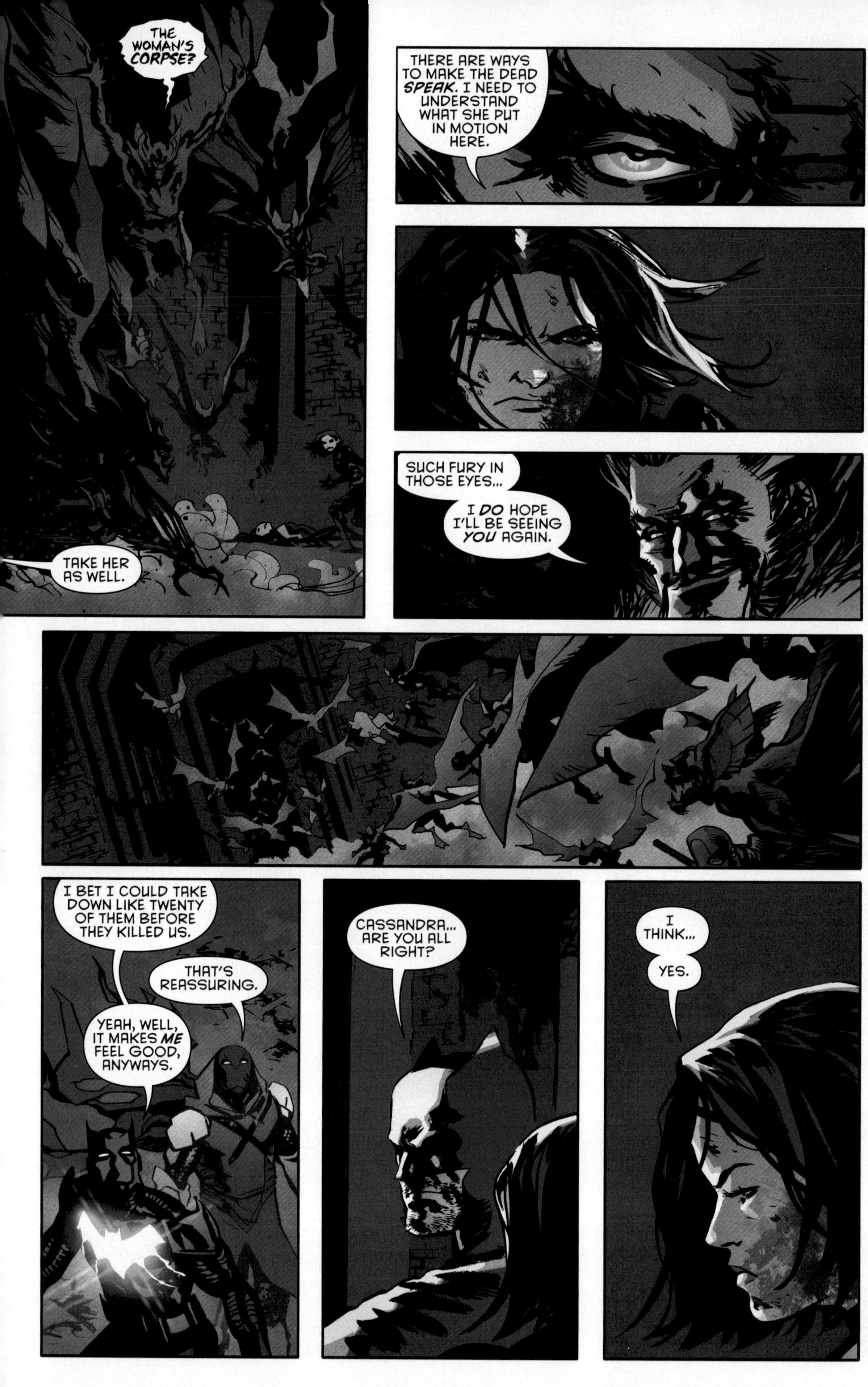
THE WOMAN'S CORPSE?
TAKE HER AS WELL.
THERE ARE WAYS TO MAKE THE DEAD SPEAK. I NEED TO UNDERSTAND WHAT SHE PUT IN MOTION HERE.
SUCH FURY IN THOSE EYES...
I DO HOPE I'LL BE SEEING YOU AGAIN.
I BET I COULD TAKE DOWN LIKE TWENTY OF THEM BEFORE THEY KILLED US.
THAT'S REASSURING.
YEAH, WELL, IT MAKES ME FEEL GOOD, ANYWAYS.
CASSANDRA... ARE YOU ALL RIGHT?
I THINK...
YES.

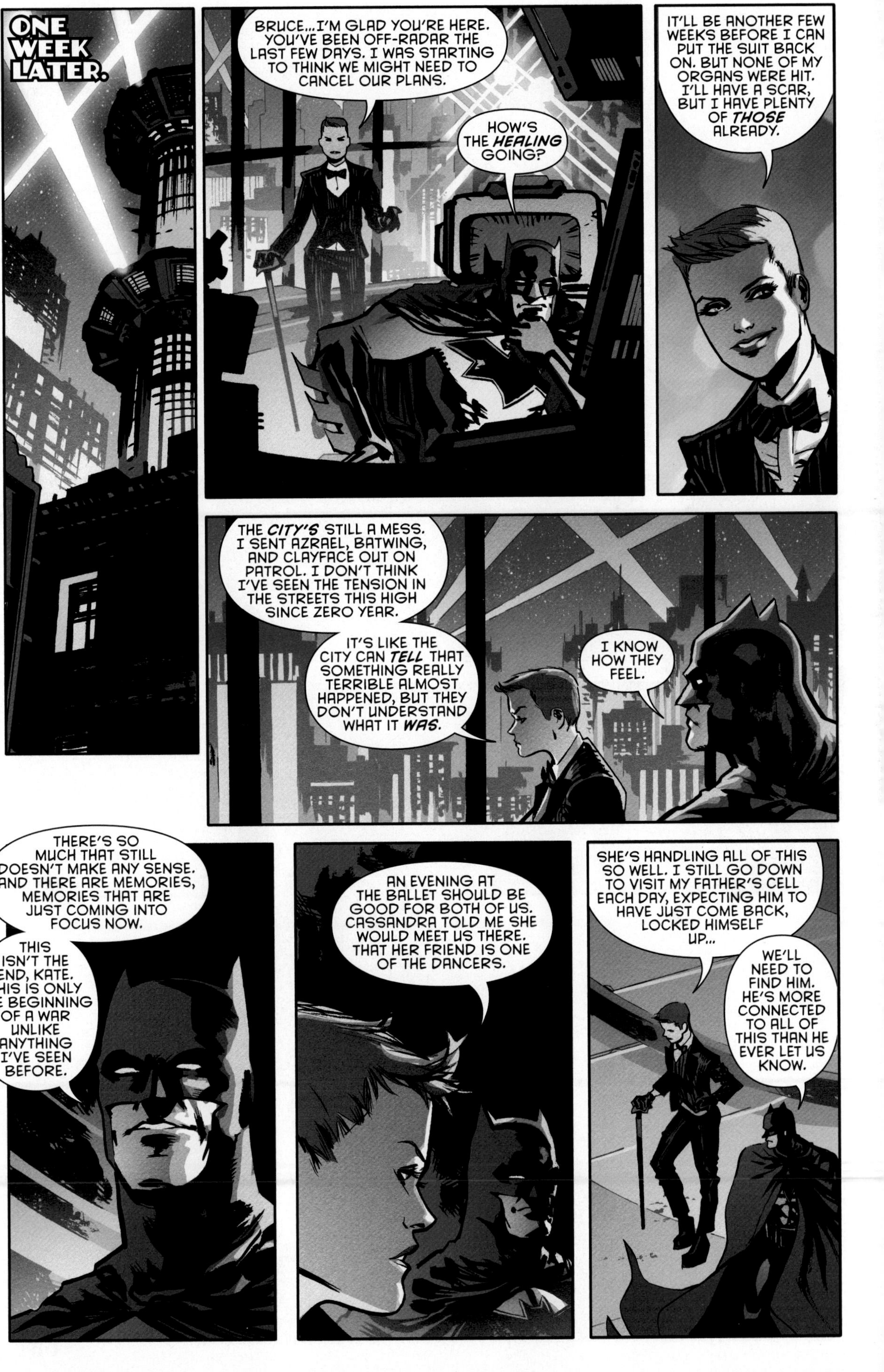
ONE WEEK LATER.
BRUCE...I'M GLAD YOU'RE HERE. YOU'VE BEEN OFF-RADAR THE LAST FEW DAYS. I WAS STARTING TO THINK WE MIGHT NEED TO CANCEL OUR PLANS.
HOW'S THE HEALING GOING?
IT'LL BE ANOTHER FEW WEEKS BEFORE I CAN PUT THE SUIT BACK ON. BUT NONE OF MY ORGANS WERE HIT. I'LL HAVE A SCAR, BUT I HAVE PLENTY OF THOSE ALREADY.
THE CITY'S STILL A MESS. I SENT AZRAEL, BATWING, AND CLAYFACE OUT ON PATROL. I DON'T THINK I'VE SEEN THE TENSION IN THE STREETS THIS HIGH SINCE ZERO YEAR.
IT'S LIKE THE CITY CAN TELL THAT SOMETHING REALLY TERRIBLE ALMOST HAPPENED, BUT THEY DON'T UNDERSTAND WHAT IT WAS.
I KNOW HOW THEY FEEL.
THERE'S SO MUCH THAT STILL DOESN'T MAKE ANY SENSE. AND THERE ARE MEMORIES, MEMORIES THAT ARE JUST COMING INTO FOCUS NOW.
THIS ISN'T THE END, KATE. THIS IS ONLY HE BEGINNING OF A WAR UNLIKE ANYTHING I'VE SEEN BEFORE.
AN EVENING AT THE BALLET SHOULD BE GOOD FOR BOTH OF US. CASSANDRA TOLD ME SHE WOULD MEET US THERE. THAT HER FRIEND IS ONE OF THE DANCERS.
SHE'S HANDLING ALL OF THIS SO WELL. I STILL GO DOWN TO VISIT MY FATHER'S CELL EACH DAY, EXPECTING HIM TO HAVE JUST COME BACK, LOCKED HIMSELF UP...
WE'LL NEED TO FIND HIM. HE'S MORE CONNECTED TO ALL OF THIS THAN HE EVER LET US KNOW.

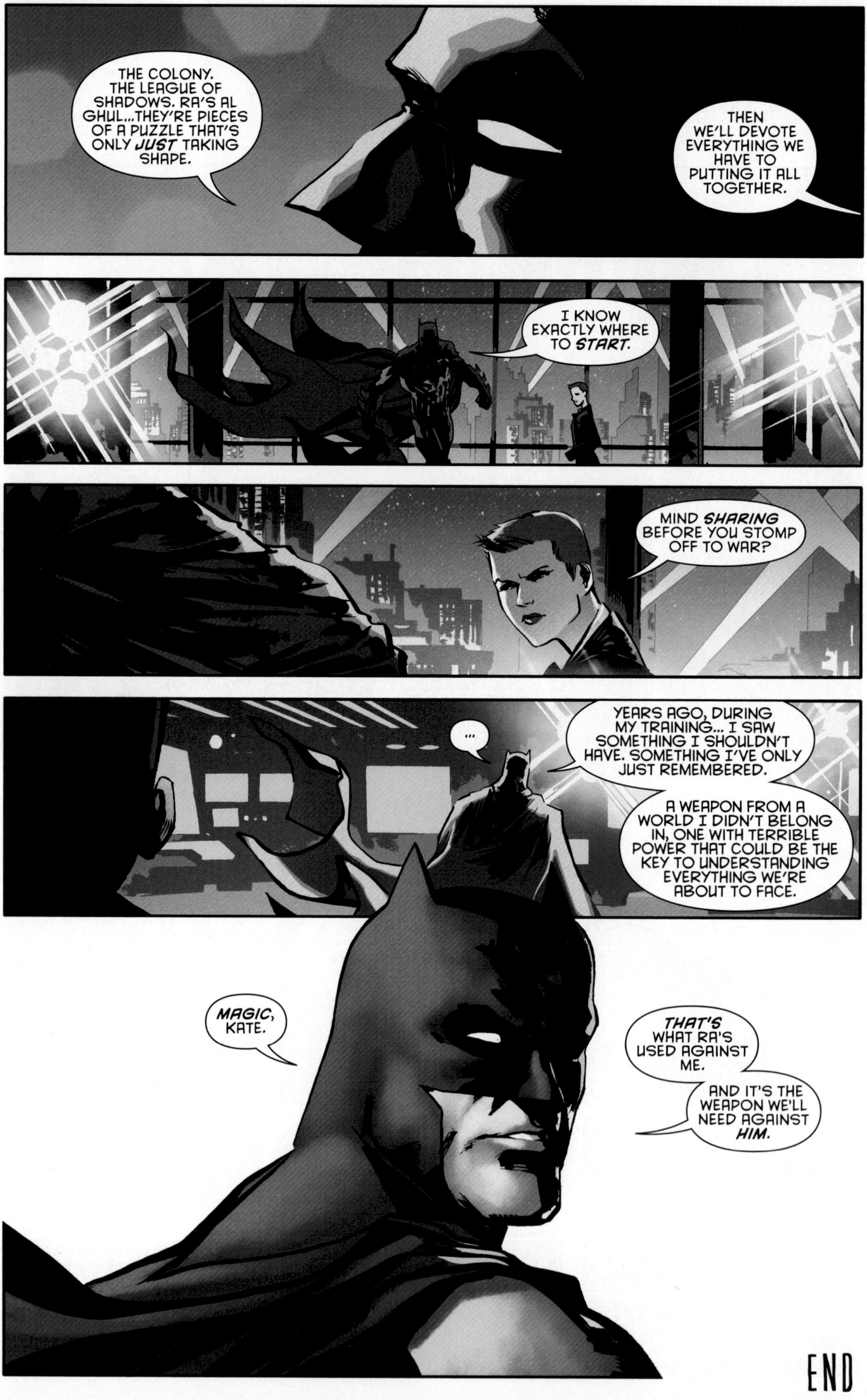
THE COLONY. THE LEAGUE OF SHADOWS. RA'S AL GHUL...THEY'RE PIECES OF A PUZZLE THAT'S ONLY JUST TAKING SHAPE.
THEN WE'LL DEVOTE EVERYTHING WE HAVE TO PUTTING IT ALL TOGETHER.
I KNOW EXACTLY WHERE TO START.
MIND SHARING BEFORE YOU STOMP OFF TO WAR?
...
YEARS AGO, DURING MY TRAINING... I SAW SOMETHING I SHOULDN'T HAVE. SOMETHING I'VE ONLY JUST REMEMBERED.
A WEAPON FROM A WORLD I DIDN'T BELONG IN, ONE WITH TERRIBLE POWER THAT COULD BE THE KEY TO UNDERSTANDING EVERYTHING WE'RE ABOUT TO FACE.
MAGIC, KATE.
THAT'S WHAT RA'S USED AGAINST ME.
AND IT'S THE WEAPON WE'LL NEED AGAINST HIM.
END

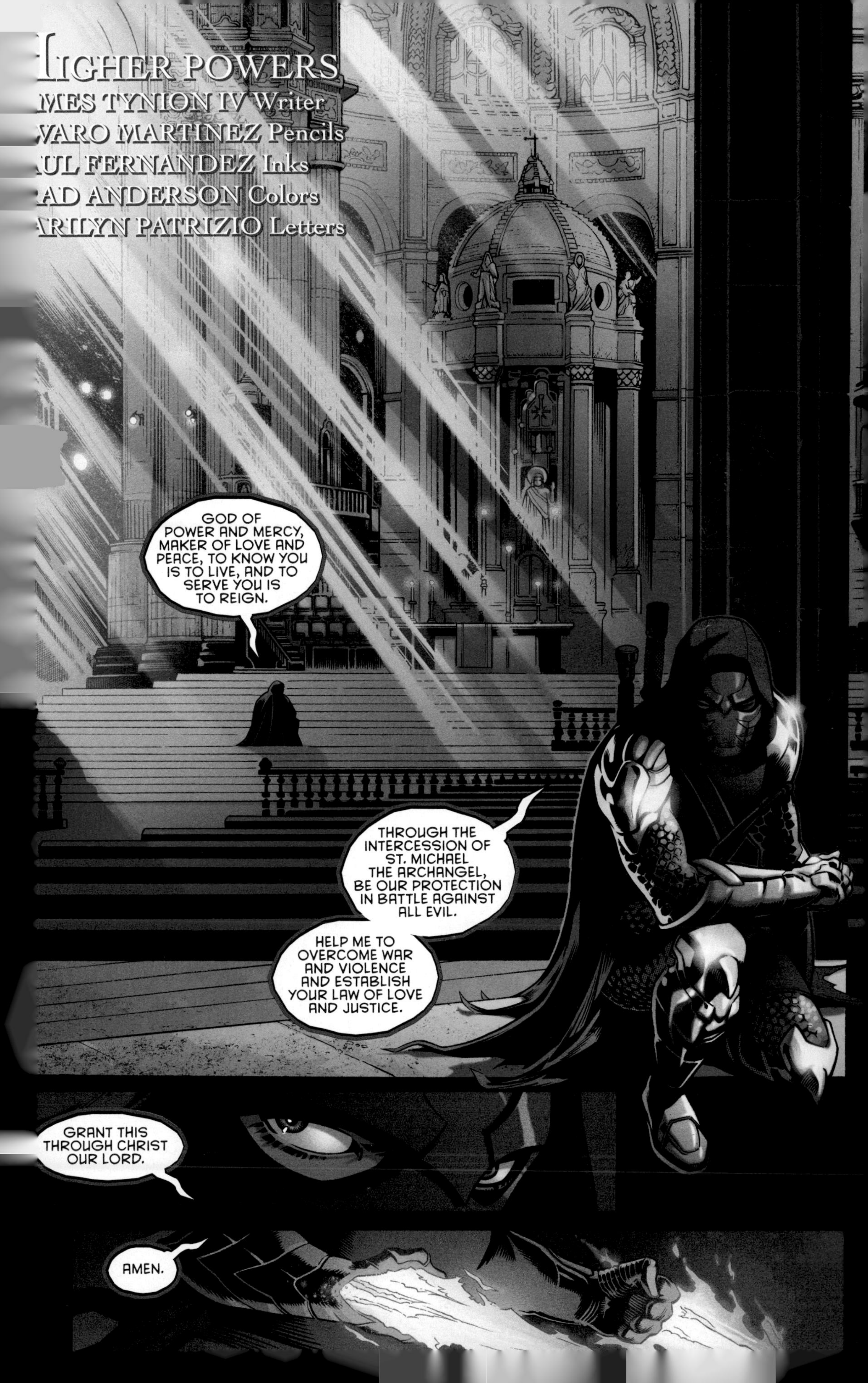
HIGHER POWERS
MES TYNION IV Writer
VARO MARTINEZ Pencils
UL FERNANDEZ Inks
AD ANDERSON Colors
ARILYN PATRIZIO Letters
GOD OF POWER AND MERCY, MAKER OF LOVE AND PEACE, TO KNOW YOU IS TO LIVE, AND TO SERVE YOU IS TO REIGN.
THROUGH THE INTERCESSION OF ST. MICHAEL THE ARCHANGEL, BE OUR PROTECTION IN BATTLE AGAINST ALL EVIL.
HELP ME TO OVERCOME WAR AND VIOLENCE AND ESTABLISH YOUR LAW OF LOVE AND JUSTICE.
GRANT THIS THROUGH CHRIST OUR LORD.
AMEN.

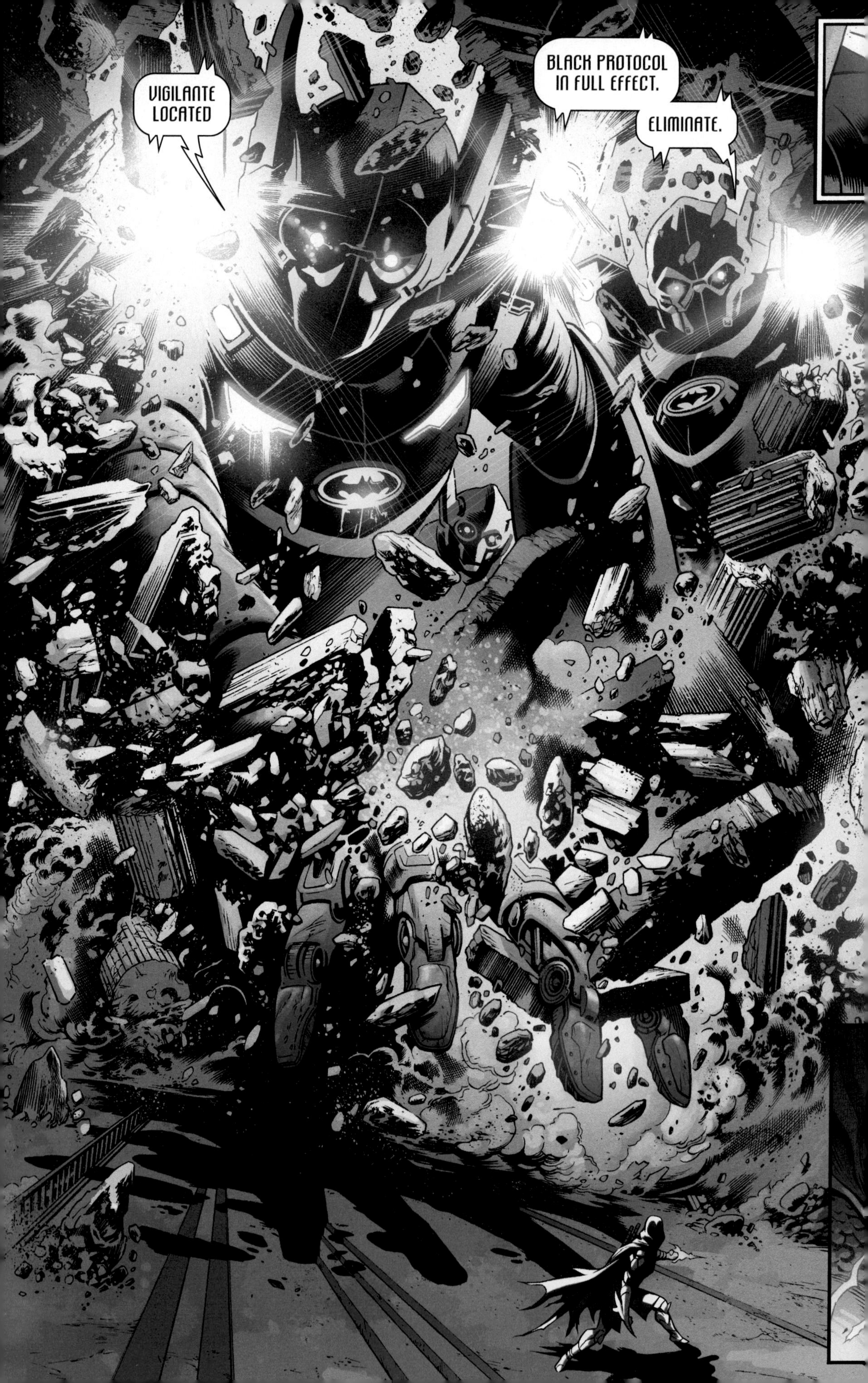
VIGILANTE LOCATED
BLACK PROTOCOL IN FULL EFFECT.
ELIMINATE.

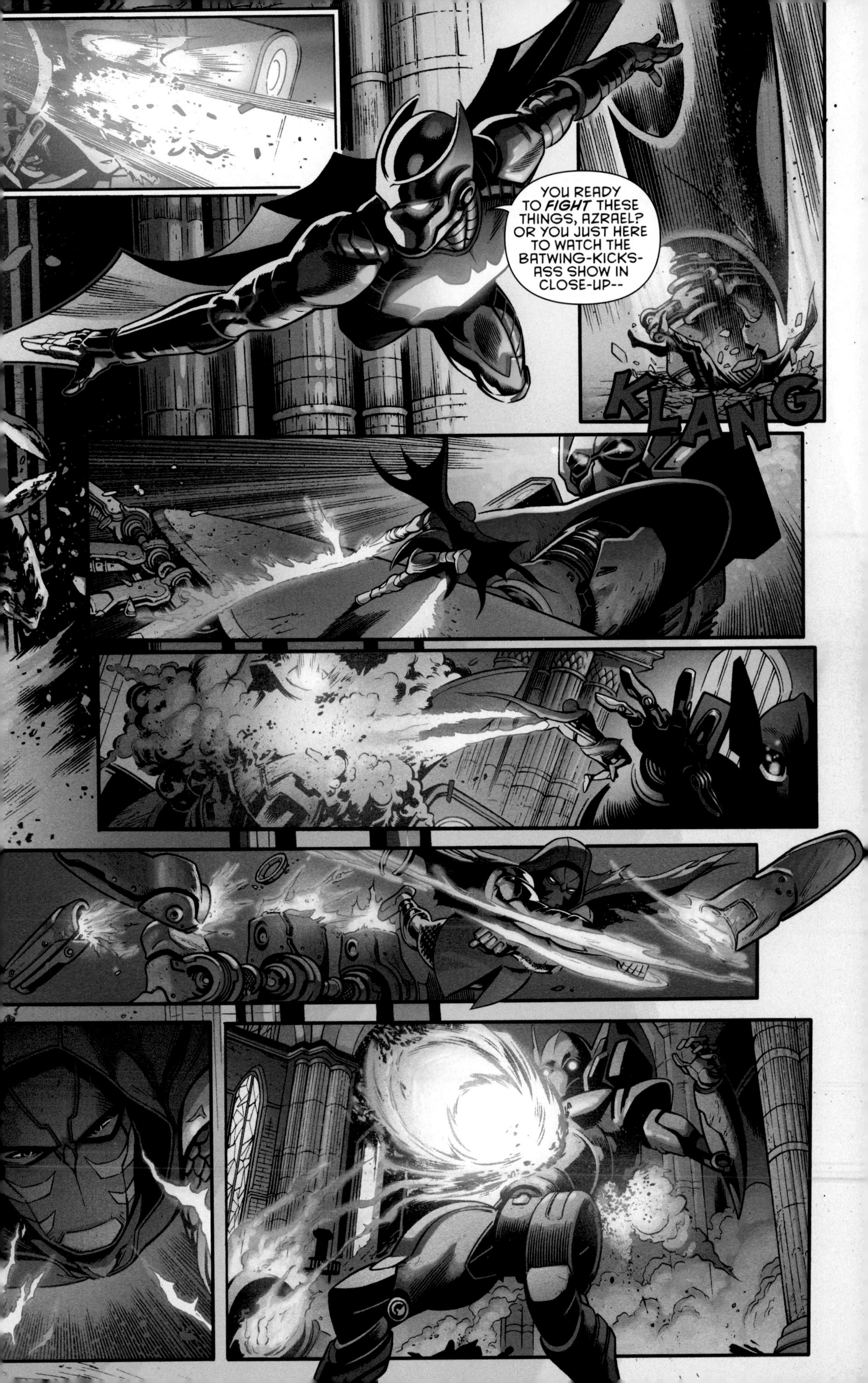
YOU READY TO FIGHT THESE THINGS, AZRAEL? OR YOU JUST HERE TO WATCH THE BATWING-KICKS-ASS SHOW IN CLOSE-UP--
KLANG

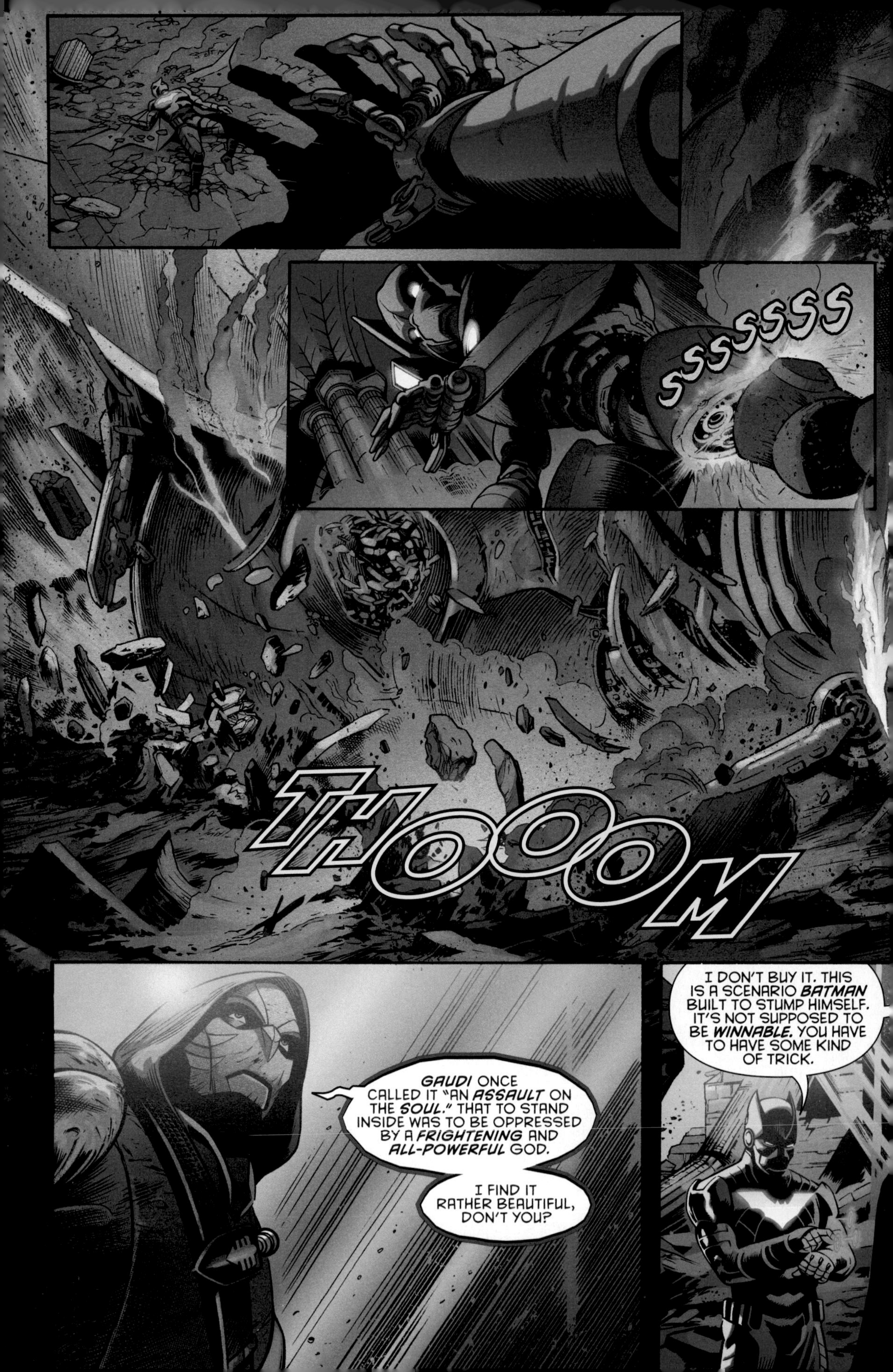
SSSSSSS
THOOOOM
GAUDI ONCE CALLED IT "AN ASSAULT ON THE SOUL." THAT TO STAND INSIDE WAS TO BE OPPRESSED BY A FRIGHTENING AND ALL-POWERFUL GOD.
I FIND IT RATHER BEAUTIFUL, DON'T YOU?
I DON'T BUY IT. THIS IS A SCENARIO BATMAN BUILT TO STUMP HIMSELF. IT'S NOT SUPPOSED TO BE WINNABLE. YOU HAVE TO HAVE SOME KIND OF TRICK.

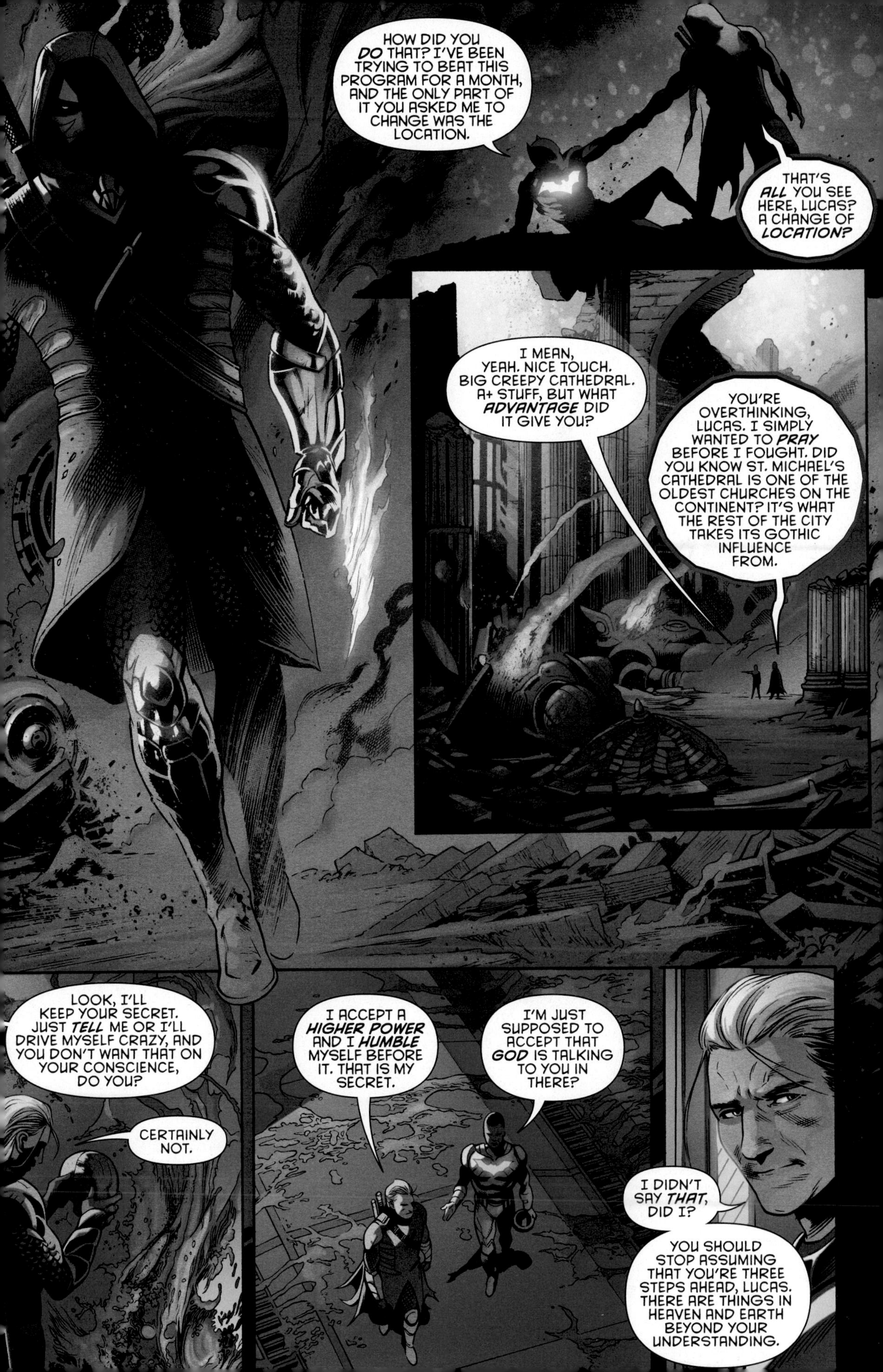
HOW DID YOU DO THAT? I'VE BEEN TRYING TO BEAT THIS PROGRAM FOR A MONTH, AND THE ONLY PART OF IT YOU ASKED ME TO CHANGE WAS THE LOCATION.
THAT'S ALL YOU SEE HERE, LUCAS? A CHANGE OF LOCATION?
I MEAN, YEAH. NICE TOUCH. BIG CREEPY CATHEDRAL. A+ STUFF, BUT WHAT ADVANTAGE DID IT GIVE YOU?
YOU'RE OVERTHINKING, LUCAS. I SIMPLY WANTED TO PRAY BEFORE I FOUGHT. DID YOU KNOW ST. MICHAEL'S CATHEDRAL IS ONE OF THE OLDEST CHURCHES ON THE CONTINENT? IT'S WHAT THE REST OF THE CITY TAKES ITS GOTHIC INFLUENCE FROM.
LOOK, I'LL KEEP YOUR SECRET. JUST TELL ME OR I'LL DRIVE MYSELF CRAZY, AND YOU DON'T WANT THAT ON YOUR CONSCIENCE, DO YOU?
CERTAINLY NOT.
I ACCEPT A HIGHER POWER AND I HUMBLE MYSELF BEFORE IT. THAT IS MY SECRET.
I'M JUST SUPPOSED TO ACCEPT THAT GOD IS TALKING TO YOU IN THERE?
I DIDN'T SAY THAT, DID I?
YOU SHOULD STOP ASSUMING THAT YOU'RE THREE STEPS AHEAD, LUCAS. THERE ARE THINGS IN HEAVEN AND EARTH BEYOND YOUR UNDERSTANDING.

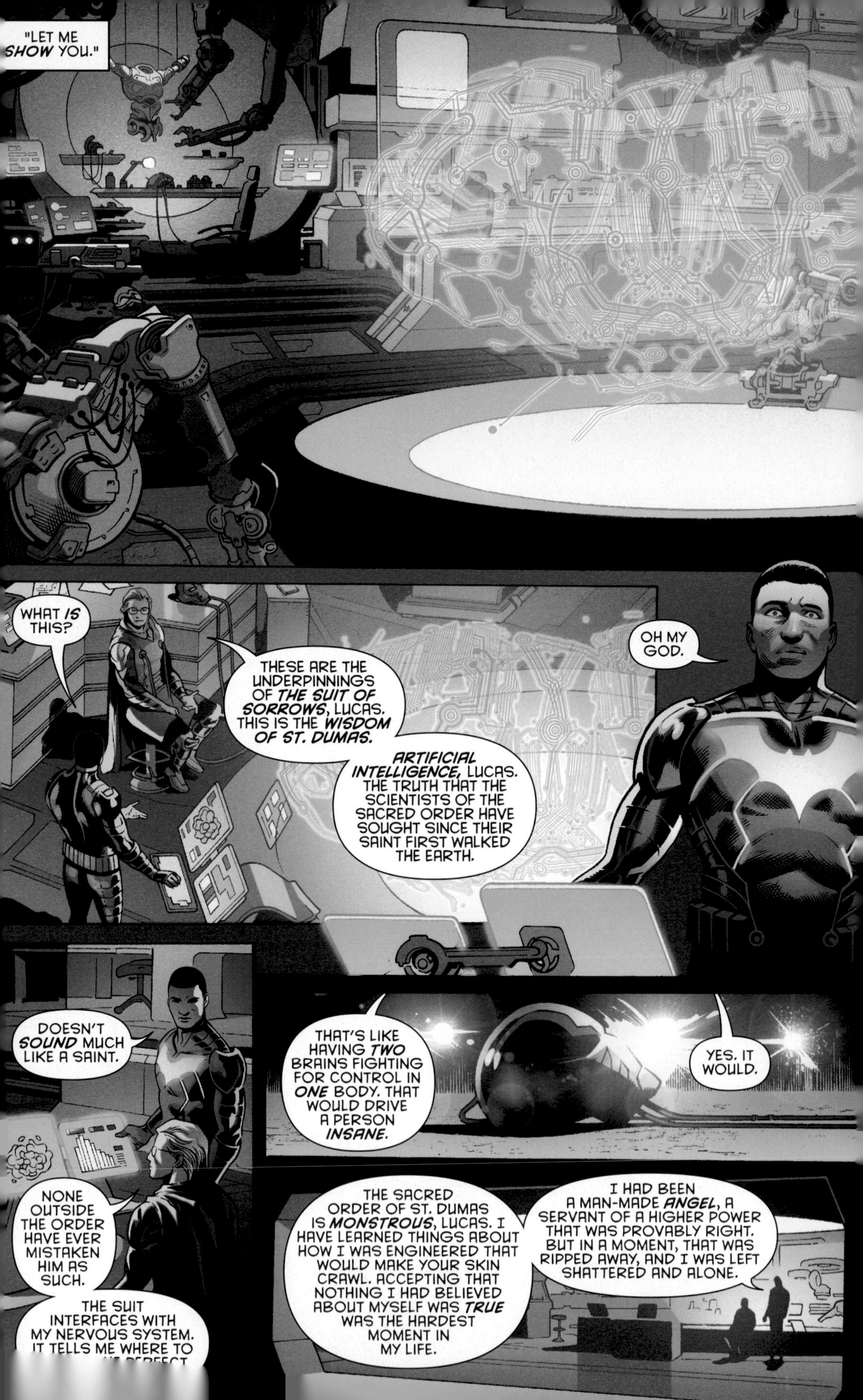
"LET ME SHOW YOU."
WHAT IS THIS?
THESE ARE THE UNDERPINNINGS OF THE SUIT OF SORROWS, LUCAS. THIS IS THE WISDOM OF ST. DUMAS.
ARTIFICIAL INTELLIGENCE, LUCAS. THE TRUTH THAT THE SCIENTISTS OF THE SACRED ORDER HAVE SOUGHT SINCE THEIR SAINT FIRST WALKED THE EARTH.
OH MY GOD.
DOESN'T SOUND MUCH LIKE A SAINT.
NONE OUTSIDE THE ORDER HAVE EVER MISTAKEN HIM AS SUCH.
THE SUIT INTERFACES WITH MY NERVOUS SYSTEM. IT TELLS ME WHERE TO
THAT'S LIKE HAVING TWO BRAINS FIGHTING FOR CONTROL IN ONE BODY. THAT WOULD DRIVE A PERSON INSANE.
YES. IT WOULD.
THE SACRED ORDER OF ST. DUMAS IS MONSTROUS, LUCAS. I HAVE LEARNED THINGS ABOUT HOW I WAS ENGINEERED THAT WOULD MAKE YOUR SKIN CRAWL. ACCEPTING THAT NOTHING I HAD BELIEVED ABOUT MYSELF WAS TRUE WAS THE HARDEST MOMENT IN MY LIFE.
I HAD BEEN A MAN-MADE ANGEL, A SERVANT OF A HIGHER POWER THAT WAS PROVABLY RIGHT. BUT IN A MOMENT, THAT WAS RIPPED AWAY, AND I WAS LEFT SHATTERED AND ALONE.

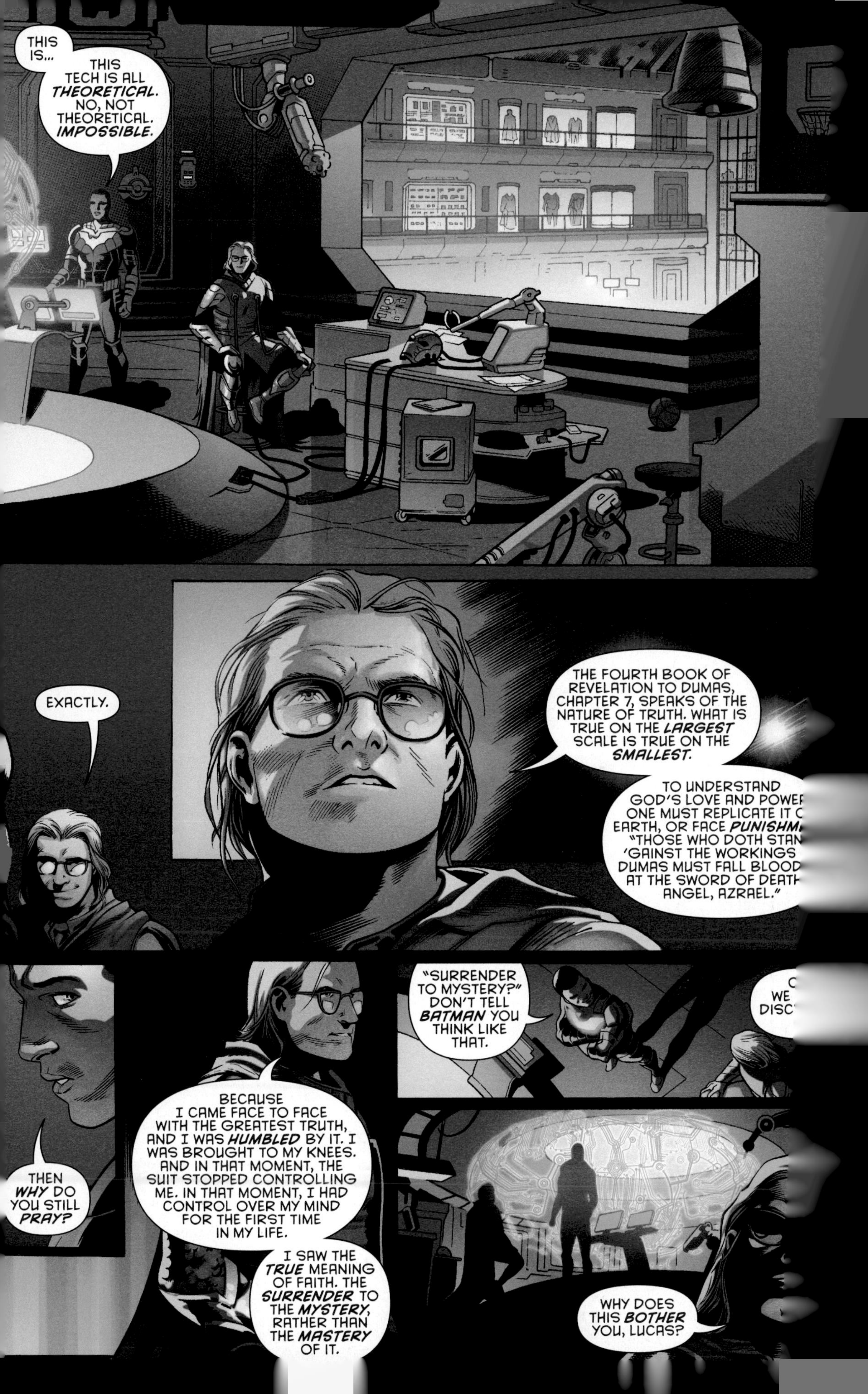

THIS IS...
THIS TECH IS ALL THEORETICAL. NO, NOT THEORETICAL. IMPOSSIBLE.
EXACTLY.
THE FOURTH BOOK OF REVELATION TO DUMAS, CHAPTER 7, SPEAKS OF THE NATURE OF TRUTH. WHAT IS TRUE ON THE LARGEST SCALE IS TRUE ON THE SMALLEST.
TO UNDERSTAND GOD'S LOVE AND POWE ONE MUST REPLICATE IT EARTH, OR FACE "THOSE WHO DOTH 'GAINST THE WORKINGS DUMAS MUST FALL AT THE SWORD OF ANGEL, AZRAEL."
THEN WHY DO YOU STILL PRAY?
BECAUSE I CAME FACE TO FACE WITH THE GREATEST TRUTH, AND I WAS HUMBLED BY IT. I WAS BROUGHT TO MY KNEES. AND IN THAT MOMENT, THE SUIT STOPPED CONTROLLING ME. IN THAT MOMENT, I HAD CONTROL OVER MY MIND FOR THE FIRST TIME IN MY LIFE.
I SAW THE TRUE MEANING OF FAITH. THE SURRENDER TO THE MYSTERY, RATHER THAN THE MASTERY OF IT.
"SURRENDER TO MYSTERY?" DON'T TELL BATMAN YOU THINK LIKE THAT.
WHY DOES THIS BOTHER YOU, LUCAS?

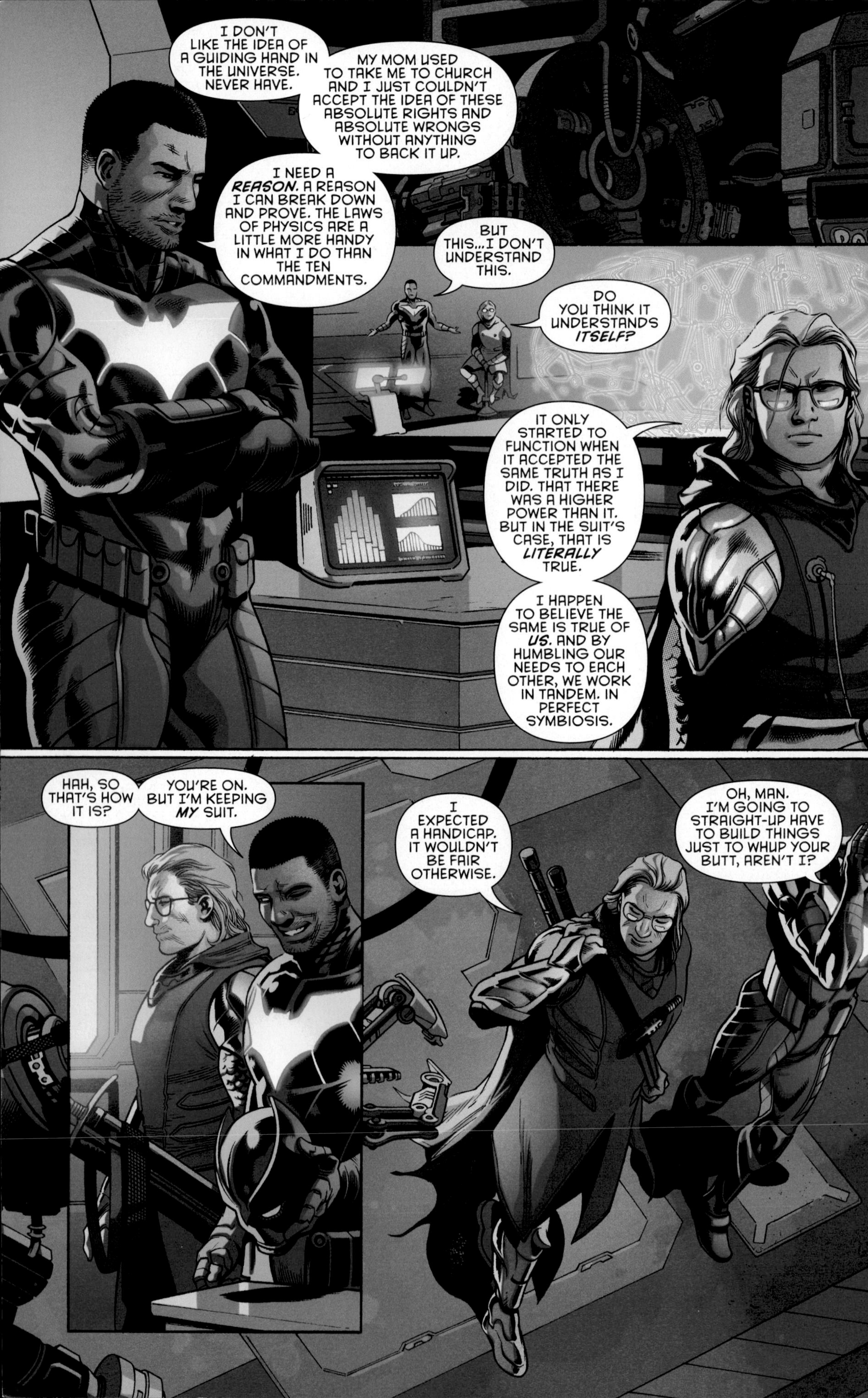
I DON'T LIKE THE IDEA OF A GUIDING HAND IN THE UNIVERSE. NEVER HAVE.
MY MOM USED TO TAKE ME TO CHURCH AND I JUST COULDN'T ACCEPT THE IDEA OF THESE ABSOLUTE RIGHTS AND ABSOLUTE WRONGS WITHOUT ANYTHING TO BACK IT UP.
I NEED A *REASON*. A REASON I CAN BREAK DOWN AND PROVE. THE LAWS OF PHYSICS ARE A LITTLE MORE HANDY IN WHAT I DO THAN THE TEN COMMANDMENTS.
BUT THIS...I DON'T UNDERSTAND THIS.
DO YOU THINK IT UNDERSTANDS *ITSELF?*
IT ONLY STARTED TO FUNCTION WHEN IT ACCEPTED THE SAME TRUTH AS I DID. THAT THERE WAS A HIGHER POWER THAN IT. BUT IN THE SUIT'S CASE, THAT IS *LITERALLY* TRUE.
I HAPPEN TO BELIEVE THE SAME IS TRUE OF *US*. AND BY HUMBLING OUR NEEDS TO EACH OTHER, WE WORK IN TANDEM. IN PERFECT SYMBIOSIS.
HAH, SO THAT'S HOW IT IS?
YOU'RE ON. BUT I'M KEEPING *MY* SUIT.
I EXPECTED A HANDICAP. IT WOULDN'T BE FAIR OTHERWISE.
OH, MAN. I'M GOING TO STRAIGHT-UP HAVE TO BUILD THINGS JUST TO WHUP YOUR BUTT, AREN'T I?

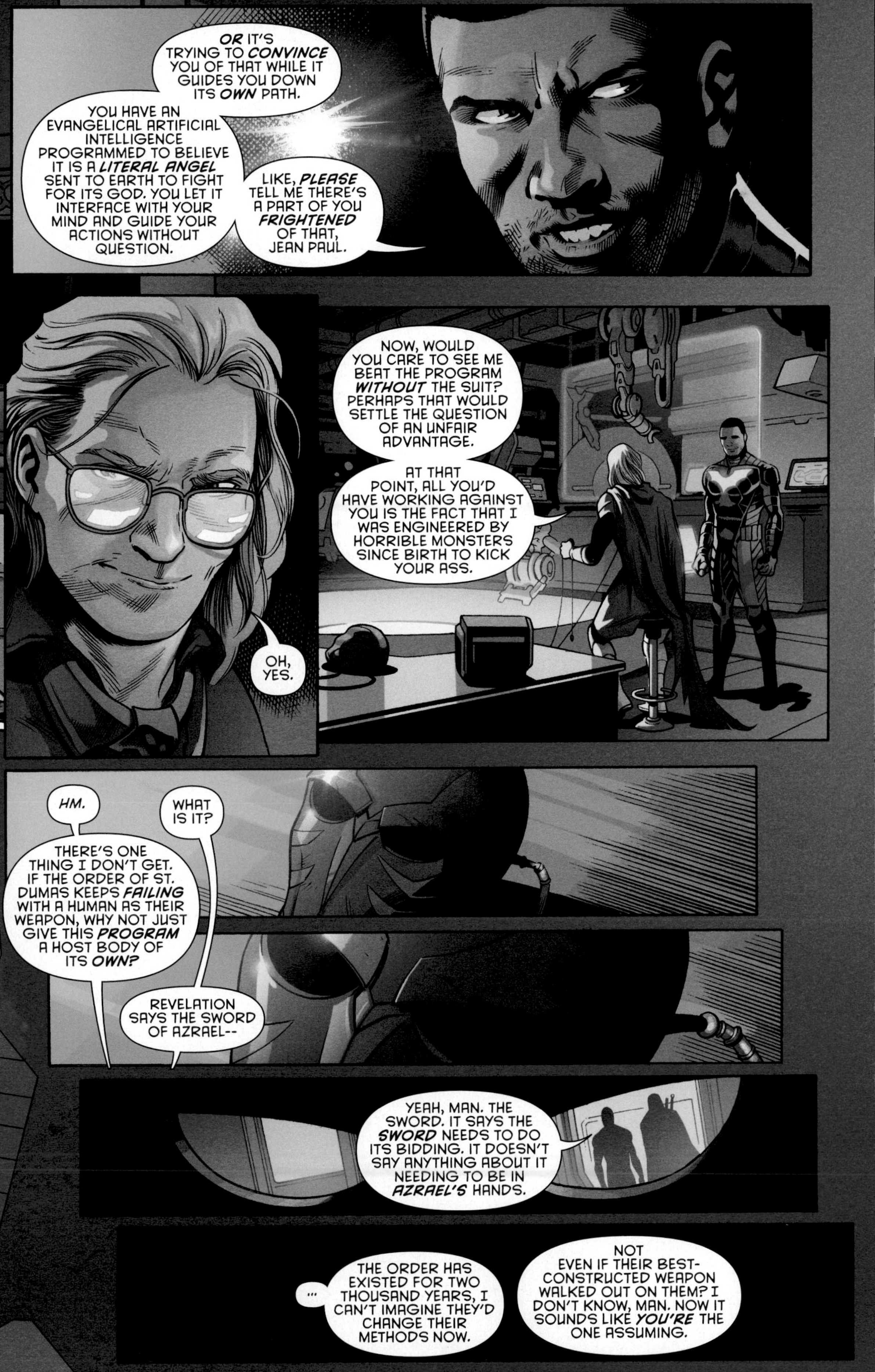
OR IT'S TRYING TO CONVINCE YOU OF THAT WHILE IT GUIDES YOU DOWN ITS OWN PATH.
YOU HAVE AN EVANGELICAL ARTIFICIAL INTELLIGENCE PROGRAMMED TO BELIEVE IT IS A LITERAL ANGEL SENT TO EARTH TO FIGHT FOR ITS GOD. YOU LET IT INTERFACE WITH YOUR MIND AND GUIDE YOUR ACTIONS WITHOUT QUESTION.
LIKE, PLEASE TELL ME THERE'S A PART OF YOU FRIGHTENED OF THAT, JEAN PAUL.
OH, YES.
NOW, WOULD YOU CARE TO SEE ME BEAT THE PROGRAM WITHOUT THE SUIT? PERHAPS THAT WOULD SETTLE THE QUESTION OF AN UNFAIR ADVANTAGE.
AT THAT POINT, ALL YOU'D HAVE WORKING AGAINST YOU IS THE FACT THAT I WAS ENGINEERED BY HORRIBLE MONSTERS SINCE BIRTH TO KICK YOUR ASS.
HM.
WHAT IS IT?
THERE'S ONE THING I DON'T GET. IF THE ORDER OF ST. DUMAS KEEPS FAILING WITH A HUMAN AS THEIR WEAPON, WHY NOT JUST GIVE THIS PROGRAM A HOST BODY OF ITS OWN?
REVELATION SAYS THE SWORD OF AZRAEL--
YEAH, MAN. THE SWORD. IT SAYS THE SWORD NEEDS TO DO ITS BIDDING. IT DOESN'T SAY ANYTHING ABOUT IT NEEDING TO BE IN AZRAEL'S HANDS.
...
THE ORDER HAS EXISTED FOR TWO THOUSAND YEARS, I CAN'T IMAGINE THEY'D CHANGE THEIR METHODS NOW.
NOT EVEN IF THEIR BEST-CONSTRUCTED WEAPON WALKED OUT ON THEM? I DON'T KNOW, MAN. NOW IT SOUNDS LIKE YOU'RE THE ONE ASSUMING.

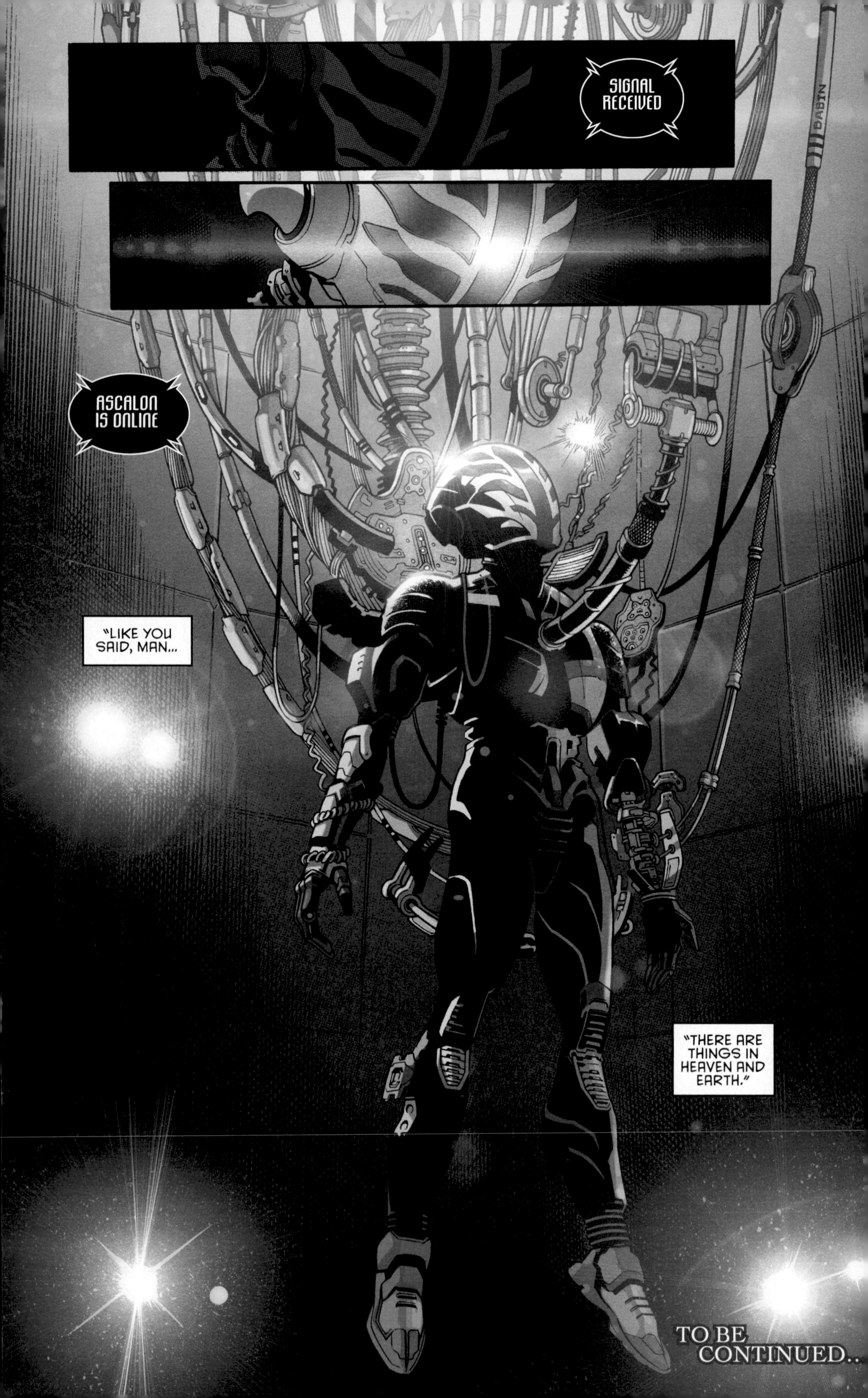

SIGNAL RECEIVED
ASCALON IS ONLINE
"LIKE YOU SAID, MAN...
"THERE ARE THINGS IN HEAVEN AND EARTH."
TO BE CONTINUED...

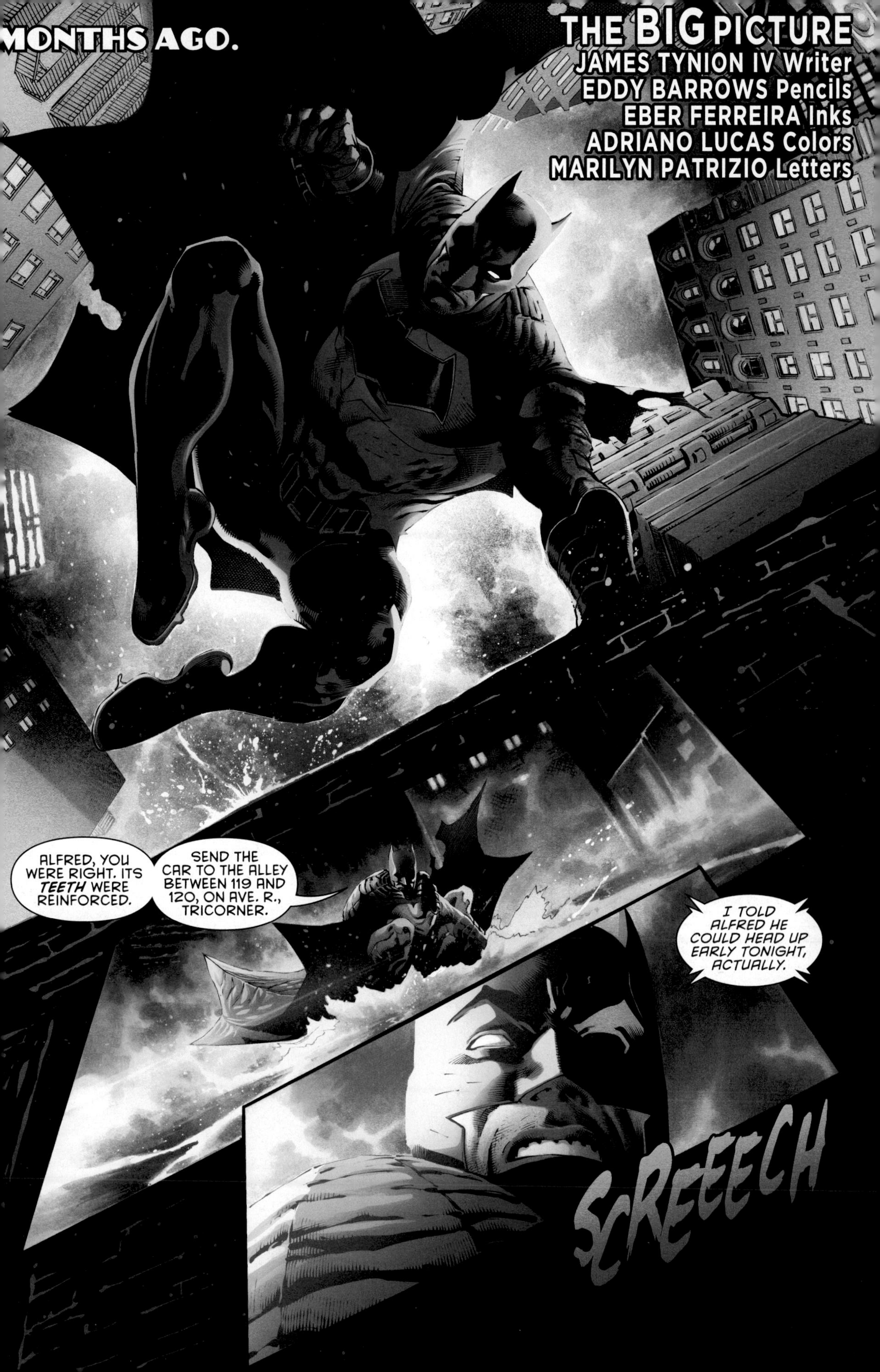
MONTHS AGO.
THE BIG PICTURE
JAMES TYNION IV Writer
EDDY BARROWS Pencils
EBER FERREIRA Inks
ADRIANO LUCAS Colors
MARILYN PATRIZIO Letters
ALFRED, YOU WERE RIGHT. ITS TEETH WERE REINFORCED.
SEND THE CAR TO THE ALLEY BETWEEN 119 AND 120, ON AVE. R., TRICORNER.
I TOLD ALFRED HE COULD HEAD UP EARLY TONIGHT, ACTUALLY.
SCREEECH

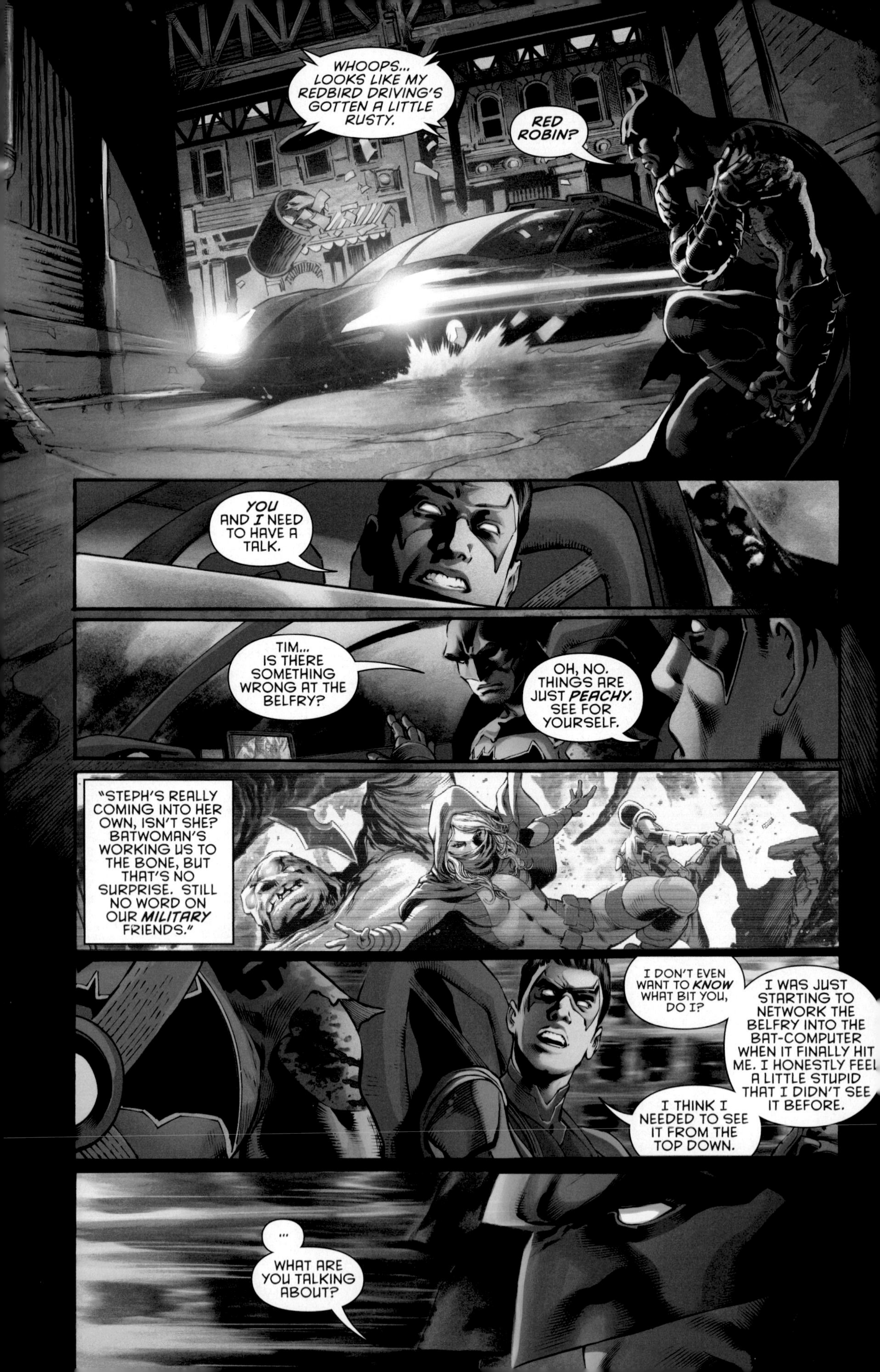
WHOOPS... LOOKS LIKE MY REDBIRD DRIVING'S GOTTEN A LITTLE RUSTY.
RED ROBIN?
YOU AND I NEED TO HAVE A TALK.
TIM... IS THERE SOMETHING WRONG AT THE BELFRY?
OH, NO. THINGS ARE JUST PEACHY. SEE FOR YOURSELF.
"STEPH'S REALLY COMING INTO HER OWN, ISN'T SHE? BATWOMAN'S WORKING US TO THE BONE, BUT THAT'S NO SURPRISE. STILL NO WORD ON OUR MILITARY FRIENDS."
I DON'T EVEN WANT TO KNOW WHAT BIT YOU, DO I?
I WAS JUST STARTING TO NETWORK THE BELFRY INTO THE BAT-COMPUTER WHEN IT FINALLY HIT ME. I HONESTLY FEEL A LITTLE STUPID THAT I DIDN'T SEE IT BEFORE.
I THINK I NEEDED TO SEE IT FROM THE TOP DOWN.
...
WHAT ARE YOU TALKING ABOUT?

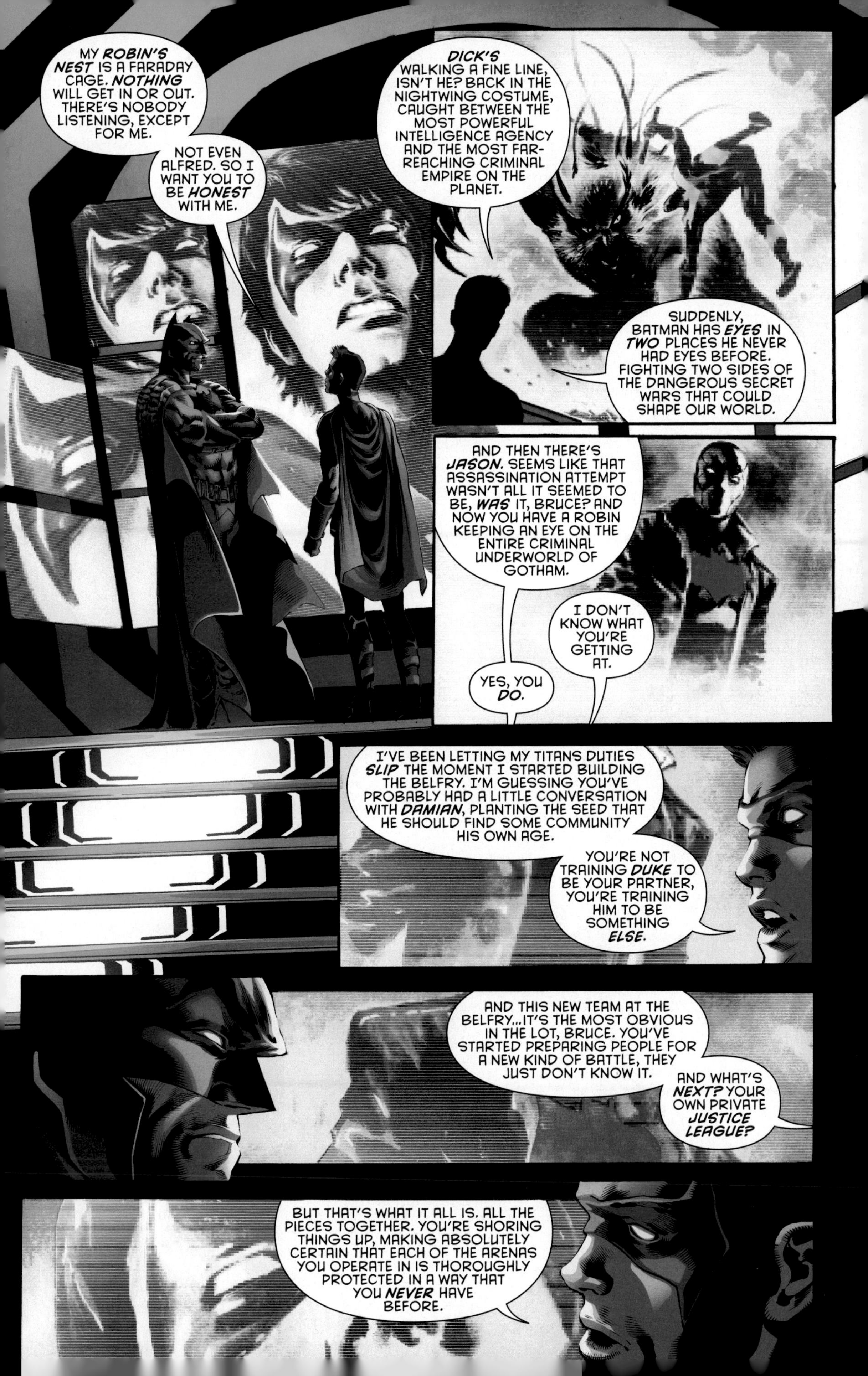
MY ROBIN'S NEST IS A FARADAY CAGE. NOTHING WILL GET IN OR OUT. THERE'S NOBODY LISTENING, EXCEPT FOR ME.
NOT EVEN ALFRED. SO I WANT YOU TO BE HONEST WITH ME.
DICK'S WALKING A FINE LINE, ISN'T HE? BACK IN THE NIGHTWING COSTUME, CAUGHT BETWEEN THE MOST POWERFUL INTELLIGENCE AGENCY AND THE MOST FAR-REACHING CRIMINAL EMPIRE ON THE PLANET.
SUDDENLY, BATMAN HAS EYES IN TWO PLACES HE NEVER HAD EYES BEFORE. FIGHTING TWO SIDES OF THE DANGEROUS SECRET WARS THAT COULD SHAPE OUR WORLD.
AND THEN THERE'S JASON. SEEMS LIKE THAT ASSASSINATION ATTEMPT WASN'T ALL IT SEEMED TO BE, WAS IT, BRUCE? AND NOW YOU HAVE A ROBIN KEEPING AN EYE ON THE ENTIRE CRIMINAL UNDERWORLD OF GOTHAM.
I DON'T KNOW WHAT YOU'RE GETTING AT.
YES, YOU DO.
I'VE BEEN LETTING MY TITANS DUTIES SLIP THE MOMENT I STARTED BUILDING THE BELFRY. I'M GUESSING YOU'VE PROBABLY HAD A LITTLE CONVERSATION WITH DAMIAN, PLANTING THE SEED THAT HE SHOULD FIND SOME COMMUNITY HIS OWN AGE.
YOU'RE NOT TRAINING DUKE TO BE YOUR PARTNER, YOU'RE TRAINING HIM TO BE SOMETHING ELSE.
AND THIS NEW TEAM AT THE BELFRY...IT'S THE MOST OBVIOUS IN THE LOT, BRUCE. YOU'VE STARTED PREPARING PEOPLE FOR A NEW KIND OF BATTLE, THEY JUST DON'T KNOW IT.
AND WHAT'S NEXT? YOUR OWN PRIVATE JUSTICE LEAGUE?
BUT THAT'S WHAT IT ALL IS. ALL THE PIECES TOGETHER. YOU'RE SHORING THINGS UP, MAKING ABSOLUTELY CERTAIN THAT EACH OF THE ARENAS YOU OPERATE IN IS THOROUGHLY PROTECTED IN A WAY THAT YOU NEVER HAVE BEFORE.

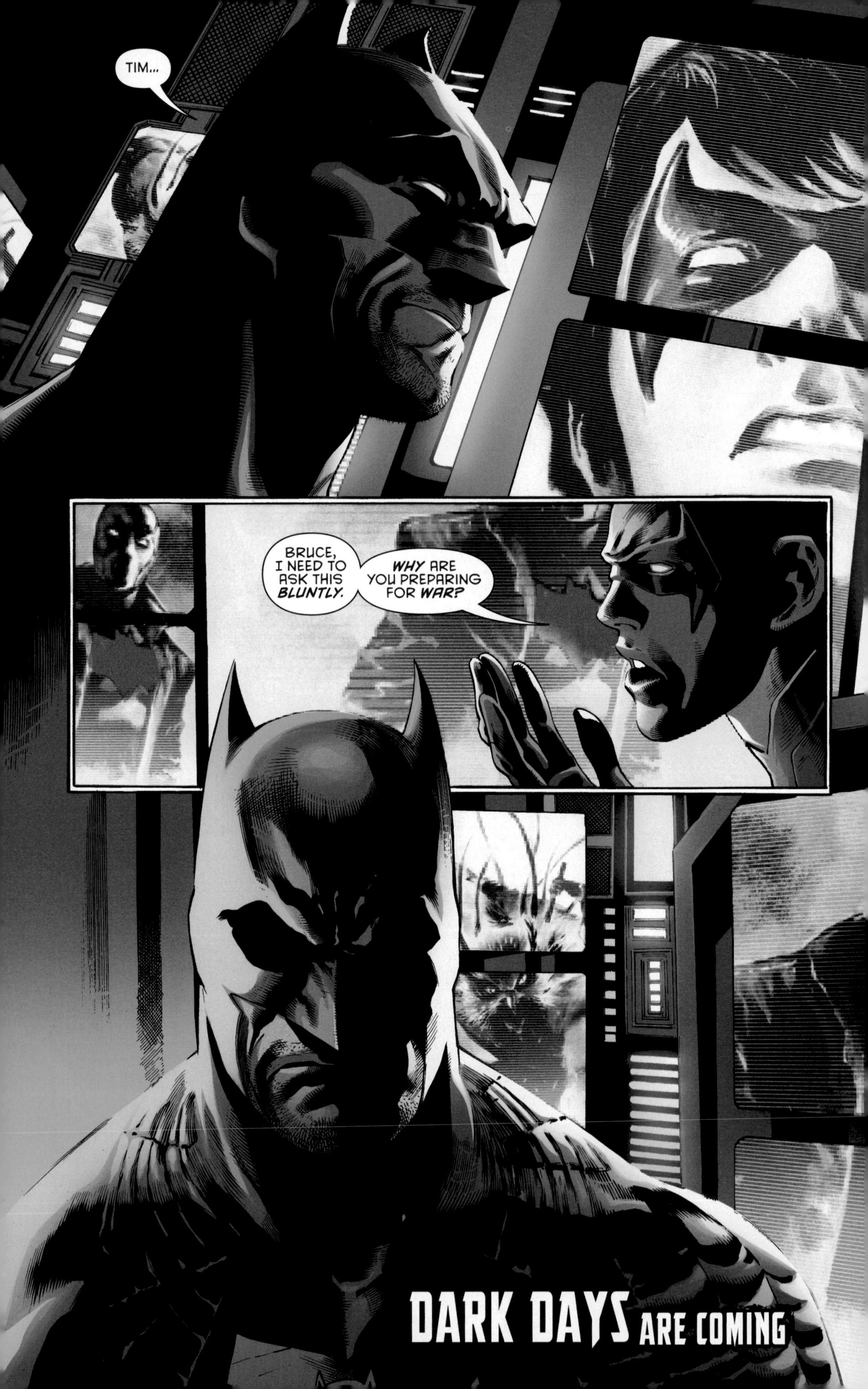

TIM...
BRUCE, I NEED TO ASK THIS BLUNTLY.
WHY ARE YOU PREPARING FOR WAR?
DARK DAYS ARE COMING

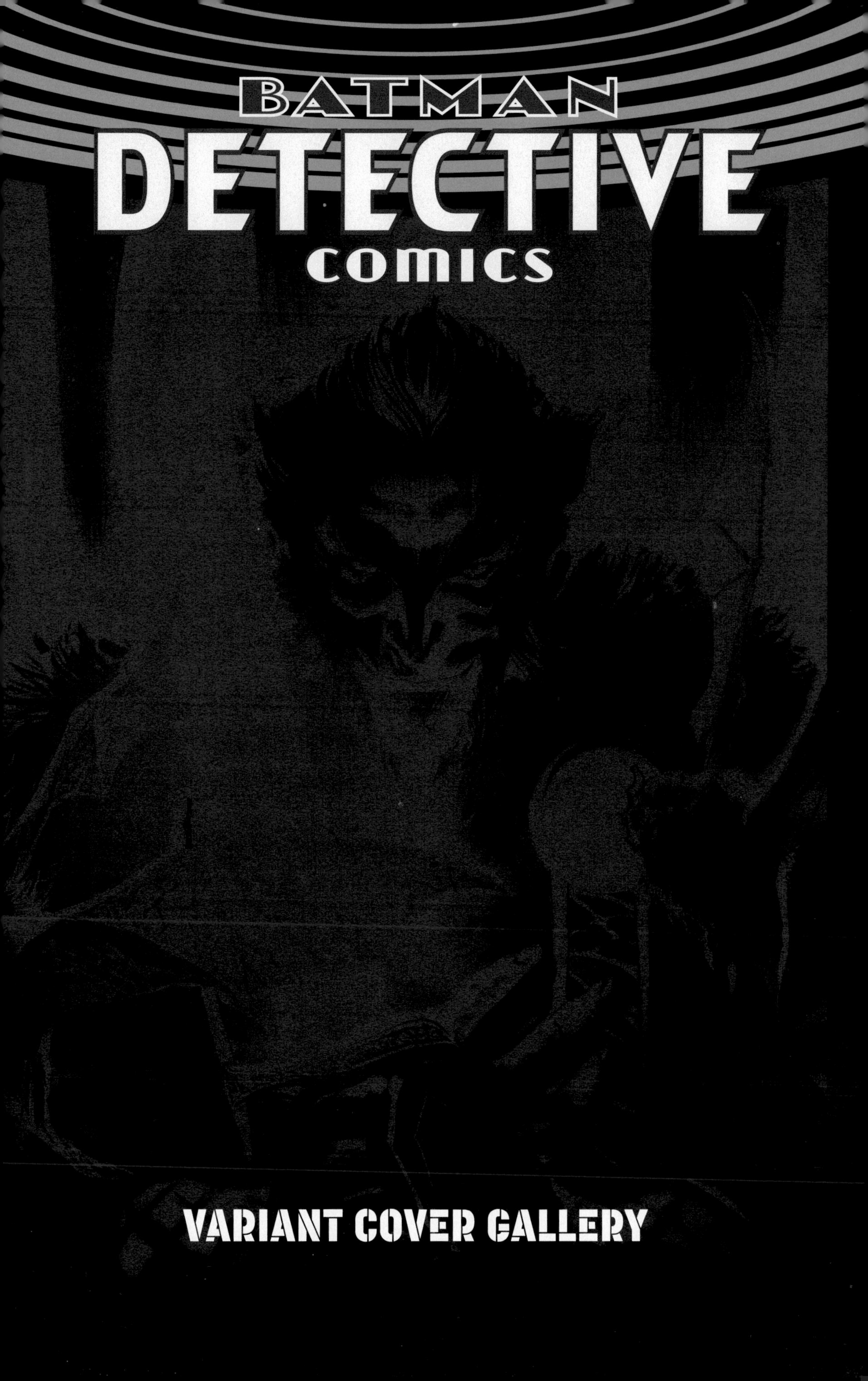
BATMAN
DETECTIVE
COMICS
VARIANT COVER GALLERY

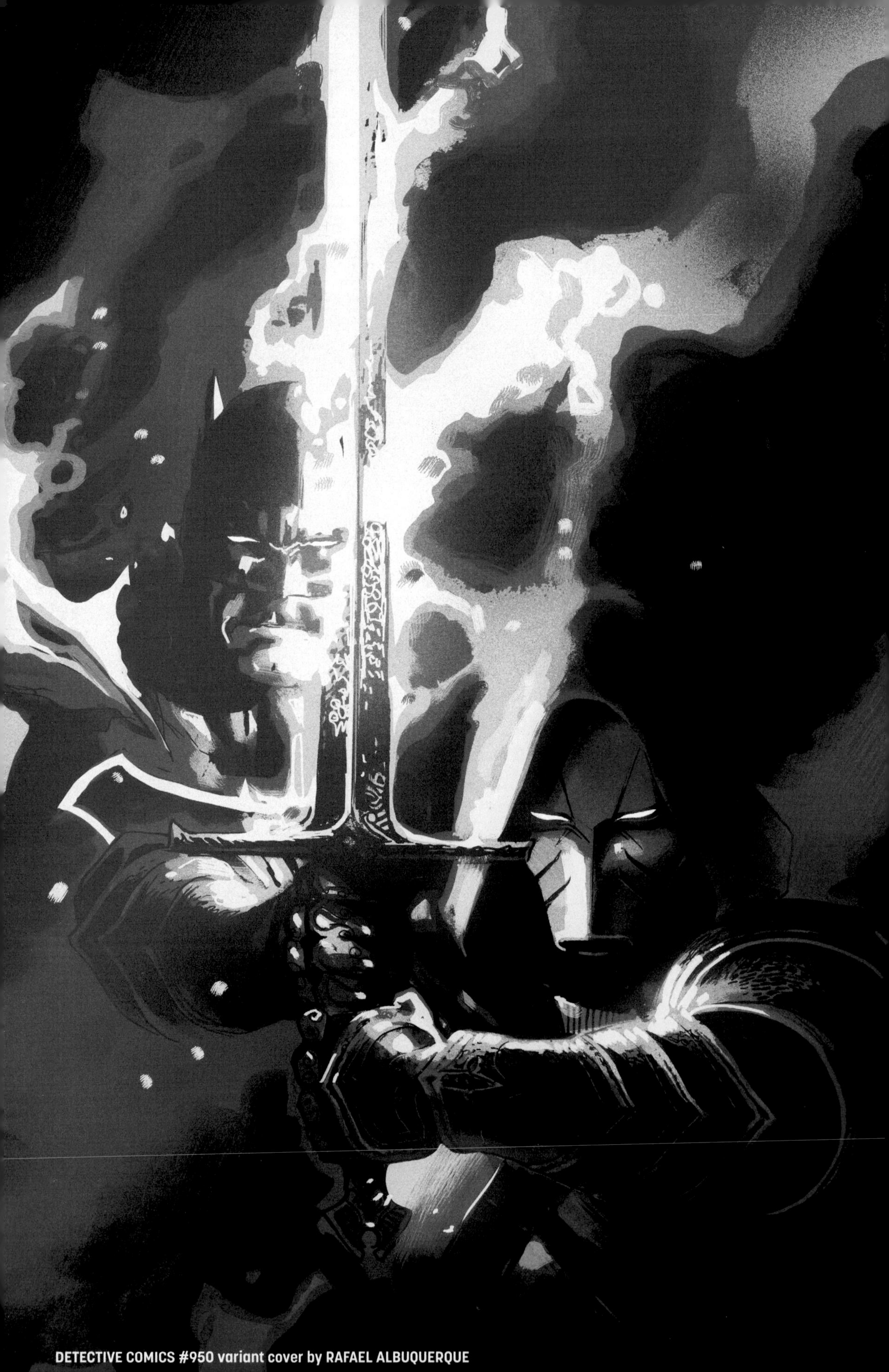

DETECTIVE COMICS #950 variant cover by RAFAEL ALBUQUERQUE

DETECTIVE COMICS #951 variant cover by RAFAEL ALBUQUERQUE

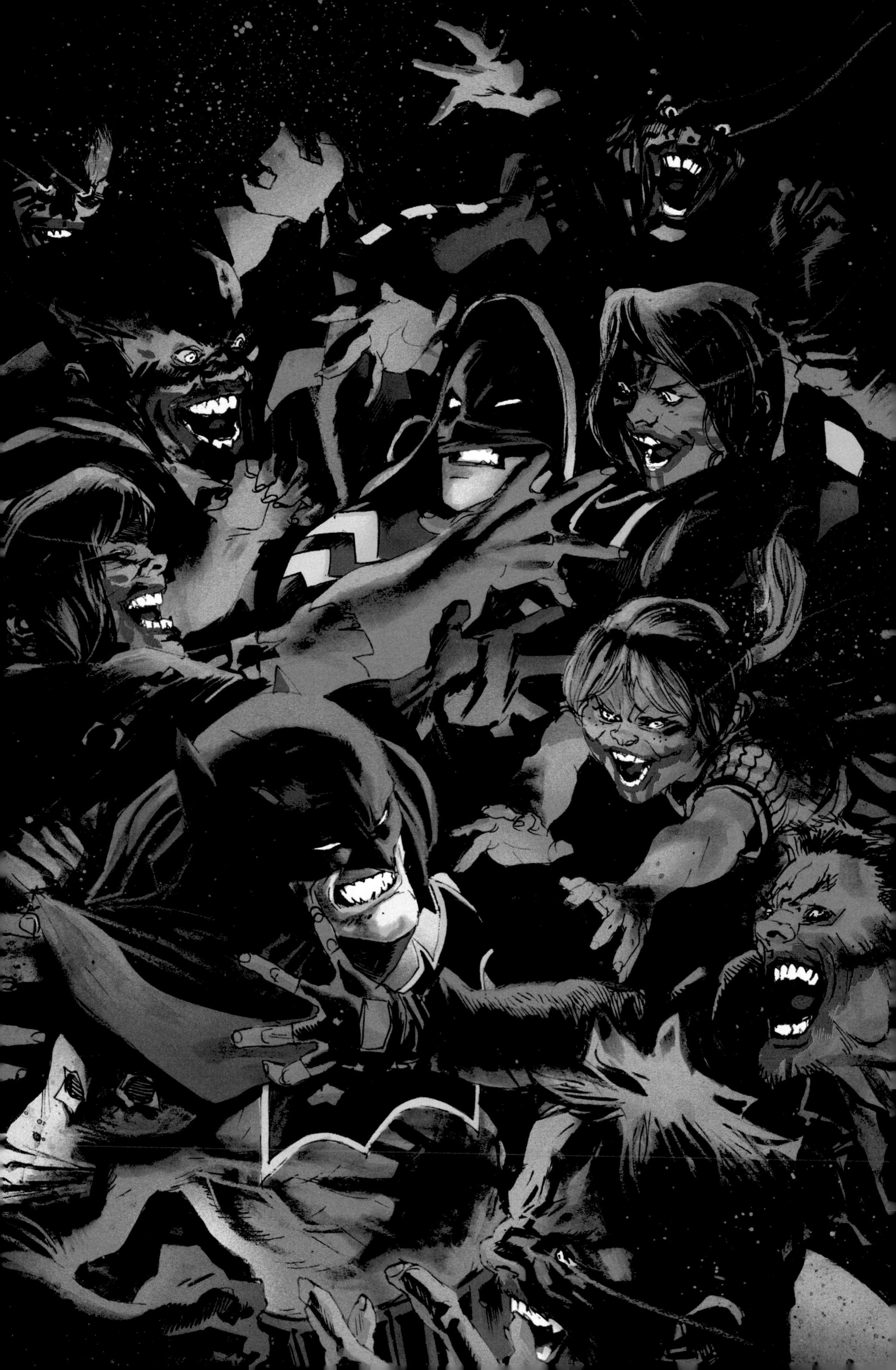

DETECTIVE COMICS #952 Variant cover by RAFAEL ALBUQUERQUE

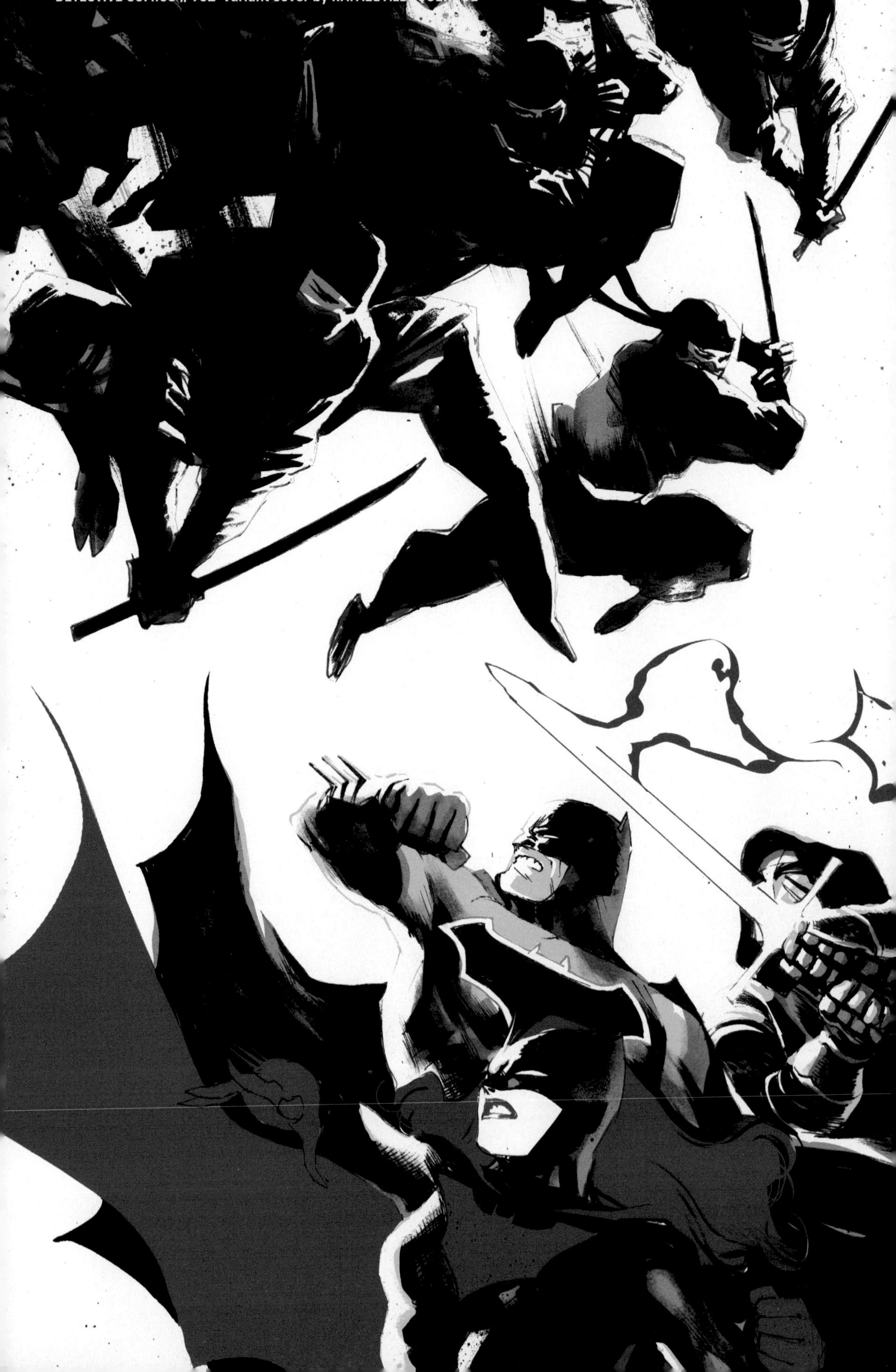

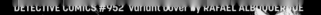

DETECTIVE COMICS #953 variant cover by RAFAEL ALBUQUERQUE

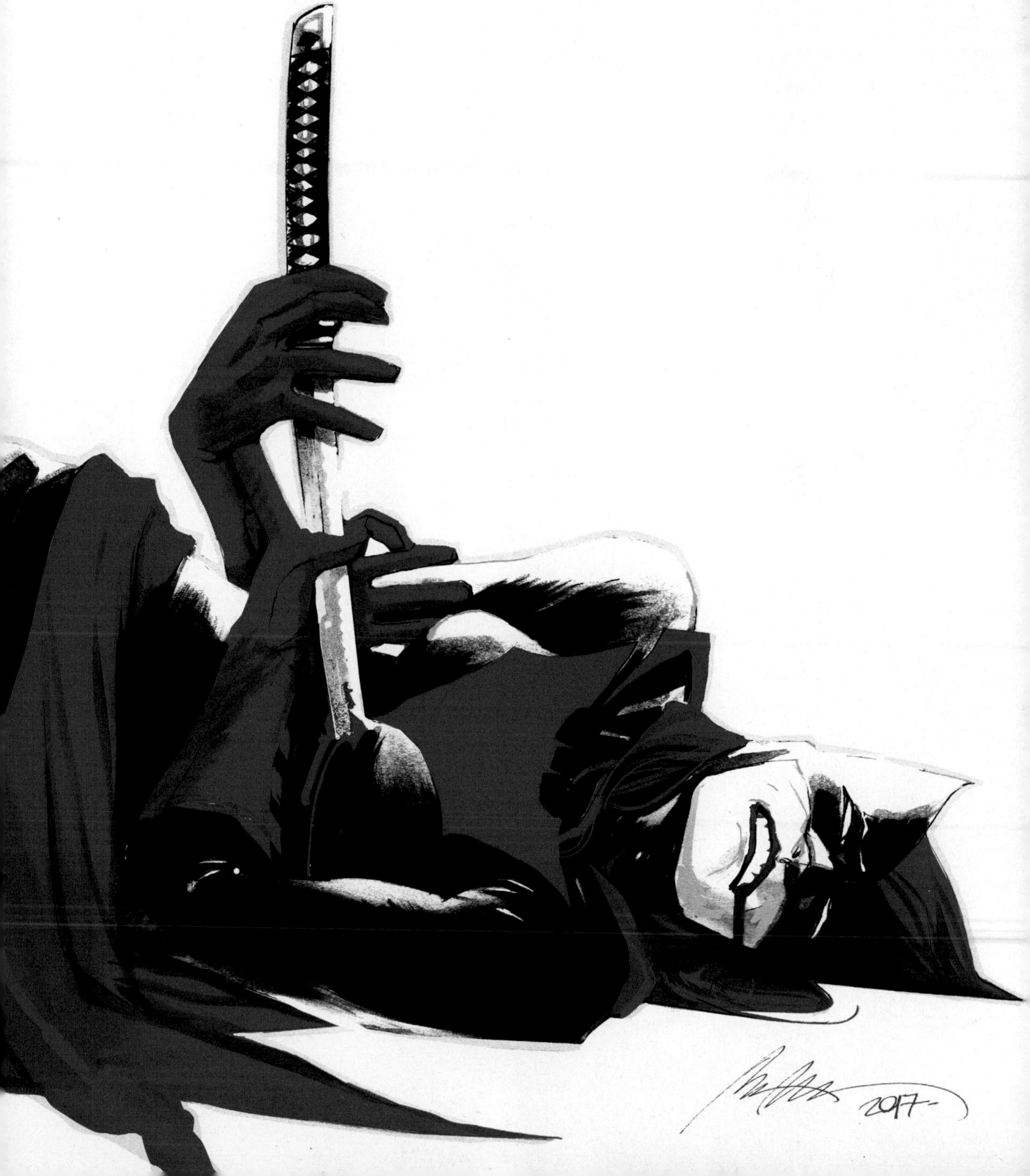
2017

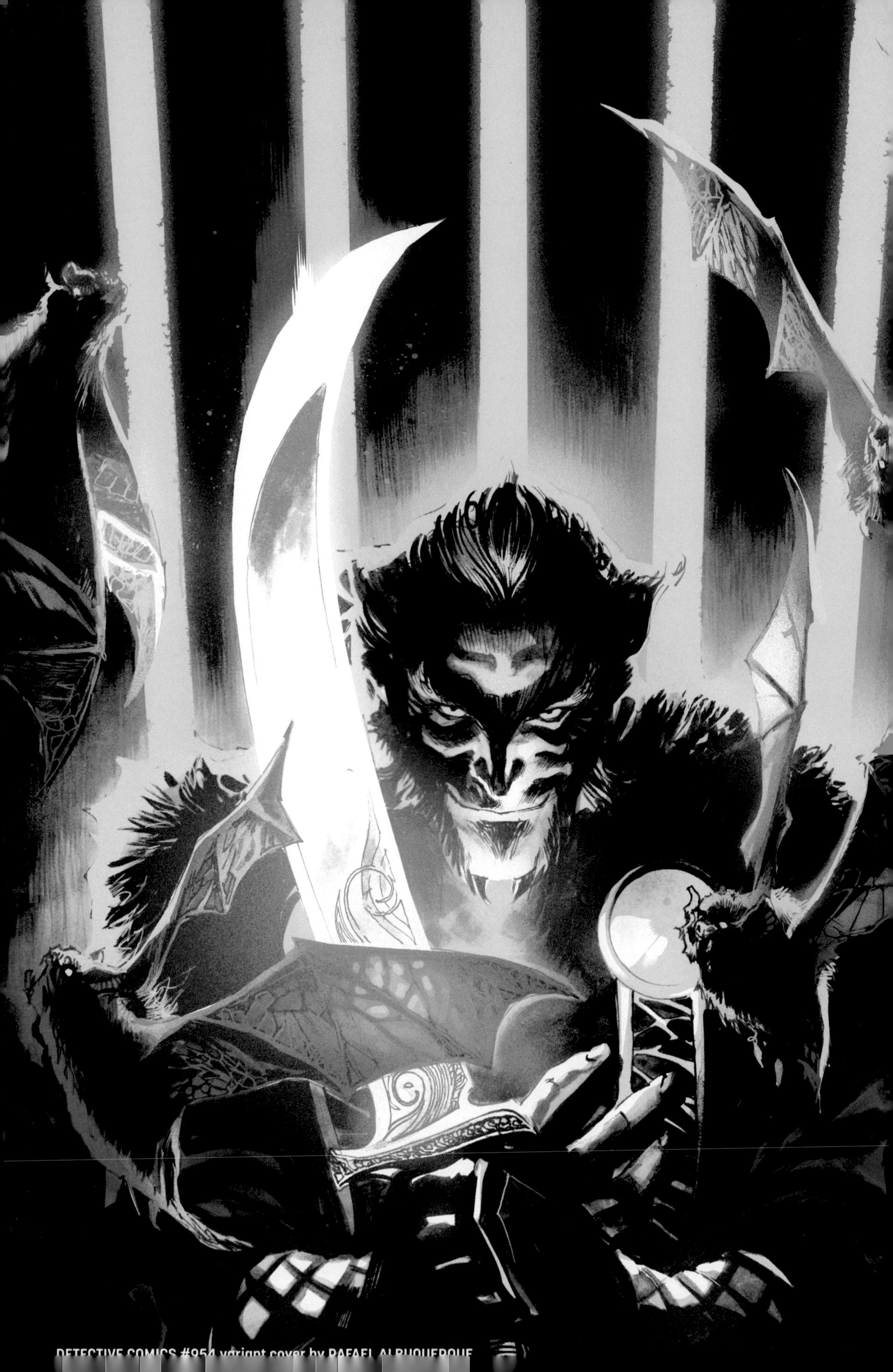

DETECTIVE COMICS #954 variant cover by RAFAEL ALBUQUERQUE

DETECTIVE COMICS #955 variant cover by RAFAEL ALBUQUERQUE

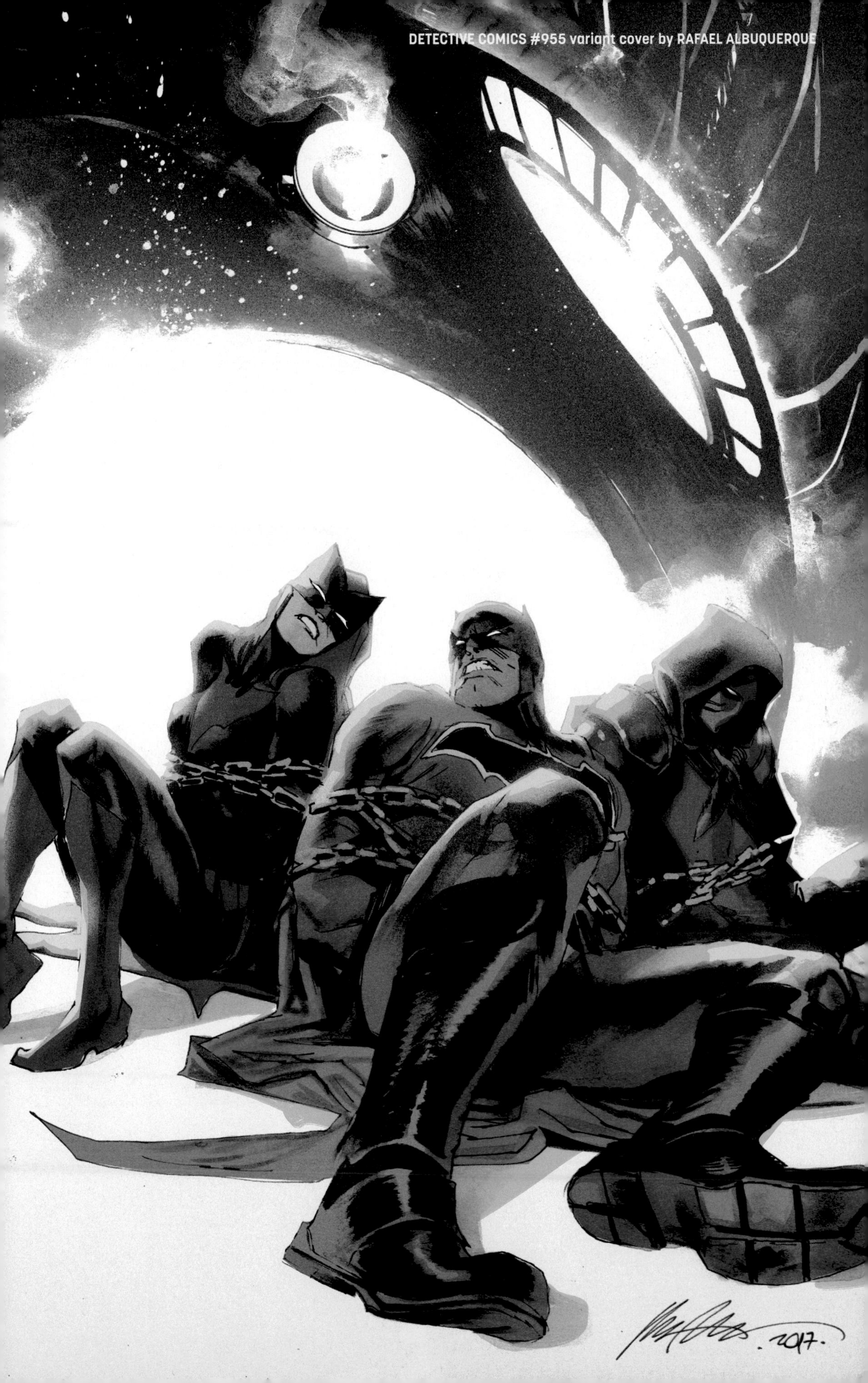

DETECTIVE COMICS #956 variant cover by RAFAEL ALBUQUERQUE

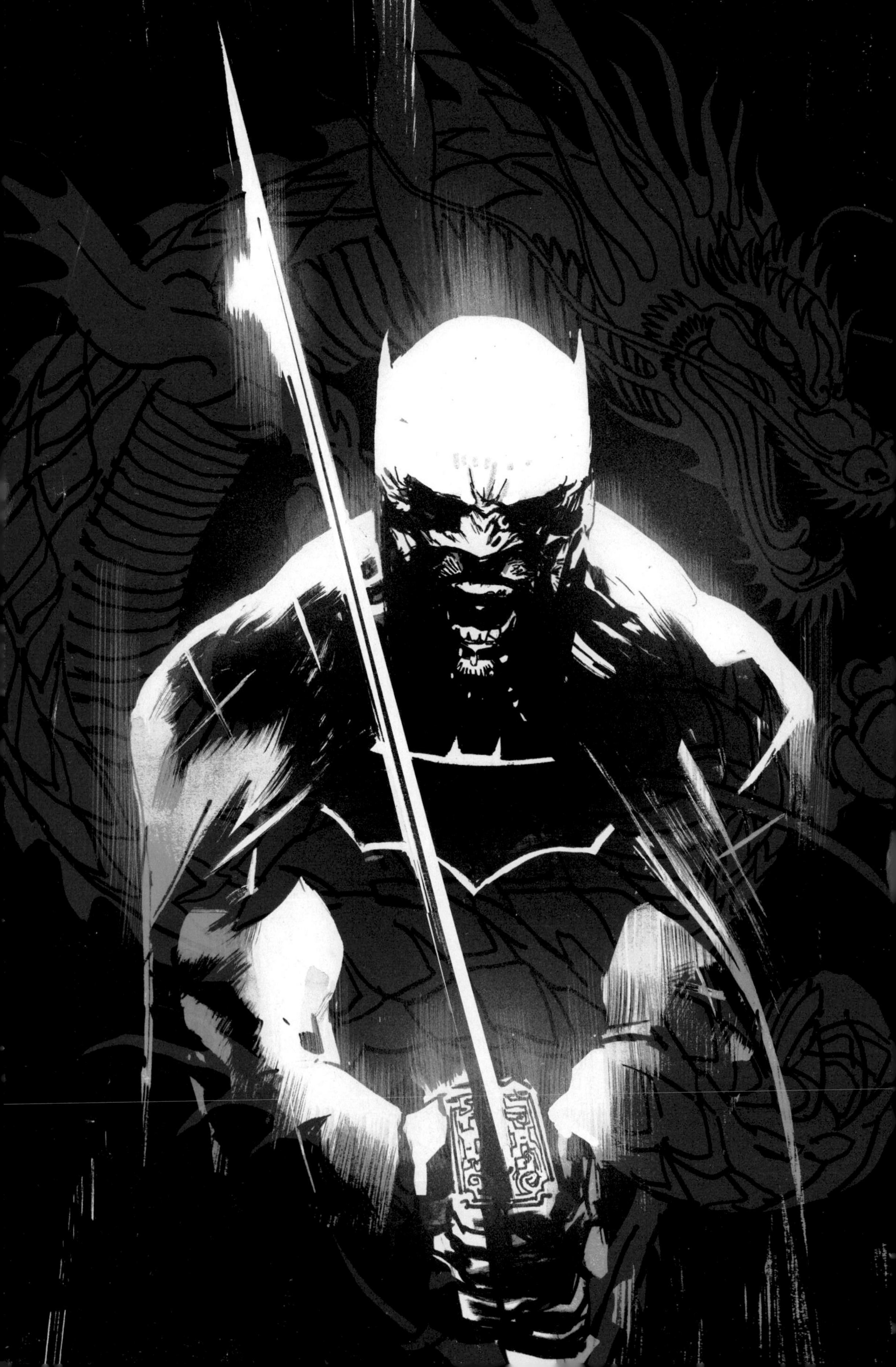